AF241609

Helen Gordon

... because of how she lived

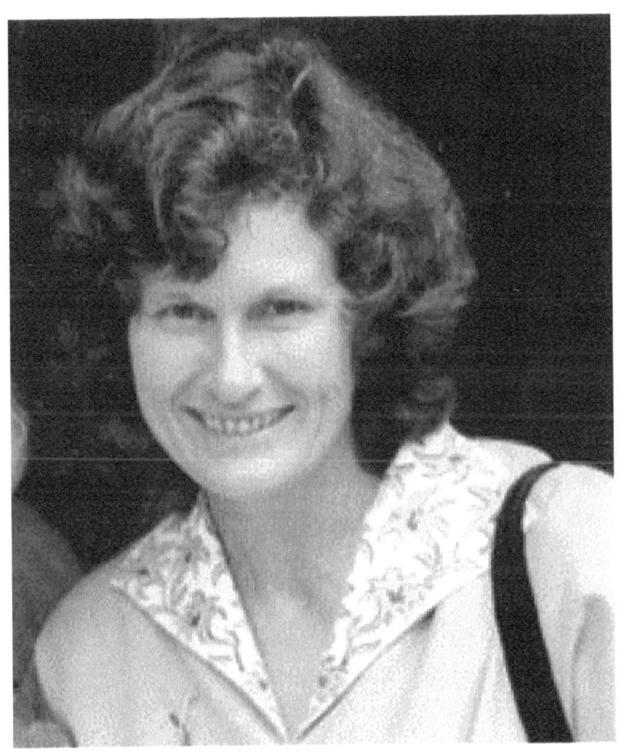

Compiled by Don Gordon

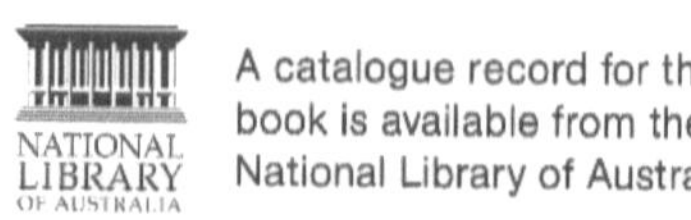

A catalogue record for this book is available from the National Library of Australia

ISBN-13: 978-1-922727-46-6

Publication details

Title: Helen Gordon – "… because of how she lived"
Author: Compiled by Don Gordon
Date: July 2022

Copyright © 2022 Don Gordon
All rights reserved.

Copies available from
Amazon and all good bookstores, or from
Don Gordon - Email: don.gordon1@hotmail.com

Other publications regarding Helen Gordon:
Picture book of Helen's artwork – "Let your spirit fly!"

Information

Details about Helen's life and work can be found
in the profile of Helen Mitchell in www.billandmavismitchellfamily.com

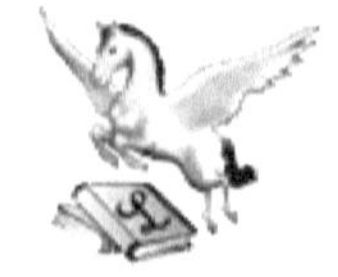

Linellen Press
265 Boomerang Road
Oldbury, Western Australia
www.linellenpress.com.au

Contents

*** *Stories told by Helen*

Preface

Dear readers,

You might be Helen's family, friends, artists, Baha'is, or indigenous women. Or you might have been a resident of the various communities where she lived or visited. You might have participated in Helen's workshops. Perhaps you worked beside her. Or maybe you never knew her personally but want to learn how she went about encouraging others. This book is intended for a diverse readership of those whose lives have intersected with Helen in some way. No matter who you are, as you browse these pages, you will find parts of great interest and relevance to your own journey – and other parts might be new ground for you.

I had thought of compiling separate books about her faith, about her creativity, and about her connections with people in various places. But it makes sense to draw all these together into one book as Helen saw these as inseparable .... because that is how she lived.

At a gathering in the days after her passing, her son, Ben, said, "We are not here because she died, but because of how she lived".

Helen did not see herself as exceptional and would not push herself out in front of people, so I wonder what she would think if she held this book in her hands. How keen would she have been for others to read about her experiences? She would wonder what the fuss is all about. Like most of us, she did whatever she thought was best for each day – without trying to be someone special – but it has all added up to what you will find in these pages.

More than half of this book are stories written by Helen. But who was she writing for? She just left the diaries in a drawer. She didn't bother even sharing these within the family. They were not particularly personal, so I have now taken the next step of making available what she has written. The stories are windows into the sort of person she was – and how she lived.

This compilation is four books in one.

Stages: The chronology of seven phases of Helen's life – childhood, youth, marriage, motherhood, life in various locations and her final years - <u>what</u>, <u>where</u>, <u>when</u>, and <u>who</u>. These have been written by myself (in the third person), and provide the contexts for other parts of this compilation.

Stories: There are twelve narratives about specific occasions or periods. These give extra significance to the <u>what</u>, <u>where</u>, <u>when</u>, and <u>who</u> of the stages of Helen's life. Most were written by Helen (in the first person). They are interposed amongst the stages in this compilation. Everyone loves a good story. Readers can go directly to these because they are in red font in the contents page - Chapters 2, 4, 6, 9, 12, 15, 16, 17, 18, 24, 25 & 33.

Inspirations: Helen was driven by her commitment to four dimensions: her family and friends, her creativity, community service and Baha'i activities. This is <u>why</u> she did what she did.

How to … Helen laid out eight sets of instructions for <u>how</u> to undertake these activities.

I have also compiled a companion picture book – of her creativity – 'Let your spirit fly!'

As I have been preparing this in the year since Helen died, I have reflected on her life and our forty-seven years together. Even though we had been married for so long, I am still discovering more about her. I think that you, dear reader, will also make discoveries as you turn these pages.

<u>Thanks</u>: I am immensely grateful for the many gifts Helen gave me. Foremost among these were the rich connections with her

family and friends. In our time together, I have got to know so many impressive people – too many to give adequate acknowledgement in this book. Some have contributed to this compilation and the companion picture book: Mahshid Ferdowsian, Maxien Bradley, Verona Lucas, Ronnie Naughton, Maryam Bell, Elizabeth Hof, Allison Stewart, Charmaine Burke, Ellie McLean, Lorraine Injie, Violette Brentnall, Lorraine Lobo, Trish Halloran, Dianne Isgar, and Charlie Pierce. Also, Helen's siblings: Beverly, Cynthia, John and Russell. Our children: Ruth, Ben and Joe. Our grandchildren: Oirae and Hannah (photography), and Weyburn, Jasmine, Luca, Dara and Kai for being such inspirations.

<u>Feedback</u>: Comments are always welcome.

Don Gordon (husband)
don.gordon1@hotmail.com
August 2022

..ooOOoo..

Brief biography

Helen Gordon, nee Mitchell

14th Aug 1945 – 3rd July 2021

Helen was born as Helen Margaret Mitchell in Geelong in 1945 and she grew up in Perth.

She qualified as an Occupational Therapist, and also studied medicine for three years, and completed a BSc in human anatomy.

Helen embraced the Baha'i Faith when she was twenty-five years old. This was in the earliest days of the Faith in Western Australia.

In 1974, she married Don Gordon when they were each on working holidays in Scotland. On returning to Western Australia, Helen was alongside her husband in his social work with indigenous people. Their first five years were in Laverton, Derby and Kununurra. They lived in Narrogin for two decades as their three children, Joseph, Ben and Ruth, grew up and completed all their schooling. Then three years in the remote aboriginal community of Blackstone was followed by a decade in the mining town of Tom Price. On eight occasions, she lived for extended periods with non-western communities – indigenous, gypsies, and Pacific islanders. Her final decade was in Kelmscott.

Wherever she went, she lived by the principles of her faith and pursued arts and crafts – her own work, but particularly engaging others in a wide range of community arts. She often worked with indigenous women and children.

Helen died in 2021, aged 75 years.

..ooOOoo..

1

Getting started in life

Helen Mitchell – from 1945 to 1974

Helen's childhood, university, and occupational therapy in Perth

Written by Don

Helen's mother was Mavis, nee Renshaw. From her mother, Helen learnt about getting organized, love of handicrafts, and the centrality of families. Helen's father was William 'Bill' Willaton Mitchell. He became the public relations advisor to the Charles Court, the Premier of Western Australia, and was important in the development of ideas and policies. From her father, Helen learnt to stand up for what she believed in – and the confidence in getting things done.

Bill was working with the *Ballarat Courier*, before he enlisted for the Second World War. He served as a radio operator in Papua New Guinea. While on leave, in October 1944, he married Mavis Renshaw in Geelong before returning to PNG. Bill was discharged some months later and resumed work with the *Ballarat Courier*.

The family ancestry is in:
www.billandmavismitchellfamily.com

Helen was born in the South Geelong Hospital on the 14th August 1945. This was the day World War II ended in the Pacific.

Mavis described the circumstances of the birth. Just before her baby was to be born, she was left alone in the ward for quite a while – perhaps because staff were distracted with the excitement around the hospital celebrating the ending of the war. She could feel her baby coming, and began to worry that there would not be any midwife to assist her. However, help arrived in time for Helen to be bought safely into the world that was now at peace – and all the bells were ringing.

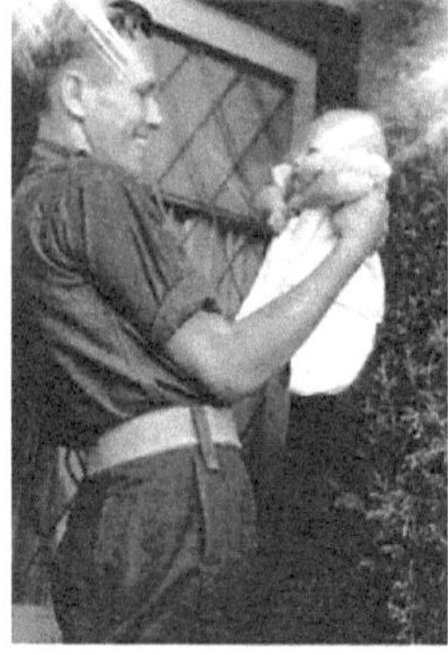

Although Bill and Mavis were establishing their home at Lake Wendouree in Ballarat, Mavis had come back to Geelong to have Helen. Bill's mother lived in Ballarat, but Geelong was familiar to Mavis because this was where she had always lived. Her own mother had died many years before, but she had an older brother, Albert, sister Enid who was a nurse, and a younger sister Audrey.

Helen's christening was at the South Geelong Anglican Church. Her christening gown, might have already been a family heirloom, and also adorned her younger siblings in later years. The gown is still held by Don.

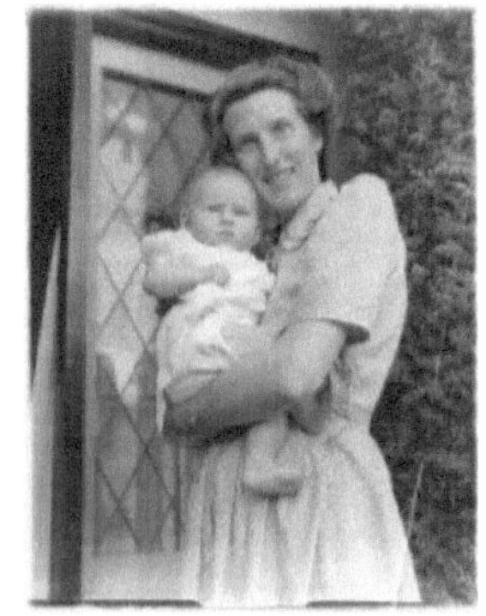

In 1947, her sister, Cynthia, was born when Helen was eighteen months old. Soon after this, Bill obtained work as a journalist with the ABC in Western Australia. The arrangement was that he would go ahead to get things ready for Mavis and the two infants. A few months later, Mavis arrived in Perth by plane with baby Cynthia in her arms and little Helen toddling at her side. They were greeted at the airport by Bill's new boss, who told her that Bill was in the Hollywood Rehabilitation Hospital with a relapse of tuberculosis which he had previously contracted while in PNG. He was to be in the hospital for a long time.

Bill had rented a house in Inglewood for the family. Mavis described these as tough times. She was alone in a strange place. Her husband was in hospital, and she didn't have the support of the family who had been around her in Geelong. She didn't feel confident about the right ways she should be caring for her two little children. There were long trips to the hospital where they were able to see Bill through a window but were not able to get physically close to him because he was in the infectious diseases section.

Because of this difficult beginning, Mavis was particularly appreciative of the support of Mr and Mrs Parsons who became firm friends of the family. They were like grandparents for the 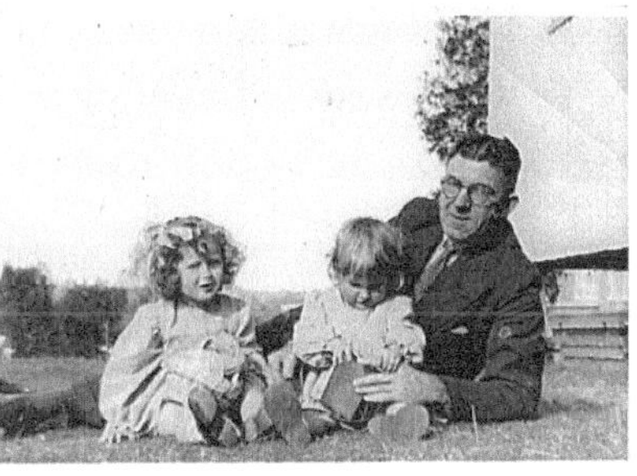 children. Mr Parsons in photographed (above) with Helen and Cynthia. Later, life-long family connections also developed with the Wilkins and Nelson families.

Mavis would have been glad to have visits from her youngest sister, Audrey, and Bill's mother, Elsie.

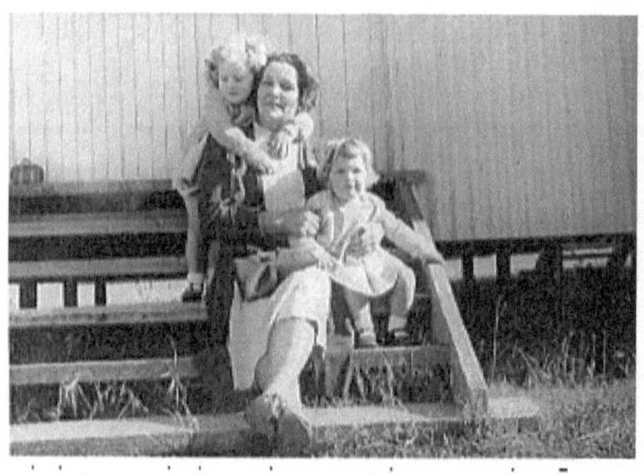 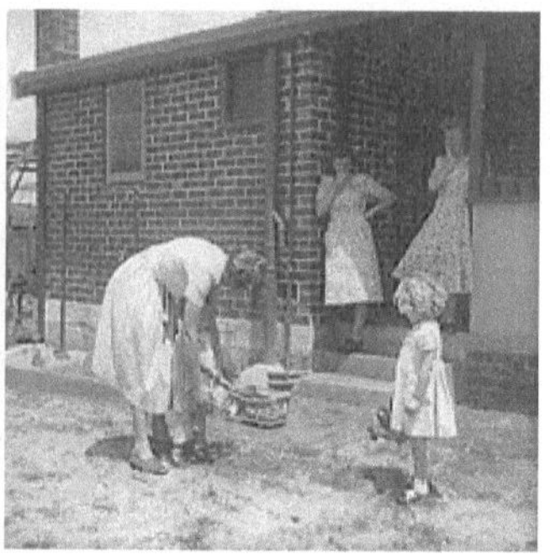

These photos with Helen and Cynthia indicate that these visits might have been before Beverly was born. The photo on the left, with Elsie, was probably at the Hollywood Hospital – perhaps not long before Bill was discharged. On the next page, with Audrey, might have been soon after they had moved from Inglewood to Kensington. This was a Housing Commission house – 11 Bourke Street. It was to be home for the family for about a decade.

While Bill was a patient, he started an in-hospital newsletter – he was always doing something! He was the first in WA to receive a new drug – Streptomycin – and he was eventually discharged after two years and returned to his work at the ABC.

Beverly was born in 1949 when Helen was four years old.

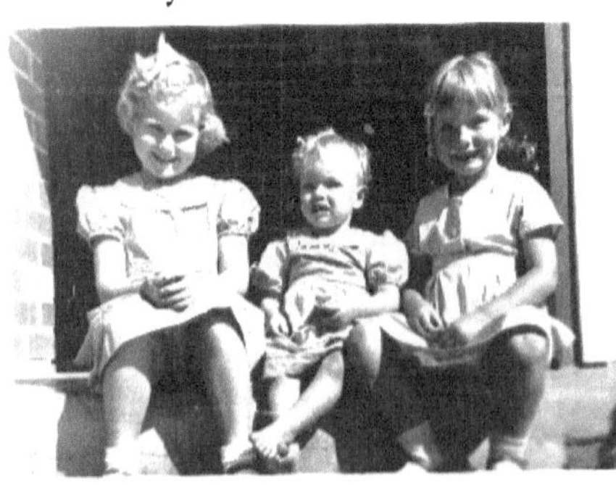

The photo (left) is Helen, Beverly and Cynthia – on the back steps of the Kensington house.

The following photo is Helen in the front of the house about 2000.

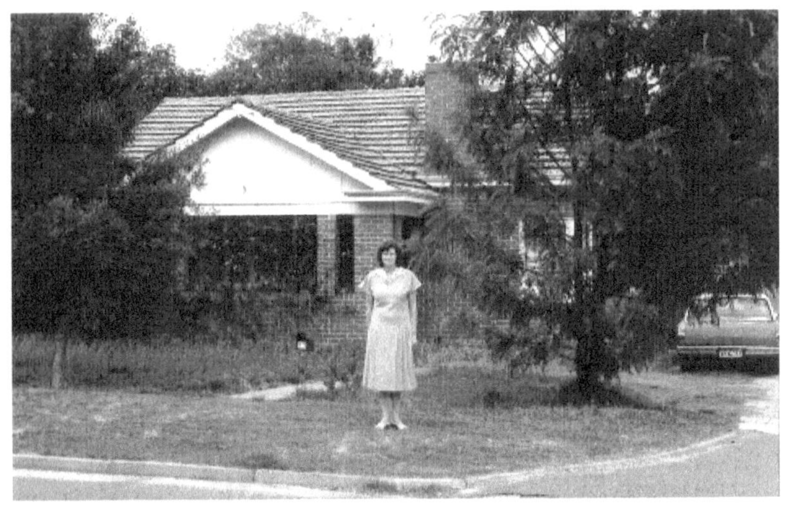

When Beverly was a toddler, she took a liking to eating snails from the garden and Helen had to extract them from her mouth. The three girls got on well, but there were the usual sibling arguments over special things like the show bags from the annual Royal Show. They shared one bedroom and Beverly remembers squabbling over opening and closing their window. Cynthia recollected how Helen used to read to her and tell her what she had learnt at school. The children liked making up concerts and Mavis helped them with their costumes and their performances.

Helen commenced her schooling at the Kensington Primary School in 1951. Her brother, John was born in that year.

When she was almost eight years old, Helen was devastated when her six-month-old brother, Douglas, died of pneumonia. For Mavis, this remained with her as a deep loss – she recalled that it was one of the most difficult things she had to face throughout her life, as this kind of loss was not fully appreciated by the community in those times. It might have prompted Mavis and Bill to think of getting their own home as the Kensington house had sad memories.

Bill purchased five and half acres in the Willeton area that was called Riverton at the time. This seemed such a long way from the centre of Perth – across the old causeway (before the Narrows and Mount Henry bridges) and about eleven kilometres from where they were living. They wanted this land so that Cynthia could have a horse. The family referred to it as 'The Block' and the children used to visit the block as can be seen in this photo with John at the front and Beverly, Cynthia and Helen at the back. Bill designed a large house that he progressively built over many 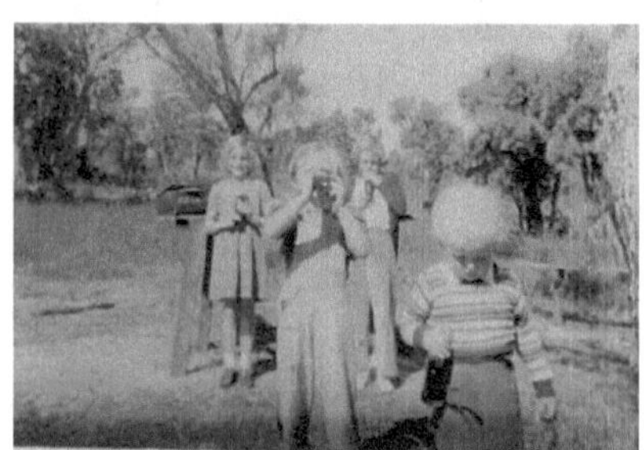 years while the family were still living at Kensington. The children loved being there while Bill was busy building. They had fun carting bricks and had competitions to see who could carry the most at a time – Cynthia aways won that! They also fossicked through the blue metal looking for 'fool's gold'.

At Kensington, the children often enjoyed playing in a pine plantation in the next street. They swept pine needles on the ground to form 'rooms' to play their games.

The family attended the Methodist church. Bill had previously been active in the Methodist church in Ballarat. Mavis attended the South Geelong Anglican church with her family when she was growing up. Initially, the Mitchells attended the Kensington Methodist church and later the Rossmoyne church where Helen taught in the Sunday School, ran a youth group, and played the organ for many years as a teenager.

The girls attended Brownies and Mavis was 'Brown Owl'. This next photo has Helen on the right of the leader. Elizabeth Hof (nee Wilkins) is on the other side of the leader. It is probably Cynthia next to Elizabeth. Beverly was in the back row, fourth from the left. Rebecca Wilkins is in the middle row, second from the right. The portrait on the right is Helen at 11½ years.

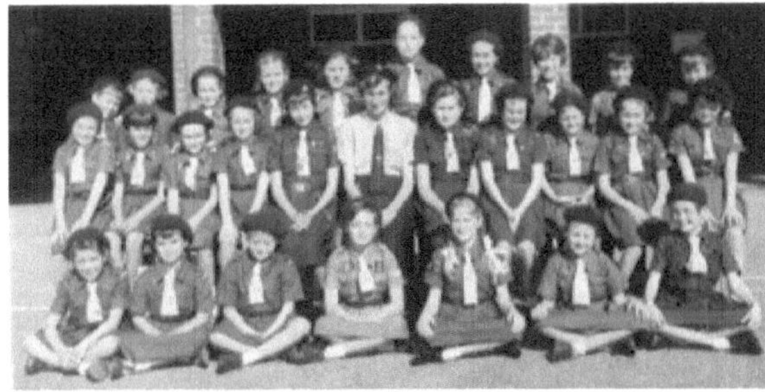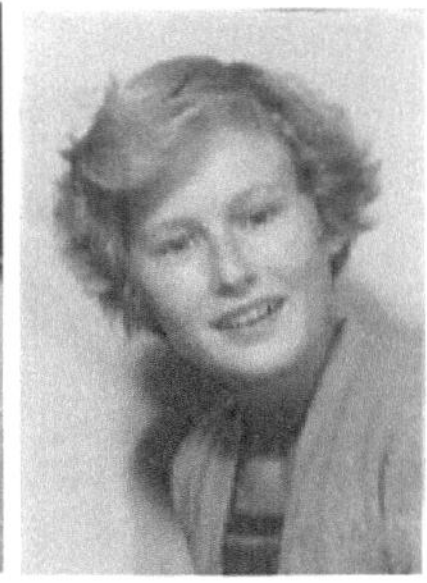

In 1954, Bill changed from the ABC to become a journalist with the *West Australian* newspaper in Fremantle. He became more involved in politics with the Liberal Party.

Helen attended Kent Street High School from 1957. In the photo with the girls in their uniforms around 1960, Helen is on the far left and Elizabeth Hof (nee Wilkins) is on the far right. In the photo at the school reunion around 2000, Helen is the third from the left, Cynthia is on the far right, and Elizabeth is at the front right.

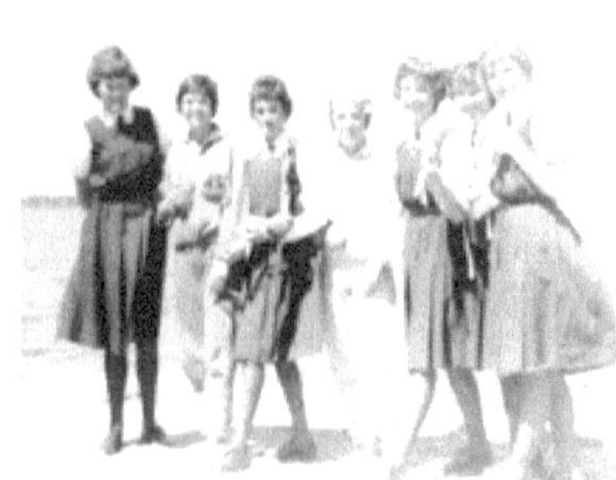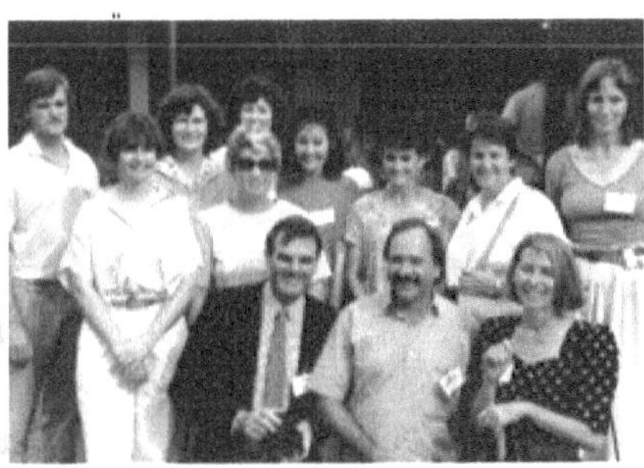

Russell was born in 1959 when Helen was fourteen years old. As she was the eldest of so many siblings, Helen helped her mother care for the younger children. They were crowded into two bedrooms and a 'sleepout' – an enclosed verandah – at the Kensington house. Helen recalled that, *We lived in a tiny two-*

bedroomed house, but I don't remember feeling deprived in any way. It was quite a lively sort of neighborhood, full of very interesting people as I was growing up.

Helen and Elizabeth used to attend the Herbert Edwards School of Tennis in Subiaco for lessons together on Saturday mornings during the warm months. They used to take the bus into Perth, from where they would get into a tram for the second half of the journey to Subiaco. One time the girls spent their return fares on White Knight peppermint chocolate bars and they had to walk back such a long way from Subiaco to their homes in Kensington. It is not hard to imagine the stir this caused amongst their parents.

When, in 1961, the family finally moved to their Willetton home, they felt the contrast to the old house. Now the five children each had their own bedroom. It was not yet fully complete – there weren't any doors for a while, no back or front doors. Bill liked to try new things and he used a new type of cladding for the internal walls and ceiling. The cladding was called Stramit – it was compacted straw and was said to be fire-proof.

At the time of this move, Helen was fifteen years old and in her third year of high school. In Kensington, they had been living quite close to the high school whereas Kent Street High School was quite a trek (10 kilometres) from Willetton. Sometimes Bill would drive the three girls to school and he

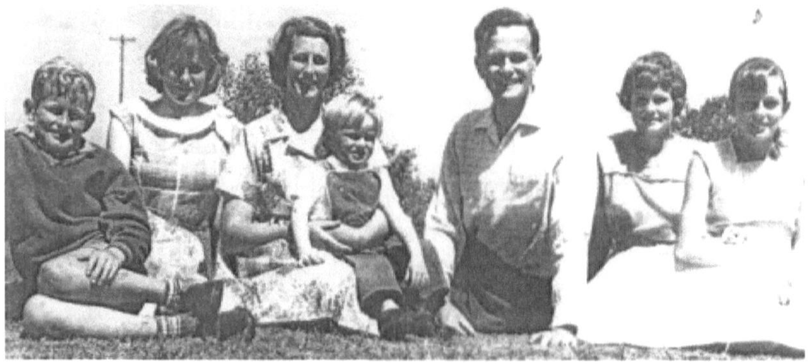

would almost drive past the school because he was so preoccupied with writing his next speech in his head. The girls would have to shout at him, "Hey, Dad, stop. Here's the school!"

The family went on several long camping trips. One memorable journey was going across the Nullabor (not yet a sealed road) in a VW Micro Bus. Bill had made a full-length roof rack that was long enough and wide enough for the three girls to sleep up there comfortably. He made hinged struts that, when they were folded into an upright position, they made the top of the bus look like a covered wagon and had enough room for the girls to sit up. Mavis made the cover for it on her trusty Singer sewing machine. John slept on the front bench seat and Russell at the back on a platform there. Their mum and dad slept in the middle section by removing the centre bench seat, turning it around and placing it on the ground next to the floor to form a double bed under an awning that came out from the 'covered wagon'.

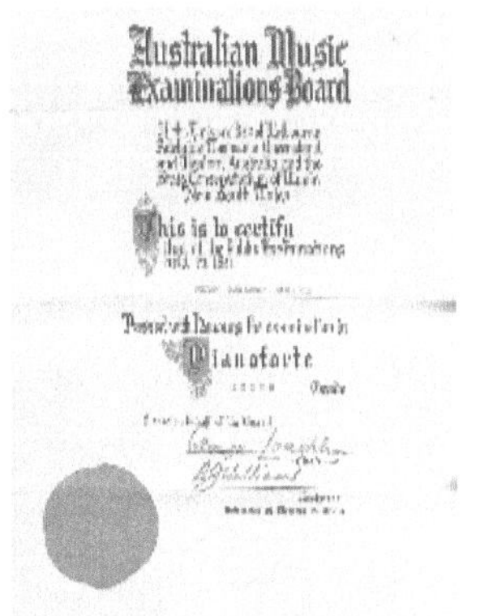

Helen completed grade six in piano in 1961. Music always played an important part in her life.

She matriculated at the end of high school in 1962. Her tertiary studies included medicine for three years, Occupational Therapy for two years, and BSc in Anatomy for one year. This is how those eventful years unfolded.

Helen was fortunate to win a scholarship and started studying medicine at the University of Western Australia in 1963. Among her fellow students were Jane James (with whom Helen retained a friendship when Jane was a GP in Denmark), Anne Durack, Annette Finn (who was a witness in Helen's wedding in Scotland), and Fiona Stanley.

Fiona became a prominent medical researcher after whom the Fiona Stanley Hospital was named – and Helen was treated there near the end of her life.

In one of her university holidays, Helen worked at the Kununoppin hospital. She was shocked when a ute skidded to a halt at the hospital with panicked youths who had been on a kangaroo hunt. One of them had been shot while standing on the back and leaning over the top of the cab. A rifle inside the cab had accidentally gone off and had shot the youth in the head. On another occasion, Helen was required to take part in a simple operation because they said, "Oh, you are a medical student. Please do this …"

Drama struck in 1965. Mavis had been drying a mattress near a radiator and the bedding fell against the heater while she was outside hanging out the washing. Within minutes the whole house was on fire. Bill was driving home, and someone called out, "Hey, Bill, your house is on fire!" He thought it was a joke until he arrived home to find the fire brigade trying to save whatever they could.

The fire was so hot that the bricks changed colour and the glass in the windows melted – so much for Stramit being fireproof!

The neighbours rallied around. That night the family were able to shift into the Panizza's old house that was literally down the road from their burnt-out house. A neighbour who lived up at the top of Elgon Hill, Bill Gilliland, worked for Joyce Brothers and had beds delivered for them all. They went for dinner at another neighbour's and then were able to sleep in Panizza's house. Beverly, who was only fifteen, remembers how relieved she was that the family were still together, and no one had been injured.

Only a few items could be saved from the fire and there are some stories some of these.

The piano was lifted up to safety by a crane, and years later, Helen arranged for it to be taken to Kununurra when she was living there. It is now at Russell's house.

In her room, Helen had a skeleton for her medical studies and there is a family story that the police raised questions about how this skeleton was found in the burnt ruins of the house.

Helen's grade six piano certificate has a couple of scorch marks (see previous page).

In those times, Helen loved going ice-skating, so she was pleased that her skates survived the fire. A few years later, when she was in Scotland, she had the idea of skating there. In the final months of her life, when she could not concentrate on anything much, she took comfort in watching hours of videos of beautiful formation ice skating. At her funeral, these ice skates were placed on top of the coffin and were buried with her.

Helen's books and study notes were burnt in the fire. This is when she was about to sit for her third-year medical exams. Fortunately, fellow students lent her their notes – and she passed okay.

Although she managed to pass, Helen wrote about this period of her life: *It was a time of crises, and I started thinking deeply about why I was studying medicine. I heard about an Occupational Therapy school starting up in Perth and, the more I found out about this, the more I felt this was closer to my calling, as I was also very interested in, and good at, arts and crafts. So, I investigated transferring my scholarship, but they said this couldn't happen as it would be going backwards from Uni to TAFE. So, I firstly worked at Claremont Mental Hospital as an OT assistant for a year and then applied for a scholarship which bonded me to work with the Mental Health Services (MHS) for two years after completing the course. I accepted. I was credited the first year because of my previous studies, so I entered the second year of the OT course in 1968, and completed it the following year.*"

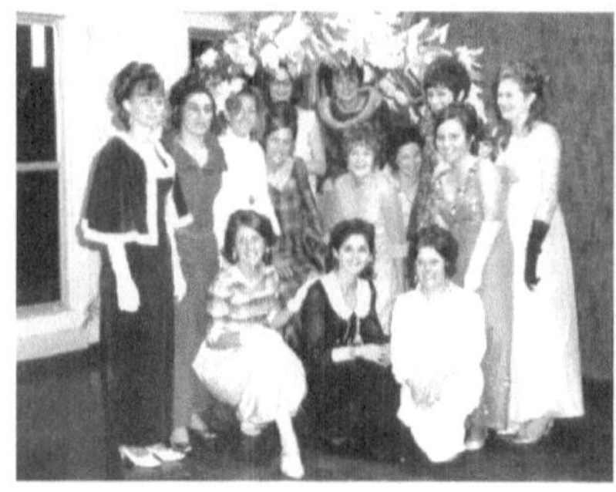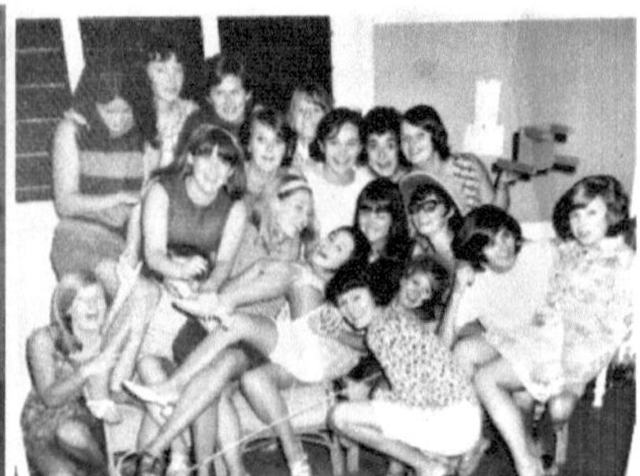

In the photo of the OT students' ball, Helen is on the far right. Maxien Lethbridge (now Bradley) is second on the left – and Ronnie Becker (now Naughton) is seated on the left. In the 'messing around' photo, Helen is in the back row, third from the left. Maxien is the head, the seventh from the left, in the back row, and Ronnie is kneeling sideways.

Ronnie's memories of Helen:

Memories of Helen go back as far as 1968 and our OT student days where, as OT students, we received training in theoretical subjects as well as many practical. One of the projects was to set up a small business venture and Helen, as well as Cynthia nee Green and Marian nee Foster, and I were engaged in screen printing and then selling packs of notepaper and cards.

As I got to know Helen, it became quite obvious that Helen had a gift for creative and artistic pursuits and that continued throughout her life.

Helen became a close friend mostly due to the love of the arts, including music and outdoor adventures which we both shared. Helen often also welcomed me into the Mitchell home, which was always a hive of stimulating activity and enterprise.

Helen, Cynthia, Marian and I formed a close friendship,

and on one term holiday break in 1968, we decided to tour the NW Pilbara region in an oldish VW Combi bravely loaned to us by the Mitchell family for our adventure. We had absolutely no idea what to expect in the outback with our limited mechanical knowledge, and had numerous challenges on the way. We travelled mostly on unsealed roads and experienced various mechanical breakdowns, relying on passers-by to rescue and assist us. Our major goal was to film and record on tape our incredible journey, which we achieved. Helen, in particular, was full of confidence that we would succeed and make it back to Perth safely.

It seemed to me that Helen would always be ready to embark on some worthwhile artistic project with a community focus and often inspired me with her aspirations and endeavours.

There were gaps in contact during child-rearing years but we reconnected again following the 50th OT group reunion. Those recent get-togethers and opportunities to reminisce and share will be treasured always.

Helen will also be remembered by me for her gentle nature and extraordinary capacity to listen, absorb and demonstrate enthusiasm for the speaker's story. It was always evident that she had a deep faith and a belief in the hereafter.

You will remain in my prayers and thoughts for evermore.

Rest in Peace, dear friend, Love Ronnie Naughton nee Becker

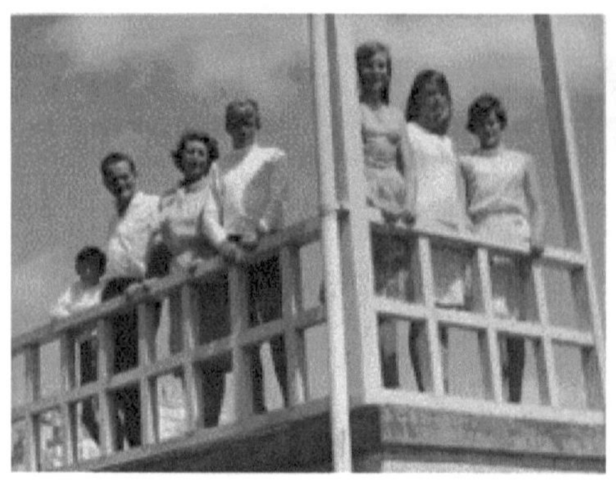 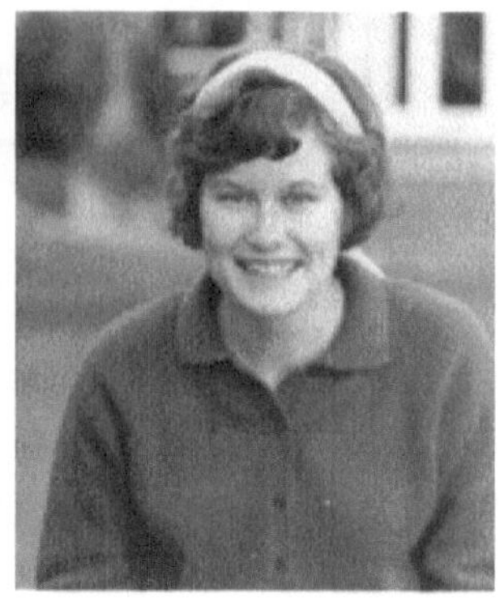

After the fire, the house was rebuilt on the original foundatons. Subsequently, Bill and Mavis sold off most of the five and a half acres and ended up with half an acre at 9 Elgon Hill, Willetton. That area is now prized as it is near the highly regarded Rossmoyne Senior High School.

In 1968, through her friend, Verona Mauger (now Lucas), Helen became interested in the Baha'i Faith. She was attracted, but not prepared to fully commit herself for several years. Helen details her journey as a Baha'i in chapter 25, but her first steps in this direction are in the following account.

Around this time, Helen moved from home into a house in Cottesloe that she rented with a few other Baha'i youth. It was an old house, with make-do electrical wiring and an external dunny out the back. It was a great time playing music and talking excitedly through the night. This confused the neighbours, who suspected that there were drugs, and they called the police.

Helen finished her Occupational Therapy course in 1969 and at the end of that year, she went to the Baha'i Summer School at Yerrinbool which is south of Sydney. She holidayed with Verona and 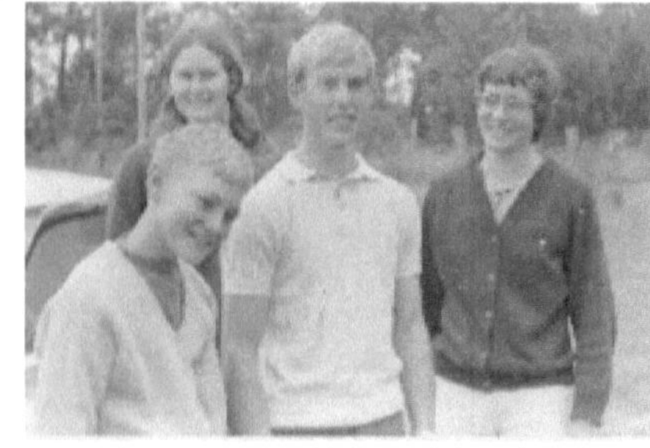

her brothers in Sydney where Verona had moved to. On this trip, she decided to become a Baha'i at the beginning of 1970.

On returning to Perth, Helen moved in with Maxien, with whom she had studied Occupational Therapy. This was Maxien's mother's flat – in Mount's Bay Road.

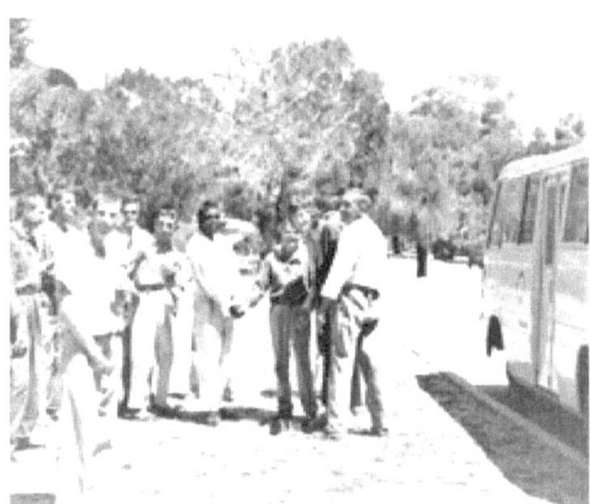
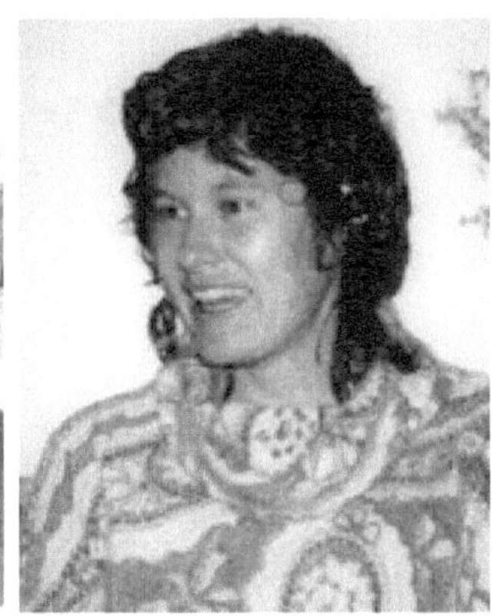

Helen returned to work at the maximum-security section of Claremont Mental Hospital in 1970. She had previously worked there as a therapy assistant in 1967, but now she came back as a trained Occupational Therapist – for her bond with the MHS. On one occasion, she had the patients playing volleyball and somehow she fell. The patients, who were considered dangerous, gently carried her to safety – she felt so well cared for.

She suspended her two-year bond at the end of 1970 to go back to university to complete a Bachelor of Science with a major in Human Anatomy. This was her favourite subject because she had gained a particular interest in this during her medical studies. Helen completed this in one year because she was credited with her previous passes.

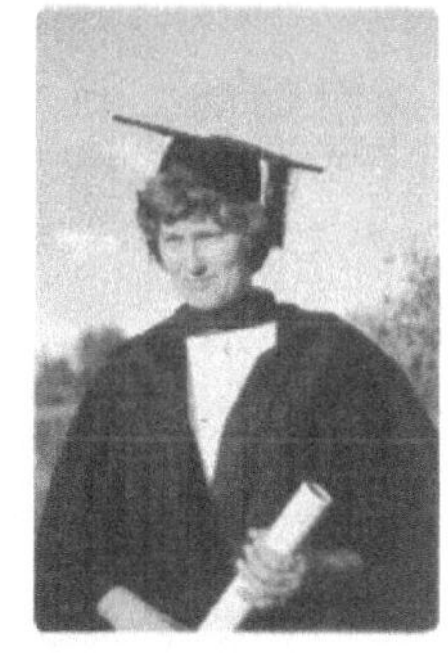

During this year, Helen established the UWA Baha'i Society.

Around this time, Bill purchased two Zeta cars - Bill could not resist a novel idea. Everyone was amused as Helen drove around in this quaint contraption. These were produced by the Lightburn washing machine company and were powered by a noisy motor-bike type two-stroke engine inside a light fibreglass body. Gearing was up for first, down for second, then back up for third. The petrol gauge was a plastic pipe in the dashboard

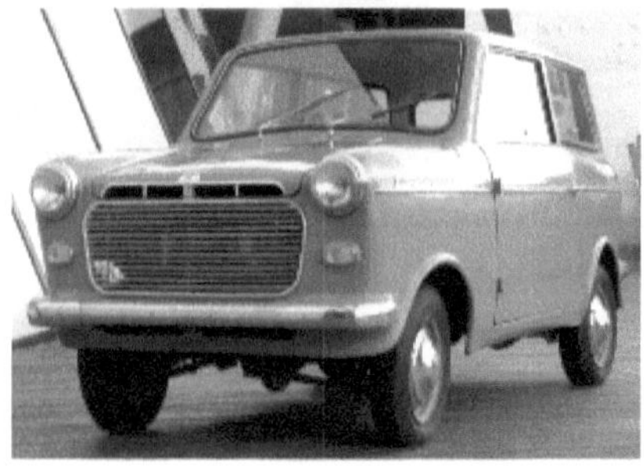

in which the fuel went up and down so Helen was never sure how much she had left. Fortunately, it was very easy to push. Once she was in awkward parking spot and passer-by lifted the car out.

In May 1971, Helen went to Fiji for the Baha'i Oceanic Conference. She got Dengue fever there but recovered quickly.

In 1972, she resumed her work with Claremont Mental Hospital for another year because she was obliged to complete her bond with MHS.

Then she was off to New Zealand for a working holiday in 1973. In March of that year, she had quite an adventure on the Routeburn track, which she was unprepared for – and barely survived to tell the tale. She recorded this in diary form[1].

On her tour around NZ, she happened to strike up a casual conversation with someone in a park in Nelson. This lady, who was working in a science laboratory, mentioned that they were in need of a lab technician. So Helen worked there for a few months.

Soon after returning to Perth, she was off to Northern Ireland for Maxien's wedding, and then to St Andrews in Scotland...   ooOOoo..

---

[1]   Helen's adventure on the Routeburn Track is Chapter 2.

2

The Routeburn Track

A mountain adventure in New Zealand in 1973

Written by Helen Mitchell

"You must go on the Milford Track
You must go on the Milford Track
You must go on the Milford Track
Even if you don't go anywhere else ---
You must go on the Milford Track"
says Bob Goodale, and he knows!

From Aukland to Queenstown:
"Have you been on the Milford Track?"
"Yes," "No," "No," "Yes," "Would like to?"
"Not interested?", "What's it like?".
"Fantastic,"– "Tremendous scenery."
"Didn't see anything for rain,
 just trudge through mud."
"Okay, but the Routeburn Track is much better,
 cheaper, shorter, much more interesting."

Lorraine Orme, Jan Plume and I arrived in Queenstown at about 5:30 pm, Thurs 15th March 1973. It was raining and cold. Getting thoroughly wet, we trudged with all our belongings, half a mile around the lake to the Youth Hostel.

We had brought the sunshine with us all the way down the west coast – and Queenstown did not disappoint us – three days of sunshine and glorious weather.

It's Friday – let's get up early and find out what is involved in the Routeburn Track or the Milford Track – they were still just names to us.

Information from the Tourist Bureau and Public Relations Office: $57 for the Routeburn Track and $82 for the Milford Track. These were paid guided tours that provided sleeping accommodation and meals and a bus trip back to Queenstown or TeAnau at the end of the journey. A bit much for our pockets, and we had met many people who had done the tracks on their own.

Information from the Lands and Survey Dept: Boat leaves Queenstown at 9:00 am on Mon, Wed & Fri and connects with a bus at Kinloch which drives you to Bryant's Lodge and the beginning of the Routeburn Track. Cost $3.50. The use of the National Park huts for $2.00. You had to carry your own food and sleeping bag etc. Milford Track – no information – enquire at TeAnua.

Thus, having at least some information on the Routeburn Track and it getting very close to the end of the season for doing these treks, we decided to start out on the following Monday – across the Humboldt Mountains.

Using a rough map and details regarding the track on a small pamphlet given to us by the Lands & Survey Dept, we began to prepare for the journey –

Food: Dried everything – as light as possible

Clothing: Be prepared for snow! Gosh- already had a windproof nylon top with a hood. So, on finding a pair of baggy nylon trousers in a sports shop, I considered that was adequate.

Shoes: Well, my boots have always been most comfortable for walking in – they're warm and fairly waterproof – had Tope souls and heels put on before I left Perth – so they were in good condition.

Well, even though I packed the bare minimum – one change of clothes, food for three days in dried packets, with my sleeping bag – I was carrying about 35 lbs (16 kgs). Incredible! Yet what could I throw out? Nylon cord? No, could come in handy. Torch? No. Peanut paste? Perhaps, but that's good protein and I like it. Well, in the end, we each managed to collect a small bag of goods we didn't really need, and this we freighted to TeAnau.

All set to go – it's Sunday – a day to fill – wandered through Queenstown yesterday – well, it does say on the bottom of the pamphlet that you should contact the ranger in Glenorchy before setting out. To Glenorchy! On a Sunday! No buses – literally a one-horse town – and about 30 miles (48 kilometres) away. Hitchhike? Never done it before – and three of us.

Well, we set out – walked about three miles until we heard a car coming up behind us. Tried to put my thumb up in the manner that hitch-hikers do – failed miserably and ended up waving in a friendly manner as the car passed by. But – miracle of miracles – about 100 yards (90 metres) down the track, it slowly came to a stop. "Would you like a lift? How far are you going?" Two dear old ladies who had been in the army together and were out for a few days picnic to chat about old times – and they <u>never</u> pick up hitch-hikers - but weren't those girls so friendly waving to them like that!

Well, they would take us all the way to Glenorchy and even to 'Paradise', after the Paradise duck. Any time we wanted to take photos we were to just let them know and they would stop. And – my goodness – I saw some of the most beautiful scenery I have seen since I have been in New Zealand. They even waited for me to do a few quick sketches. (We passed an artist with his oil paints and easel merrily painting on the side of the road – a real professional.)

It being fasting time for us Baha'is, I left the others having lunch and walked a half mile down the track to the ranger's cottage – 'Mt Aspiring National Park'. "You want to do the Routeburn? It's a good track – well used – might snow though." That was about all the information I got from the ranger – apart from another pamphlet exactly the same as the one we already had.

Mon 19th March:

Three smiling faces framed by assorted colours of rucksacks and sleeping bags appeared at the Queenstown jetty.

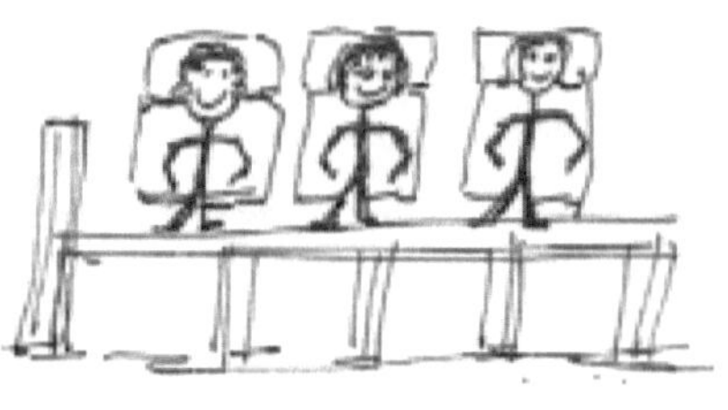

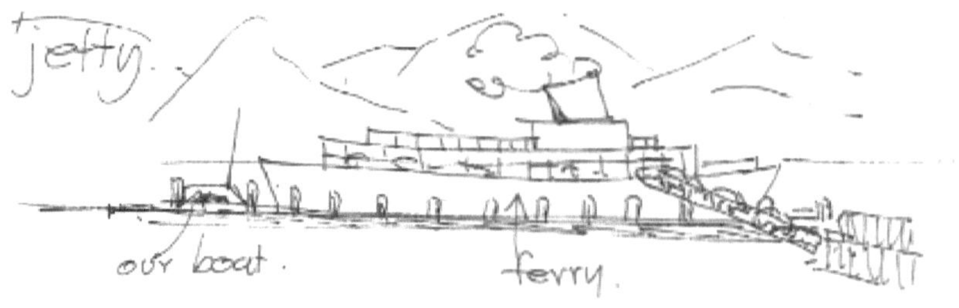

While waiting to buy our tickets a very large ferry pulled in – it was packed with … sheep. As the sheep were being off-loaded we assumed that we would be on-loaded directly after. Pondering on the smelly conditions, we hardly noticed another much smaller boat pull in down the other end of the jetty. Well, that was it – about 25 feet (8 metres) I suppose, and the deck some 2 feet (60 cms) out of the water.

There were eleven of us altogether heading for the Routeburn Track that day. Since the boat was down there and we were up here, none of us knew quite what we were supposed to do about getting on. And then 'it' appeared – bounding with one step from boat to jetty – *"Morning. Can I give you a hand?"* It took me a while to recover from the sudden appearance of this fellow in his blazing red anorak flashing **'Carlton Science'** across his back. Yes, sure we needed a hand – in fact a ladder would have been better – but somehow we passed our rucksacks down and then half-fell onto the deck of the boat. There was sort of slat-seats that propped up from the side of the deck – just enough room as one was broken – and there we all huddled with our rucksacks piled in a heap in the middle, settling down with feet outstretched, relaxing on the rail, ready for a three-hour cruise up Lake Wakatipu, viewing the beautiful mountain scenery.

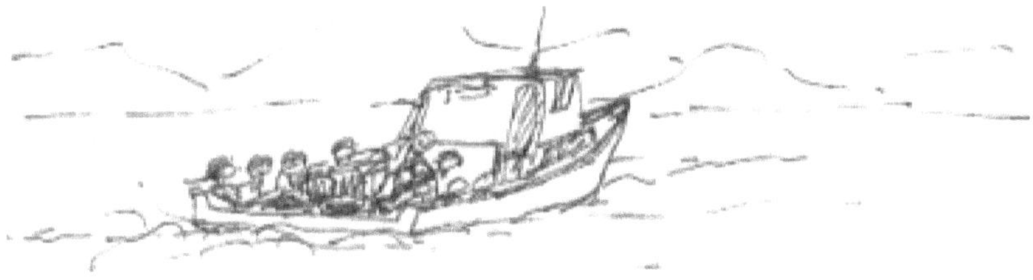

Isn't this great!

Wow – and then the wind hit us – it was like being on the ocean. I hurriedly put on my nylon top and pants although I was already wet. Our skipper threw us down a large canvas cover to wrap our rucksacks in. Well, it got so wet and rough that we all ended up squeezing into the cabin with the skipper – my eyes nearly popped out of my head – there he was, perched on the high stool driving the boat with his feet. Puffing away on a cigarette and twiddling with knobs with the other hand, he chatted away – *"... and there is Mount this and Mount that ... and they had an avalanche there last winter and there's Pig Island in the distance ...."* At this point, he jumped off his seat and asked us if we would all like tea or coffee. At the same

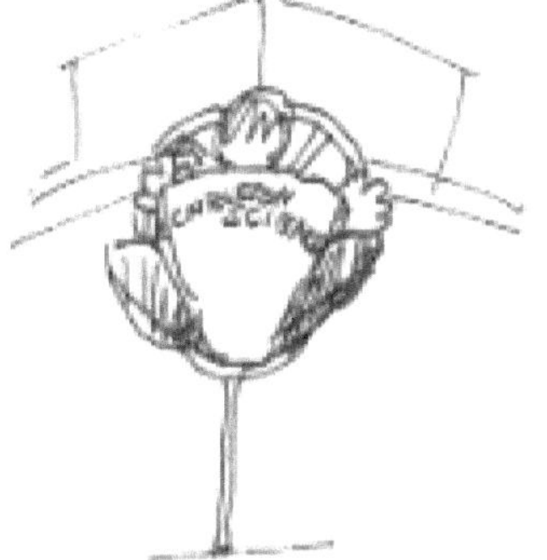

time, he grabbed me and asked me to steer the boat *"between the big island and the little one"*. There being so much spray splashing over the front window of the cabin and me being short-sighted, I just couldn't see "the little island", so I headed for the big one – well, tried to – we zig zagged around for a while until I realized that the steering on the boat over-steers considerably. Eventually, I got the hang of it – between the two islands because I had at last caught sight of the little one – and there's a sand bank on the left – and allow for the wind. We made it – whew! – not bad with everyone teasing me constantly – every time I laughed, the boat headed off in another direction. My last effort at steering the boat was when we were nearing Kinloch – and then the skipper just disappeared and left me to it. He seemed ages and the jetty was getting closer – and then suddenly the steering locked and I couldn't turn the wheel – Oh boy! Where's 'Carlton Science'? – and then I heard a roar of laughter – a couple of boys were holding the chain that connects the wheel with the engine steering. And then up pops 'Carlton Science' just in time to bring the boat smoothly into the jetty. Wow! And that was only the beginning.

And there we were – this was Kinloch – which seemed to consist only of a house and bus shelter. Anyone living here? Ah! A hand was waving out the window of the house and a voice echoed down the hill – *"Cup of tea ready!"* My stomach leapt with delight at the thought. But it was only for 'Carlton Science' who immediately bounded up the hill, calling back to us as he went, *"The bus will be here soon – the bus driver's gone for a short run."* A run? Where? I couldn't see any roads that went anywhere?

It was noon and the sun was shining, so we all settled down on the ground, resting against our packs. And then it appeared! THE BUS.

A 1942 Chevrolet bus. Well-kept celluloid windows but no roof! Painted red with a neatly painted label on the side. Water leaking profusely from the

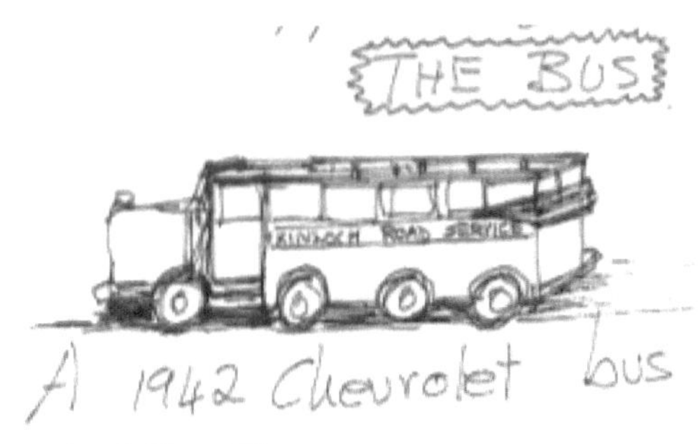

radiator and running down the hill as if to greet us.

And then the door opens – and out jumps friendliness itself – all dressed up in cap, tie, white shirt, polished shoes as any proper bus driver would be. Tottering on his feet a little and with a smile from ear to ear, he walks over to tell us he is the bus driver and that is his bus – but – we will have to wait until he has had his cup of tea – and there was the hand waving out the window again.

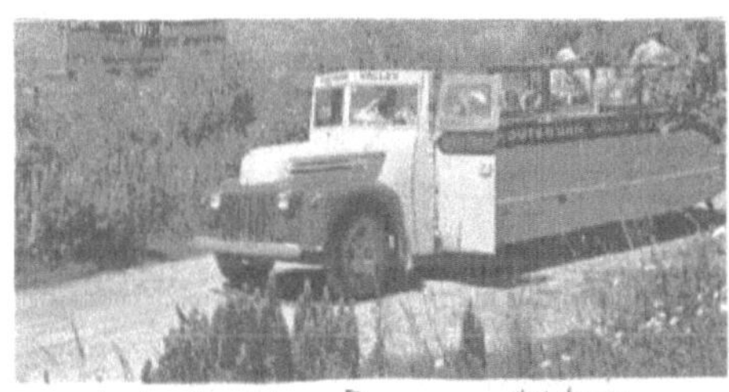
Kinloch – Routeburn Bus – owned & driven by Harry Bryant – for the past 48 & yrs.

After half an hour, Harry reappeared (we learned later, that was his name). Ceremoniously he opened the door and told us we could now get on – but no rucksacks on the seats – as they may tear the upholstery. As we were loading on, Harry was constantly disappearing behind a clump of bushes and then reappearing with cans and buckets of water – Ah! – He tells us, "… the only thing wrong with this bus is that it has a leaky radiator" – did it ever!

Well, radiator full, Harry seated like a king at the front, one turn of the key and we're off. As we rattled from side to side, Harry proceeded to give us a conducted tour of the countryside. "… and there's Mt Earshaw," he would say, taking his hands off the wheel and not only pointing but turning right around to chat away about every inch of history concerning every landmark that appeared on the horizon, while passengers gazed concernedly at the road and the approaching narrow gateway.

Harry had been driving this bus for precisely 43½ years – along the same road, backwards and forwards – approximately twelve miles. He had named every pot-hole in the road and spoke to the sheep and cows we passed as if he knew them individually.

We were informed that he had the only truly air-conditioned bus in NZ – and it was delightful on a sunny day; looking at the scenery without glass reflections, we looked over the windows in this bus. But what happens when it rains?! That's what the hood at the back was for – one of those fold-down types like they have on prams except it was extendable – and I have since been told by a friend that it really works!

Whoops! We're stopping. Engine trouble? No. Nothing to worry about, "… just have to fill the radiator before climbing the next hill – a bit of a steep one."

Eventually, we arrived – at Bryant's Lodge (after Harry Bryant – the one and only bus driver on the Routeburn-Kinloch Road) and the start of the Routeburn Track.

Note: The Routeburn-Kinloch Road was part of a route originally planned as access to the pioneering settlement at Martin's Bay, but the road was incorrectly routed and no further construction was carried out.

My first attempt at putting my rucksack on laid me flat on the ground with all that 35 lbs on top of me. Amidst much amused laughter and the help of a friend, I managed to load up. Feeling decidedly unbalanced, I tottered forward like a child learning to walk – 23 miles!

Discovery number 1 was that they don't make mountains out

of sand here – they make them out of rocks! – and thin-soled high-heeled boots weren't exactly designed for this kind of rambling.

Discovery number 2 was that I was quite unfit or I was carrying too much weight – or both. Only 200 yards down the track and I'm puffing – and oh boy! – my shoulders – they're aching!

Distances were measured in walking times – 2½ hours to the Routeburn Flat Huts, and 4 hours to the Routeburn Falls Hut – and it says in the pamphlet that most people make it to the Routeburn Fall Hut on the first afternoon! Well – never say die! I had to think of a way of doing this without killing myself.

I found that I could walk for fifteen minutes before feeling absolutely compelled to collapse on a rock and allow my poor muscles to recover. So I would not allow myself a rest until fifteen minutes was up. And the only way I got through was to aim for a log or bend and say to myself, "Look, Helen – just a bit further – only from here to there," and then I'd look for another point to aim for. What a miserable way to enjoy the countryside!

About an hour passed and I had well and truly arrived at discovery number 3. Warm woollen slacks and jumper were not quite the thing for tramping, no matter how cold the temperature was. The perspiration was trickling down inside my clothes and I frequently stopped by the cool mountain streams to cool my face and gulp down some water. Shorts and a light top would have been quite adequate.

The supposed 2 ½-hour walk to the Routeburn Flat Huts took me 3 ½ hours and there were all the others resting against their packs laughing and talking and having a bite to eat. "How come you took so long?" they said. I just pulled my shoulders in, and let my pack fall to the ground – and almost fell down with it.

"I can see the Routeburn Falls Hut!" someone was saying, pointing vertically upwards as if at a cloud.

"Where?"

"See, just on the side of that waterfall near those dump of trees."

And there it was – a neat wooden speck shrouded by mountain mist. The sign said casually '1½-hour walk'.

"Oh, God! If you have any angels to spare today could you just allow them to lift me to the top of the mountain!"

Another 1000 feet almost straight up! Well, it took me three hours. It was dusk by the time I got there – and my goodness! – I nearly didn't – twenty steps up and a 5-minute pause to pant and puff – it is difficult to estimate progress at that rate.

The Routeburn Falls Hut consisted of a central cooking-eating area with two small bunk rooms, one on each side – quite civilized with a kerosene, two-burner cooker and a washing sink with water laid on. Even tables and benches for meals. And luxury of luxuries – a mattress to sleep on!

As I was last in line to cook my tea, it was about 9:30 pm before I sat down for a meal – just as well, because I couldn't have eaten before that.

Everyone else seemed to have had trouble climbing the last bit, and so we all sat around discussing our sore backs, aching feet etc. In the midst of it, the assistant manager, who lived in a room attached to one end of the hut, came in and collected our $2.00 fee for the huts.

Well, to bed, but not much rest – it rained all night, and there was a wild party going on in the ranger's room until all hours.

The dawn brought the Kea parrots with their wild screeching. Time to rise and stoke up the energy supplies again.

The pamphlet warns that the next bit of the track is very exposed and dangerous in bad weather, and you are not supposed to tackle it unless fine weather prevails. Luckily it had stopped raining – even a patch of blue sky. Still, a bit misty up there but the ranger assured us that the forecast was fine.

By the time we had cleaned up and packed, it was 10 am. Well, off we trudged again to climb from 3,300 feet to 4,200 and cross what is known as the Harris Saddle.

It wasn't long before my feet were soaking – the track was only made of rocks – it was a stream. You just waded through water, mud and rocks – all the way. On one occasion, I slipped in a mud patch. One leg fell knee-deep in mud, and I could feel the mud trickling down the inside of my boot. One hand landed on a sizable rock which was all that saved me from sliding in completely. I felt like just sitting in the mud and crying – but there was no one around to listen! Oh gosh! Struggle up – and on again – all muddy and wet – yuk!

And now we're climbing up – puff, pant -and up a bit further and a bit further.

Whew! Time to collapse on a rock. And, as I looked back, I saw what looked like a blue shirt with a backpack and legs. He was leaping up the mountainside – literally running up the mountain.

I knew there was a guided tour in front of us. They have their own huts with meals cooked for them, properly made beds, showers etc. and so, as he approached, I asked, "Are you on the guided tour?"

Quite unpuffed, with a fresh smile, he replied, "I am the guide!" He had cleaned up the hut while the party went on ahead and then he ran to catch 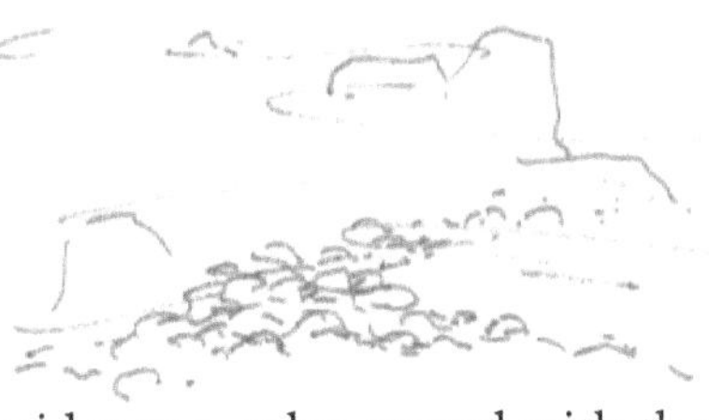 up with them. There were other guides too, who stayed with the climbers. He paused and chatted for a bit – this was the 30th time he'd done the trek from one side to the other. He laughed at my high-heeled boots, saying that the next bit was hard going and I'd be lucky not to break my ankle or worse! And off he leapt up the mountain again, leaving me still gasping by the side of the track with that pleasant thought of what was ahead.

Plodding on and on, up and up, wading through mountain mist until – my God, the sign! – '4,200 feet – the highest point of the track'. One would expect here to gaze out upon infinite horizons but, alas, only mist and vague rocks.

Another few hundred yards of crawling inch by inch around the face of the cliff and I managed to catch up with the others – the guided tour party was there as well – all eating, drinking and talking. The blue-shirted guide I had met on the way up took pity on me as I stumbled over the last few rocks – he came and lifted my pack off my back – RELIEF.

It was about 12:30 – 1:00 pm and the sign stated, '3½ hours to the Lake McKenzie Hut'. If I made the same rate of progress as previously, I would be lucky to get there before nightfall. But of course – it was more-or-less downhill from now on – 1000 feet almost vertically down. At least when you're going up, you can't see where you might fall!

Hanging on to trees and gradually lowering myself to the next rock – truly – it was worse than the steepest climb – much greater chance of slipping – and controlled bending brings into action muscles I don't think I have ever used before. Every muscle in my body was tense, trying to control what could have been a rather rapid descent.

The Montane Beech forest, with its large exposed roots and damp bark covered with lichens, filtered sunlight over the rocky ground from a multitude of half-lit patches – just the right setting for elves and leprechauns – and ghosts.

About halfway down, there was a sign pointing nowhere stating, 'Deadman's Track' and then a little further on a plaque nailed to a rock, 'In memory of …. who died of exposure on this spot …' Oh dear!

I was now starting to tremble with the tension of controlling each well-aimed fall to the next rock below. If I had landed wrongly, I certainly would have "done an ankle in or worse". And my feet were so sore – every rock seemed to be pressing on bare skin. And my shoulders were aching.

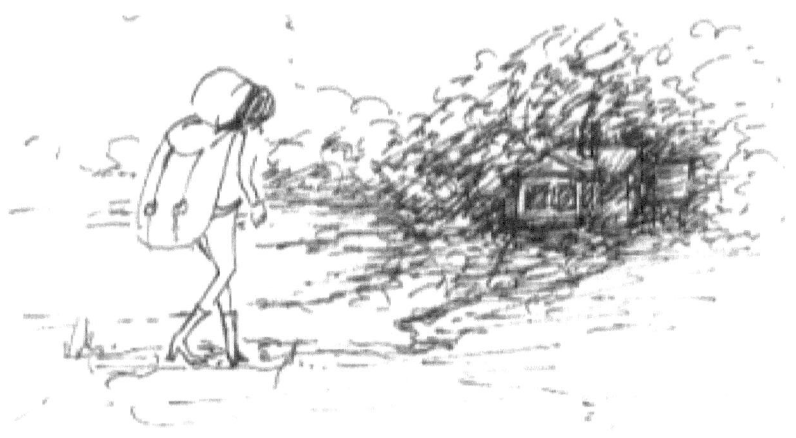

The afternoon light was fading when, slipping and sliding in mud, I emerged from the Beech trees into a cleared, grassy space, with a lake in one corner and – and – over there, a hut! – with smoke coming out of the chimney! The wonder of that sight will never be forgotten. If I could choose the eighth wonder of the world, that would be it.

My spirit danced in front of me as, painfully, I put one foot in front of the other and dropped my burdened body another 100 yards.

The MacKenzie Hut was much more primitive than the

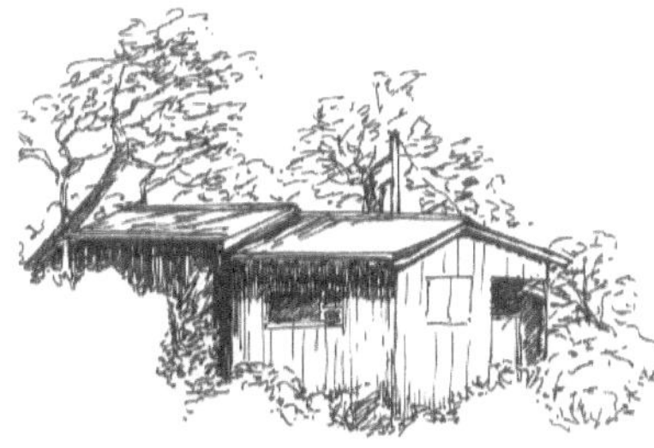

previous one – there was a small cooking and eating room with most of the space being taken by a large wood stove. There were two small bunk rooms off this, the bunks being wooden frames with a piece of heavy matting slung across from one side to the other – no mattresses.

'*Washing*' – there was a sign at the front of the hut – down at the lake. Being covered in perspiration and mud, I gathered my soap, towel and clean clothes – down to the lake – stripped off – and dived in. I'm sure the water was close to freezing point because I was quite numb by the time I had finished washing. But it certainly relieved my aching muscles.

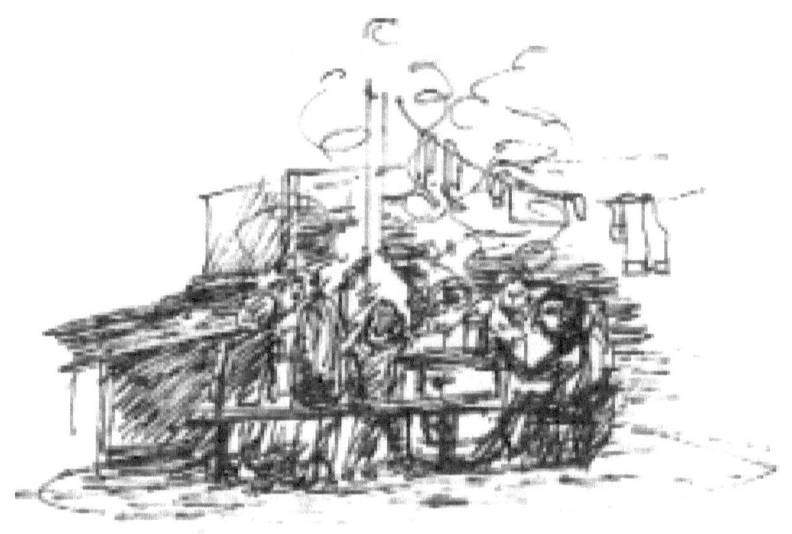

Back at the hut, everyone was cooking tea so I prepared my billy of dried everything and joined the throng of starving faces sitting on benches, almost leaning on the stove or in it, occasionally rising amidst the smoke and steam to stir their brew.

Bloating our stomachs with cup after cup of billy tea, we chatted away with stories of nearly falling down waterfalls and just thank God it didn't rain or snow – well, I'm sure I wouldn't have made it if it had. Anyway, the worst was over.

And as the embers began to lose their warmth and the candles dwindled, we all slowly drifted off to bed – not so much to sleep though, with those cold, hard mats and the guy above me constantly turning over and over as if he was caught in a washing machine – nylon scraping of matting makes the most awful noise – and there were the snorers sounding like pigs trying to harmonize.

The morning air was freezing cold in the valley when we set out again, but the day soon warmed up – or I did, anyway.

The next hut was at Lake Howden – not quite as far – a drop in altitude of about 1000 feet but over a much longer distance than the previous descent, with much milder grades. There was a little more time to stop and enjoy the scenery – the Earland Falls were certainly a wonderful sight – the water must have dropped from some 300 to 400 feet above us. My legs and muscles were aching before I had even left, and had barely recovered from the previous day's ordeal, so it was again, with much relief, that I stumbled my way into the Howden Hut.

This was even more primitive than the previous hut – just one big room – an old stove in the middle and matting bunks around the wall. Anyway, it was cosy.

After a couple of hours on the track the following morning, we made it to the Milford-TeAvau Highway. Flagging down an empty bus, we caught a ride to Milford Sound – Wow! – What magnificent scenery – the road was bordered by high, snow-capped mountains, the stony ground illuminated by brightly coloured lichens. The road took us through the Homer Tunnel – one-way for a whole mile or more of rocky mountain. You can only go through at certain times either way. A real engineering feat – they started tunnelling at each end and met exactly in the middle – not bad at a slope of 500 feet per mile.

Milford greeted us with a swarm of sand flies – they really eat you alive. However, Milford Sound is really a beautiful spot, situated on the margin of Fiordland National Park. Barren, rocky peaks rising steeply out of the cold, still water, continuously changing colour with the time of day. The occasional boat is seen chugging its way in or out of the fiord.

Well, it's the Baha'i New Year's Day for me! A little confused, the others wished me *"Happy New Year"* without asking too many questions. A friend bought me a 10-cent bar of chocolate and a cup of tea in the café. What a way to celebrate Naw-ruz (new year) – filthy dirty, wet feet set in muddy boots, and plastered with Aeorguard to allay the onslaught of sandflies.

We caught the last bus back to TeAnau that afternoon. It was just our luck to find that the hostel was full, and after a quarter-mile trek to the caravan park found no room there either and to had to walk with all our luggage around to the motor camp one mile down the lake. But who should we meet on the way – 'blue shirt with long legs' – the Routeburn guide – just couldn't believe that I had made it in my high-heeled boots.

Well, at last, hot showers, good food and a mattress to sleep on – luxuries or necessities?!

Epilogue:

At 11:30 am, we discovered after getting up late that there was no room in the motor camp the following night and the bus for Invercargill left at 11:45 am. We ran down to the phone and asked the bus company to put the luggage we had sent on onto the bus and asked it to stop at the motor camp on the way through. Well, ten minutes to pack! – I just threw everything in – to discover that my billy of chicken broth had emptied itself over everything – yuk!

So Invercargill was a day and a half of washing and drying – it was raining all the time so we had to use heaters inside. And thus, clean clothes in our packs and muscles in slightly better condition, we left Invercargill ready for the next adventure – up the east coast.

..ooOOoo..

3

Wedding of
Helen Mitchell & Don Gordon

at St Andrews in Scotland on 13th July 1974

Written by Don

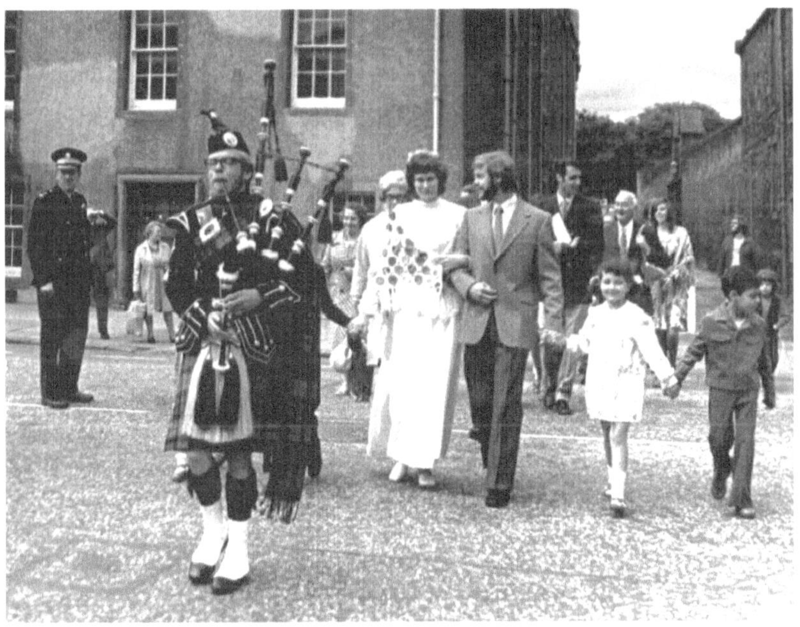

After Helen had completed her bond with the Mental Health Services by working at the Claremont Mental Hospital, and had been in New Zealand for a working holiday, she went to

Northern Ireland to attend the wedding of her friend, Maxien Lethbridge to Jim Bradley. This was Lurgan, Craigavon, in June 1973.

She toured around Northern Ireland during the troubles between the Catholics and Protestants. This was the first time she had seen armed police walking the streets. At one point, she had been taking photos and was told by a policeman to remove the film from her camera.

She looked forward to seeing the sun go down on Galway Bay (after one of her favourite songs) and was disappointed to be there on a cloudy day when the sun could not even be seen.

Helen then went to St Andrews in Scotland to assist with the small Baha'i community, and she lived with Mrs Tingle at 43 Argyle Street. She worked as a servant for a family in the town.

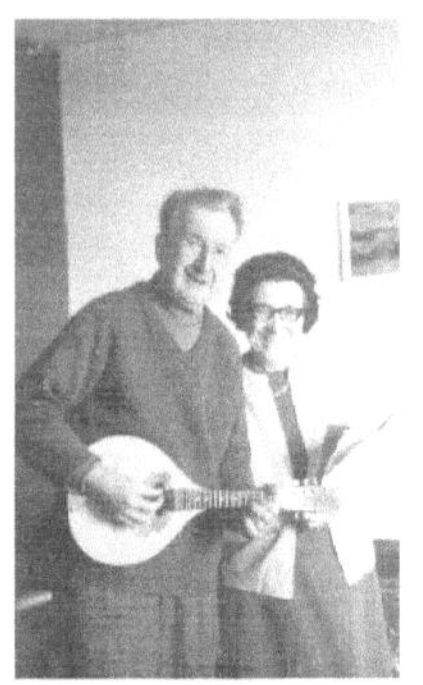

In that time, he developed many close friendships, including old Mr and Mrs Bain of Paisley near Glasgow (pictured right).

How they met

Helen and Don were at the University of Western Australia at the same time in the late 1960s and early 1970s. Although not close friends, they knew each other because of many mutual friends. They were both members of the university's Evangelical Union – a large Christian group. They both knew Milton McGhee, a close friend of Don's. Helen attended Don's 21st birthday in 1967 as the partner of Don's best friend, Kevin Seaton. They both knew Peter Nichols and Tuan (Don, Kevin & Peter were at Hollywood High School together). Don ran the Aquarius coffee lounge in the middle of Perth. This was through the YMCA, and so he knew Helen's brother-law, John 'JT'

Thornton, who was a key figure in the YMCA. John's band, 'JT and the Jazz Men' was the top dance band in Perth and Don helped the roadie setting up on several occasions. Don needed a female member for the Aquarius committee and JT was going to suggest Helen, but she was not available so he suggested Ronnie Becker (now Naughton), who was one of Helen's fellow Occupational Therapy students. The Baha'i singing group, led by Charlie Pierce, performed at Aquarius occasionally. Don got to know many of the Baha'is, including Tony Deamer, who fixed Don's VW Beetle. Also, Don knew several of the OT students, and was an escort with a few of them for formal outings. Don had been to the Mount Street flat where Maxien and Helen were staying. He knew Helen's sister, Cynthia, with her old duffle coat at Uni. Another connection was that Don's brother-in-law, Max Beckitt, worked in the same WAIT accounting office as a prominent Baha'i, Saheil. And, as noted below, their fathers knew each other. These connections were at that time, but there is a subsequent connection in Narrogin, with Aileen, who had been in Helen's high school, married Doug Sawkins, who was in Don's class – in schools that were on opposite sides of Perth.

So, Helen's and Don's paths crossed and recrossed in many ways. This indicates what a small community Perth was at that time. The crucial link was a little later when Helen was already in Scotland and Don, who had been working in Derby with the Department of Community Welfare, was booked to go to the UK for a working holiday – it is what many young people did in those days. Just before he left, he bumped into JT on the Rottnest Ferry and, on hearing that Don was about to leave, JT gave him Helen's address – in case Don went that way.

Don initially stayed a week in Kent with a friend from Derby and then in Quainton with Frank Baines, who had been a work colleague in Derby but had returned to the UK. While staying there, Don worked for a few months in a bifurcated rivet factory in Aylesbury. Then he toured up to Scotland and visited various places and passed through St Andrews but had misplaced Helen's address. He went back to Glasgow to get the address and visited Helen in January 1974. Straight away, Don got work as a gardener with the University of St Andrews and hired a caravan at a site on the hills overlooking the town. This was while he was enquiring about opportunities for courses or work experience in community development. By March, he obtained work as the live-in warden at a new Heathery Knowe gypsy site, 120 kilometres to the southwest, near Glasgow. He travelled back to St Andrews on the weekends.

A romance quickly developed. Three months after Don had arrived in St Andrews, they decided, on 21st April, to get married.

They rang their parents with the great news, not caring that, in Western Australia, it was the middle of the night. The parents then rang each other to politely introduce themselves. But after their call, they realized they already knew each other because the fathers were on the same board of management for Jason Industries – they had sat through many meetings together. So they rang back and spoke on familiar terms. Helen and Don had thought of a quiet wedding with just local friends, but quickly the parents decided to come.

Helen went on pilgrimage to the Baha'i World Centre in May.

The Wedding

In addition to all four of their parents, Don's grandmother also came. And other Australian acquaintances happened to be in the UK, including Annette Finn, with whom Helen had studied medicine. Other attendees were Mr and Mrs Bain. Don's boss, Donald Barbour (a giant of a man

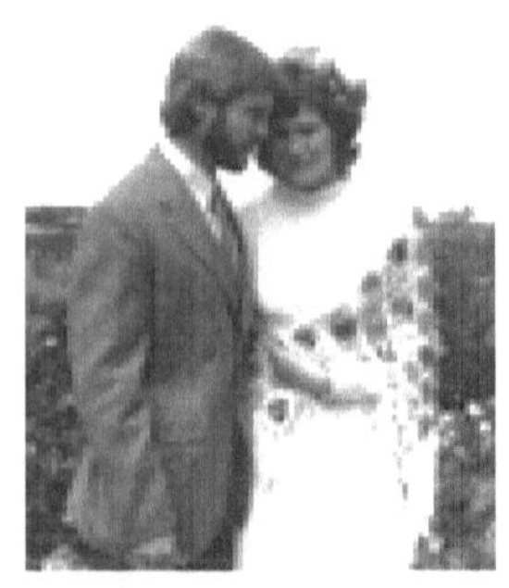

with a petite wife) elegantly danced a highland fling at the reception. And, of course, there were many local Baha'is. Soon after, Helen's sister, Bev, toured the UK and visited Helen and Don.

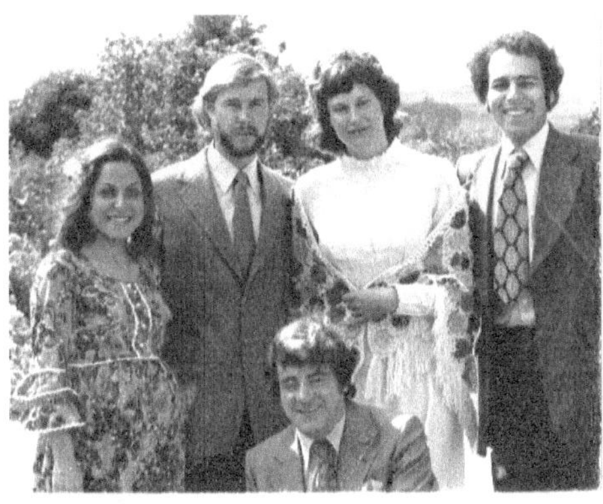

The wedding was in two formats – firstly, the formalities in the registration office, and then the Baha'i ceremony held at the Catholic presbytery, officiated by Ronald Taherzadeh. Then there was a wonderful parade through the streets, led by a bag-piper (Roddy Grant from Stornaway), to the reception. The photo has Ronald Taherzadeh and his wife Mercedes, with kneeling Roddy Grant.

Helen's father captured this all on Super-8 video.

"Out of the fusion of two souls a third and subtle entity is born. Though invisible and intangible on earth, it is the composite soul of two lovers. The progress of the one mysteriously influences the other. They become the tutors of each other's souls. Distance or death, mere physical forces, cannot cause its disintegration" 'Abdu'l Baha

They honeymooned on the Heathery Knowe gypsy site[2].

Three months later, with Helen pregnant, they returned to Australia. They went to Laverton, where Don had obtained work, at the beginning of 1975.

---

[2]   Helen described her time at the gypsy site in Chapter 4.

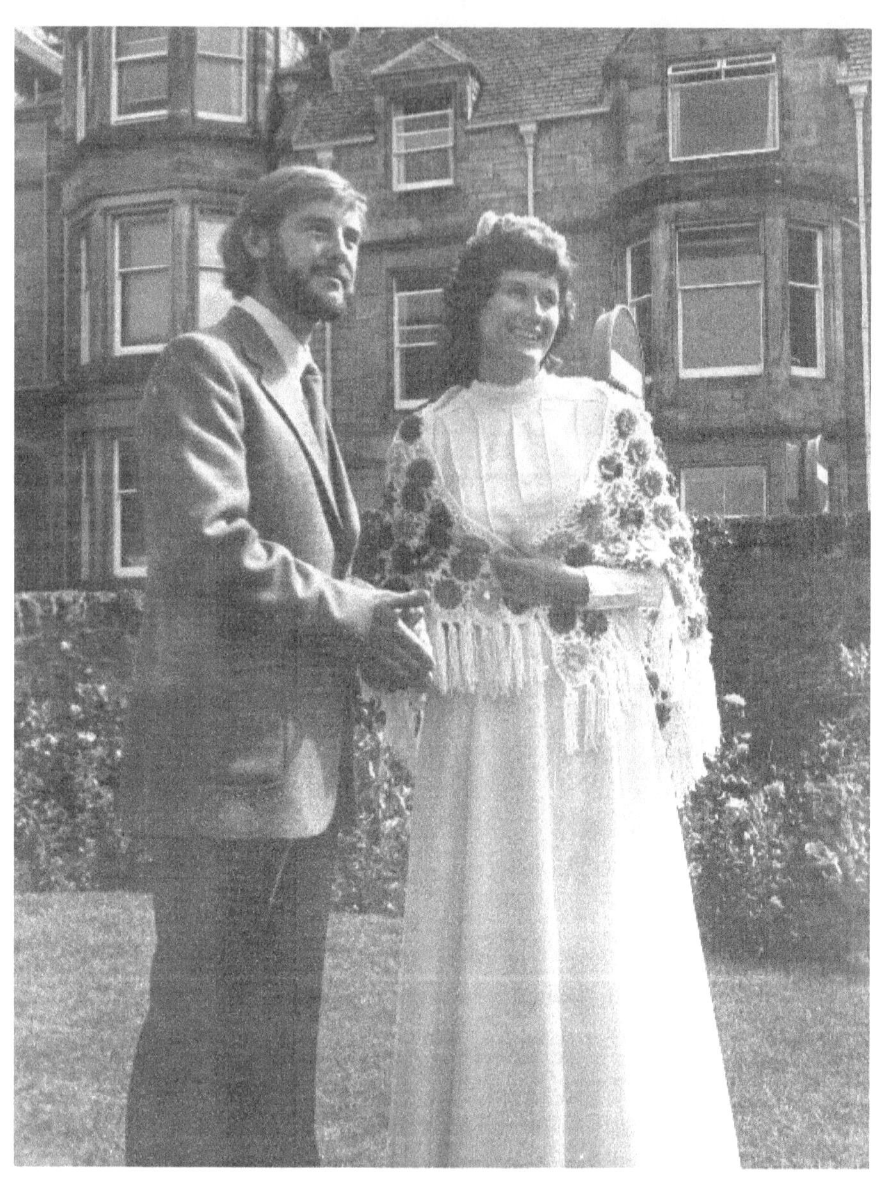

..ooOOoo..

4

Travellers in Scotland

Living for 3 months with 'gypsies' in 1974

Written by Helen

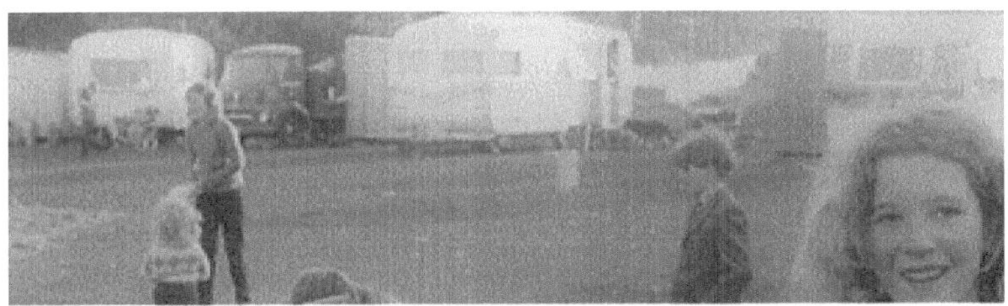

We were married in St Andrews but then moved to near Glasgow, where Don was working as a warden on a gypsy caravan site.

The Heathery Knowe site was a circle of twelve caravans with just a communal water tap, a small shed containing a primitive chemical toilet and no shower or bath.

After a week or so, the smell of the chemical toilet made me quite nauseous and I longed for a good wash. The caravan was so small we had no room to store anything. So we thought, how could we solve these difficulties? We would take out the wood fireplace, which took up a lot of space and replace it with a kero heater and a cupboard. And, with a tiny room at the end, we would make a bathroom. We bought a gas ring and a large urn and then proceeded to make a bath. We used a disused bath thrown on the tip as a mould, and buckets of fibreglass from a fibreglass factory only walking distance away. We asked all the gypsies to decorate our bath with felt pens before putting on the final coat of fibreglass. They then all watched in amazement as we squeezed our flexible bath into the caravan. And I thought very soon they would learn from us and want us to help them make a bath and improve their living conditions.

After a couple of weeks of enjoying our lovely hot baths, we began to realize why gypsies mostly have wood fires in their caravans and, even in the best of caravans, never keep water inside. The sun doesn't shine much in Scotland, and the steam from the urn seeped into the wood and it started to grow mould and smell damp all the time. The kero heater wasn't strong enough to dry it out.

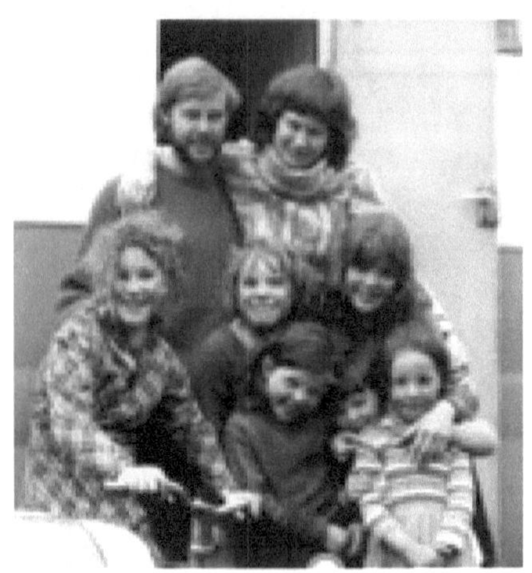

That was the beginning of a continual exchange of learning between ourselves and gypsies. The children couldn't read or write; they couldn't tell the time and didn't know the days of the week. So, starting in our little caravan and then moving into a disused double-decker bus which one of the gypsies towed to the site, we started a school for the children. We taught them to read while they taught us how to use other people's rubbish. Our school desks and chairs came from the tip, still in good condition. The books, six huge bags full, were being thrown out

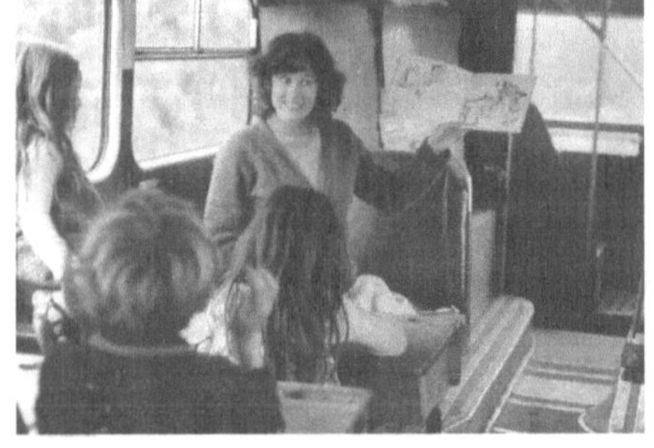

by the library because they were finger-marked. With no help from the local school – they just weren't interested – and us stumbling on trying out different teaching methods, the children started to learn. They were quite undisciplined but bursting with enthusiasm and were very creative and imaginative.

Life was based on relationships, not ideologies. When life is in the raw, words without actions are meaningless. One lady, Isa, had eleven children and her mother dying of cancer, all living together in one small caravan. She cooked and washed all day but even had time to bring me a bowl of soup when I was sick. Another family of six lived in a primitive tent made from an old tarpaulin wrapped around sticks. I felt I was just beginning to learn what life was all about, not passing exams, but sharing and helping each other. All the learning and knowledge you might gain is worthless without it.

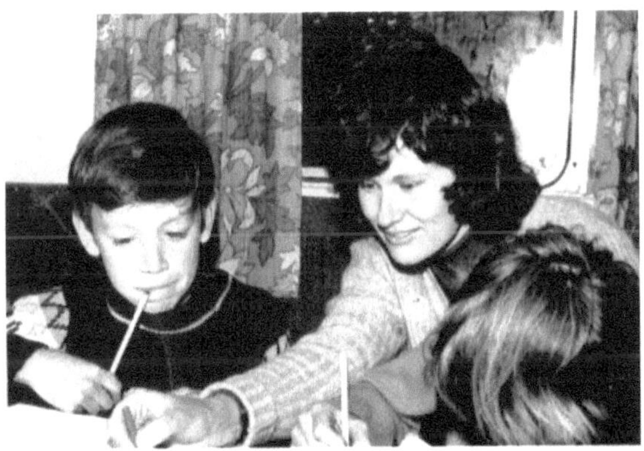

The campsite was now working fairly well. Don had established regular meeting procedures whereby they could consult and make decisions about how they wished the campsite to be run. This was the first permanent site in Scotland where gypsies could legally reside so a warden had been appointed to make sure everything went well at the beginning – to solve the initial difficulties as, while most gypsies wanted a place where they could stay, they were not accustomed to working together except in small tight-knit family groups. And so, the time came when a full-time warden was no longer necessary. The social work department was close to getting a full-time teacher to continue the children's education.

I was pregnant with our first child and suffered quite badly from morning sickness. So we decided to move back to Australia. It was hard to say goodbye. They insisted on us taking some of their treasured possessions – little crystal vases and ornaments. There were hugs and tears on both sides.

..ooOOoo..

Background – notes by Don

The above account was read at Helen's memorial celebration following her death in 2021 because it would have been news to the audience. Although it was forty-seven years ago, it set a pattern of living that Helen developed in place after place. Wherever she went, time and time again, in different settings, she drew out the hidden capabilities of disadvantaged women and children through art, crafts and the Baha'i Faith. She supported their abilities, personal expression and growth – and thus community transformation.

This was a subculture of families who kept on the move. They were not Romany Gypsies but were known as 'travellers' or 'tinkers', and they called themselves 'going about folk'. A few had flashy caravans towed by a Range-Rover or Ford Transit van, but most were very poor, and some lived in tents or a cart pulled by horses. They would camp in small groups wherever they could – on the verges of motorways or the bottom of a farmer's paddock – before they were forced to move on. Never welcome, always pushed on, always moving.

By 1974, there were already several legal gypsy sites in

England, but the Coatbridge Social Work Department established the first in Scotland. The project was driven by Donald Barber of CSWD.

It was expected to be subject to criticism from townspeople, so it was arranged that Don Gordon would live there to help set it up so that everything was working okay, to avoid controversy.

Don was a social worker on a working holiday from Australia. He lived on one of the standings in a caravan provided by CSWD. He was designated as a 'warden' and his role was to help the travellers establish basic processes for who would use the various standings and how they would live together. Each standing was quickly taken up, and there was less coming and going than had been anticipated. Don convened community meetings, and everything went surprisingly smooth.

The site was on Gartcosh Road and was known as 'Heathery Knowe'. It consisted of a circle of twelve caravan standings and an adjacent area for tents ('bivvies') and horses. Each standing had a small shed for storage and a bucket toilet. The contents of the toilets were emptied into an in-ground tank in the middle of the circle. There was one communal tap.

The travellers dealt in scrap metal and so there was area set aside for them to sort different items. Some went off potato picking, and others did small bituminizing jobs.

Reciprocity was fundamental to how they connected with each other. It was a complex network of obligations they owed each other. It bound them together because they could always count on other travellers to assist them because each was already (or soon will be) indebted to the other. Don began to understand this, and knew that he would need their help when his old car would inevitably break down. He was useless as a mechanic whereas they could fix anything. So he made sure that he always had a basic set of tools which he took every opportunity to lend. In this way, Don knew that the travellers would have to help him the next time he needed their mechanical skills.

Don was there for five months. In the middle of that time, he married Helen and they had their honeymoon at the caravan site. The photo on the next page is Don crossing the threshold of their first home with his new wife.

They got on well with everyone and became close to many of the families. Helen did a lot with the women and children. Education was an issue, and the travellers towed an old double-decker bus onto the site for this purpose, and Helen started teaching some reading and writing (not very successfully).

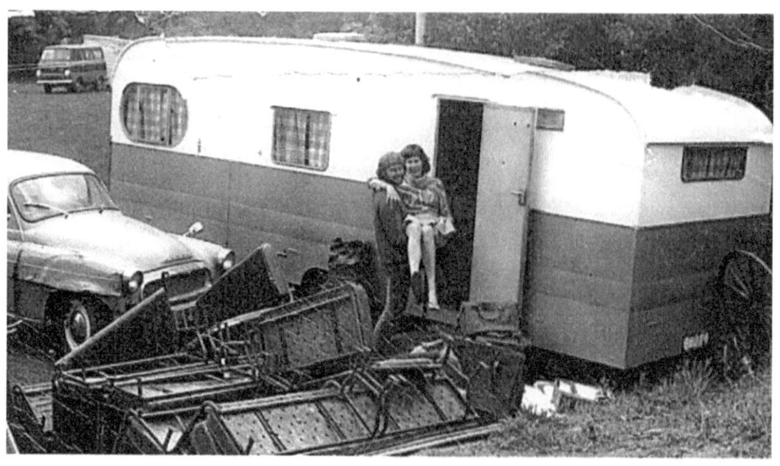

By the time they left to return to Australia, things were going well, and a live-in warden was no longer required.

It is not known what happened in the long term, but Donald Barber and others would have left full documentation within the records of the CSWD. There might also be some reports by Willy Guy, who was an anthropologist who visited the site many times.

Gypsy Traveller History in Scotland was compiled by Shamus McPhee, 2017 – published through Iriss (Institute for Research & Innovation in Social Services). This was an intriguing account that identifies significant developments over the centuries.

There is information about the years 1968 and 1984, but Shamus might not have been aware of the important initiative of Heathery Knowe between these years, in 1974.

..ooOOoo..

5

Early years of marriage
Laverton, Derby & Kununurra
1975 to 1979

Births of Joe, Ben & Ruth

Written by Don

After their wedding in July 1974, Helen and Don lived with gypsies for a few months before returning from Scotland to Western Australia.

Previously, in 1972, Don had commenced working with the Department of Community Welfare (DCW)[3] in Derby in the Kimberleys, in the far north of WA. He was the first social worker north of Geraldton. This was a time when the department was transitioning from the Department of Native Welfare. He had a role in the establishment of a new aboriginal community at Luma. After 1½ years in Derby, he took a year's unpaid leave to gain an understanding of community

---

[3]   During the 26 years Don was employed with the organization, it took various forms – Native Welfare Department (NWD) changed to Dept for Community Welfare (DCW) in 1972, Dept for Community Services (DCS) in 1985, Dept for Community Development (DCD) in 1992, Dept for Families and Children's Services (DFCS) in 1995, Dept for Community Development (DCD) in 2001. Throughout this book, it is referred to as DCW.

development. He went to England and Scotland, and soon after catching up with Helen in St Andrews, he obtained work as a live-in warden at a gypsy site.

Laverton – 6 months in 1974 & 1975

When they arrived back in Australia, Don resumed working with DCW – this time in Laverton. This is a small mining town on the edge of the Gibson Desert, about 1000 kilometres east of Perth.

They were in Laverton for only six months but it was a momentous time because the police provoked an incident with the aboriginal people at Skull Creek. This resulted in a Royal Commission. Don was a key witness.

Derby – 18 months in 1975 & 1976

Don was promoted to Supervisor for the Kimberley, based in Derby. So he was back there after the lapse of 1½ years – this time as a married man.

Joe was born in April 1975. He was going to present as a breach birth, so Helen had to fly down to Perth for the delivery.

Helen described her Baha'i activities in an interview in 2015[4].

When he was previously in Derby, Don had been a base grade social worker, whereas he came back in a management role. He was the supervisor responsible for over fifty staff in six offices spread across a huge area with many complex social issues.

This was a time of major changes with aboriginal people. They had recently become eligible for award wages and social security. This resulted in their having to leave cattle stations where they had been 'paid' rations rather than wages. This led to the formation of indigenous settlements on areas that had to be

---

[4]   Helen's description of her time in Derby – see Chapter 25.

sectioned off from cattle stations. There were high hopes of these communities developing the processes for self-determination. The department's homemaker program was a positive response.

By his own admission, Don was not up to this senior role. He requested a demotion back to a social worker position, and he transferred to Kununurra with DCW.

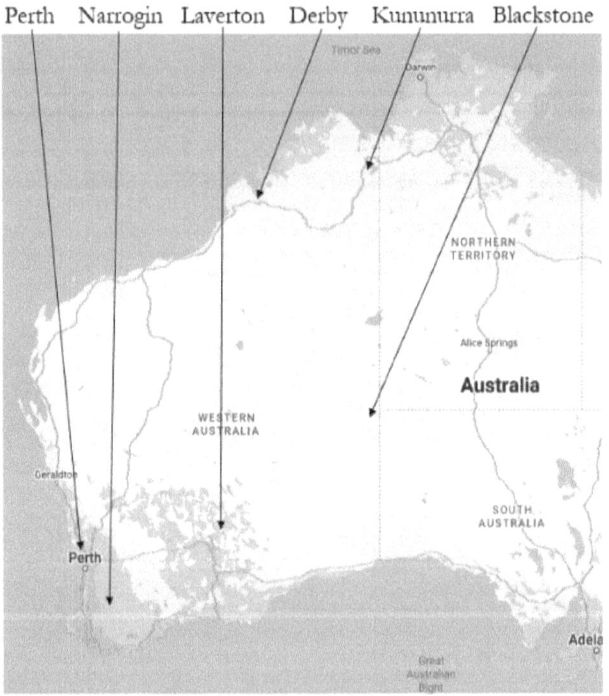

Kununurra – 3 years in 1976 to 1979

The town of Kununurra was on the other side of the Kimberleys – the most northerly town in WA. It had been commenced about fifteen years before – a huge irrigation scheme with the Ord River, serviced by a small diversion dam, and the massive Argyle dam.

Kununurra was one of the hottest towns in WA and the

house rented from the DCW was not air-conditioned – only had fans and hopper windows.

Ben was born in May 1977.

There was an aboriginal 'reserve' called the Mirima village. It was a circle of about fifteen basic houses, a few kilometres out of the town. Don and Helen set up a little shop for some day-to-day essentials. It was staffed by local girls. A senior lady, who was not numerate, sat with them to make sure the girls were not subject to pressure to favour their relatives.

The aboriginal people living in town did not connect so much with the more traditional people on the reserve, and Don saw a need for an aboriginal organisation for those living in the town. This resulted in the formation of Waringarri, which became a major aboriginal organization.

Don also helped establish a small settlement at Yardingarl.

Helen and Don became infected with hepititis from Don's efforts to fix blockages in the Mirima toilet system.

Helen was pleased to have some of the neighbouring aboriginal children come to play at her home.

Helen and Don conducted many activities with the aboriginal youth – at the town hall and at the diversion dam. This was done without direct encouragement from DCW. Don ran afoul of his employer when he did not prevent his indigenous staff from taking part in a protest march when the youth activities were opposed by some public figures. Racial feelings ran high within the town.

Helen was involved with the Women's and Children's Centre, which was servicing the needs of the non-aboriginal people in the town. She designed the layout for the building for which they were seeking funds.

They had some ducks in their backyard. When Joe was four years old, he was always climbing, and he climbed up on the duck fence and onto the roof of the house – and called out to other children in the street.

In late 1977, the little family were in the Marshall Islands for three months[5].

Ruth was born in 1979.

They had been in Kununurra for three years, and after Ruth's birth, Helen and Don decided to move closer to the grandparents and to settle in a town for the children's schooling. They decided on Narrogin because this was close to Perth – but not too close. This was a move from the hottest to the coldest parts of the state.

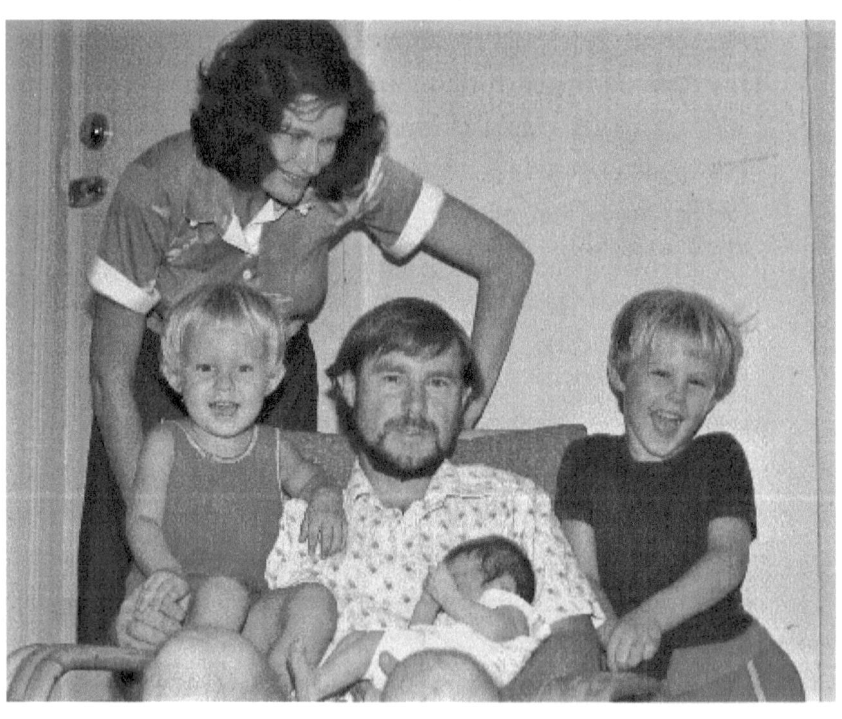

.ooOOoo..

---

5   Helen described the time on the Marshall Islands – see Chapter 6

6

The Marshall Islands

On a Pacific atoll for 3 months in 1977-78

The diary of Helen Gordon

The Beginning

In 1977, I was living in Kununurra, at the top of Western Australia, with my husband, Don and two young children – Joseph (2½ years) and Benjamin (5 months). Don worked for the Community Welfare Department. He was due for three months holiday and we wanted to go to one interesting place and stay there. I wanted to be somewhere that I could teach the Baha'i Faith. We decided that we could go anywhere, as long as people could speak some English, and that there were medical facilities close by for the children. As it happened, neither condition was to be.

We heard about the Marshall Islands through a Baha'i friend, Jackie Aippersbach, who had been in the Marshalls on a teaching trip. She was now on Elcho Island near Darwin and we had visited her there.

The Marshall Islands is a small nation of about 55,000 people. It is part of Micronesia, in the Pacific Ocean, a third of the way between Australia and North America. It is a cluster of tiny atolls, with narrow strips of islands around sheltered lagoons with deep ocean on the outside. No places are higher than just a couple of meters above sea level. The atolls are spread across a vast expanse of ocean – lots of water and very little land. The capital is Majuro. We stayed at Laura and later at Long Island, which is a few kilometres on the road from Majuro. Mainly we were at Mwejrik near Pikarej, which is on the Arno atoll, forty-five kilometres from Majuro.

Sadly, the Marshalls are best known for the USA atomic tests on Bikini and other atolls in the 1940s & 1950s. It is now at risk of rising sea levels with climate change.

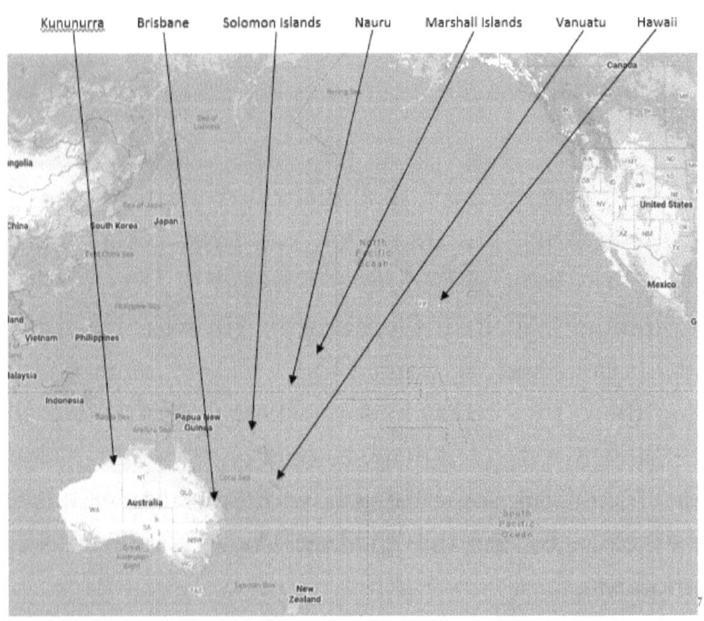

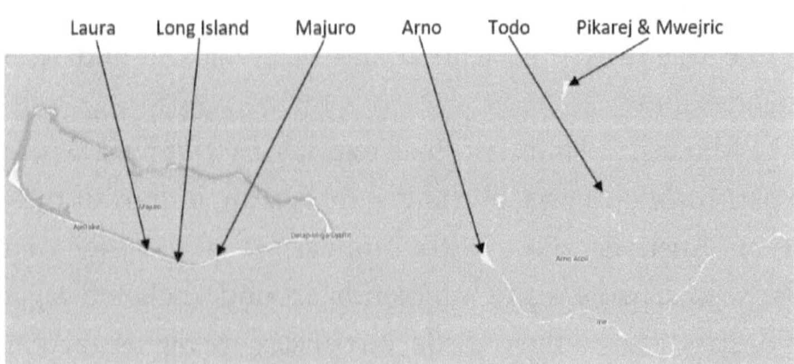

Getting there

October 1977

I had written to the National Spiritual Assembly of the Marshall Islands but received no reply. We found out that letters can take four months by sea mail, so I contacted Judge Benson (counsellor for Micronesia) in Guam, the largest island in Micronesia. He contacted the National Spiritual Assembly (NSA) in the Marshall Islands and we awaited a response.

We were so sure we were going there that we paid for our tickets. The next day a telegram arrived from the NSA to say we were welcome.

To prepare for our trip, I made small canvas beds for the children that could be rolled up to pack, and supported by rocks or cans when we got there. I had a whole suitcase of peanuts and muesli so I could keep my milk supply going for Ben. We also took medicines, although the usual tropical diseases are not prevalent there. I packed a small silkscreen and some ink, thinking it might be useful. I made some sandals with car tyre bases. We had the minimum of clothes because we would be near the equator.

Nov 5th

Left Kununurra at 6 am. In Darwin rang Bill Washington – he had heard of the Marshallese Baha'is – gave glowing reports. Saw Carol and Persian Baha'i. Did some shopping – about four hours in Darwin then on to Brisbane. Got a room at People's Palace in Brisbane. Raining, but had a walk around town. Good sense of being relieved to be on holidays but everyone (except Joseph) at the point of exhaustion.

Sun Nov 6th

Brisbane to the Solomon Islands by mid-morning. Honiara is

the capital, on the largest island, Guadacanal. Enquired about Bruce Saunders (Jackie's advice) but he had left for Australia the day before. Got a room in Blum's old hotel – very nice. Honiara has many traditional-style houses in small clusters – first impressions of similarity with aboriginals. Couldn't see much of Honiara because it was raining but a terrific feeling of being somewhere exotic and distinctly different – suddenly in another world (anticipations of Majuro). Asked an Islander girl (from Gilberts) if she knew of Baha'is … she said she was a Baha'i and she (Theresa) rang the Blum's and arranged for us to visit Mrs Blum. There we went with Bob and his wife, Jo, an American couple retired (ex-military) in the Solomons. Also taken to the temple site by a NZ couple. At the Blums, we met Eadie, a girl from Malaita Island. *[Later note: Little did we imagine that years later, our son, Ben, would marry Eadie's younger sister, Violyn, and they would establish their family in the Solomons for ten years.]*

Went to tea at Saunder's house – a magnificent mansion being looked after by Mrs Blum (his mother-in-law) while they were away.

Mon Nov 7th to Thurs Nov 10th

Honiara to Nauru in late morning. Spent three days in luxurious hotel – expensive but gave us the rest we needed. The hotel is one of the few substantial buildings in Nauru. There are few evidences of the financial rewards from phosphate mining. Didn't enjoy Nauru much – didn't have the kind of atmosphere that Honiara had. After two days, we met up Bwebwe – a Gilbertese Baha'i girl who is nursing at the phosphate company's hospital. Only had a couple of hours with her – lunch at the hotel. Really nice girl – gave us shell necklaces from Gilberts. Many Gilbertese are at Nauru working under very poor conditions and low pay doing work the Naurians don't want to do ($1.38 per day!).

Majuro

Thurs 10th

As our plane was about to land in Majuro, we looked out the windows and could just see ocean on both sides – no land. We found out that the airport, as with everywhere in the Marshalls is just a narrow strip. The atolls are a circular edge surrounding a lagoon. Arrived in the early evening – great anticipation before arriving – wonderful welcome from Majaro Baha'is. A little difficulty with visas – but hopefully we can stay the full time. Taken by John (from Fiji) to Francis and Farateu Reimers's home and made very welcome. Went to Baha'i Centre and met many Baha'is and introduced ourselves. Met the famous Betra Majmeto (counsellor), John, Vinson Jamir (a pioneer from the USA and working as a lawyer with the Peace Corps) and an American couple from Guam just passing through.

Tremendous relief that we were expected and given such a welcome. Hopefully, we can be of some use to their community. Still very exhausted.

Fri Nov 11th

Generally organised ourselves. Reimers is an interesting household – many relatives living there – Reimers and four children, Dawnise, Merna, Djugajuorr and her husband and baby. They all seemed to go about their lives freely and helping with the children and housework. We were surprised how little English is spoken. Francis and Farateu speak English very well and are very much at ease with our culture, but none of the others can speak English except to say "Hello" etc. Saw Reimer's shop. It is the biggest in Majuro and they must be very well off. The business was commenced by Francis's father, who lives next door. They also own other buildings (including the biggest and newest, which is being rented by the Post Office) and they also own a lot of land and have other businesses too.

The business centre of Majuro is called Rita.

Merna and Dornice are from Killi Island (orginally inhabitants from Bikini). Merna is deaf and dumb – a symptom of the radiation that affected many people after all the atomic testing in Bikini Atoll – radioactive ash fell on many islands and was ignored, and people were eating radioactive fish – their staple diet.

Celebration of Bahau'llah's birthday at the Baha'i Centre. (Went to Laura – a wider land area at one end of the atoll – with Francis to pick up some people beforehand.) Many Baha'is from all over Majuro came – a great spirit, and we had what Don called "a real feast". They had supper first so the children could sleep through the talks. Myself, Vinson and Betra gave talks covering the life history of Bahau'llah. There are very few of the writings translated into Marshallese, so people learn everything by heart.

Sat Nov 12th

Rest day.

In the morning, I went to learn from some ladies how to make fans with palm leaves. One of the ladies' daughters had gone into hospital to have a baby so we went to the hospital to see the baby and, after waiting some time, the news came that the baby was born dead. The dead child was wrapped and passed from grandma to the other relatives who nursed it tenderly and talked to it gently and looked at it as if to say why should it be dead. It was then taken back on the back of the truck with us all and placed on a snow-white cushion on a mat, with great reverence, in the middle of the lounge floor. All afternoon the relatives sat around, and the children looked at the baby and talked to it and lay next to it. The Baha'i funeral took place in the evening. Some prayers were said, and then the baby was placed in a coffin and the lid nailed on. It was then carried to the front of the mother's house and buried there. Children are always buried close to the house.

Met with the National Teaching Committee (NTC) in the evening concerning plans for our activities.

Sun 13th

Don stayed at Reimers with Joseph and I went with Betra and other Baha'is to Long Island. We talked to many people about the Faith – many showed great interest and three people declared. Benji is always our best means of communication. Everyone here loves babies and they were impressed with how well he was growing on my breast milk – they referred to him as 'kalib ning a ning' (big baby) and already many offers to adopt him. Our 10-kilo ning-a-ning was no feather and I was exhausted on arriving home that night.

Mon 14th

Shopping and looking around. Learnt more about making fans.

Laura

Tues 15th

Hired a car and all went to Laura to investigate the possibility of staying there. Met up with many Baha'is, including a boy, Jacob, who offered to translate for us. Had a brief discussion with the Baha'is at Laninburlong's house. Found out that Jacob's sister had a house which we could use! Arrangements were made for us to come and stay tomorrow.

Earlier in the day, we had been to a nice picnic spot with beautiful blue water right at the end of the island. Two ladies who came with us never stopped making fans all day.

Spent the day shopping and preparing for going to Laura. Spent a little while with Vinson regarding speaking Marshallese. Straight after tea, we left for Laura. Francis and Farateu and others came with us. Jacob and many other Baha'is came around and we spent the evening with them. I spoke about Local Spiritual Assemblies (LSA).

Thurs 17th

Jacob spent the previous evening with us and also this evening. He is a policeman and travels to Rita for work. We are staying in his sister's house. It is made of concrete bricks and a tin roof. However, that's all it is, being unfinished. The windows are boarded over and the floor is coral rocks with a few boards over one section. There is one rather rusty bed where I sleep and Don takes a mat on the floor while the children have their homemade stretchers we brought with us. It was impossible to buy a mattress here – everyone sleeps on the floor on sleeping mats. Floor space and its use is quite amazing. You never walk into a house with shoes on and never walk on a sleeping mat. A sitting mat is treated with less reverence. The floor is used for everything – sleeping, eating, all activities. Chairs and tables are most uncommon. The floor is always being cleaned and kept spotless.

The sea is never far away. We are only about twenty or thirty feet from the water's edge. It is lovely clean water, unlike the waterfronts near Rita, which are very polluted. The coral shelf extends out about 100 yards or so and then drops sharply into the ocean.

The people in Laura mainly subsist off fishing and land produce (breadfruit, bananas, limes, pandanus fruit, coconuts and tarrow). They also sell some of this in Rita. The coconut tree is used for so many amazing things:-

- Coconut water – a refreshing drink from the young

coconuts – have to climb the tree to get them

- Coconut milk – from squeezing grated copra
- Coconut meat – whole and grated
- Coconut shell – for cups
- Coconut sap is made into a slightly alcoholic drink called *toddy*
- Husks – for fires
- Young leaves – for making baskets, plates, fans etc.
- Mature leaves – for roofing, mats, baskets, fans etc.

There is no water or electricity laid on. We rely on rainwater for drinking. Washing is in the sea or from a nearby well. We wash clothes in large basins – by hand. Our toilet is a little hut set over a huge hole about 20 ft from the house. We use a campfire for all cooking and boiling up all drinking water. We wash in the sea and in large basins. Much of our living and activities (washing clothes, cooking etc.) is done out of doors and we have a large mat we place on the coral rock concourse around the house – for the children etc. Benjy is just beginning to edge his way towards objects as he lies on his tummy.

The whole environment is idyllic – wherever we look we can see fruit trees, and there are very few trees that do not bear edible fruits – coconuts, breadfruit, pandanus, banana, pawpaw, and lime. There are no dangerous spiders or insects; flies are no worry and mosquitoes are controlled by use of mosquito coils burning at night. There are no apparent health hazards, and the people seem healthy here.

In the evening, Robert came around and we spent several hours trying to talk Marshallese. He was very patient and seemed to enjoy it. There was a sense of friendship despite language barriers. Others could not come because it was raining very heavily.

Friday 18th Nov

Tried to make bread in the camp oven without much success because we couldn't get a good fire. Wood was damp and doesn't burn to good embers here because it is soft wood.

At lunch time Betra came around with Jim and Rita (Rita assists Betra). They were trying to locate a venue for a food program for the old people – and were successful.

Betra is a cheerful soul who always seems to be laughing and relaxed. They had their baby with them – Jim looks after it during the day.

In the evening, a truckload of Baha'is from Rita and Laura came to have tea. They only stayed about two hours altogether but in that time they cooked a magnificent island-style rice meal cooked in coconut milk and served on 'instant' woven platters of coconut leaves. A wonderful friendly atmosphere left us with a sense of being very much the receivers and not the givers. These people have so much to teach us about generosity etc. Also, their ample use of the natural endowments of their island (e.g. by weaving coconut 'plates') is a real inspiration.

Saturday 19th Nov

We went for a walk and discovered a little – very little – shop just down the road and then went to visit a very old man Junyoung who was a Baha'i. We sat under a large lime tree (propped up by sticks) and he called over various relatives, mainly grandchildren, who spoke English. One was a boy called "King" who went to Michigan Uni to study law and was home on holidays. Quite fascinating. He seemed to be related to almost everyone in Laura.

We shared some lunch with him. He really adored the children and spent much time talking to them. He lived in a very small home that didn't seem very waterproof.

As we were leaving, a young boy, James, asked if we would

like some coconuts and within seconds had skimmed up a tree at least fifty feet high and knocked down some coconuts. He husked them and then opened the tops so we could drink the fluid. The young ones are best for water.

Saturday night, we were expecting Jacob, but he didn't come and no-one else did. So we had an early night.

Sunday 20th

Went for a walk to the main part of Laura – well, not exactly the main part because Laura doesn't seem to have a real centre – but we walked along a section with a lot of activity around the Presbyterian Church, Missionaries' homes, Assembly of God Bible College, public elementary school. Church services were proceeding and we had a look into the Assembly of God – people singing hymns in Marshallese in a particular local style. The man prayed and his voice sounded much like churches everywhere. We curtailed our walk because it was very hot.

In the mid-afternoon, two men and five youths came and sat themselves down near our fire. The two men (Larry, the dentist and another man who was a fisherman) and one of the boys were from the family complex thirty yards away – we had not met them up to this point. Larry was the only one with much English and he was very good and interpreted for the others. He surprised us by announcing that they were all Baha'is. I spoke to them about the main figures of the Faith. They didn't seem to have even a basic understanding of the background of the Faith. Perhaps they knew more than their ability with English allowed them to display. They said they always met here on Sundays and that they and others would come back at night, but they didn't.

Monday 21st

Settling into our new lifestyle with mother nature as our constant companion. Joseph is enjoying this very much.

The day was completely occupied with cooking bread, washing etc. Bread was a miserable failure. This life is really acceptable, but one has to adjust to the fact that daily activities such as cooking take very much longer.

In the late afternoon, the boys who had come the previous afternoon came after work. They work in a youth employment training scheme. – because of the lack of jobs around here – they get paid about $5 per week to do community tasks such as making seats for public roadsides – and acquiring some skills. The boys climbed a nearby coconut tree and got us some drinking coconuts.

Tuesday 22nd

Don and Joseph went to town to get supplies. I stayed here with Benjy and read some books. Life is easy without Joseph – he is so active and so demanding all the time. Don caught up with people in Rita – we may be going to Arno? A friend, Gena, brought him back – he owns a small shop near us and is continuously travelling back and forth to keep it supplied. We held the Feast in the evening on our own.

Wednesday 23rd

Went for a long walk before breakfast and saw all the fishermen with their long nets catching small fish caught on the reef at low tide. The fishing people also go further afield in boats of an unusual design – they have outriggers to steady them in and out of the waves.

After breakfast, an old woman appeared and whisked away our washing, saying she would do it. Her name is Ngarbit and she lives with Junyun. We had no water as it hadn't rained for days so she went next door and made some arrangements. We went over to see what was happening and came into conversation with Larry and others, and I did handicrafts with the women in the cooking hut. They were cooking breadfruit. In the meantime, Ngarbit was down at the well doing our washing. We then returned home after a car pulled up at our place with the owners of the house. They were pleased to meet us and happy we were living there and didn't want any rent. They went away and then called back briefly to give us some young coconuts.

We cooked some bread successfully today with many intrigued onlookers from next door. We were happy to be able to give them some bread as they had sent over previously some cooked fish and hot breadfruit. We felt happy we were making some closer contact with people. Ngarbit stayed all the day doing all the chores and for this we fed her. She seemed happy just to be around and useful. We would have liked to pay her but it sets precedents and then people think you are rich westerners and it affects how you relate to them. Old people have no pensions and if they are not attached to a family they can live very poorly. We made sure she ate well, and I think she was very grateful for this.

Thursday 24th

Despite our protests, Ngarbit arrived bright and early and the washing disappeared again. I was going to catch the bus to town but missed it. In the meantime, we met up with many people under the big tree near the shop. A little girl was playing a four-stringed guitar with a blues melody and quite complicated rhythm. We came back to find Ngarbit had chopped firewood and done the dishes. Decided to go for a walk along the beach – met up with Nomno, who invited us to his home – most enjoyable time. The law student lived here too. Nomno was finishing carving out a boat from a breadfruit tree trunk.

Friday 25th

Was hoping for rain as we were down to our last gallon of water and did it rain! Filled up several drums. Last night about 2 am, Larry from next door woke us to give us two fish. We didn't realize that the idea was we cook them immediately – that's what they do. He then came back again about 6 am to ask if we had cooked the fish. As it was pouring with rain and had been all night there was no hope of lighting a fire, so he offered that we come over to his place and use his kerosene stove. Much to our embarrassment as we didn't really know how to cook the fish properly. He was quite amazed we weren't cooking rice with it and then sort of puzzled that we cut the head off and cleaned it and then it disintegrated as I turned it over. The fish had gone off – in this climate, you have to either put them on ice or cook them straight away. So we left hurriedly.

Ngarbit, our old lady, came and did the washing about midday. We then lit a fire inside and cooked lunch of rice and coconut with tinned meat.

In the evening, Larry asked Don to go fishing with him. They set a net then sat on the beach, ate raw fish, and talked for an hour or so then collected the net. This time we cooked the fish straight away under Larry's instruction. You scale them and cook them whole in plenty of oil and make shallow slits in each side and salt. Magnificent! Really delicious. Feeling very happy, we collapsed into a deep slumber with the rain pouring down.

Saturday 26th Nov

Drizzled all morning so we baked some bread inside the house – most successfully. A boy called round just to sit and talk, then Robert arrived. Faithful Ngarbit had done the washing so we all sat down to fresh bread and Spam for lunch. Robert is a lovely old man – it is a pity we can't speak Marshallese better. Communication is difficult. He told us all the Baha'is are coming around tomorrow. The people who owned the house then arrived. He was an electrician in Rita and had moved down there because of travelling difficulties. He spoke English quite well. He told us the government had given him a grant to build the house, but the grants had run out so maybe the house would not be finished. They were most happy we were living there and didn't want any rent. We took a walk and visited Larry, who was busy mending his fishing net, and his wife was making baskets.

Don went fishing with Larry again tonight – fish for tea again.

Robert called in and lit the kerosene pressure lamp for us then left. People just seem to come and go without explanation and everyone here spends a long time just sitting, not saying much. Most activities seem to just happen without any planning and generally in groups rather than individually.

Sunday 27th

Household chores in morning – baked some bread. Ngarbit didn't come. Baha'is from Rita, including Fred (a Gilbertese man who was on the NSA – wonderful sense of humour – would always ask Joseph where his coat of many colours was), Farrateu, and Nailin arrived and then a lot of Baha'is from around Laura. We talked about 'Abdu'l-Baha, then about LSAs. Then Farrateu asked me to talk about the Baha'i laws. Then I told the story of the Bab. It was good to have the nicely-cooked bread to hand around – happy atmosphere.

Fred and Farateu told us this afternoon that we were to leave for Arno tomorrow. However, Francis hasn't come to pick us up as expected. Said goodbyes to everyone – made many friends in Laura, particularly Junyung, the old man, and our washer lady, and Larry the fisherman-come-dentist.

Monday 28th

Francis hasn't come – pouring with rain. Nairgit arrived and was so sad to see our bags packed – she really liked coming to do our washing! Towards afternoon it had fined up so we took a walk to Jacob's to unlock the padlock for the house (which Joseph kindly shut up for us) and a book I'd lent him. Met up with his wife, who somehow understood our smattering of Marshallese.

Met Jacob on the way back, playing volley ball – the street is a hive of activity close to sunset – children sitting around playing ukuleles and singing, a game of volley ball in a small clearing, the owners of the tiny shop looking for a few last customers, the fisherman setting out with the coconut leaf baskets to go fishing at night, a few teenagers loafing under a large breadfruit tree near the shop, women walking their babies and general chitchat in the fading light. Once the light is gone, activity ceases and people sleep, except the fishermen.

We had managed to get a lift to town and were waiting on the roadside when along came several Baha'is from Majuro and Francis and Farateu with the truck. So we loaded up in a rather disorganized fashion and went back to Majuro.

Tues 29th

Spent the day organizing our visa extension (only one month at a time), plane tickets and a plane to take us to Arno. Shopping in the evening – a month's supply of food. Also bought a lot of handicrafts to take back. Francis and Farateu drove us around all day.

Arno, Mwejrik & Bikarej

Wed 30th

Shopped in morning. Managed at last to find the pilot who agreed to take us to Arno at midday. Funny chap. Apparently spends most of his time chasing girls and having a good time and rarely visits his office. So off to the airport. We had chartered a seaplane to get there as there was no other way of getting to that part of the island we were to stay on. What an incredible journey – to see Arno Atoll spread out below us – the islands like tiny dots and lines on a huge blue ocean.

We were to stay at the small island of Mwejrik which is close to a much bigger island, Bikarej. It is a walk of a few kilometres at low tide – otherwise by boat.

We landed in the small lagoon – and Peter and two boys (one being Farateu's brother, John) came to meet us. Peter and Tsuata and their child, Akiki, were the only people living on this island and we were to stay with them. John and another boy were also staying for a short time. They took our luggage by boat across the lagoon and we walked to the house.

The house was a two-roomed fibro and masonite affair with a tin roof, cement floor – no sewerage (just the whole Pacific Ocean) and of course no electricity – but lots of rainwater gathered from the roof into a large tank.

Everyone except Tsuata spoke good English – and she spoke none. All are Gilbertese but have left Gilberts over a decade ago. It was a great relief to see that we could communicate so well – in contrast to Laura. Also, in contrast to Laura, they seemed more active Baha'is – in fact, John had come over from Majuro several weeks before to strengthen the Baha'i community here.

We quickly settled into their set-up – e.g. helping (somewhat artlessly) to cut out coconut meat as part of the copra-making process. Joseph almost immediately made good friends with the little boy Akiki (5 years old) and so Joseph seemed in much better spirits.

We had a most magnificent meal of crabs which had been caught in about half an hour.

Slept in a small room on a concrete floor (with the inevitable mat).

Thursday 1st Dec

I went with Peter and John by small boat to Bikarej while Don remained with Joseph – went for a walk around the island – very thick undergrowth – you can't walk unless you cut your way, so they followed existing paths and along the beach.

At Bikarej, I met most of the Baha'is. At the end of the track through Bikarej lives an American man with his local wife. They invited me in. Many people there and they were fascinated by me – where I came from – and they had a lot of fun with my small smattering of Marshallese. All adored Benjy and were surprised that he was totally breastfed. Many women in the Marshalls now bottle-feed their babies – probably because they feel it is better for the baby. Then suddenly, a fellow appeared, having climbed a coconut tree to bring me a much-appreciated thirst-quenching drink – coconut water – and then put a shell necklace around my neck.

Meeting with the Baha'is was good and they seem really interested in hearing more about the Faith. One of them, the teacher on the island, can speak English. It is hoped an LSA will be formed before I leave. They suggested I come back next evening. I was back at Mwejrik by lunchtime.

Cooked bread in the afternoon.

Evenings we have a meal and go virtually straight to bed after talking for a short time.

Friday 2nd

I went fishing with John and Peter. The fish are netted by blocking their path to the sea on the outgoing tide. We caught about thirty – each several pounds – an amazingly simple operation.

John and Peter took some of the fish to give to the people at Bikarej – we went by boat. Fishing is much better on this island than on Bikarej. On their return, the boat went back again carrying Don, me, kids and John.

Magnificent meal of delicious ("enno") fried and boiled fish in the home of Absolem. Sat on floor mats as usual in the partly enclosed area for cooking and eating most of the houses seem to have – very pleasant. Eating is an international language.

Baha'i meeting with about eight adults. I explained the basic teachings of Baha'ullah. Then followed questions mainly about sin and hell.

Slept in a quaint semi-traditional hut with pandanus matting roof, all tied together with string made from coconut fibre – no nails. And the hut was laid with mats all ready for us – with two pillows on the floor and mosquito coils burning and a little lamp – felt like honoured guests.

Saturday 3rd

Breakfast with Absolem – pancakes.

On the way through the village, we met up with the policeman. He wanted to know who we were and when we would be coming again. He was blowing his whistle to wake everyone just to let them know a policeman was around. He also blows it at night and 10 pm, and all young boys have to be in their homes by then.

We went back to 'our' island by the small boat first thing.

An uneventful day. Feeling very comfortable in this setting, but exceptionally frustrating morning because I was attempting to do the washing but was interrupted continuously by the children. I am feeling edgy because of the frustrations of getting the simplest daily chores done with the demands of the children and the absence of proper washing facilities etc.

The men caught more crabs for tea. And we baked more bread.

Very exhausted. Just slept and rested. Cool rainy day – first rainy day since we've been here. Peter was up at 1 am to catch fish. Peter and Tsuata are amazing people. They are very adept in the skills of natural living – catching birds and fish, using the coconuts for so many different things – like making string out of the husks of the coconut. They make copra for selling here too but only get about 5c/lb for the copra – this is not much. A boat comes about every three months to pick it up and also brings a few goods for the little store at Bakarej.

Peter was saying today there is a lot of stealing in Bakarej and the boat always loses some goods when it is in dock, so they don't like coming there. Also, there is stealing from amongst each other, even from Peter and Tsuata's little island here where no one else lives. They come and take things when they are away. This seems odd in such a small community of only about eighty people.

The children are really thriving – particularly Joseph. Very happy with his little playmate and eating like a horse – starting to fill out again. Benjy is still fully breastfed – starting to feel it a bit of a drain as he is quite a monster. However, will persevere as it is so much easier and safer under these living conditions. I think he possibly would be better now with some solids. He is sitting up almost by himself, but when he loses balance he really topples and gets most upset. We have worked out a little seat for him now, which is a blessing as I had nowhere safe to put him down – dogs, pigs, chooks, cats roam freely around the area.

There are very few natural animals (except crabs) on the island – all being imported and the only dangers are falling coconuts and sharks (maybe) and barracuda in the water. While I was first at Bikarej, John was telling me about a typhoon that hit the island many years ago and three waves as tall as the coconut trees went right over the island. Only a few people survived and that was by tying themselves to trees or some such. The island was totally stripped.

Mon 5th

Very wet day – wondering if we would get to Bikarej. We left when there was a dry spell hoping for the best. Peter took us across as the engine is not the best – it needs a new spark plug. The usual gracious welcome by Absolem and Chlora. Our little house was all ready for us. We took a walk to the end of the island – as Don hadn't seen much of it. There was a lot of activity this evening – a whole group playing or watching volleyball. Don joined in for a bit. John was sick with diarrhea so was continuously paying little visits along the way.

We got back after dark to find a tea of chicken and rice beautifully laid out awaiting us. Not as many people were there for the meeting as the copra boat was in on the next island and the men had taken their copra down. However, it was a good evening. I talked about the history of the Faith and then to Chlora about Bible prophesy. There is such a need for more translation of the writings into Marshallese.

Tues 6th

Peter arrived in the morning to take us back. He couldn't get the engine started so he had walked back around the edge of the lagoon dragging the boat. After a pancake breakfast, we left to return to our little island.

Spent the day cooking bread or sorting things out. Went for a walk around the island. The men went fishing and were back with some beautiful fish for tea. Some fish are poisonous so you have to be careful.

Wed 7th

A busy day making copra as the boat is coming soon – they

think. Had a good talk with John and planned our next meeting – decided to talk about the Feast Day. The men went fishing again and, in an hour or so, came back with a big haul of fish.

Thurs 8th

Over to Bikarej just after lunch for another meeting. Some fishing boats from Majuro arrived not long after we got there. Not many Baha'is came, but the fishermen all sat around and listened. There seems to be some problems with John's translations – this was made obvious when one of the fishermen who spoke English was always helping out. It is difficult as John's native language is Gilbertese, and he doesn't speak Marshallese or English with great fluency.

John decided to go back to Majaro with the fishermen so we gave him a long shopping list. The fishermen go out about 5 am to catch big tuna, put them on ice and take them to Majuro

Fri 9th

Benjy and Joseph awake very early. Pancakes for breakfast. Chlora and Absolem are most hospitable. Peter arrived and we returned to Mwejrik. He was saying the Baha'is were most unhappy with John's translation and didn't think more meetings were worthwhile while he was translating.

In the afternoon, Peter, Tsuata and Akiki went to Bikarej to tee up a boat for transporting their copra, and we had the island to ourselves all day. Good not to have to worry about having our washes in private. They came back late afternoon with Cullington and a large open boat (oversized rowing boat) in tow.

Sat 10th

We loaded the copra in the morning – 20 bags worth about $200 – three weeks' work by Peter and Cullington with help from John and Tsuata and us. Loaded at low tide. The boat was very leaky and they had to shift the cargo around so that the worst leaks were above the water line. They left at the rising tide about midday – quite a spectacle with the small boat with a one-and-a-half horsepower motor towing the lumbering and heavily laden 'barge' sitting low in the water.

Copra production is hard work – and very poorly paid at about 5c/lb. The ground is cleared and the fallen coconuts are husked. They are then taken in a sack back home where there is an area set up for cutting out and drying the copra. Each coconut is then cracked open with a long knife then the 'meat' is taken out with a small knife. This means often many cuts as the knife occasionally slips or penetrates the outer shell. They are then dried in a special kiln using husks and the shells as firewood. They are then bagged. The big difficulty for Peter and Tsuata is to estimate a good time to take their copra to Bikarej as the ship is so unreliable.

During the afternoon, Don took Benjy and Joseph for a walk so I could do some reading. After becoming engrossed in my book, I looked up and suddenly wondered where Don was as it seemed a long time since he left, and the sun was getting low in the sky. I walked in several directions as far as I could – it being high tide – and couldn't find them and began to get panicky. Retraced my steps – petrified of falling coconuts from very high trees in the centre of the island – and still couldn't find them. Started imagining all sorts of things – the sun was nearly set. So took a torch and resolved to walk around the island. Just as I set out, Don and the kids walked around the bend as happy as can be. I was so relieved – stupid me – 'bwebwe'.

For the first time, we opened a tin of chicken for tea – not very nice in comparison to the 'real' chickens Peter has killed. Last night we had one of Peter's chickens with garlic – 'enoh'.

Peter did not return until very early the next morning – on a favourable tide before the sun rose. He had missed the ship and was very disappointed – has stored his copra at Bikarej for the next boat. Absolem charged him $15 for use of the barge, which upset Peter because Peter had given him fish and other favours.

Peter had talked to Alden about the feast (Sunday) but didn't get a clear reply so it looks as though the people at Bikarej will not participate in the feast.

Sunday 11th

Peter got the radio working with batteries he bought in Bikarej and we heard the news for the first time in over a month. The first item was that Australia had had another election and Liberals in again. We had forgotten there was going to be an election. Mostly the radio just has very low-grade stations from California and American music.

Pedro walked from Bikarej to see if we had taken Flora's bible – we hadn't, and he left soon afterwards.

Feast with Peter and Tsuata at night. Very nice. I explained the Baha'i calendar and the meaning of feasts. Had a few prayers in English read by me (Peter can't read English or Marshallese and we didn't have any prayers in Gilbertese). Despite this, he seemed to have a good understanding of the basics of the Faith – in contrast to people at Laura and Bikarej. Talked about problems of teaching at Bikarej and decided that I should speak to Alden myself.

We now have very little petrol so we can't get to Bikarej very easily. We could walk but difficult with the kids.

Monday 12th

I did a little sketch of the house in the morning – very difficult to get any uninterrupted time without children. I went to help Peter for an hour or so (with Joseph) cleaning the forest floor and collecting coconuts. Joseph happy looking for crabs and carrying hermit crabs around everywhere in a glass jar. Joseph and Akiki had many 'swims' at the water's edge. Water is getting low but looks like a good rain tonight.

Tues 13th

Torrential rain last night – the water tank is full again. Ben is waking three times every night for feeds – maybe it is time he was on solids. I was hoping to get through at least the next month without giving him anything else.

Rained most of the day. Don is still trying to make his fence. Joseph and Akiki wander around in the rain with their crabs – putting them in jars and playing with them.

Wed 14th

Magnificent loaf of bread today – using coconut milk. Have mastered camp oven. Don took the kids for a walk while I did some painting and reading. Trouble getting the washing dry. In the afternoon went into the middle of the island – Peter, Tsuata and Don were clearing and collecting coconuts and there were crabs everywhere. Tsuata was cooking them on the fire as they were burning off. Coconut trees were about 100 feet high – petrified of falling coconuts. Didn't stay long as Benjy fell asleep so took him back home – too many mosquitos. Garlic chicken for tea – yum! Peter and Tsuata are good cooks.

Joseph blossoming – doesn't use his bottle now except on odd occasions and is eating like a horse and seems to have grown a lot, physically, emotionally and mentally. Akiki teases him a lot but he is learning to cope with this.

Thurs 15th

Don is getting stuck into his fence after trying many different methods – using uprights of coconut frond stems. Don took the kids for a short walk while I did some painting. Rained a lot. Talked with Peter in the evening about Bikarej.

Fri 16th

Don got up very early as the kids woke up and took them to see the sunrise. Peter was already up cracking coconut husks. About mid-morning, Peter and Tsuata made a sail out of a couple of sticks and an old sheet. Very effective. Off they went to Bikarej. We all went for a walk and had a great time swimming in the nude. Benjy loves the sand and water.

After the usual prolonged effort, we lit a fire and cooked some lunch. Joseph devoured the whole can of corn (our ration) before the rice was cooked. Peter and Tsuata arrived back having towed the boat home – with an umbrella made of coconut leaves to keep the rain off their shopping. Tinned food for tea. Don had a good talk to Peter tonight.

Sitting writing this with a hurricane lamp beside me, in our little room on the mat that covers the concrete floor which is our bed, radio playing music from the Gilbert Islands.

Sat 17th

Made bread using fermented coconut tree sap – magnificent.

    Yeast – 1 cup sap in morning

           1 cup sap in evening

           1 cup salt water

           a little flour

           leave overnight

Peter and Tsuata were up early – before we arose, they had the bread on the rise and caught a whole pile of fish.

Don did a little more on the garden fence – slow going but the end product will be OK and learning a lot as he goes.

Will be going to Bikarej tomorrow.

Sun 18th

Buckets of rain last night – literally, and rained all day so no journey to Bikarej. The children were getting mischievous having to spend more time indoors. Peter caught more fish as usual. Did some handicrafts with Tsuata. Don still working hard on his fence. Unusual late afternoon – the first time we had seen reflections in the lagoon – perfectly still. Life is very steady here with an easy rhythm.

Don said that an amazing thing happened. He was sitting with Joseph by the water, and Joe reached over and put his hand on Don's knee. It might seem such a small thing but it really struck Don. Joe had never responded to cuddles or shown affection before. He was stiff when we held him, he didn't melt into us. It made such an impression on Don. Joe had not known how to express this, but now he can! Maybe it was from the difficult birth and his first days separated in a humidicrib, but now, this simple life on the island has enabled him to feel this closeness.

Mon 19th

Still no sign of John's return or any messages from Majuro. Rain again today so didn't get to Bikarej again. Tsuata was cooking fish for most of the day – fish, fish cakes, and pancakes – ennoh!

I learnt a few handicrafts from Tsuata – a quick way of making a carry-basket from coconut fronds – also yeast from coconut sap.

Suddenly John (and Collington) have returned. A boat dropped them several islands away, and they walked here. Have a lot of stores for us left at the island, which we will have to get somehow.

John said he didn't do much in Majuro because of bad weather – which also prevented him from returning earlier. As it was, his boat trip seemed quite risky in this weather. John didn't have much news but said a Baha'i travel teacher from California arrived a few days ago and will be going to Kwadjalin.

Tues 20th

Awake most of the night feeding Benjy and settling Joseph. Up at the crack of dawn but not before Peter and Tsuata. The bread, using coconut sap for yeast, was on the rise. John had gone back to the boat during the night and also back to Majuro. Peter and Tsuata took the boat to Bikarej and picked up all the supplies. The lagoon was very rough. There was a letter from the NTC saying that they had chartered the boat Johnny came on to bring us supplies and suggested we might go back on it, but it was too late and the weather too rough anyway. It also said that the pilot of the seaplane was away on holidays so it might be difficult for us to get back.

Today Tsuata taught me how to make a sleeping mat from pandanus.

Wed 21st

Went to Bikarej and spoke with a man about his boat taking us to Majuro in two weeks' time – he said he would – for $100. I am afraid that the trip may prove rough or dangerous and we requested the pilot to take all precautions.

Saw Alden – said he would translate and indicated he had no problems or reservations about this. Meeting arranged for Friday.

Once again, we were receivers of fantastic hospitality and generosity – e.g. the boatman offered us breadfruit (tastes like cheese) and pork which he was evidently intending on eating himself. Had homecooked bread and pawpaw at Absolem's – served with great warmth. I was only asking about coconut rope and Pedro gave me a large quantity despite my protests. Alden offered us his walky-talky when we asked him if he could send a message for us. Unfortunately, couldn't get through when we tried back at Mwejrik.

Thurs 22nd

Peter caught a mountain of fish again so took some across to Bikarej. He came back late that night without Tsuata, and Akiki had spent the night there. Don did a bit of clearing and fencing. Spent the day preparing for talking about Bible prophesy on the Friday night.

Friday 23rd

Went to Bikarej in mid-morning. Presented a raisin loaf to Clara, which we had baked in the morning. Pretty rough crossing to Bikarej because of the wind – even small waves made the going difficult.

At Bikarej, watched people (mainly men) at Absolem's house playing 'Trouble' (Ludo) – identical rules to the game we know but it had a different name. They play for money.

Had salted fish for tea. They partly unsalted it by soaking it in water and then boiled it – tasted OK.

Tried to get in contact with Majuro by walky-talky but no luck.

Alden said he would translate for the meeting that night but didn't show up – clearly not interested. No one came either, so I tried to communicate with Clara by use of a dictionary – very difficult but we certainly learnt that Clara is definitely interested.

I spent a while in the late afternoon with Clara learning Marshallese. She seemed to enjoy it.

Pedro gave us a shark's backbone necklace – most generous.

Christmas Eve

Pancakes for breakfast.

Peter picked us up late morning to take us back to Mwejrik.

Tsuata had a whole lot of fish cooked for us on arrival, which we consumed with vigour. Tsuata doing more on her mat – quite a complicated sequence.

Peter & Tsuata suddenly announced that they were going to Bikarej to spend the night – left mid-afternoon.

Spent afternoon doing routine chores. Joseph spilt all of a nice fruit salad I had made!

Christmas Day – Sunday

We started early to clean up the yard in Peter and Tsuata's absence so that we could surprise them on their return.

They returned in mid-morning – we hadn't quite finished the clean-up and they made no comment, but I guess they were pleased.

I made a 'Christmas cake' which was very successful and a nice change in our diet. Had Spam patties for Christmas lunch.

Children had a swim in the afternoon – that's not unusual except that we went with them and took photographs – Benjy enjoys kicking the water and eating the sand. Joseph and Akiki were insatiable for 'round-and-round' whirlies in the water.

Boiled chicken at night.

Boxing Day – Monday 26th December

Tsuata finished her mat today and ceremoniously tied it in a bundle and gave it to Benjy – these people give so much – we know so little about generosity.

Talking to Peter much more now – about the Faith and religion in general.

Benjy now waits for his dip in the ocean and gets very excited when he sees the water. Joseph has grown a lot physically and emotionally but has been a bit whingy of late – although Akiki does tease him. We come closer and closer to Peter and Tsuata. They are becoming very good friends, and we are all just the one family. There is a good happy feeling here.

Great excitement when we saw the lights of a ship on the horizon – our rescue ship? – no – it passed without seeing us.

Tuesday 27th Dec

Baked a cake while Peter and Tsuata fished for most of the morning. Did a little more to my painting and Don to his fence. Don made a swing for the boys – another thing for them to fight about. Fine sunny day – looks like the stormy weather has gone for the time.

How can we get back to Majuro?

Wednesday 28th Dec

Went to Bikarej first thing in the morning for the 8 am CB radio scheds but arrived too late. Asked Alden to send a message for us (advising Francis about the travel arrangements we have made). He said he would do it but isn't an enthusiastic type of person.

Spent half an hour or so with Clara. Peter talked to her and Absolem about the Bible and Baha'i Faith.

Returned to Mwejriki in the late morning

Almost straight away, Peter made a sail and he and Tsuata sailed across to Bikarej (Tsuata didn't come with us on the first trip). They returned late afternoon. They seemed to like going to Bikarej at any excuse, but Peter thought the sail could save fuel (they had to motor back though because of adverse winds).

In the afternoon, Don did more on the fence and I did more on my painting. Joseph played around happily in Akiki's absence. When with Akiki, he grizzles and cries continually.

Thurs 29th

Finished my painting. Don dug a big hole for his garden and filled it with rubbish. Only one more side of the fence to do.

A plane flew low over the island and circled as if to land – we immediately assumed that Baha'is had sent the seaplane to pick us up. However, it was the army plane looking for a lost fisherman.

We are concerned about getting back by 6th Jan as that is when our visa has to be renewed. We are playing with windy weather and approaching low tide.

Tsauta and Peter sailed across the lagoon to Bikarej. They seem to enjoy going there. Yesterday they won some money playing Ludo and bought some flour.

Benjy loves watching the animals. As soon as he even hears the pig, he sits bolt upright. Tonight, he watched the chooks being fed sitting in his chair and was totally enthralled. Joseph becoming a really wholesome little boy and quite affectionate towards Benjy. Really happy. Although sometimes he whines and grizzles when Akiki is around. There is quite an age difference between them and Joseph has no speech, even in English.

Friday 30th

Went to Bikarej – not early enough and missed the first (8am) walky-talky schedule. Alden kept trying for us all morning. We went for a walk to the end of the island for an hour or so to fill in time. A nice clear channel between the islands. Met a woman getting water and "chatted" as best we could. She had a child in her arms, which is a good point of contact.

About 12 noon Alden was able to get through to Majuro to someone he knew – who said he would get Francis at 1 pm. However, nothing came through at 1 pm and we tried until after 2 pm. Alden gave us some salted fish and rice for lunch. While waiting for the radio, I watched Alden's wife make a coconut leaf mat, and Joseph played happily with children and looked for crabs.

Peter came about 2:30 pm and we spent some time with Absolem and Clara (eating pancakes) and then returned to Mwejrik.

Did a big wash – went to sleep early – exhausted.

Saturday 31st

Across to Bikarej early again. Alden had made contact with someone else the previous night, and he was expecting Francis to come on at 8:30 am. Once again, no contact – presumedly Francis had not been told. We kept trying for an hour or so and then they were about to give up when someone else came on who said they would get Francis – yet again, no contact despite trying for another three hours.

Had lunch of chicken with Alden in their magnificent little eating and cooking hut that Alden had designed and built himself. Seem to be getting to know Alden much better – seems less remote than when we first met him. He asked me for Baha'i books the previous day and he read some that I brought over today.

Met up with Therabus while Alden was on the radio. Therabus had run out of gas but didn't tell us until specifically asked – thus our transport to Majuro is in doubt. Previously we had been trying to contact Francis to tell him not to do anything because we had things under control for transport from this end, but now it seems that we need Francis to arrange something from Majuro. Getting worried about how we will return.

Therabus is waiting for a ship to bring fuel which he hopes to get by Monday to take us but it seems doubtful it will arrive in time, and in any case, if the ship does come, we would be better to go on that – cheaper, safer etc.

Went back to Absolem's and met up with Peter. We were discussing our dilemma when Peter saw Francis's brother's fishing boat (Vincent) – we rushed out but couldn't attract his attention. Then another boat went past and Absolem flashed a mirror and it stopped. It had been travelling in duo with Vincent's boat.

It was very low tide and Peter and Don walked to the edge of the reef and Peter swam over to the boat – seemed very dangerous because the waves were breaking against the edge of the reef then drawing back, exposing the ghastly, deep, jagged rock face. Getting back seemed even more dangerous but Peter has done it many times and he was not worried. It took all Don's strength just to stand near the edge of the waves and on sharp coral rocks.

The men in the boat said they would contact Vincent and either he would return tomorrow or as soon as possible.

Thus we went back to Mwejric with hopes of imminent departure – a day of mixed fortunes of raised hopes and disappointments.

Began preparing to leave.

Had Feast with Peter and Tsuata – very good with Peter asking lots of questions about Baha'i view of Christian concepts like heaven, hell, sin etc.

Sunday 1st January 1978

I finished my picture and frame and we put it in Peter and Tsuata's room in the late afternoon. They didn't see it till after dark and examined it piece by piece by lamp and torch light. They were very pleased.

No boat from Majuro.

Virtually finished the fence.

Peter caught a lot of fish with a net set close to the beach near the house.

Tsuata made two coconut mats – she is very fast.

Monday 2nd Jan

Still no boat or message.

Did some more on the fence.

In the afternoon, Tsuata and I did little decorations using

shells and pandanus leaves. Tsuata made Benjy a pandanus ball which he loves and played with for two hours. He is sitting up very comfortably, is moving around a lot, trying to climb over onto my lap from the floor and shows signs of beginning to crawl.

Tuesday 3rd Jan

Don completed his fence and the peanuts were planted. These were the last of the seed peanuts we had brought to eat from Kununurra. Don was very satisfied with his effort.

Went to Bikarej to find out if any news of boats – but none at all. Very disappointing. Came back and baked bread. Peter and Tsuata went fishing on the ocean side – very rough, winds still strong – and caught a big haul of fish while we baked bread. Supplies are getting low. Joseph grizzling less and playing much better with Benjy.

Wednesday 4th Jan

Quiet day – nothing much happened

Benjy showing more signs of crawling and more activity. Tsuata has made him a crawling mat.

Saw some lights of people crabbing at Bikarej and thought it was a signal that they had some news for us so resolved to go there on Thursday.

Thursday 5th

To Bikarej in mid-morning. Weather seems to be deteriorating.

Tried to find Alden to see if he had any news – but couldn't find him. Pedro and the others had no news so it was decided that Don should stay at Bikarej and I would take the children back with Peter. Don would try to contact Francis on the 6 pm and 8 am scheds. Getting anxious now about our visa terminating.

The wind was very strong and had only gone a short way when Peter decided it wasn't safe to go on. So we came back and I stayed back with Don while Peter took Akiki back. Watched the boat bounce around the edge of the lagoon but they arrived safely. Peter has spent most of his life on a boat as a ship's captain and we are indebted to his knowledge of the water. An unskilled person could run into a lot of trouble even on this small lagoon.

On arriving back at Clara and Absolem's, Pedro decided to come with us to see Alden. He was in and playing Ludo but his wife told us of a message over the radio – from the Baha'is – to say they were trying to get a boat to come, but the weather was too rough and if the weather continued, they would send a big ship. Wonderful news – just to know they are concerned and thinking of us – made us feel better but still no closer to getting back. Anchoo's boat is on the other side of the Arno atoll but even it can't get back to Majuro because of the bad weather. So maybe it won't get to Bikarej until next week.

Asked about supplies and managed to get tea and mosquito coils but sold out of everything else – even rice and flour. Went on to Tabal's place. He also had sold out – no food on the island except what nature provides. Tabal gave us his usual royal welcome with pandanus fruit. (Benjy loved it) and then coffee and doughnuts followed by eggs, rice and dried fish – such hospitality! A very interesting man – with a very orderly garden and well-built house. While we were there, Clara and Absolom came and bought chicken with them – for our tea. So we bought two more and took them back alive as a small token for all their hospitality. We know so little of generosity. These people give when they have nothing. They gave us their own food.

Tried the 6 pm sched but couldn't reach Majuro. When we returned to Clara and Absolom's, Peter, Tsuata and Akiki were there. They came over to give us the radio message. We all slept the night in our little pandanus hut – Benjy woke six times for feeds despite his oatmeal porridge and pandanus during the day – I think he was thirsty.

Friday 6th

Weather unsettled at night. Also, I had to feed Benjy six times! So I was very tired in the morning.

It was low tide so Peter wanted to leave early. We had to walk back. Peter pulled the boat carrying me and the children along in the shallows and Tsuata and Don walked along – took only about an hour.

After we got back, it became very windy and it looks as though the weather of the past days has reached its climax and will blow itself out – therefore, expect much rain tonight.

A lazy day – I rested because I was feeling very run-down. Don read.

Tsuata cooked us breadfruit and Benjy had some.

Getting back to Majuro

Sat 7th

Weather seemed to be better after a fairly windy and rainy night. Hopes high for a boat in the afternoon, but nothing.

About 5:30 pm, we heard an announcement over the radio for us to get the regular seaplane at Todo on Monday at 11 am.

Also, Pedro and Collington came over from Bikarej to tell us in case we hadn't heard – wonderful that they came so cheerfully (even though unnecessarily).

We are worried how we can get to Todo. The alternatives are:-

See if Therabus or Tabal have enough gas to take us by boat to Todo.

If not, for Don to go to Todo – by either walking to Todo or going by canoe – to ask the pilot to return to Majuro via Mwejrik to pick up me and the kids.

If Archoo's boat is available.

If pilot will not go to Mwejrik, Don will go into Majuro on the plane and then make arrangements from there – to charter a boat or plane.

Sun 8th, Mon 9th and Tues 10th – Helen's version

Don left for Bikarej early in the morning with a few bits and pieces in case he had to walk to Todo – just water, some rubber and nails in case the sandals I had made broke (Don's had been taken earlier by Johnny) and a mosquito coil and matches for sleeping overnight on one of the islands. However, we almost expected to get a boat with enough petrol to get to Todo – either Tabal or Therebus.

Waited anxiously for his return, expecting to pack straight away. Was very disappointed when Peter returned alone. A very anxious day and night – up most of the night with the children – couldn't sleep anyway. Was glad Pedro had gone with Don. He is a really nice fellow and speaks English and is good company.

Monday morning was up, packed ready waiting for the plane to call in at Mwejrik on the way to Majuro. Waited anxiously till 2 pm then got the washing out of the boat after realizing nothing was going to happen that day. Then in the middle of the night, Alden arrived to say Don and Pedro had contacted him on the walky-talky from Majuro to say the plane would be coming at 8 am that morning. He asked if he could come on the plane too. Was overjoyed – slept peacefully for the rest of the night. We had nearly run out of supplies, and our visa expired that day.

Todo is fifteen kilometres from Bikarej. As can be seen in the map, most of this can only be walked at low tide, so we tried to get a boat.

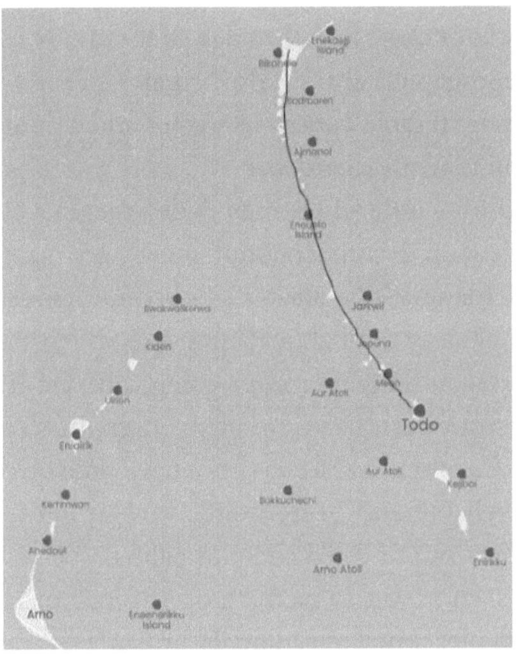

At Bikarej. we first went to see Therebus but he had no fuel to get to Todo. He said Tabal would have some, and so did everyone else. So Pedro and I went off to see Tabal in high hopes. Along the way, we called in to see Alden to see if he had any news. He said that Tabal had gone to Todo yesterday to take his sick wife to hospital – curses. That also meant that we couldn't have the use of his canoe in his absence (no one to bring it back anyway). No news of Anchoo's boat either. No luck anywhere, so we commenced to walk.

The tide was already well on its way in – we realized that we should really have left about one and a half hours earlier but decided to go as far as we could on this tide and then stop (there are islands every few hundred yards) and wait for the next low tide then finish the rest off on the morning tide.

The first half was easy walking over flat rocks on the ocean side, and we kept walking as fast as possible and got as far as a largish island just over halfway – about 12:30 pm. Along the way, we saw the waves crash into the edge of the reef then suck back, leaving a large gaping abyss. Also, small (2-foot round) holes filled with an incredible variety of shapes and colours of coral – very beautiful miniature gardens.

We rested for a little while, then Pedro caught a coconut crab which we devoured with coconut meat and pawpaws (from Bikarej). We made a little shelter of coconut leaves because of light rain. Half slept until about 7 pm – checking the tide every half hour or so – anxious to get going, but the tide declined slowly. I was not keen to go on in the dark, but Pedro felt we should because otherwise, we may not have time on the morning tide. The torch batteries were a little low so Pedro made two enormous flairs out of dried coconut palms.

The first section was to be the most difficult of all, and I was soon in difficulty when the sandals broke. Pedro lent me his thongs and he went barefooted. I was getting nervous and was stumbling all over the place. The rocks were very uneven – small boulders about a foot high, and many seemed to move – had sharp edges etc. The flares worked very well – they burned bright when pointed towards the wind and slower when pointed away from the wind. There was no moon. We made such poor progress that the flares burnt out when we were less than a third of the way – Pedro had expected that we would make quicker time. I kept on losing my balance and lurching along like a drunk man and gave most of my things to Pedro so that I could use my hands to keep balance – a pathetic sight. About halfway across this 400-yard stretch, there were four-foot holes in the reef and we had to work around them. In one of them, a bit of rock gave way and I lost the wedding ring off my finger – Pedro found it by use of the torch in the very clear waters. He said he would hold it until we got to Todo. We clambered on, and somehow we made it to an easier section past the first island.

We kept going, and it was easier in that I didn't need my hands to balance but I was still continuously at the point of falling. I thought we should stop on an island and wait until light but Pedro pushed me on. He was fantastic – just kept encouraging and not ridiculing my inept clumsiness. He kept on saying hopeful things like, "Just a little further now", or "just to this next island and after that it is easy" etc.

It did get easier, and about 11 pm, we slept on the island just prior to Todo. There were several huts there, and Pedro had hoped for a feed – he had kept on talking about it as we walked (to encourage me) – but no one home – probably at church in Todo.

Used one of the huts for sleeping. All night little sand crabs kept crawling all over the place and got cheeky about climbing over us, so I got into a sleeping bag Peter had lent me.

Walked to Todo across fairly easy rocky reef – all along, I kept hoping that the pilot would hear sense and go to Mwejrik for us.

Had some rice at Tabal's son's house and at another house. Waited about one and a half hours and then saw the plane coming.

Todo is a beautiful island – much neater and better laid out (more compact) than Bikarej. While we were there, Tabal took a canoe out into the lagoon. Very picturesque and beautiful blue skies across the lagoon. We were in good spirits.

The pilot knocked me down by refusing to go the extra distance to Mwejric. I pleaded with him. Told him the difficulties we had been having in making arrangements and that Helen was desperate. He just didn't seem interested – said he didn't have enough fuel which is hard to believe.

So we went into Majuro with him. No one met us at the airport – got a taxi into town.

Found out that the weather had been worse than we had thought, and boats had not been able to go to Mwejrik. And Vincent's boat was out of action with a hole in it. So chartering the plane seemed the only way to get Helen in. The pilot couldn't fly in the afternoon because of the wind so we arranged it for the next morning.

Spent the afternoon buying provisions for Peter and Absolom – also, Francis decided to send out Johnny, Pedro and another boy to Nemo on the plane, so they got some provisions for them too.

Spoke to Alden on the walky-talky to see if he wanted anything for his store.

Went to a movie at night with Pedro because it was his only night in town.

Back to Majuro

Tues 11th (Helen's diary continues)

We were running three-quarters of an hour late for the plane because of difficulties getting fuel and kerosene for Peter. The pilot was angry but took us anyway.

Arrived at Mwejric about 9:30 am. Joseph was excited to see the seaplane with Dad in. Plane taxied to near the house and Peter brought the boat out to it. The boys and provisions made the boat very low in the water. In the air, we circled around and I took photos of the atoll then we were back in Majuro in fifteen minutes.

Francis met the plane and took us back to his house.

We went into Immigration and got our visas extended with no difficulties, much to our relief.

Went shopping and I devoured some fresh fruit and Joseph also went mad on oranges.

Wed 11th

I went for a walk in the morning to get some bread – met up with one of the Baha'is who invited us back for breakfast. There we met up with Vinson and had a good talk. The Baha'is here had done so much to try to get us back. Twice going out in boats and having to turn back as the sea was so rough. They had seen the regional administrator, who said he would grant us an extension on our visa until we returned. If only we had been able to communicate.

A day of relaxation and catching up.

Thurs 12th Jan

Didn't do much, just relaxed – went for a walk on the reef – Joseph saw some of his beloved crabs he hadn't seen for three days. Don read *Zen* and the *Art of Motor Cycle Maintenance* and *One Flow over the Cookoo's Nest* another day).

In the evening, Vinson came around and talked about the possibility of Helen talking at the Teaching Conference on the coming weekend. They had a good discussion about teaching and deepening with Francis, Farateu and Vinson.

Friday 13th

Went shopping and met up with Robert from Laura. The Teaching Conference started in the evening – not as many people as had hoped but a good spirit.

Saturday 14th

Very tired. Slept in. Gave a talk on the Baha'i Calendar. Stayed at the centre all day. Come home and bathed and fed the children. Benjy off to sleep so we went back to the centre. Met up with Junyung from Laura today and gave him a message for Nargit.

Sunday 15th

Very very tired. Gave a talk on the Baha'i fund. Just had to lie down and sleep in the afternoon. Exhausted. Just lay down on the floor of the centre and slept soundly. The atmosphere is always very relaxed and this is not considered rude. Felt too tired to go back in the evening but Don encouraged me. Only there ten minutes when Joseph ran into a bench seat and cut his lip badly. So we all went home. He was very upset for a while but calmed down and slept well.

Monday 16th

Went to the beach near Eastern Gateway Hotel – good but a poor comparison with Mwejrik – especially the pollution and the fact you have to go by taxi.

Joseph's mouth is not too bad. He is quite at peace with himself.

Wrote diary in the evening.

Tuesday 17th

Bought some material and took it to the Marshallese Community Action Group where some ladies do dressmaking. Sent telegram to Mum and went to Long Island to arrange our tickets home. While there found that the plane we wished to leave on went straight to Port Vila, so decided to see if Barbie and Charlie Pierce would like a visit. Had a swim and then took our sleepy children back home.

Long Island

Wed 18th Jan

Went shopping on my own – so easy without the children.

Sent a telegram to Barbie and Charlie and then met up with Vinson, who told us of the National Teaching Committee (NTC) meeting the previous evening and of their decision for us to spend the rest of our time at Long Island. Feast in the evening – about thirty people there. Farateu came – looked very sick. She has been staying in her room all day and seems to be getting worse. The children being sick too hasn't helped matters. I think it is best we were leaving their home as maybe we are a burden to them – even though they insist we aren't.

Thurs 19th Jan

John picked us up early to take us to Long Island to see our house. It is a little pandanus roof hut badly in need of repair, but it should be fun and plenty of sun, clean sand, water and lots of crabs for Joseph. The Baha'is all live very close. We should be able to do something here. Don went shopping in the afternoon to get supplies and later went to a meeting at the ICA.

Friday 20th Jan

Shopping and generally getting ready to go to Long Island most of the day. Things made difficult because of water restrictions in Rita – water on only intermittently so use of toilets and washing etc. a bit awkward – not a problem when using mother nature at Long Island.

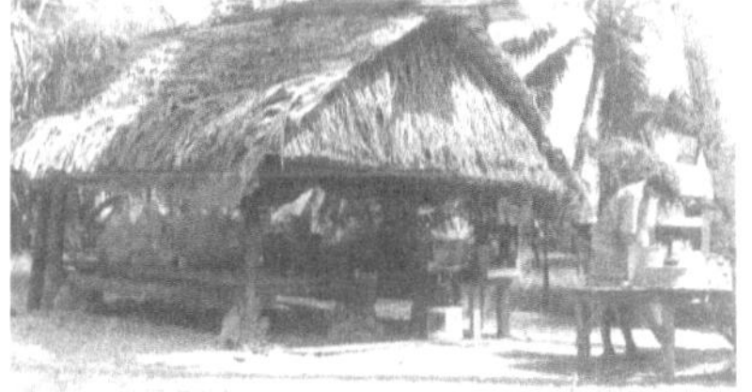

Took taxi to Long Island in late afternoon.

George had repaired the roof.

Don tried out a small primus stove, which was in a cupboard here. The cardboard box it was in to provide wind protection caught fire (not surprisingly) and the stove was destroyed.

I developed breast fever in the afternoon and felt very sore, weak and worried. Couldn't feed Benjy on one side. Feverish all night.

Steven and another Baha'i girl visited and it looks as though good contact can be established.

Couldn't go to meeting in Rita – for Rose – because of my fever.

Saturday 21st

Went into Rita to hospital. Doctor gave me some antibiotics. Benjy hungry because I cannot offer both breasts. Tried him out on bottle but a distressing day – especially with me feeling weak – but fever subsiding. I tried to rest all day but not easy with the demands of both children.

Don bought a new kerosene stove.

Sunday 22nd Jan

Steven came several times in the morning to make arrangements for the meeting of the Baha'is of Long Island. Some Rita Baha'is came out in the afternoon with Rose for the meeting. Rose spoke – all in Marshallese but the meeting sounded positive – people obviously enthralled and asking questions.

Monday 23rd

Easy day. I was trying to rest but things are quite a hassle – even simple things – so not much rest. But feeling very much better – expressing milk to discharge infected milk.

Benjy showing signs of not being well – slightly infected eye, rash on shoulders and upper arms, temperature, slightly runny nose, clinging to me, can't be left.

Tuesday 24th

Benjy still not well. Spent the day nursing him. Steven and his wife and son came around in the morning. We discussed the meeting. Rose is to speak on Thursday evening and decided to hold it in his house. I went over to see Marina and gave her some books she asked for. At lunchtime, all the children coming home from school called in – to see Benjy, who sparked up for a short time, responding to their doting affection for him.

Wed 25th

Benjy still sick. The school children called in again. Don took Joseph with him to Rita and got supplies and medicine from Francis' place for Benjy (I had left it there). Farateu still very sick.

To describe this place a little better: It is a small island joined by a US Army manmade causeway to Rita and Laura. About twenty families live on the island. There are no facilities and people live a native-style of life, although many have jobs in Rita.

There are five long-standing Baha'is here: Tatake and Tilate (Marina), Loktok and Steven, Tiritoa and George – and several new Baha'is who are at present inactive and know very little about the Faith – one being Jalot. An LSA was formed, but three members have moved away from Long Island. They are aiming to gather enough active Baha'is together to have a by-election and re-establish the LSA.

Thurs 26th

Benjy is a bit better – so didn't give him the medicine. Rose was supposed to be coming, but about 6 pm Steven arrived with a letter and news that she was not coming. Most unfortunate – George had knocked off work early to come, and Marina was looking forward to it. However, we decided to prepare more for her coming on Sunday evening and give invitations to all the people in Long Island.

Fri 27th

Met Farateu's mother who has come from Kwajalin (or Ebeye) to look after the household while Farateu is in hospital. Really nice, homely woman.

Don went down to Air Nauru to fix up about our flight to Port Vila.

Benjy much better. I went into Rita to see Rose and arrange for Sunday. She said she would definitely come and wrote out an invitation in Marshallese for me. Wrote out some invitations that night.

Sat 28th

Benjy greatly improved. Finished off the notices and then went to Steven's place. He took me to many houses in Long Island and we invited people to come to the meeting and talked to them about the Faith. Many people showed great interest.

Sun 29th

Steven came and took the rest of the invitations to distribute. Spent most of the morning talking with George. Very interesting fellow – reads a lot and has many books – subscribes to the National Geographic – unusual for people here. Also found out his grandson is Akiki. Peter and Tsuata used to live in the next hut to this one – now broken down – and adopted George's grandson while they were living there.

Went over to Tatake's home in the afternoon and met up with his relatives who were all drinking, one particular being very talkative and friendly. He gathered the others together and they sang Gilbertese songs for us and served us a meal. It was good atmosphere there and we enjoyed the afternoon. We returned to our house to prepare ourselves for the meeting. I cooked up some pancakes for supper. Rose arrived on time with many Baha'is from Rita. Many people came, although most of them were Steven's family. He has thirteen children. It was a good meeting and many non-Baha'is asked questions.

After the meeting, Loktok gave Rose and me a headband and flowers. These people are so thoughtful and generous. Even after the meeting, they went and got water for us from one of the town supply taps as I mentioned we were low in water.

Mon 30th

Washing. Baked bread. I showed Merinda how to bake bread – worked out magnificently – the best we have made – used Kingee wood which is hard and makes good coals.

A fisherman from across the road called in and we were able to offer him some fried rice we were cooking and also some bread – it's good to be able to do something for someone else for a change.

I took some bread over to Merinda's house, and they gave her a plate of breadfruit (cooked with onion and coconut milk) – delicious. We were sitting on the beach eating the breadfruit when some fishermen (including the one we had met earlier) caught some very small fish with a throw net – a fascinating sight. They gave us some small ones. We didn't eat them because we feared pollution from the lagoon water.

Later, Steven's wife brought us more water.

I spent part of the afternoon with Merinda and, while she was there, about six young people called in and became curious about the Baha'i Faith. I took the opportunity. Very good.

Tues 31st

Lazy day. Saw Miranda in the afternoon and talked a bit about Baha'i. Don took Joseph into Rita and did some shopping and caught up with people. Water restrictions are bad there – only water for a couple of hours each day – people are queuing for water. Sanitation must be bad. We are very lucky to be out at

Long Island. People are even coming from Rita to wash and collect water from the well over the road from us. Don stopped a taxi to go to Rita and what a surprise – in the back was Tabal from Bikarej. Don and he had a good chat via the taxi driver.

Wed 1st

Washing, baked bread – worked out very well.

Merinda came over in the afternoon and just chatted. She translated part of a booklet on camp life.

Both children are very happy. Joseph could do with a playmate – but nonetheless seems to occupy himself quite well looking for crabs etc. Benjy is getting more active – wanting to be in everything. These times have marked quite a turning point in Joseph's behavior. After having no speech when we arrived, he had started talking in Marshallese while playing with Akiki and now starting to talk in English, and for the first time showed affection towards us. This had not happened after a very traumatic birth that separated me from him for some time. Emotionally he became like a baby with Ben, wanting cuddles and affection, catching up on what he had missed. What a blessing! This gave me considerable insight into autism and associated disorders. When we arrived here, Joseph was certainly on the edge, with difficulty in communicating and no speech.

Took some good photographs of the children near the well.

Thurs 2nd Feb

George was sick this morning but went to work later. Visited Steven in the afternoon because a girl I had met earlier and lives down the road was washing at the well and offered to drive us down. She is Gilbertese and her husband is at present working at Enewetek. They have built a really wee house with a pandanus roof (but using a dressed timber structure) and walls from wooden packing cases layered like louvres then filled with some sort of filler, and a concrete floor. A really neat-looking cottage. Jalot, a new Baha'i, stays with her as her husband is in Arno. It was good to be with Steven's family again – generally a good happy atmosphere. They were cooking breadfruit. They have a very primitive small house for so many children – thirteen, and some of them are married with young children.

Steven was really apologetic again about neglecting us and wished he'd had time to build a little hut near his house for us to stay in so we would always have company. He looked tired and had been to some other islands in this atoll, taking votes for the recent election for a magistrate from Laura and DUD. He drove us home, giving us one of their precious breadfruits for tea. He was then almost deciding not to go to Kwajelien tomorrow as planned as he wished to stay here until we left. However, we told him to go if it was best for him – he was going there to help finalise a lease of some land for a Baha'i property there.

George home early and not well. People in and out for the buckets of water from the well. The water situation is still not good.

Friday 3rd

It began raining last night and our water problems are over – we have stacks of nice clean rainwater – but we boil it to be absolutely certain.

Fred called in in the middle of the night on his way from the airport – arrived back from Kwadjalein after his NSA meeting. He had a letter for George from his son on Kwadj.

In the morning, Francis and Fred came out with John Thurston – pioneer from Gilberts – on their way to the airport to meet Judge Richard Benson. John knows Gus Morrison, and so I gave him a quick letter to take with him when he goes. John has been in Gilberts for six years – is American. Is building a big catamaran (trimaran) to do freight runs in the Gilberts.

On the way back, they stopped in with Judge Benson. He is very soft-spoken – warmly expressed pleasure at meeting us and interested in what we had been doing.

They also bought out a letter from Mum Gordon.

After they left, Steven arrived and said he was not going to Kwadj after all – he wanted to stay here until we left.

After him, to complete the procession of visitors, John Milne called in to see how we're getting on.

George was sick this morning – maybe food poisoning, but he managed to go off to work as usual – not expecting to actually do work, but to spend time of day with the people he works for.

In the evening, I went into a meeting in Rita with Merina. Women in Steven's family also went, but they were very late. Rose has been conducting these meetings every day. About forty women there – good spirit, speaking Marshallese. Afterwards, they practiced dances for a future event. I also spent time talking to Judge Benson afterwards.

Saturday 4th Feb

Merina called around in the afternoon and just chattered. She and I are becoming good friends. She translated some of Betra's booklets.

In the evening, I went in with many young people from Tatake's and Steven's houses – to a social evening of Baha'is in Rita – to honour ourselves, Judge Benson, Rose and John Thurston. Fabulous traditional dances and songs – a magnificent spirit. I sang *Little Lake of Troubled Water* as my item. Unfortunately, Don didn't know the evening was for us, and he stayed home to protect the house from stealers.

I arrived back exhausted but thrilled.

Sunday 5th Feb

George has now recovered from his sickness – he spends most of his time with his employer's family.

Baked bread and washed.

Waited for Rita's teaching team to come, but evidently, they were not planning on coming – some mix-up.

In the late afternoon we went around to Steven's house. He said they had been thinking of asking us to 'sponsor' little Rosina (his oldest daughter's child) for education in Australia from five years old. We said we would be happy for her to stay with us but not until she was twelve years old and that he should also think of alternative places for her to do her schooling – perhaps closer to home (in culture and distance) and with her friends. There would probably be difficulties with Immigrations. But we could correspond about this as time goes on.

Steven took us for a drive along the Laura road – we saw the houses etc. with new eyes. We had not seen it since the experiences of the past two months, and we now understand more of what we see.

Gave Steven's family the loaf of bread.

Tea of fried rice and banana fritters. Bed.

Monday 6th Feb

Went into town in the morning. Saw Francis at his shop. He said Richard Benson would be coming out to see us in the afternoon. This cut short our shopping trip, but we got handicrafts as gifts for relatives.

Richard Benson stayed about one and a half hours – a soft-spoken man and good listener.

A wonderful feast that night – with Steven and his family, George and Jalot. Tatake, Tibit, and Marina were coming, but Marina's baby arrived that night.

Tuesday 7th Feb

Judge Benson came again and sat and talked for about a couple of hours. Found out Marina had a boy. We spent until 2 am talking to George and packing.

Wednesday 8th Feb

Had just got ourselves organized when Betra arrived to say everyone was meeting at the airport at 10:15am. This was much earlier than we expected. However, managed to just make it into Rita to visit Marina and her baby. She was so pleased to see me and asked me to give the baby a name. After consulting Don, we chose 'Kimberley'.

Then a mad rush back to Long Island. Everyone was waiting there, so we got all our things on the truck and 'goodbye Majuro'. Fred had a letter from Jackie for us – wonderful to get news from her but sad to hear of her misadventures. So many people were at the airport to see us off. Benjy was whisked away and passed from one admirer to another. Judge Benson was also leaving at the same time. I will never forget Fred holding Ben in his arms and saying "But, Ben, you can't leave yet – the goals are not won." And certainly Ben was our passport to everyone's hearts there. And also Joseph – Fred teased him again about his coat of many colours. *[Later note: And it is interesting that, years later, Ben spent ten years in the Pacific – the Solomons Islands, married to an islander, on the NSA, and living in a remote village just like we did then.]*

To Vanuatu

It was not easy to hop on the plane, but we were so soon in Nauru that Majuro almost seemed like dream.

Nauru was a good catching up time - washing and cleaning

After all this time with no mishaps in the Marshalls, Joseph nearly electrocuted himself in the motel room – on a lamp that had no globe in it.

Rang the NPC hospital, but Bwebwe had gone back to the Gilbert Islands.

Thurs 9th Feb

Up early (4.30 am) to catch the plane. Left some of our hand baggage in the airport lounge and discovered this as the hostesses were going through their safety routine – they very kindly opened the door and let us get the bag.

Two hours' flight to Port Vila.

Barbie and Charlie met us – had sent a telegram which we hadn't received. They are very busy – but had arranged for us to stay with them. Charlie has been working very hard as NSA secretary. Barbie is doing kindergarten teaching.

Friday 10th Feb

Went into town in the morning to fix up our on-going reservations. We were struck with the Frenchness of the place. This condominium idea is crazy.

Didn't do much – just caught up with washing etc.

The man who fixed up our tickets was a Baha'i! – found out when we had to give an address for contact. Some of Barbie and Charlie's friends came for tea, including an anthropologist, Kirk, who is in charge of the museum here. He brought many slides of his journey into the bush of Malockeula Island – very primitive tribes. Very entertaining fellow – just bubbling with enthusiasm for his anthropological work.

Saturday 11th Feb

Charlie and Barbie shouted us to a lovely lunch down by Lake Lagoon. However, had badly overeaten the night before so couldn't eat much. That night we spoke at the Baha'i Centre – Don on aborigines and myself on the Marshall Islands. A really good night – everyone showed great interest.

Sunday 12th Feb

Went to an ocean beach at a place called Dry Creek. Very relaxing. Charlie is very overworked, and very tense. His job in the statistics department doesn't really suit his temperament and then he does all the NSA secretarial work.

Monday 13th Feb

Took a trip on a glass bottom boat – a real tourist gimmick but still interesting.

Tuesday 14th Feb

Went to Olive's fireside – she is a very delightful person. She is the dentist and her husband is at present in England studying to be the first NH magistrate. Just arrived home when Benjy started crying and crying. Walked up and down with him all night. The hospital just gave him sleeping medicine which seemed to have no effect.

Wednesday 15th

Took Benjy to a private doctor in town. He had an ear infection, so he gave him an antibiotic for it. He was much better by the evening and slept well. Went to visit a spastic boy – he is seven years old, can't talk, toilet himself or walk but is very lovable and has a pleasant disposition. I gave them some ideas to help him develop a bit. The family were infinitely patient in their care of him.

Thursday 16th Feb

Spent the afternoon with Mildred and Enid teaching them handicrafts. Met up with Meg and Bryn Deamer – they came for tea. They had spent considerable time on Malakeula Island. They had a Baha'i Summer School there.

Friday 17th Feb

Spent the day at the Baha'i Centre with Meg and Bryn

Saturday 18th and Sunday 19th Feb

Off to Brisbane

A long tiring journey. Then up to Noosville to spend Sunday with Jackie, who has been staying with Gertie and Gerhard Schmelts – Lot 15 Duke Road. Enjoyed a whole day of fresh fruits, nuts and veges. Gertie is a natural healer and has some very interesting ideas.

Monday 19th Feb

To Darwin. Spent the afternoon with Penny and Bill. Then to Kununurra and home in the evening.

Ya Baha'u'l-Abha!

..ooOOoo..

7

Narrogin

19 years from 1979 to 1998

The children growing up

Written by Don

Summary

At the end of 1979, after the birth of Ruth in Kununurra, Helen and Don decided to move closer to grandparents and to settle in a town for the children's schooling. They decided on Narrogin because this was close to Perth, but not too close. Don was transferred in his work with DCW.

Helen became involved in many community activities. She ran a silk-screen business from home and taught calligraphy. As the children grew older and were at school, she took on several part-time jobs.

House

Initially, they rented a house in Clark Street – this was provided by Don's employer. In 1980, they purchased the cheapest land in Narrogin – a 1½ acre block near the creek. They designed their own passive solar house and engaged a builder. However, the builder pulled out and this idea was discontinued. This was fortunate because it could have ended up very expensive, and the passive solar processes might not have worked. Instead, in 1982, they arranged for a timber-framed house to be transported from Attadale. The house was cut in half and came to the block on two large low-loaders, which required a police escort. The two halves were repositioned together and mounted on stumps.

Don and Helen spent some years renovating the house and developing the property.

In the first year, there were very heavy rains, and stormwater from the road flowed onto the block. Also, surface water seeped from the hill behind the house and pooled around the stumps under the house. To drain the water away, Don arranged for a backhoe to dig a channel from the house, across the paddock, down to the creek. However, the paddock was so waterlogged that the sides of the channel kept on caving in, so the operator had to dig the hole wider and wider. When he started to dig close to the house, there was panic when one the stumps fell in. The backhoe itself got bogged and had to be towed out by a long chain. The problem was solved after the town council brought fourteen truckloads of fill to build up the verge to divert stormwater. And, to control the seepage from the hill, Don dug a deep drain around the house, with a pipe taking water to the creek.

Over the years, the family made good use of a large vegetable patch, chook yard, small orchard, paddock and creek. They had a series of five horses – also goats, turkeys, ducks, and guinea pigs. They planted many bushes and trees and took great pleasure in the rural setting.

They had intriguing experiences with animals. A kookaburra believed that his reflection in the windows was a rival invading his territory. He positioned himself on the washing line and repeatedly dived at the windows with tremendous force every few minutes. He would do this for hours, and it went on for at least four months. He actually broke two windows! Staff at the insurance company must have wondered about the truth of the claims – but they paid up. Then there was the mystery of the nanny goat who got pregnant twice even though the family did not have a billy goat. Somehow, a stray billy must have made some secret visits. Another mystery arose many years later when Don and Helen were renting out the house while they were in Blackstone. Tenants (a doctor and his family) believed the house was haunted because of strange sounds they were hearing at night. They actually ceased their tenancy because of this. It was some time later that it was discovered that some noisy possums had taken up residence in the ceiling.

Don's work

Soon after they moved to Narrogin, a major controversy came to a head back in the Kimberleys. Aboriginal people opposed access to mineral exploration on the Noonkanbah Station. Land rights and sacred sites became hotly debated across the nation. Helen's father, Bill Mitchell, was a key figure in supporting the mining company.

Don's work with DCW was mainly, but not exclusively, with aboriginal people. This included juvenile offending, domestic violence, child protection, fostering, and financial assistance. He initiated a budgeting service in Narrogin, and financial services in Albany and Collie. He conducted parenting courses and a Helping Services Expo. He facilitated community organisations working together by convening regular meetings, and he issued newsletters. He linked rural social workers in Australia with a newsletter. He helped set up a counselling service for farming families, based in Hyden. He compiled major proposals for Gnowangerup, Wandering, district planning, a service with stolen generations, and the relative standing different field officers.

In 1984, Don trained as a primary school teacher with Murdoch University (externally), but he decided that a teaching career was not for him. He continued with DCW, but later, from 1992, he worked as an aboriginal organisation trainer with TAFE for two years, then with Community Mental Health and Disability Services, where he set up Inroads family support service.

Community involvement

Over the years, Helen was involved in numerous local organizations, particularly in arts, theatre and music. Some of this was through her various employments but mostly was voluntarily to encourage the children's interests and activities — pony club, recorder group, schooling, scouts, theatre sets and dancing. She was member of Yoga and Tai Chi groups.

Arts & crafts

Helen made posters, community banners, and the Scout calendar. She organised community festivals and art exhibitions. She was employed by TAFE to teach crafts with aboriginal people. She conducted a wide range of activities with elderly people in the hospital and aged care. She developed a weaving loom that could be operated by people with one arm. She also developed effective papier-mache leg splints.

Music was a big part of Helen's life in Narrogin where she was in a recorder group with Ruth and she learnt to play the flute for the performance of *The Sorcerer*.

For many years Helen and Don did Scottish country dancing with Hazel McMaster.

In 2022, after her death, the *Helen Gordon Retrospective*

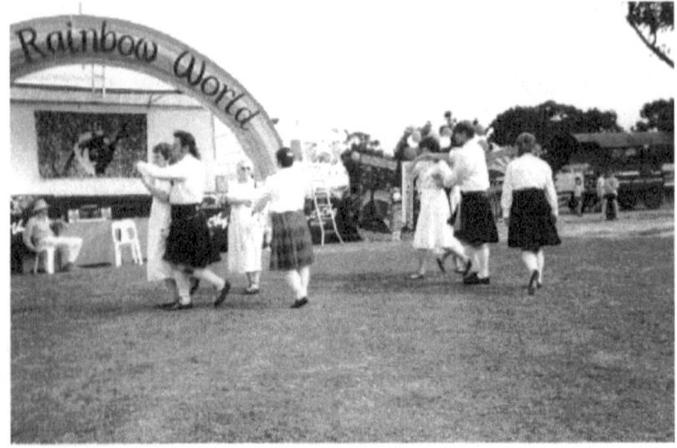

exhibition was held in Narrogin – a display of her impressive range of arts and crafts throughout her life.

Baha'i activities

For most of the time, Helen was the only Baha'i in Narrogin. She kept a diary[6] of Baha'i activities while she was there. Highlights included the displays at the agricultural shows. There were many visits from Perth Baha'is, including for a community soccer game and, in 1994, Rainbow World Spring Festival. In 1991, Mrs Moshirian visited many towns in the southwest and spent a week in Narrogin[7]. Also, in 1991, the SW Regional Women's Conference was held in Narrogin. In 1992 Helen placed a message in a 25-year time capsule[8] which is placed at the slit rock in Gnarojin Park. She was a speaker at the Sai Baba Conference in 1995. In 1996, there was an *Everyone Contributes* camp.

Helen entered 'Baha'i Thoughts' in *The Narrogin Observer* for sixteen years and she edited *The Bush Eagle* newsletter for isolated believers.

---

[6] The diary of Helen's time in Narrogin is lodged with the NSA archives. Don also has a copy.

[7] Mrs Moshirian in pages 67-69 in the diary.

[8] Time capsule: Don has copy of Helen's message.

Helen's employment

Helen had her own silk-screen business.

Commencing in 1985, for a decade, Helen was with TAFE, teaching silk-screening to aboriginal. She ran calligraphy classes at TAFE and also privately.

In 1988, she worked part-time managing an art and craft shop.

For two years from 1991, she worked part-time organizing activity groups, including craft, music, social events, at the Narrogin Hospital and later at the Karinya Cottage Homes.

For four years, from 1993, she worked as a Laboratory Technician at the Science Department at Narrogin Senior High School.

The children

Joe, from a young child, was enthusiastic about Lego, Mechano and electronics – and then robotics. He was a Scout and was keen on go-karts. He had difficulty with reading – dyslexia, which was assisted with the Distar reading program and coloured glasses. When he was eleven years old, Joe had a severe immune response that developed from a simple throat infection, then chilblains on his legs, and then kidney failure. This led to neurological complications, and he couldn't walk for a few months.

Ben had an early interest in *Masters of the Universe*. Later he developed skills in wood turning and ballet. He enjoyed scuba diving, horse riding and Scouts. When he was ten years old, he stayed with his grandparents in Brisbane for a few months. When he was sixteen, he went on the *The Leewin* sailing vessel for a week.

Ruth played the recorder and was dancing for many years and

she entered the Regional Eisteddfods. She loved ponies and had a series of four ponies. She produced stage-set designs for the local productions of *The Sorcerer*, *Grease*, *Nun-sense*, and *Showboat*.

Friendships & holidays

Close friendships developed with other families with children of similar ages – in Perth and southwest – Bunbury, Collie and Albany. There were numerous weekend trips away and many people came to visit Narrogin. Summer Schools in Perth were an annual highlight. Don took the boys on long bike excursions to Williams, Collie and Bunbury. In 1988, they had camper-vanned over east with an extended stay at St Leonards near Geelong and then up to Brisbane with all spots in between.

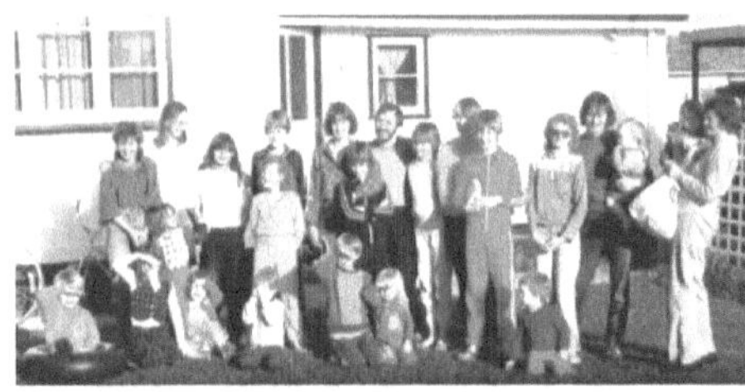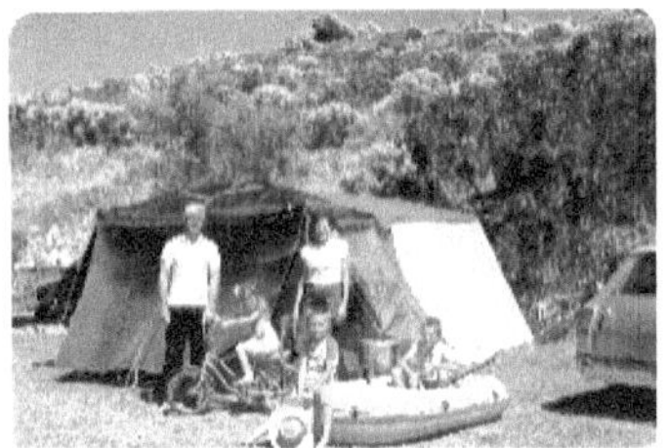

Leaving

By the end of 1998, the children had completed all their schooling in Narrogin, and they left home to further their studies in Perth. They each did much better in the tertiary education than they did in their school years. With the children no longer at home, Helen and Don decided to go to Blackstone.

..ooOOoo..

8

Living in another world

Blackstone – 1989 to 2001

Women in a remote aboriginal community

Written by Don

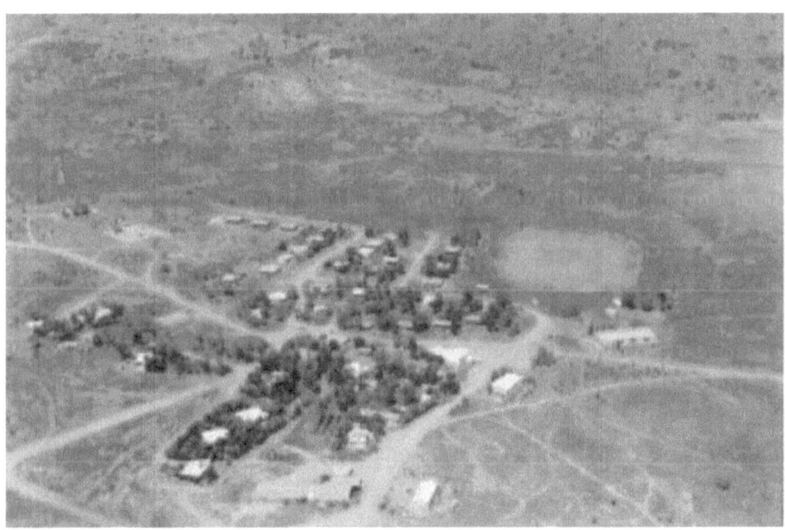

By 1998, the youngest child, Ruth, had flown the nest and was now in Perth, with her two older brothers, Joe and Ben, studying. Don had always worked with indigenous people as a social worker, community development and other roles, and now he was keen to go to the outback again.

Helen and Don jointly applied for jobs in the remote

community of Blackstone. They flew there for the 'interview' for a few days. Helen immediately got together with the women making bush baskets – this connection might have been a significant reason for the community deciding to employ them.

Don was the Community Development Advisor (CDA) which meant he was, in effect, managing the community. Helen was office manager and Women's Centre coordinator.

Background

The next chapter (Chapter 9) has Helen's detailed account of her time in this community. She also related some Blackstone stories when describing her experiences as a Baha'i (Chapter 25). Another chapter (Chapter 10) explains her development of crafts there. And there are instructions on how to make these (Chapter 30). But firstly, it is useful to lay out the context for all this.

Blackstone is in the semi-desert near where the three states meet (WA, NT and SA) - just 75 kilometres inside the border of Western Australia. It is 1700 kilometres northeast of Perth and it takes a few days to get there – half of this journey is on gravel.

It is also known as Papulankutja, and is one of about eight communities in the Ngaanyatjarra Lands.

The community started just two decades before Helen and Don arrived there. Everything had already been set up in terms of physical infrastructure, support services and staffing. There were, of course, many issues yet to face, but at least the basics were in place. The Gordons had plenty to work with.

There were about 180 traditionally orientated full-blood Ngaanyatjarra-speaking people. Most had moved there from the Warburton Mission back to their homelands some twenty years previously as the government started to provide services in these places. In contrast to most of Australia, the Ngaanyatjarra people had never been dispossessed of their lands. No other people had ever settled there. So traditional cultural practices were still strong.

In 1998, Centrelink presence was minimal. The main income was the CDEP work-for-the-dole scheme. There was no income generated from anything the community was producing.

There was still no internet or TV – even radio reception was limited. Communication was by phone and fax.

Fortunately, people were generally law-abiding – the nearest police were in Laverton, 750 kilometres away[9]. It was a 'dry' community. There was no tolerance for drugs; alcohol was banned, and this was supported by the majority of the community. Avgas was used – there was no petrol, so there would be no means of petrol sniffing – a severe problem in the neighbouring Pitjantjatjarra lands.

There had only been two CDAs prior to the Gordons. The main one was Murray Wells, who had grown up in the Lands as the child of missionaries. His father was a truck driver bringing supplies out to this area. He trained as a teacher and was the first school teacher at Blackstone, staying for about six years. He then became the first Blackstone CDA for about eleven years. Jim Hair followed for a number of years, prior to handing over to Don.

Even though the community was fairly 'new', in this short time, it had become well-endowed with infrastructure for those times. It had an office, community store, community school, community clinic, women's centre, mechanical workshop, CDEP workshop, community hall, a 25-metre indoor swimming pool, a grassed oval with lights, and a basketball court. There was a sizable orchard. There was an airstrip for light planes, which came twice a week. Flares had to be set out if the flying

---

9   Subsequently, a police station has been located within Blackstone.)

doctor plane came in at night. There were well-developed systems for electricity, water and sewerage. The roads within the community were just gravel, but they were all bituminized while the Gordons were there.

There were adequate concrete brick houses for staff, and there was accommodation for visiting staff. The housing for community members was variable. It had been started with unlined tin houses, but there had been substantial progress with replacing them with cement block houses like the staff had. Also, good wire fences were erected around each house and planting of trees was encouraged.

The community-owned the Tjukayirla Roadhouse halfway between Laverton and Warburton. When the Gordons took over the management of the community, Jim and June Hair took over the management of the roadhouse.

Stores came in by truck from Perth through NATS – weekly, with dry goods one week and fresh produce the next.

Staff consisted of the CDA, office manager/women's centre coordinator, CDEP coordinator, store manager and assistant, mechanic, two clinic sisters and four teachers.

There was a Community Council with a chairman. Most of the council members were illiterate and had had no experience with such responsibilities. In theory, the council owned and managed everything (except the school and clinic) and appointed staff (including the CDA) and controlled all of the finances of the store, roadhouse and community ($1m in the bank). However, in practice, the CDA administered all this.

Although Don's job title as Community Development Advisor indicated that he was just to advise the council about the development of the community, the role went far more than just giving advice. There were continual tensions between the CDA and the council over resources – particularly over the community vehicles.

Apart from the CDA, the major player in the operations of Blackstone was the Ngaanyatjarra Services, which covered all the Ngaanyatjarra communities. The NG Services was based in Alice Springs. They arranged the stores transport, maintenance of the electrical, water, and sewerage systems, and substantial building programs. There were many other services they provided in support of the communities. For the first years of the Gordon's time there, the NG Services even operated an air service from Alice Springs to Perth via most of the communities.

Blackstone was the only one of the NG communities to manage its own finances. This had its advantages and disadvantages and, eventually, towards the end of the Gordon's time, the books were taken over by the NG Services.

Helen's work

Helen started training some of the few literate women to work in the office. Don and Helen rearranged all the office procedures, breaking each complex task into do-able steps, in such a way that the community members, with few preliminary skills, could undertake vital tasks. Office staff, like more than 100 community members, were on a work-for-the-dole scheme. People would show up at work at their choice, and their work hours would be marked accordingly. People who did not work in the office, or any other work programs around the community, did not get paid above a basic minimum. There were a few regular workers in the office, and Helen insisted that the office could not be open unless there was at least one office worker present. On days when no one showed up to work, the door would remain closed. Community members would call out for the office to open because they wanted to use the 'book-up' system, and Helen would say that they must find someone, anyone, to come and work in the office – so that the doors could be opened.

Don and Helen had such confidence in the procedures they had devised that they could get anyone with absolute minimal literacy and no office experience to be functional within minutes. Over time, Helen trained more than ten women to work in the office, but some would be away from the community, and there could be no more than three at any one time. It was a success, but outside of Blackstone, white staff from other communities and the Ngaanyatjarra Council did not believe it could happen.

Helen's main focus was coordinating the setting up of the Women's Centre with a play group, HACC meals and arts and crafts, including painting, bush baskets, wood carving (puna), jewellery (with bush nuts), silk-screening, tie-dying, sewing etc. They had their own art and crafts shop, and the people had to buy their own materials. They could sell the items they made (but could not claim CDEP hours of their time).

The output of the people was enormous and their creativity unlimited. As well as all the crafts, they sold about 600 paintings with five exhibitions in Perth.

The highlight was the setting up of two small industries[10] – something the people were not familiar with. They made large wooden jigsaws with indigenous paintings, and they made paper out of spinifex grass[11]. For these activities, they were paid on the CDEP work-for-the-dole employment program and the money from sales kept the Women's Centre going.

Helen became very close to many of the women, and she said that when she left some three years later, it was like the end of a love affair. The connections made over that time have dragged her back many times since then. She returned to Blackstone five

---

[10] Helen's explanation of how she developed the jigsaws and spinifex paper industries – see Chapter 10

[11] Instructions for how to make spinifex paper – see Chapter 30

times. Sometimes for short visits and a few times for several months. She went with Don when he had relieving work, and she went by herself a couple of times.

At the request of the community, she returned to re-establish the spinifex paper-making industry which she had started while working there earlier. This grew into a proper industry as they won a tourism award, and have a purpose-built centre and a full-time coordinator.

Blackstone Collection

Helen wanted to preserve examples of the arts and crafts that were produced while she was at Blackstone. She had assembled items and left them for safe-keeping in the community before she left. However, on subsequent visits to Blackstone, she saw that the original collection was scattered. Helen expressed concern about this, and she wanted to assemble another collection with items she had purchased herself. Thus, in April 2021, a second 'Blackstone Collection' was packaged together. This collection includes documents and photos with the artifacts. It was sent to Thisbe Puric of NPY Women's Council in Darwin – for her to display and/or store as she sees appropriate.

Friends and family

Joe was at Blackstone for several months and worked on the computer program for the office, and he managed the swimming pool.

Ben was there for a considerable time supervising the CDEP workers in maintenance around the community. Ben and his friend Medhi had come up from Perth on their motorbikes. Mehdi worked at the community store. When they left, they rode their motorbikes to Alice Springs. And later, Ben managed the

Patjar community before going to Haifa.

Ruth married Colin in Perth in 2000. They came out to Blackstone soon after. Ruth worked with the playgroup and Colin managed the swimming pool.

Other friends came there to work for short periods – Kurt Branso to work in the store, Mahshid Ferdowsian taught sewing and hair-dressing in the Women's Centre, and Maryam Bell helped the children write a storybook.

Don's work

The community finances were not well organized and there had never been an audit attempted. There weren't coherent records that could be checked. Don arranged for the books to be audited for the first time – it took a few years for him to get the accounts to this point because he had to set up a computer system to track many types of transactions. He also arranged for business plans for the roadhouse, store and Women's Centre.

Don's reflections

We were at Blackstone at a unique time. We arrived after the first two decades when the main infrastructure was set in place. Then, during our three years there, we demonstrated how capable people are if they have the appropriate support. Now, two decades later, life seems to be difficult – people are stuck with the disincentives of Centrelink and the pervasiveness of drugs. At present, the community does not seem to be going anywhere. This is an oversimplification, but it appears that the kind of successes experienced in the time we were there, at the turn of the century, could not be easily repeated in the current circumstances.

This might sound like an over-rosy picture of our contribution. Of course, we could have done things differently, but this is not the place to dwell on negatives. The important thing, is that we seen human capacity and resilience. This was the strength of particular women Helen was privileged to work with at that moment in time.

..ooOOoo..

9

My time in Blackstone

Running an office and women's centre in a remote aboriginal community for 3 years from 1998 to 2001

Written by Helen

In this write-up, I start by setting with an overview of our time in Blackstone. This is followed by two diary-type accounts that give a sense of what it was like day-to-day – our first ten weeks[12], then highlights over the next few years[13].

After Narrogin, our children went up to Perth for university and whatever. We decided that we would do either Australian Volunteers Abroad or something like that – just for a couple of years. But we realized that it was a bit silly. We grew concerned about going to another country as we had previously been travel-teaching in the Marshall Islands with very young children. We saw some groups, like AVA, that were really not very effective. In the three months we were there, we realized we were limited in what we could do because, even though it was claimed that English was the second language, it really wasn't. It was just that some people could understand a bit of English. They talked in

---

12 Our first ten weeks – starts at page 135.

13 Glimpses of our life at Blackstone – three years – starts at page 144

Marshallese. You really need to be fluent in the language of the people. (As it worked out, we ended up in an aboriginal community where English was not their first language.) So, we started going away from that idea. Don saw some jobs for remote places in Western Australia. We felt, in that way, if something came up with our children, I'm not depending on my mum and dad to sort it out – we can just go back because we're not too far away.

So we went out at Blackstone. It was a tiny aboriginal community way out in the desert area near where the NT, SA and NT borders meet – in the Ngaanyatjarra Lands.

We were both employed. Don was the Community Development (DCA). I was managing the office and coordinator for the Women's Centre.

Looking back, I see we were there at a unique moment in time. We arrived just two decades after the community was started. Everything had already been set up in terms of physical infrastructure, support services and staffing.

Over the three years we were working there, the development of the community continued to expand its activities and work programmes. While we provided the continuous thread for this development, it was supported enormously by numerous people bringing in short-term projects and providing expertise in different areas. Our main focus, apart from keeping the community well managed, was to provide meaningful and productive activities and work programmes for community members. This included involving them in training to be effective in the skills required to manage and maintain their own community.

One of the highlights was training community members to work in the office. Over this time, ten women passed Level 1 of Office Management. We trained them and then had a lady come in from the TAFE to test them. We always had three of these ladies working in the office. They were paid for the hours they worked. If they could only work a short time, we didn't ask questions but just asked them to find one of the other girls to come in. All of them could do the basics, sorting mail, filing, cleaning, faxing forms, operating the bank/book-up system on the computer. This was complex, but Don developed a computer system they could operate. There were two women who were exceptional – Loretta Grey and Maria Munro, and they were always there unless they were out of the community. Loretta could process the pays, do the tax forms and many other sophisticated office procedures. Maria started with running the small art and craft supply shop in a small store-room within the office. She learnt to use the till and progressed to other office tasks.

Towards the end of our time at Blackstone, we had a bit of a crisis, initiated by some strange behaviour from a man who had been a petrol sniffer. Most of the white staff, including teachers, clinic nurses, and store people, left the community, supposedly for their safety. I had to run the store and the clinic, and Don had to attend to CDEP and other issues, so I asked Maria and Loretta to run the office, and for two weeks, they were on their own, doing everything. They were exceptional. In every area of work in the community, those who had done training came in to help and proved that they were very capable of doing so much. After we left, these girls continued to work in the office.

We tried to foster community involvement in decision-making. This was done through large community meetings. At one stage, we asked them to appoint some members to form a council so it would be easier to consult. Proper elections were held, and a council was formed, but it didn't last. They preferred the big community meetings. By the time we left, we had been involved in 100 meetings. Don would, along with the chairman, make up the agenda and put it on a board and then the chairman would run the meeting.

There were always offers for training to work in the store, the mechanical workshop and essential services. The school and the clinic had their own programmes of training to provide assistants.

My main focus was the development of the Women's Centre. This absorbed much of my time even more so once the girls in the office became more competent. We had two major upgrades to the building, mainly to provide an excellent facility for the playgroup and later to provide a good kitchen and dining room, shower/toilet area for the introduction of HACC. We also added covered veranda areas.

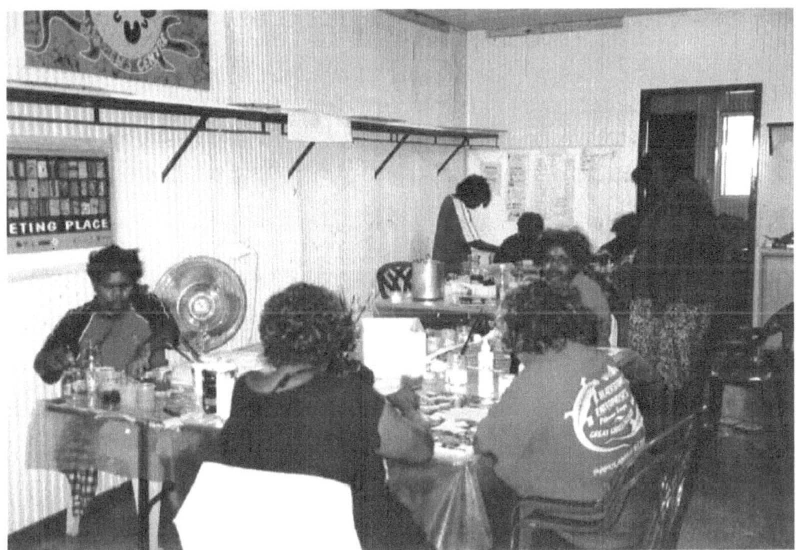

The playgroup was already running when we came there but with very limited facilities. A local lady, Beryl Jennings, had really grasped the concept of playgroups through a teacher's wife who, for a couple of years, ran this, providing local woman were there to learn. Beryl was assisted by Paula Lyons. They both continued to run this for the whole time we were there. Beryl asked Irruntju Media to make a video of how this playgroup worked. Beryl showed it at a Playgroup Convention in Alice Springs and managed to get a grant from the Commonwealth to put up a veranda and fence and other improvements for the Centre. She later became a coordinator for playgroups throughout the Lands.

Home and Community Care (HACC) was just beginning while we were there. In Blackstone, it was run by community members who would cook a meal each day for the elderly. They would walk into the centre and eat their meal there.

A second-hand shop was created in a small room in the Women's Centre. We ordered in bales of second-hand Manchester and clothing through NATS. This was greatly appreciated and some of the young girls learnt how to run it.

The art and craft shop was moved from the office to the Women's Centre.

The other activities at the Women's Centre were connected with a wide variety of arts and crafts.

I put aside some of the paintings and crafts that were exceptional, particularly those done by the older members, into storage called the Blackstone Collection[14]. The paintings were hung in the store, and the crafts were in boxes. As far as I know, some paintings are still there, but the crafts have gone elsewhere.

When we went away for holidays, a community member, Narelle Holland, would quite capably manage the Women's Centre, although she was always glad when I came back.

Up until this time, the community had grown without an overall plan. Through NG Council, a person was appointed to make a town plan. This involved a lot of discussions and finally a street plan was made, and housing plots were demarcated; public buildings were marked in.

---

[14] Helen later found that the 'Blackstone collection' had been scattered, so in 2020, she gathered together items that she had purchased herself and sent it all the Thisbe Puric in Darwin to preserve and/or display as she saw fit.

During our time in Blackstone, there was a continuous flow of people coming into the community for such a wide variety of reasons – anthropologists writing the history of the old people, scientists studying the desert environment, mining companies looking for minerals. The Minister for Education came to visit, and the ladies were pleased that he bought one of their jigsaws. The head of Mental Health Services drove in with a few others and asked where the Blackstone Hotel was. I showed them to the humble visitors' quarters and told them they had half an hour to get some food from the store and they would have to cook for themselves. This is an example of the types of people that would breeze in and out.

Many artists came organising different projects like Thisbe Puric and Nalda Searles with the Tjanpi Desert Weavers. There were also the Punu people who came with their truck, buying up the carved wooden artefacts. There were people from the churches running meetings. Sports events attracted many visitors from a wide area.

One time we were down to one operational phone, which was in the office. After finally complaining to an MP, Telstra arrived in a helicopter to fix up the public phones. This caused great excitement when it landed in front of the office.

Towards the end of 1999, a couple walked into the community with their camels on their way trekking from the furthermost west point in Australia to the furthermost eastern point – Byron Bay – to be there by the first day of the year 2000.

There were regular visits from the police based in Laverton and visiting specialists for the clinic, as well as the occasional flying doctor coming in when there was an emergency. Visitors came in through NG Air or by road.

Throughout all these activities and comings and goings of visitors and staff, there was the ongoing dramas and happenings of community life. Some of these events were joyous, others filled with sadness. We were there for births and funerals, many special events. The people were such strong individuals and yet so intimately connected.

Their deteriorating health was of considerable concern, diabetes and kidney disease being prevalent.

What it has meant to me

I don't think anything could have prepared us for this experience. We had to rethink almost everything we had learnt. Their culture was so strong and so different to everything we were used to. It was a major life-changing time for us.

We did not try to get involved in their cultural activities except when they asked us or invited us to be part of something or be of assistance. I tried to learn their language and understand something of what the women were saying. I came to respect and be in awe of just how far they had come to understand us – many learning to speak and write English – not easy.

One thing I came to love was their ability to live in the present. Conflicts could be intense but then totally forgotten. Every day started new. Life was about what people meant to each other and external appearances were not important. I also found we had much more in common as human beings living together than what our vastly different cultures might have caused us to differ.

This is by no means a complete account of events in our time at Blackstone nor even attempts to describe it in terms of how the local people may have viewed things, but hopefully, I have provided a picture, through my own lens, of this extraordinary time in the life of this community. We absolutely loved it there, and we considered it a privilege to be a part of it.

The workload is enormous, but we feel supported in that we believe this is the right thing for us to be doing at this time, and it is utilising all the experiences, talents and abilities we have developed over the years. It is wonderful to feel you can be of service where the needs are so great.

This was not the end of our involvement with the people of Blackstone. We have been back many times over the last twenty years for many reasons and always loved reconnecting with them.

Now, let's go back a bit with a snapshot of what it was like for us living there. This is what I wrote after our first break (we had two weeks off every three months). These first ten weeks set the tone for the three years we were there.

Our first ten weeks

This first ten weeks has seemed like ten years – we have had so many new and interesting things happen since arriving in Blackstone.

Papulankutja is the traditional name of the Aboriginal community here at Blackstone. It means 'meeting place'. The town has a school, community hall, covered half-size olympic pool, fully-lit grassed football oval, an office, a clinic, a mechanical workshop and works shed and store.

Blackstone is a small oasis in the middle of a vast desert situated at the foot of the Blackstone Ranges. The hills continually change colour throughout the day – from yellow green to reds, purple and blue. The red sand is dotted with low mulga trees and spinifex as well as a range of other shrubs that provide bush foods, and many delicate wild flowers.

The ground is covered with small black stones giving the town its name – most likely some type of iron ore. Many mining companies are sniffing around to see what they can find.

There is a plentiful supply of good clean bore water, which has enabled the planting of river gums, an orchard, and numerous other varieties of trees, providing shade and beauty in an otherwise harsh environment. It would normally be very hot at this time of the year, but cyclonic weather has maintained almost continual cloud cover with several thunderstorms bringing inches of rain. Over the last 24 hours we have had three inches – flooding some low-lying community houses and getting very close to our back door.

It is like another world here where two cultures are trying to merge with each other, the Ngaanyatjarra people being caught in between, trying to hold on to many of their old ways, and yet wanting to take hold of the advantages of western society like money, cars, houses etc.

We arrived here on the 6th October 1998. A few weeks prior to our arrival, the chairman of the Blackstone Community Council had been killed in a car accident and we arrived the day before his funeral. We have since found out that funerals are very big events and seem to take priority over all other community activities. People had travelled long distances to be here for this day. They had all camped out away from the town with the others, in sorry camps.

About half the houses, all those around and including the house of the dead man, had been left empty. Four people had been speared in the leg to atone for the death of this man. Someone had to be blamed. Some will never be able to live in Blackstone again. The body was flown in on a plane and taken to the community hall (the accident had occurred quite some distance from Blackstone). Only a handful of people were there in the hall, and we were beginning to wonder if they knew whether the body had arrived as nothing seemed to be happening.

Then suddenly we heard a wailing sound and a large mass of people, all together as one, walked towards the hall. Children, dogs and adults all filled the hall quickly, and wept over the coffin. The sound and the emotional impact were quite overwhelming.

A simple ceremony, partly aboriginal and partly Christian, took place. The coffin was then taken in the back of a truck to the cemetery and another small ceremony took place there. The whole town then burst into life with cars, trucks and people moving everywhere as visitors prepared for the journey home.

Since we have been here, people have been continually on the move to attend funerals – sometimes a thousand kilometres away. The 'reburial' for their chairman was to be held in a few months.

Until this time, everyone still had to remain camped in the sorry camp and were not allowed to live in the houses. On the day of the reburial, another man was to be speared in the leg, because he was in the car when the chairman was killed.

For the reburial, I helped them sew up a white sheet which was placed over the grave. It is then lifted from over the grave by the closest relatives, allowing the spirit to be released. New life begins and the grieving stops. People move from their sorry camps back into their houses.

I refer to the dead man as 'the chairman' because when someone dies it is not permitted to mention his name for many years afterwards. Our names – Don, Helen, Gordon (even our second names) are 'Kumana' – they cannot be spoken. So I was given the name Wingula, and Don was Nunjna.

Funerals and reburials seem to be happening all the time and are very important. There is a great fear of death. Houses are often burnt after someone has died, or, at least, trashed. One of the white staff, who has been here a long time, lives in a community house originally occupied by a man who committed suicide. None of the Ngaanyatjarra will live in it.

After the funeral, we were into a very intense two weeks of "hand-over" with June and Jim Hair – the previous couple that worked here – showing us what to do, particularly concerning the management of the office.

Blackstone, unlike the other communities in the Ngaanyatjarra Lands, does most of its own bookwork and is the only one that has a cheque book. This was all established by June and Jim.

One hundred community members are on a CDEP work programme for which we have to prepare pay packets each week. Others get pensions and family supplements. People are continuously on the move, so money is always being transferred from one community to another, mostly in cash on the plane. There is a lot of paperwork involved to keep track of it.

We also run a 'banking' service (not official), a Post Office and an agency for Centrelink. This is all done while being continuously interrupted by a steady stream of people with requests at the front desk and the phone ringing every few minutes.

We also assist with the running of community meetings and are accountable to ATSIC[15] for the grant they provide for the work programme, establishing work projects, and monitoring the hours people work.

Apart from this, I'm also involved with the development of the Women's Centre where they do many crafts, sewing, painting, tie dying, printing etc. Two Aboriginal ladies run a pre-school. This is done with very limited facilities. Next year we are going to improve this centre to include a toilet and shower in the pre-school and room for a second-hand clothing shop in the Women's Centre.

We are supported by a very cooperative and hard-working white staff who get along well together. Also, many of the

---

[15] ATSIC is the Commonwealth Government department for indigenous funding.

Aboriginal people are now working alongside us. One girl, in particular, has developed into an excellent office-worker and has considerably relieved my workload in that area.

Apart from ourselves, the white staff include a storekeeper, a mechanic, a projects officer, a clinic sister and four teachers. Temporary people come in from time to time to run workshops for the women, recreational programmes and also builders and service people maintaining roads, phones, electrical equipment etc. There is a continuous flow of people all the time, in and out for various reasons – all with specific tasks.

Two leaders from the Institute of Linguistics have been visiting here and have given us excellent lessons in the Ngaanyatjarra language. They are Christians and are involved in translating the Bible into this language as well as teaching Ngaanyatjarra people to write their own language, which was previously only in an oral form. Next year, language worker, Jan Mountney, will be here permanently in Blackstone and we will learn a lot more.

Blackstone has only been permanently settled since October 1977, so a lot has been done in the last twenty years. A great deal of credit must go to Murray Wells, a remarkable man, who came to Blackstone as the first school teacher, working in a tin shack the people had built themselves. He was the teacher for six years and later came back as the Advisor for eleven years. He is still in Blackstone and does relief for staff when they are on holidays and also runs the swimming pool. However, he has now taken on the position as environmental health officer for the Eastern Ngaanyatjarra lands but stationed in Blackstone.

Every day seems to be so full and eventful that I could write something each evening. However, there are a few incidents we have been involved in over the past ten weeks that reflect on the life here and the people.

The first time I gave out the pays by myself one man asked

for his wife's pay as he was looking after the children and his wife was away. I said I couldn't do that unless I had her permission, but I could give him a book-up docket for the store and they could sort it out when she got back. Either he didn't quite understand or thought I was against him, and he got very angry and stormed off. A few minutes passed and then an elderly lady went over and locked the door. I asked her why?

"He's coming back to bash you up", she said.

The next thing there was a loud banging noise on the door, as he hammered it with his wadi (a large stick with a round head used for killing animals). Don went up to the door and opened it. The man got such a surprise that he stopped, and Don invited him in to talk it over. Five minutes later, he was apologising and shaking my hand and saying we were friends. I promised that if anyone asked for his pay, I wouldn't give it to them unless I had _his_ permission.

Mostly, the people here speak their own language and only a few are literate and speak English well. It is very easy for misunderstandings to develop.

A delightful old man called Fred Forbes, who was the founding member of Blackstone, has his own water hole a short distance from the town. His dream is to have a garden there, but he has almost no idea of how to cultivate plants. When we first came, he was asking for someone to help him build a fence so his garden would be protected from camels and kangaroos etc. Don agreed that, if he could get the support of some of the young men to do the work, he would provide the materials and allow the project officer to assist. This eventuated, and Don went out one evening to have a look at the garden and help him plant seeds. Fred was planting all the seeds in one hole so we explained that he had to allow more room for the plants to grow. His English is very poor, but as we explained things, mostly through drawings on the ground, he would say, "That's the one!

That's the one!"

Finally, he asked me to take a picture of himself and Don in his garden. He goes out every day to water it and report about how high the plants are growing. He is the only one so far who has any vision of cultivating plants. So we want to encourage him.

Life is very exposed here. People's emotions and thoughts are right out in the open. Community meetings, mostly held outside, sitting on the ground with dogs and children walking around, are usually quite heated events with strong feelings being expressed until finally a decision is reached. However, a strong pattern is developing where, if there is a problem, we have a meeting and talk about it.

Once Don was threatened with a machete for insisting on a meeting before he would allow a community truck to be taken out. However, the man cooled down fairly quickly.

Perhaps one of the most difficult times was when Don went to Alice Springs and I was looking after things here. In the evening, I heard what sounded like large stones being thrown on a roof nearby. I was going to have a look myself but decided to ring the project officer and get him to check up. It was a young man of about twenty years old who had had a history of angry outbursts and probably some sort of mental illness. (Many children have been affected by petrol sniffing – they have severe mental deterioration – one has epileptic fits). Keith, the project officer, tried to calm him down, but the chap threatened him with a machete. Keith was concerned as he had seen his behaviour changing for some time – driving cars very fast putting others at risk, and had pulled the large doors off the community hall. We rang the police and advised them to come but, as it is quite a distance, they didn't feel it was justified unless someone was hurt. At 8:00 a.m., the boy's father came to my house and asked me to ring the police and put his boy in gaol.

The police talked to him on the phone and convinced him that it wasn't urgent, that the matter could be dealt with later. I talked to him for some time to try to understand why he should want his son put into gaol, and it seemed that, if his boy kept misbehaving, then he would be speared in the leg for allowing his boy to behave in this manner. Finally, I went to the office and life continued as normal when suddenly there was a loud noise as a large stone was thrown the project officer's vehicle window, smashing it. Carlton, this young boy, attacked the car first and then the project officer with a knife. People were running everywhere, screaming. Keith managed to get away and lock himself in the pool building. I locked the women and children in the office. I rang the police and told them they had to come this time. It took about three hours for them to come from Warburton, by which time Carlton had sought out the storekeeper with whom he'd always had a good connection. The storekeeper managed to get him into his car and drove him out of town to let him cool down. The police finally caught up with him there and took him away. It will be a bit of a worry if he comes back.

This is a 'dry' community. In fact, alcohol is banned for all the Ngaanyatjarra communities. Life here is manageable without alcohol and petrol (avgas is used instead). When the men particularly get to Kalgoorlie occasionally, they often binge themselves out with drink. It is hard to understand why they do it, particularly the teenagers. I asked one lady and she said, "It's because the parents don't talk to their children and they let them run wild".

We really love the children. They respond immediately to some attention. They are not bad but just totally wild, as the parents don't discipline their children. They are left very much to wander around and fend for themselves – often getting into mischief. Most young children wander around naked and women very unashamedly walk around with one breast dangling and a child attached.

The people here still do a lot of hunting and collecting of bush foods – yellow berries, quandongs etc. Mostly they use cars and rifles for hunting.

Cars have to be seen to be believed. They would rarely last a month – often only days. When hunting, they use them like tanks ploughing through the scrub. As long as the car goes, they will use it, forgetting that it needs water and oil to keep it going. However, they are fast learning a lot about cars — even the women.

Life is still very immediate and lived for today, without much thought for tomorrow. Material things don't last long, mostly because they have no idea of caring for them. They find it hard to stick at the same job continuously for a long time.

The Flying Doctor came last night to take the clinic sister to Kalgoorlie Hospital. She had been bitten by either a snake or a redback while sleeping and was very sick. A venomous snake was found and killed in her kitchen but there were also redbacks around.

The children are always trying to pinch my grapes but, so far, I have managed to get them to ask for them and share them around nicely. If I refused them altogether, I'm sure they would just take them. They may as well learn some manners along the way.

We have been amazed at the honesty of most people here. They often put pressure on you to lend them money, but they would never take it.

In our busy times, we have had a lot of support from the Aboriginal people, who have often worked late into the night and weekends to get the job done. It has been very rewarding, and you feel it is all worthwhile. The idea is that they can run their own community, but it is a long way from that yet.

While we don't want to change the Aboriginal people into white people, it is inevitable if they are to live in a settled community that they learn the principles of work and cleanliness and have the ability to administer their own affairs. I get the feeling they have learnt more about us than we have learnt about them.

I just hope we will be guided and have the wisdom to develop this community in the best possible way. We have been fortunate that the white staff who were here before us have set a very good basis for us to work from.

The rain has gone, the sky is clear and I can hear the children all happily playing basketball outside. I must now get on with other matters like cooking tea, cleaning house etc. And now someone is knocking on the door.

I hope this has given you some idea of life at Blackstone.

Glimpses of our life in Blackstone – 1999 & 2000

19th October 1999

We arrived back in Blackstone from away on holidays. Everyone seemed pleased to see us – although many were away at NAIDOC week in Laverton and funeral at Warburton – a young boy committed suicide in his cell, and then the father died of a heart attack.

21st Sept to 19th Oct

Holidays were an interesting time with completing a sorting out of our last few boxes of material possessions.

We also spent a couple of days in Narrogin, seeing many friends. We also got to know Colin better, and time was spent discussing the forthcoming marriage with our daughter, Ruth. Our son, Ben, seems more relaxed and happy than ever. He is planning his motorbike ride to Blackstone with his friend Medhi.

Also, quite a lot of time was spent organizing the Blackstone
Art Exhibition.

20th Oct

I had one of the most stressful days ever today trying to sort
out details for the exhibition. However, it all ended happily and
everything is progressing well.

Lynette and Melissa worked by themselves at the Women's
Centre and produced some very good quality garments.

22nd Oct

Everyone is sad today. Vera Woods is ill – <u>very</u> sick in Perth
hospital. Her husband Brian went to Kalgoorlie with her but
took off drinking and doesn't even know she was sent on to
Perth.

Melissa and Lynette are doing very well with their sewing and
looking after the centre.

A health competition is on for the best painting about health.
Six paintings are being done by each community and there will
be prizes.

Joseph, our other son, is here from Alice Springs.

29th Oct

Have come out of a very difficult time with the organization
of the exhibition of Blackstone art at the Kings Park Gallery.
Not happy at all with the way things are being done, but we will
have to see it through, and I am having to get tougher and more
assertive in my dealings with people there. A lot of things have
come out of it. My liaison with Chellany and Drewfus Gates –
they have assisted me greatly by getting paintings valued. And
Zelda Vea Vea has aroused interest from Edith Cowan for
running workshops there.

Today Cynthia Ward took over running the second-hand

shop – and is doing this very well.

About six ladies have started painting again.

The playgroup has been run for a whole week by Paula while BJ is away.

It has been raining non-stop for over a week – and everyone camped out in 'sorry camps'.

4ᵗʰ Nov to 12ᵗʰ

Melissa, Lynette, Mary and myself all set out for Perth to attend the opening of the Blackstone art exhibition. They were very shy at first but gradually became more talkative. The exhibition was very successful – one-third sold on opening night. We also conducted many successful workshops at Banksia Hill, Graylands, and Curtin Uni. Edith Cowan Arts Dept are interested in holding workshops at Blackstone in the future.

We also went to the beach, the markets and shopping. The girls had a great time.

We had some rather difficult meetings with Aboriginal Development and sorted out some business issues.

It was good to have that week with the family. Ruth and Colin are finding their own way. Ben is growing into a gorgeous fellow. Shadi came over and has grown into such a lovely talented young lady. Joe is still in Alice Springs.

14ᵗʰ Nov

Back in Blackstone, many difficult issues here, with the clinic sister and one of the teachers under threat by one man. He has been taken by the police now. However, the clinic has been closed temporarily, until things are sorted out. Don is very tired and under a lot of pressure.

31ˢᵗ Oct, Sunday

We took Lynette, Melissa and Mary and a young cousin out

for the afternoon. We caught goannas and cooked them on the fire; also bush plants and foods for the exhibition. We also found a mountain devil. After the two weeks of non-stop rain, we found a lot of rock-holes filled with water. The girls were looking for wild turkey but didn't find any. We went past the Brown's old hunting grounds on the road to Tjuntuntjarra.

21ˢᵗ Nov

A lot has happened over the last week. Amanda has left and I am on my own in the office – not as much time for the women's centre.

However, have signed all the girls (seven of them) on to do the Cert 1 in Office Administration. Hopefully, this will work out.

Also, Chellinay Gates has offered to do all the marketing of jewellery, crafts and paintings for Blackstone – a great relief. I hope she fits in with the people here.

At the beginning of the week, a small cyclone swept through the town uprooting some of the largest trees and throwing them to the ground. Trees were hanging off power lines and there was no power for some time. Mack and Des very bravely got up in the cherry picker and cut the branches down. The people in sorry camp managed to escape, but their tents were blown away.

This weekend we have had a busy time catching up on book work. Maria Munro came in and gave me a hand – she is excellent!

28ᵗʰ Jan 2000

So much has happened since October. We have been so busy I have come home so tired I haven't written in my diary.

The art exhibition was a success. Mary, Melissa and Lynette attended the opening, flying down with me. They were all very excited and dressed themselves up except for shoes. They stayed with Ben and Ruth at their house, and we did several workshops in painting at Banksia Hill, Curtin Uni and Claremont Aboriginal Psych Unit. The girls really enjoyed themselves, going swimming in the sea, buying things at the second-hand shop. They enjoyed having showers and baths and continually used the washing machine.

There were some difficulties with my dealings with ABS so Chellinay Gates has taken on the marketing of Blackstone art and craft. She had another exhibition in December and is holding another big one on February 13th & 14th. Another 40 paintings were sent down. Sylvia Benson is also doing some magnificent woodwork – sent down a sample.

We left to go on holidays on the 20th Dec. Amanda and Brian relieved us.

Our daughter Ruth's wedding was a highlight of our holidays – a truly enjoyable and relaxed event but was still very dignified – all under the oak tree in grandma's garden.

7th Feb

Don moved the new filing cabinets into the office. However, the children had removed the keys which had been stuck on the side in small bags. Young Jackie said she had seen them playing with them. One was found stuck to the top of the door, another was outside on the ground and the last in the swimming pool. The children dived for it.

8th Feb

A really enjoyable day with all the women busy sewing at the women's centre, and then a successful evening, collecting honey ants along the Tjuntuntjarra road. The honey ants are to be sent to the art exhibition (Desert Stories) at Chellinay's and Drew's.

9ᵗʰ Feb

Another good sewing day with the ladies taking more responsibility and having their own ideas on how to finish off dresses. Lynette is putting on pockets. Janet is putting a stretchy band around the waist.

We all went out at lunchtime to collect more honey ants and bush foods to send down for the exhibition on the Thursday plane. We went out to Morgan's Bore and got many honey ants, bardies and yellow berries.

10ᵗʰ Feb

A good day at the office and LC. Packaged everything off to Perth. They were given the wrong time for the plane and missed it. Fortunately, I had arranged for Keith to take them to his hotel, so they are going to pick them up there. There seems to be many obstacles.

11ᵗʰ Feb

The honey ants and bardi grubs etc. finally arrived at Chellinay's. She has been to a lot of trouble to set up the exhibition – trying to get media coverage – very difficult.

13ᵗʰ Feb

Not many people came to the exhibition on Saturday, but a lot was sold. Hopefully for more on Sunday but the phone is out so can't get through to find out.

Mehdi had an interesting experience going to supposedly get a rucksack or some bedding for Spencer from Linden Bore. This was a ploy to get them all out hunting and he was taken along an almost non-existent track until they got there – and then nothing was at the bore. It was late and dark when they got back and had a flat tyre on the way.

This weekend we organized the office for about the tenth

time. Ben helped putting in the shelves etc. Big clean-up at the same time.

It is pouring with rain and cold – a great relief after two weeks of intense heat. There have been floods and roads put off everywhere.

12th Feb and 13th Feb

The weekend of our 'Desert Stories'. Not as many sales as we had hoped but covered costs of the last lot of paintings and sending out invitations.

The boys have been out on some more trips looking for people that can't be found. This will be the last trip – they had so many flat tyres and people are using it as an excuse to go out hunting.

14th Feb – Monday

I've developed a very heavy cold and am dragging myself around. The ladies are doing very well in the women's centre. Lots of sewing, the school jigsaws, HACC meals & playgroups.

29th Feb

A lot has happened over the past two weeks. Ng Services has come out to look at the books. They were impressed with Blackstone and all the girls working in the office but are very keen to take over the store and roadhouse, and they don't want to provide us with an accountant to do an internal audit. Very nice ladies but with a rather arrogant, know-it-all approach that didn't leave us with a feeling of support – once again.

Today was meant to be the final interview for the Project Officer and his wife as an office trainer. They were interviewed and, without our knowledge or discussion, were sent to Kiwikurra – very disappointing.

I felt very down at the end of last week and talked Don into going for an outing to Wingellina – despite heavy downpours of rain. We made it alright with half a dozen community members in the back. However, going there, we started sliding all over the road because there had been another inch of rain since we had left. We ended up with a delightful afternoon, evening and morning tea with Amanda and Brian. They are enjoying life in Wingellina.

We nearly got back to Blackstone on the Sunday when we caught up with the Hollands in a bog, and boys on their motorbikes. Mehdi had gone back and, about two kilometres out, had run into an obstacle and landed on his head and shoulders in a mud puddle. The storekeeper from Wingellina, fortunately, was going past and picked him up and took him to the clinic. He had broken his collar bone and severely bruised and lacerated himself. Medhi is in a sorry state, but it could have been worse. On the way home, we realized how important it was to have a break and get out.

11ᵗʰ March

So much has happened over the past two weeks. The women's centre is blossoming – the sewing is of a high standard and they are now designing and cutting out their own clothes. They have decided to extend HACC meals to include workers and bake their own bread. Jigsaw puzzles are becoming popular – sold some to Wingellina and Blackstone schools.

Ben had taken over as Project Officer and is doing an excellent job – getting a lot of young men working – repairing their houses.

The fast has started and Medhi and I get up early and pray and breakfast together.

There has been a lot of rain – the roads are cut off, but the weather is mild and very pleasant. Everywhere is green and lush. The boys have had some interesting times pulling people out of bogs.

Amongst all the good things that are happening, we are under a lot of pressure from the head of Ng Council to hand over our books to their rather inadequate bookkeeping service. The community has become involved and, as a result of one person who has authority over-reacting to our refusal to give her, her brother's pension cheque and this lady has convinced these ignorant (in the sense of bookkeeping) people into sending the books to Alice Springs. Don is really worn down with it. I just hope the matter is resolved soon.

Chellinay is doing a great job of selling paintings etc. – seeking out other avenues for marketing.

20ᵗʰ March

The time of the fast has been both very fulfilling and many tests.

Thisbe, Megan and Dan have arrived to make a giant basket (6m x 4m) for a world expo in Germany. They have taken over the hall – are making the structure out of bamboo. A lot of women are helping.

Don is under a lot of stress with a very abusive approach from Ng Council & Ng Services. Our Project Officer and bookkeeper have been sent to Kirrakurra – without us even being told.

All the plants are growing at the women's centre and Lynette is looking after them and is very excited to see the seeds coming up.

They have started meals for workers as well as old people.

Second-hand was a great success, with three bales arriving at the same time. Everyone was very well behaved after a few anxious moments while they were being sorted. In two hours, they bought $2,200 worth of clothing and bedding. Another $200 was sold today. Already we have made $600 profit.

Ben is doing a great job as Project Officer. Medhi had done some time with the recording studio.

25ᵗʰ March

Thisbe has been here from the Women's Council and is still making a large basket to send to the world expo in Germany. It is held together with bamboo and string. They have taken over the hall and about twenty women were working on it.

Don is very weighed down by the issue of the books and Peter Rapkin's continual abusive letters.

David and Margaret have arrived, and John, Leanne and Lauren.

Ben and Medhi are preparing to leave. We had a really nice evening with them.

NawRuz was a very happy and joyous evening. We invited many people from the community over for a meal.

8ᵗʰ April

We have had a few storms over the past two weeks.

Sylvia Benson trying to take over the office and sack all the white staff. In a very emotive manner, she called a council meeting and demanded that all the books be sent to Alice Springs. Everyone agreed and Don has been forced to give up the system he has created. We still can't see how it is going to save work and he is bitterly disappointed, particularly as the local office staff are becoming so good at their jobs.

Ruth is working towards another exhibition of Blackstone work while I'm on holidays. The title will be 'Desert Tracks'. She is doing it as one of her projects in the new TAFE centre.

Some musicians are here and have with them some instruments made from tyres, polypipe, wooden marimarers, and xylophone from metal pipes.

May

We have now returned from holidays – all spent in Perth helping Ruth with the exhibition 'Desert Tracks'. And helping Joseph settle into his flat at Brownley Towers – painting and moving furniture.

There have been many interesting developments since returning: the community has divided itself into seven groups, and each will have a portion of a trust fund into which money is divided according to the number of people in each group. Money goes into the trust fund from store profits and other sources. The people are all very happy with this and are now putting $5/wk back in for family cars.

There have been a few break-ins at the store and teacher's houses and some of the teenage boys have become very abusive – mainly with language, and we think some are on drugs.

Serena Woods died while we were away – a young lady only 24 – from a diabetic coma. Yesterday Narelle Holland told me the story of how she died: Jessie and Aaron and Serena were out in the bush collecting honey ants. When they came back to the car, the battery was flat. They started walking home. Serena suddenly collapsed. Aaron tried to give her some water, but she couldn't drink it. He ran all the way back to the community to get help. By the time the sister came, she had died. The community blamed Aaron and Jessie. Aaron was speared in the leg, and they were going to bash Jessie up, but she locked herself in the house. So they hit Narelle but just with their fists – no sticks. Aaron and Jessie have gone to Tjukurla now and won't come back until after the second funeral. Everyone was in sorry camp for about three weeks.

Early in the morning on the 9th May 2000, Mr Brown died – the oldest man in the community. There was some wailing but only a few close relatives camped out in sorry camps. It is more accepted when an old man dies. Mr Jackie Brown had a big family – four wives and many children and grandchildren. There are now arguments about where the funeral will be – Blackstone or Wingellina.

Xmas 2000

So much has happened at Blackstone this past year. Despite attempts at keeping a diary, this has not been consistent and even this record would be inadequate to explain the process of development that is happening here, of which we are just a small part. What we think is just impossible, happens, and what we predict will take months and years of development happens in days and weeks.

When we came here, we started a process to train and encourage more involvement of local people in the running of their community. This process involves setting up structures that enable the work to be done easily and accurately by the local people, as well as training in skills and increasing understanding of issues involved to maximize decision-making.

We started with the office and just took in anybody who wanted to have a go. The office work was very complex, with many different types of money transactions – banking, book-up, credit, buying and selling.

We were fortunate to have Joseph with us last year, and while he was there, he worked with Don to set up a computerized office system. This is used to record and connect all money transactions. It is user-friendly and enables the local staff to totally manage the office's day-to-day transactions.

..ooOOoo..

10

Initiating craft industries
in a remote community

Jigsaws and spinifex paper in Blackstone

Written by Helen Gordon

Jigsaws

The Blackstone Women's Centre started to make jigsaws as part of a work program from 1998 to 2001.

At that time, there was no funding to keep the Women's Centre going. Even though many members of the community were involved in painting, basket-making, punu, and gum-nut jewellery, these were all individual activities for which they were paid as things were sold. With these activities, they paid for the tools and raw materials to pursue these activities and then when they were sold all the money went to the individual artist. We had a small shop that sold canvas and paints, raffia, wools, woodworking tools etc. This mostly just broke even. There were a few collective activities where the goods produced provided funding for the Women's Centre, such as hand-dyeing T-shirts and sewing. We also had a small secondhand shop.

Another issue was a great interest in painting, but not everyone was going to get into the fine art market. As it was, we had set up a community fund to pay people for their paintings and then the community would on-sell them. Some paintings would be much harder to sell than others, and it was really hard and often precarious work as we had no established Art Centre at that stage. The thought was to divert the painting efforts into more easily saleable products. Thus the idea of jigsaw puzzles. As long as they had some simple iconic objects on them and a reasonable background, they would pass as a saleable product.

My interest was always in providing dignified and meaningful work for the people of Blackstone. We could sell them to schools and other interested groups by advertising and marketing our product directly from Blackstone. The MDF board was cheap and easy to bring in on a truck. The only expense was the scroll saw – not too expensive. The idea was that people would be paid on CDEP to work on the jigsaw project and the money from sales would go back to support the Women's Centre.

To present this idea, I painted six boards 60cm square with a white background ready for painting. We had bought in a scroll saw. However, when I talked about the idea and showed them the boards to be painted, they all started whining like little children complaining that other communities pay people on CDEP to do their painting and give them the money for the painting afterwards. I briefly explained why we had to do it this other way, but they again started moaning, so I just told them they could run their own Women's Centre. I had a lot of office work to do, but I wasn't paid to do the work at the Women's Centre. I completely detached myself from it and left. A short time later, they asked me to come back and immediately started whining again. I just left without saying anything, thinking that it was not going to work. However, at the end of the day they begged me to come back. I very reluctantly went and was almost blown away by six magnificent paintings done on the white boards. I was almost trembling at the thought of cutting them up but had to follow it through.

We sold our first jigsaws to the local schools, and they were very proud to know the women had gone there. This was followed by orders from other schools all over Australia. Most visitors to the community bought one. The roadhouses started selling them. Even the Minister for Education, on a brief visit there, bought one for his waiting room. We had a long list in the Women's Centre of all the places where the jigsaws were going, and they were so proud of this.

It became a really thriving work activity with some people liking one particular aspect like the scrolling or the varnishing or packaging. I remember Jennifer Forbes coming in one day and asking if she could do a different type of scrolling. I agreed, and she just took off with one of her own paintings first (the Seven Sisters, pictured) and without drawing first, just scrolled the most intricate design. She became our best cutter.

We had several different sizes. It was quite exciting to watch this development take place and with the quite substantial profits made we then branched into a sewing business, buying machines and materials. This was still done as a work program with people paid by the hour for the work they did.

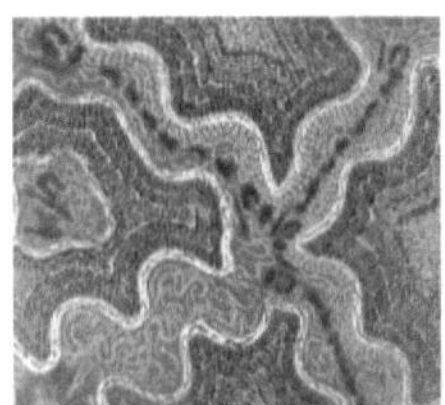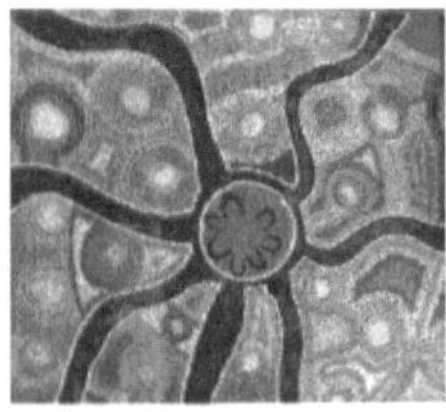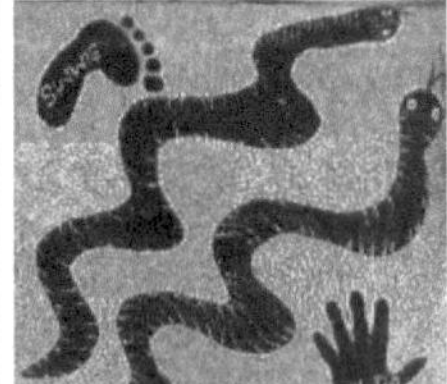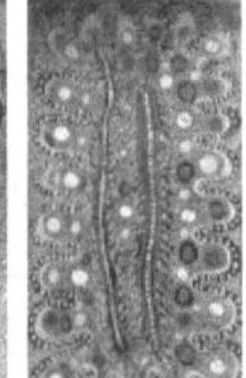

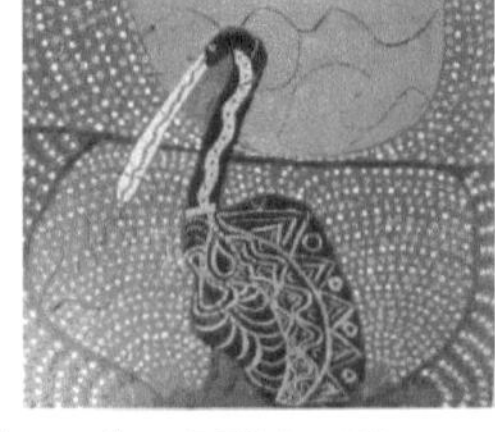

I purchased a few of these to take with me when I left. These later became part of the Blackstone collection that was sent to Darwin in 2020 – The Seven Sisters by Jennifer Forbes 60 x 60 cms, The Seven Sisters by Jennifer Mitchell 60 x 60 cms, Pukara by Hilda Simms 60 x 60 cms, Two Centipedes by May Forbes 60 x 30 cms and

Pelican – unknown artist 36 x 30 cms.

Spinifex Paper

This story started when my husband and I went to work at Blackstone in 1998. Even though my main task was to manage the office, I was also asked to be the coordinator for the Women's Centre and try to find meaningful work for the women. Over time we developed many opportunities for work, including painting, sewing, tie-dyeing, basket-making (this was already happening through NPY Women's Council), punu and community work. However, I was always trying to think of some marketable product that could be made from the natural resources in the community environment. We dabbled a little with bush medicines and I kept trying to imagine something that could be made from the millions of small black stones on the ground. I had almost given up when I had a dream about making paper from spinifex grass.

I was not a paper-maker so on one of my breaks in Perth, I looked up the WA Papermakers' Society and they welcomed me to come and learn from them. The chairperson had me over to her house and we made paper from grasses. She had actually made paper from spinifex in the Pilbara.

When I returned to Blackstone, I brought with me some of the essential ingredients and tried it out. It worked really well, but the formula involved using caustic soda to break down the grass. This was untenable in an environment where children were always around and where it could not be controlled.

I started doing some more research and read where it was possible to use soda ash for some fibres. I tried this, and it worked. This is quite safe and easy to use.

One of the community members was really interested in working with me on this. So Narelle Holland and myself dragged old frames and doors from the tip to make benches on the veranda of the Women's Centre. We used concrete bricks for a press. I ordered in a variable speed four-litre blender (rather than the usual Oak Park beater used in commercial paper-making, which costs some $10,000 and has to come from America). We already had some portable electric elements for heating the water.

Soon we were making paper and all the ladies became quite excited. Everyone who visited the community wanted to buy a piece of the paper.

We started to paint on it and do embossed paintings with glue and the red sand. We ordered in some cheap frames and coloured card so after doing a painting they could frame it. They sold really quickly straight from the community.

We still had a very make-shift set up for making it and had not advertised it when we started getting orders from outside. Native Title was prepared to pay $5 for an A4 sheet and wanted 100 sheets to put on the front of some documents for mining companies. A gallery wanted some sent to Sydney. Some print-makers were interested in it.

Unfortunately, this was at a time when we were leaving. I was so sad to be leaving this project just as it was beginning. I taught it to the new lady starting, but she didn't stay long. However, Blackstone was fortunate that Diana Isgar eventually took over this role and stayed for many years. She invited me to come back and set this up as an industry. We were in Tom Price by then, so I packed the car with everything I needed, including a really good press made by an engineer in Tom Price. I was there for about three months setting this up, making proper drying racks, and establishing better ways of making the paper and creating marketable products and labels.

It was wonderful to work on this project with no other responsibilities to think about. I came back again in 2004, and by then, the school wanted to have the children involved as part of their school programme. Also, Dianna had found funding to build a purpose-built building for the paper-making and to employ a full-time coordinator to manage this. It was a while before the building finally happened, but that is the present Blackstone Art Centre.

Diana wanted me to be the coordinator, but I couldn't stay so she asked me to find somebody. A friend of mine who was an artist and had grown up in the desert and been involved with Indigenous people was interested. Within a few weeks, Erin O'Connor came out and managed the project for nearly two years. I passed on to her all that I could and offered to support her as best I could.

In that time, they spent two weeks at the WA Museum demonstrating the paper-making and selling their products. After Erin left, others took over for a time, but it eventually slowed down. Dianna then left and became the HACC coordinator.

I went back to Blackstone in 2016 and set up the paper-making again for their Arts Festival. Later, in 2017, while Don was doing relieving work at Jameson, I talked with Narelle Holland who now lives there and she was keen to do the paper-making again. We set it up on the veranda at the Women's Centre in Jameson and organised it as Narelle's own business. Jameson and Blackstone are under the same art centre, so it was easy to move the equipment there. Unfortunately, the art centre was in a phase where they had had a number of relieving coordinators and was barely keeping itself together, so there was no interest in the paper. I still keep in touch with Narelle and see her when she comes to Perth, but I think, at the moment, it is not happening.

..ooOOoo..

11

Life in the Pilbara

In Tom Price for 10 years from 2001 to 2011

Written by Don

In 2001, after three years in Blackstone, then five months in Mulan, Helen and Don moved to Tom Price, where Ruth and her husband Colin (who was a teacher) had Matthew, the first grandchild.

In the decade they were in Tom Price, Don had three jobs. He was back as a social worker with DCW for four years. Then he was a project officer with Gumula Aboriginal Corporation for three years and then with employment services through Ashburton Aboriginal Corporation for three years. These three positions entailed many visits to remote aboriginal communities.

Baha'i activities

There was an LSA in Tom Price. Some of the members were inactive members, but nonetheless there were many Baha'i activities such as devotional meetings, Feasts, holy days, and Ruhi study circles. There was a large banner in the street parade for the annual Nameless Festival.

There were rich friendships with the other Bahai's in Tom Price – Shone and John Ernest, Lorraine Lobo, Andrew Shanks and, of course, Ruth and Colin. Also, there were warm connections with others in the Pilbara cluster. Helen conducted BESS classes at North Tom Price Primary School with Ruth and Sarhouz Ardestani. Many others visited, lived and worked there for short periods – including Chantelle Burke, Navaab McLean, Shadi Ferdowsian, Bahroos, Peter and Genevieve Swinstead, Allison Stewart, Doris Allen and Barbara Pierce. The Artworks group performed and made murals in the swimming pool and community hall. Felix and Clara from Artworks stayed on for a while. Helen arranged for Joyce Injie and Tadjee Limerick to attend the annual Summer Schools in Perth. She helped connect isolated Baha'is throughout Australia as she edited the *Bush Honey*[16] newsletter with the Outback Project.

Helen and Don, along with other members of the cluster, completed a course in socio-economic development[17] in 2006.

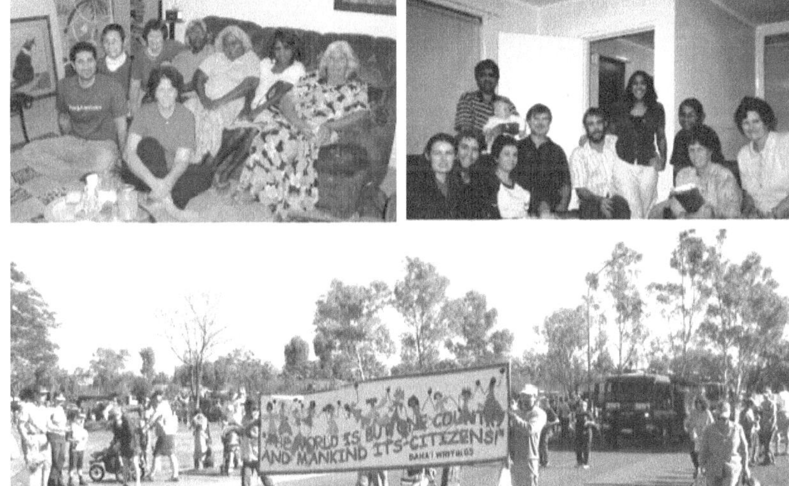

---

16   Copies of Bush Honey are held by Don.
17   The course in socio-economic development was through FUNDAEC.

Community arts & crafts

Murals:

Helen engaged children and community members in painting many murals around the town – bus shelters, drive-in theatre, sports pavilion, schools, and hotel. Ruth was involved with several of these.

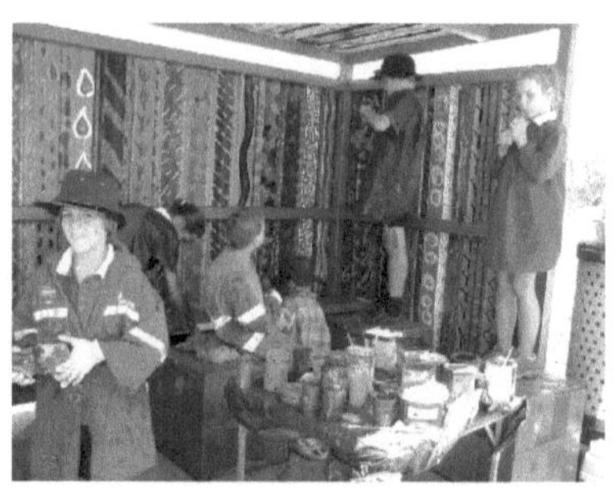

Cultural Centre:

Helen was the central figure in the establishment of the Tom Price Cultural Centre. Helen wrote: *In October 2004, the Cultural Centre began as a germ of an idea around the craft table at Wakuthuni from discussions between several indigenous people and myself as the project worker in the community at that time. Richard Savage from Rio Tinto was also at this meeting. We looked around for a suitable place, and found that the old Scout Hall was no longer being used and had fallen into a sad state of disrepair. The building had no ceiling, was full of cobwebs and had layers of dust everywhere. The toilets smelled, roots were growing out of the hand basins, slime was in the kitchen sink from an eternally dripping tap, broken glass lay over the floor from smashed windows, and doors didn't open – so it was anything but inviting. In early 2005, it was decided to call a meeting there. It was thought that if ten people walked into the building as it was, and agreed that it was a good idea, then a committee could be formed. Exactly ten people came. They were not daunted by the condition of the building but saw that it was basically a very well-constructed place and just needed cleaning, painting and a new kitchen and a ceiling. On that night, they drafted the concept and objectives of the Cultural Centre – with a vision of activities that bring people together – learning from each other and working cooperatively, regardless of culture or colour. They finished the evening by enjoying a simple supper spread on a white lace tablecloth, listening to music and talking excitedly about all the activities they could have there.*

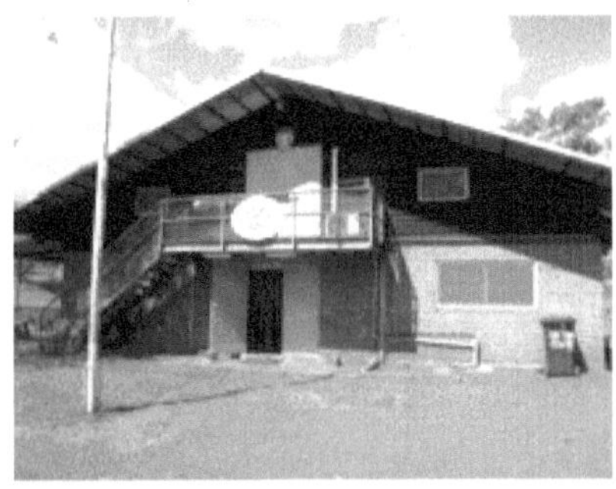

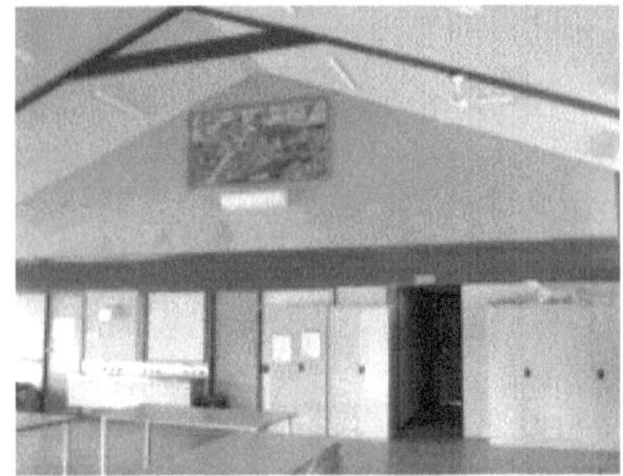

With assistance from the Pilbara Development Commission and Pilbara Iron (Rio Tinto), the hall was purchased and renovated. It became the focus for arts, crafts, the theatre group, choir, Girl Guides, Yoga and other community activities. Some rooms were rented out, and this income underpinned the centre's activities. It became an umbrella organisation to support the establishment of small groups.

PACT:

Helen was an inaugural member of a local artists group called PACT (Pilbara Artists Coming Together), and each year, they held an exhibition. *My Iron Hearted Country Art Exhibition* was the first major art exhibition to be held in Tom Price. There were seventeen local artists exhibiting ninety-one pieces of work. As one of the artists, Helen exhibited eight pieces of work.

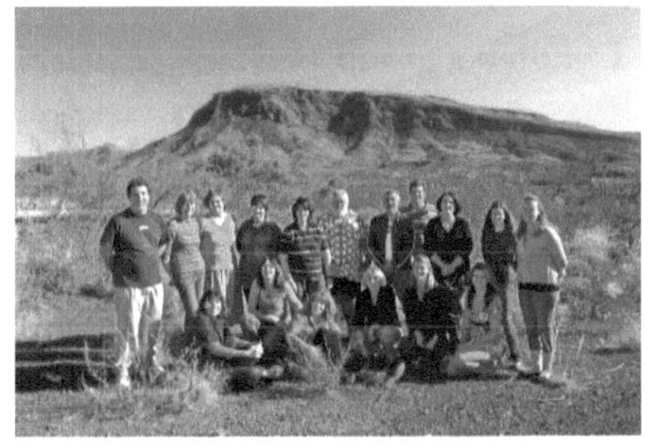

Nameless Festival:

Don and Helen were key members, along with Steve and Mary Rice, running the annual Nameless Festival for seven years. Helen helped initiate and develop the People's Exhibit for displaying art and craft from the local schools and residents. It grew over the years to display at least 250 entries plus displays of artwork from the three schools. Judges were brought from outside the town, and there was a total of thirty prizes. The judges also ran a workshop according to their particular expertise. There was no entry fee for exhibits and the exhibition was totally self-funded through local sponsorship.

Enrichment Centre:

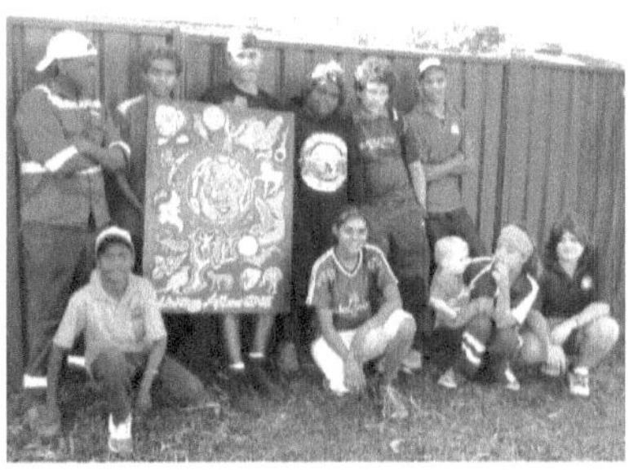

From 2007 to 2011, Helen worked in the after-school homework program – The Enrichment Centre for aboriginal high school students and Wakathuni aboriginal community. This included making a banner, designing and printing T-shirts, and a collective painting. She also tutored in science and some other subjects. Debbie Douglas was the manager of this program.

Children's group:

In the town, for four years, Helen ran a small group for crafts, cooking and games for indigenous primary school children after school. This was voluntary, but some materials were funded by the DCW. It operated from Nintirri, and later in the Art & Craft Rooms in North Tom Price Primary School.

Gallery:

In 2007, Helen and Don purchased the old Masonic Hall, which was next to the Cultural Centre. They acquired the

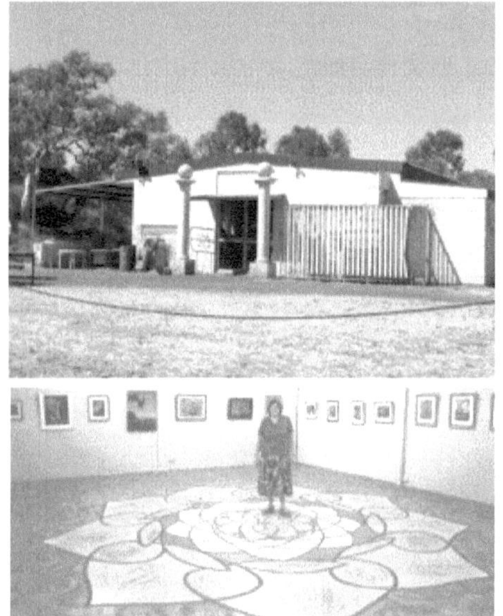

property in order to offer the Cultural Centre committee an opportunity to take it on. The committee did not take up this offer, and so the Gordons retained the property. It became their main retirement income. Helen set up a small art gallery at the hall, but did not sell much through this. She also displayed at the Pebble Mouse Studio Art Gallery

Wakuthuni

Wakuthuni is a small aboriginal community thirty kilometres from Tom Price. In 2004, Helen started working part-time as a DCW project officer at Wakuthuni. She initiated an activity program for crafts such as pyrography and papier mache bowls. This became self-funding by the sale of crafts and a secondhand clothing shop. She also ran a small playgroup. TAFE then took this over in 2005 and employed her as a part-time lecturer, and people enrolled in courses and gained accreditation for what they learnt. Helen formed a close bond with many community members – especially key figures Joyce Drummond, Maisie Pat and Brendon Cook. Helen had involvement with the nearby community of Bellary – notably with Joyce and June Ingie.

Other activities

Helen was deeply involved in many other community programs.

In 2009, she was the coordinator of the ACE Read-Write-Now literacy program for adults.

For two years, she was the secretary of the Tom Price Arts & Crafts Society.

She produced a phone and information book for Tom Price and Paraburdoo, and this was a good fundraiser for the Nameless Festival.

She produced a book of local stories called *Magical Happenings – Myths and Legends of the Pilbara.* This involved doing workshops at the schools with children and encouraging the participation of entries from the indigenous people.

She participated in an indigenous women's health group run through Nintirri Centre.

Helen and Don were members of the Rostrum public speaking group, with friends Mary and Steve Rice, who also ran the Nameless Festival.

Memorial

Not far from Tom Price, there is a lookout where, on a huge number of little rocks, people have written memorials of the departed. The memorials are scattered in piles around the lookout. The Gordons 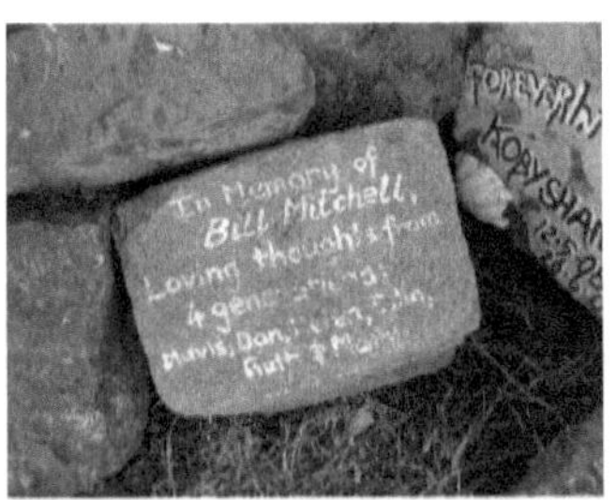 placed a rock inscribed with *"In memory of Bill Mitchell, Loving thoughts from 4 generations; Mavis, Don, Helen, Ruth, Colin and Matty".* This was when Helen's mother, Mavis, was visiting. This particular rock could not be found a few years later.

Travels

Helen and Don often travelled throughout their years at Tom Price. Helen sometimes went with Don on his tours for his employment to small aboriginal communities in the Pilbara.

Whenever they could, they went camping for a night or so in spots not far from town. There were many travels further afield:

- In 2003, to Israel and Thailand[18].

- There were stays with Ben and Violyn family in the Solomon Islands[19] – in 2004 (for their wedding – a few weeks) and then three months in 2008.

- Helen was a Pilbara delegate for the *Art in the Heart* conference in Alice Springs in October 2008.

- They went to Canberra for Joe's and Amica's wedding in 2009.

- And some weeks in the Balgo[20] aboriginal community.

- On several occasions, some months back at Blackstone.

The Gordons left Tom Price in 2011 when Don retired.

They settled in Kelmscott, but Helen returned to the Pilbara several times. She was back at Bellary for four memorials for Joyce Injie and the funeral of her daughter, June. She taught earring-making at South Hedland. She conducted community arts projects at the Karijini Experience in 2016 and 2017.

..ooOOoo..

---

[18] Israel – Chapter 12.

[19] Solomons - apart from these two visits while living in Tom Price, Helen visited two more times while she was in Kelmscott – four occasions totaling almost a year altogether.

[20] Helen described her time in Balgo in Chapter 25.

12

Israel & Thailand

Baha'i World Centre in Haifa for 4 weeks
and Thailand for 2 weeks in 2004

Helen's diary

Our journey begins with leaving Tom Price, saying goodbye at a lovely farewell gathering at Shona & John Ernest's house. They selected some paintings to give to the International Teaching Centre and they – Colin, Ruth, Matthew and the friends here – all wished us well. Also, Peter and Genevieve Swinstead were there – they were visiting Tom Price (stayed in our house while we were away) and had been working at the World Centre for many years and had met Ben before they left late last year.

We left early in the morning for our drive to Perth, and we arrived about midnight on the 9th March. – a long journey, of some 1800 kilometres.

The following evening, we proudly took our seats at Curtin University and watched our son Joseph receive his Degree with honours in Mechatronics (Robotic Engineering – a combination of mechanics, electronics and computing). He is already involved with a contract, in conjunction with his best friend Lam, to design and install a piece of electronic equipment to measure the stress on the big steel ropes that tie up the oil tankers to the big buoys off the coast of Thailand.

The next day I purchased a video camera for Ben and Violyn for a project they had in mind.

Israel

Early on the 12th of March, we set out for Israel. We met up with interesting people on the plane. We seemed to be the odd ones out. Almost all the passengers were Israeli citizens anxious to get back home before the breakout of war as America was about to attack Iraq. We were fascinated to see them stand and chant rituals at their prayer times. As soon as we had disembarked at Tel Aviv, they all rushed to the fast-processing section for Israelis, whereas we were directed to attend the slower processing of our passports as foreigners.

Ben and Violyn were there to meet us, and we all caught a *sheruit* (bus taxi) to Haifa. A friend of Ben's, Dominic Kambuga (from Tanzania) was going on holiday at the same time, and he offered us the use of his flat, so Ben and ourselves stayed there. Violyn's flat was not far away, right next to the first terrace at the top of Ben Gurion Avenue. She shared the flat with four other girls – Ildiko from Romania, Asha from Nepal, Jade from America, and Heidi, also from America. Only the last four days we had to stay in a guest house called the Port Inn.

We quickly settled in and soaked up the atmosphere. I went each day with Violyn to work on the Bahji Gardens – an early start to catch the bus for a 30-kilometre trip from the middle of Haifa to Bahji. Don assisted Ben with his maintenance work on staff houses and Baha'i buildings.

Immediate family members can stay there for a month, whereas people on pilgrimage were there for only three or nine days. It was such a privilege to come at this time, as there were no pilgrims because of the imminent war, and we were the only family visitors for most of the time. It was just us – and all the staff. We had an amazing time and did things that most volunteer workers had to wait for years. We just loved every minute of it. We felt like we had been here for years. Everyone, from members of the Baha'i Universal House of Justice (UHJ), to all the cleaners and gardeners, spoke very highly of Ben, and we seemed to have some special position in their mind because we were his parents. We also enjoyed getting to know his girlfriend, Violyn, from the Solomons. Her father was the first Baha'i in the Solomon Islands. She had come to work here as a gardener after doing a year of service at the Temple in Samoa

The custodians of the House of 'Abdu'llah Pasha, Dinya and Mehru Mehrshahi, invited us for breakfast and gave us a private tour – a grand old building attached to the prison in Acre. It was built initially as a residence for the Governor – 'Abdu'llah Pasha. After the passing of Baha'u'llah, 'Abdu'l-Bahá rented part of the building for his growing family. The remains of the Bab were kept here until they were placed in their present location. Shoghi Effendi was born here. Also, at breakfast were two men (father and son from Canada) working on the re-creation of the gardens in the walled outdoor compound. It was a bleak, windy, wet day, and the sea was spraying over the sea wall of old Acre. We walked past the prison cell where Baha'u'llah was first imprisoned, (Ben had the job of re-roofing the prison cell and doing other renovations to it) and afterwards wandered through old Acre, where time seems to have stood still for several centuries.

We went to an 'Ayyam-i-ha party in the House of Abbud. All the Northern Gardens staff were there and we had a really fun time sharing small gifts.

The day before the fast, we had brunch with Peter and Janet Khan in his home with Chris and Mike Day and Maryam Bell and Violette Haake and her husband, and Ben and Violyn.

We were invited to a wedding held at the Pilgrim Reception

Centre – a girl, called Noora from Alaska marrying a man called Roel from the Philippines. The Filipino community organised the wedding, and it was exquisitely beautiful with singing and dancing.

We went with fifty people picking up stones on the shores of the Sea of Galilee – for the paths in the gardens. This is quite a rare event, and some people have waited years for the chance to do this, so we felt quite privileged. It was such a tranquil and happy day watching the fishing boats weave their way purposefully across the sea, bringing memories of the old bible stories – it was hard to realize that the Golan Heights was only a few kilometres away.

Many people invited us for tea and we had many interesting evenings with our friends from the World Centre –

Chris and Mike Day and their son George invited us to their home – they are really settled there and enjoying their new roles: Chris with the development of a Baha'i culture and the concept of developing a Baha'i Community; and Mike with the development of a Baha'i internet news service. George cleans the steps on the terraces.

Bruce and Elham Saunders invited us for tea – with Andrew and Melinda Blake and also Behrooz Behboodi.

Others who invited us for evening meals were Ben's boss Wolfgang and his wife Mae, Dr Firaydoun Javaheri and his wife Vida (also there were Mr Kiser Barnes and his wife Nancy who think of Ben as their son – maybe because he has befriended so many African people while working there), Soheila and her husband Christopher from WA (Soheila works for the SED Dept and Christopher has been employed to do an ecological plan for the gardens), Betty Wee who is the secretary for the Works Dept – a bright soul from Singapore – we had some fun table games with her and enjoyed the view from her balcony that overlooked the terraces.

We also managed to join in with the last three-day pilgrimage in a tour of the Arc buildings. The majesty and quiet dignity of these buildings is quite overwhelming, and like many buildings in Haifa, they are set into the side of the steep slopes of Mt. Carmel, some going many stories underground.

We chose to go to work each day: Don to the workshop with Ben while I went with Violyn to the Bahji gardens. My job was to weed around the Shrine of Baha'u'llah. I took the last hour off to go to the shrine – sometimes I was the only one there as there were few tourists and no visitors or pilgrims. I was able to visit the Shrine of the Bab and 'Abdu'l-Baha several times and again have sometimes been on my own. I made a point of remembering each member of our families while I was there in the Shrine. The gardens have quite a profound effect on you – they are so exquisitely beautiful – and working there, you begin to realize the enormous task of maintaining them.

Don went with Ben on his various maintenance jobs. One thing Ben had to do was to make a room in each staff residence sealable, in case there was a gas attack on Haifa, with war threatening. Don was impressed by the way the Works Department started each day with a 'Toolbox' session. All staff, at all levels, would meet to say prayers, share information (e.g. that there had been a car accident and so everyone should avoid that area), arrange tasks (e.g. the electrical crew would need to go to some place, and the plumbers to another location, or that priority is for preparation for a particular event). But before all that, there was an open session during which people could raise issues or share whatever was on their mind. On occasions, someone mentioned a dream they'd had, and Ben got a reputation for being an interpreter of dreams – with some witty explanation that fancied everyone.

I attended a revue of the Cluster and the Institute process around the world by Dr Arbab and Dr Javaheri. I was really interested in the points raised. The UHJ has asked for everyone to support the institute process even if they don't wish to participate for whatever reason. Around the world, the use of the Ruhi books have been highly successful as initiators of self-sustaining growth and extension into the wider community. Their purpose is not that of passive education or deepening but as springboards for spiritual growth and action. There is not a single 'Ruhi Method' – all the methods used are in the writings, memorising, working in pairs etc. It is not intended to be rigidly fixed to operate in a certain way, but that a degree of flexibility is needed with different groups. I asked this question as I was previously treated almost as a heretic for suggesting that it would need some change of format to work with aboriginal people, particularly in remote communities. They liked to work in bigger groups and liked to say the passages all together etc.

It came to my mind afterwards that for some twenty years there has been a strong exploratory approach to developing the Ruhi books. And now that process has stopped. I wondered whether some of the problems which seem to have largely been connected with a degree of blind rigidity in implementing the Ruhi books could be resolved by having, at least at some level, a degree of exploratory initiative that would help it grow further and keep it alive – this, of course, would need to be done with great respect for the enormous effort that has already been put into it. So it was encouraging, for me, to hear that Dr Arbab and Dr Javaheri were making it clear that there was no single 'Ruhi Method'.

Another point raised was regarding the clusters. The whole cluster process needs to have an outward focus and be free of the demands of formal decision-making. The cluster meetings should "raise awareness of possibilities and generate enthusiasm", "reflect on experience gained, share insights, explore approaches, and acquire a better understanding of how each can contribute to achieving the aim of the Plan" (Letter to the Baha'i World 17th Jan 2003). They should end up with a calendar of activities that are to be done individually or collectively. These are not necessarily voted on as in the formal LSA meeting. For example, an individual might say they want to pursue a particular initiative. Unless it is outlandish in some way, it is written up as one of the activities. Others might offer help and suggestions but can't veto that person's idea simply because they don't like it. The role of the LSA is to support these initiatives and only interfere if they see something that is obviously detrimental or needs some guidance. An atmosphere should be created where there are no right and wrongs, no one better than anyone else. They also emphasized that growth happens very quickly when individuals or communities take charge of their own growth using their own initiatives and the institute process, and don't rely on others. Examples were given of this in the rural areas of Kenya. This doesn't mean you don't get help or ask for advice or welcome the assistance of others but it is an attitude of mind that assumes responsibility for its own growth process. The next requirement is to increase the intensity of effort.

We also went to a talk by David Walker on microfinancing in Nepal and later had lunch with him and discussed some of these issues, in regard to aboriginal communities. His method, which is in its early stages of trial, is simply a process that is set up under small committees and the rules are set to begin with but then can be changed as the needs of the group change. It is also combined with literacy programmes that have a strong spiritual and ethical component based on the writings of Baha'u'llah. There is no management structure above this, as in the Grameen Bank. Quite interesting! In its early stages yet! Don was trying to compare it with his efforts to set up structures in our small community at Blackstone to assist people with managing their finances. He felt this method probably wouldn't work with aboriginal people in Australia as they get so much assistance from the government.

We also met with Mr. Hartmut Grossmann, a Counsellor, and on the International Teaching Committee. We had some paintings from our LSA to donate to the International Teaching Centre. He was more interested in talking with us about where we had come from and our experiences. He shared some of his experiences with indigenous people in Northern Europe.

We later met with Paul Lample. We talked about some of the projects we had been involved in. He very kindly gave us a simple focus for the future – begin small and simple, keeping the focus in the right perspective; awaken the spirits of people not just establish methods and structures.

I also met with Violette Haake and spent several hours with her. She wanted to get a more intimate view of teaching work with aboriginal people, so I shared with her some of my experiences.

The Birth of the Bab and Baha'u'llah were celebrated here during the Fast, on the 5th and 6th March – according to the Lunar Calendar. Both were celebrated at the Seat of the UHJ.

We also spent three days travelling to other places in Israel with Ben and Violyn, two of the Solomon Island workers, Betty and Susie, and Adelo, Ben's flat-mate. Our first stop was the Dead Sea (yes – you do float on it – 35% salt), visiting the En Gedi Kibbutz and Field School, where people come from all over the world to study desert environments.

We climbed the Wadi David riverbed, which is in a nature reserve, and were amazed at the volume of water cascading down the dry mountainside – used to irrigate the date palms and citrus orchards. We had an interesting discussion with a long-time member of the Kibbutz, originally from Germany. She said that En Geddi was the only Kibbutz in Israel still operating in the original community style, but that it was on the verge of breaking down as had happened elsewhere. People now wanted to work for salaries, and the communal spirit was being lost. They were becoming more like commercial farms.

We also visited Massada, an ancient city built on the top of a high flat-topped mountain. It was originally a retreat for King Herod but later used as a last place of refuge for the Jews who were in revolt against Rome around 60 AD. They finally killed themselves rather than become slaves to the Romans. The story has gathered momentum in recent times with the Jews returning to Israel, and a large archeological research project has revealed the historical evidence of this place. It has become a symbol of the Jewish spirit and a popular tourist spot.

We then travelled down to Elat on the Gulf of Aqaba on the Red Sea. Here we went on a cruise that took us to the coastal waters of Jordan, Arabia, Egypt and Israel and also to view the underwater reefs through the glass bottom of the boat. Violyn and Ben went camel riding. We slept out on the desert sand for one night, cooking our tea over a fire (found an old wooden pellet on the ground that we used for wood) and singing and sharing stories. The journey down and back through the Negev – barren, desolate lower half of Israel – was interesting, with many date palm plantations and hundreds of plastic-covered greenhouses. The surrounding land had not a single blade of grass on it.

Even though there was a nasty incident while we were in Hiafa, with seventeen people killed on a government bus by a suicide bomber, the most dangerous part of being there, as far as we were concerned, was crossing the road – the traffic overspilled the roads and seemed to have a mind of its own – cars were parked all over the footpaths as the high-rise flats often had no parking space provided. There seemed to be continual beeping of horns and sirens. The streets winding up the mountain were often very narrow. We adhered to the general principle for the staff at the world centre not to go in crowded areas. Security was everywhere, even at the Baha'i Gardens, but you get used to it. We found the Israeli people to be friendly but very aware of the need to defend their country. We could feel a vibrant atmosphere there that was full of hope for the future. All youth, men and women, do several years of training as soldiers. Around Haifa, Jews and Arabs live very peacefully together.

The last day, while Don worked at the Bahji gardens with Violyn and Ben (Ben took some holidays from his normal work while we were there), I went to the Garden of Ridvan to teach Gole calligraphy. Feruz and Gole are the custodians of the Ridvan Garden. She had been wanting to learn for a long time and had no one to learn from. We also had some lovely walks around the garden.

We sadly left Ben and Violyn at the Tel Aviv airport, and after about two hours of going through security checks where Don nearly lost his toothpaste and his boots, we finally left for Bangkok.

Thailand

This was the closest we have ever experienced to a luxury holiday. We were picked up at the airport by a private taxi and taken to the Royal Princess Hotel – a five-star hotel in Old Bangkok, where a doorman waits on you and every service is offered. It was still about half what you would pay to stay in an ordinary motel in Australia. The economies are on entirely different levels.

We booked in for a number of tours which gave us a taste of Buddhist temples, the Royal Palace, ancient cities, craft industries, floating markets, and Thai entertainment and food. However, we also took off on our own several times, walking through the streets, catching government buses, river taxis and open motor-bike taxis. We found this to be just as interesting as the formal tours. It was quite remarkable to see the way people lived, and mostly with dignity, in such a crowded city. Even the traffic, with its large number of motorbikes and open taxis as well as ordinary taxis, it moved along in a complex way but peacefully with little horn-beeping. We fell in love with the people who were kind, respectful and very courteous at all levels of society. They had a great respect for their king and queen and 96% are Buddhist.

We finally managed to get in touch with the Baha'is of Thailand and Iman Brentnall – our friend from Alice Springs who works in a Baha'i School at Yasathon – about eight hours by bus from Bangkok. We decided to spend our last three days visiting him. It was a long overnight ride on the bus. We arrived at 5 am and were taken to the school by bike taxis. There is room for just one person on the back where there is a seat with a cover over it – like a pram. The man sits in front and rides you to your destination. Iman was there to meet us.

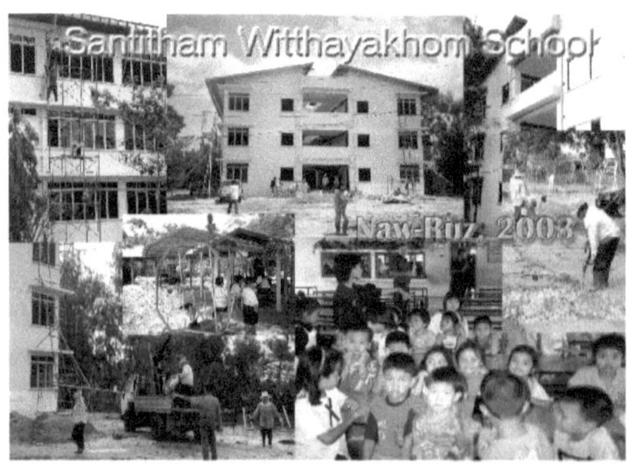

The time at the school – just two days – was the highlight of our time in Thailand. The first day was the last day of the Fast and we joined in that evening for devotions and then a Naw-ruz Feast at a local café. We met Nawarat and Naiyana Wongsopa, who have managed the school as principal and administrator for ten years. The school was started by Minoo's mother, Shirin Fozdar. They were such loving, humble people and dedicated to the school. The number of children at the school is now 700. They all seemed to be very happy and to enjoy their school. They take the children from two and half years because so many families need both parents to work. A new wing had just been built there – the builders fascinated us with their simple bamboo scaffolding going up the three-storeys where painters and others scrambled up and down. They had built this concrete building with no more than an ordinary concrete mixer – there was no other mechanized equipment. They were like a big extended family, and everyone worked, old and young, living in tiny, temporary tin-roofed huts next to the building.

The next day was the last day of the school year and also a celebration for Naw-ruz. We joined them in the open-sided meeting hall where they had singing and a festive lunch. Some of the classrooms are still thatched huts with open walls.

We busied ourselves by tidying up an area of garden that had been used as a dumping ground for rubbish, for which, no more than a few hours work, people seemed to be everlastingly grateful.

We had some interesting talks with Nawarat about his ideas for the development of the school. They are trying to lift the level of education and have a strong component in moral development. They play uplifting songs in the playground, and around the gardens are hung the human virtues in Thai and English – like truthfulness, kindness etc.

We left on the bus that night, the 21st March, with several members of the Baha'i community who were going into Bangkok for an NSA and other meetings. The auxillary board member, Gole Jafari, drove us to the bus.

The following day we had the privilege of meeting with most of the NSA members of Thailand, Mrs Atchara Walton, Mr Nasser Jafari, Mr Chaiwat, Yaowa Papong, Mrs Nida Starr (her husband is Mark Starr from Australia), Mrs Sunantha Smith, Mr

Edward Chang and Nawarat Wongsopa.

We felt very much at home in Thailand, but it was time to leave, and we were looking forward to meeting up with the family again in Australia.

Joe was there to meet us, and the family had gathered to welcome us back and say farewell to Joe, who was leaving on the 27th March. I then took Don back to the airport, and he set out for Brisbane that same night to visit his family there. The next few days, we spent getting Joe organized for his trip, which takes him to Thailand with his work and then around the world visiting friends and working in many countries.

Where will it end?? Who is next?? Wherever – there is no doubt that "the earth is one country and mankind its citizens".

..ooOOoo..

13

Back in the city

in Kelmscott 9 years from 2012 to 2021

Written by Don

They moved from Tom Price when Don retired in 2011 and settled down to suburban life after four decades out bush.

Initially, Don and Helen spent a month with their son Joe and his wife, Amica, who were coordinating an educational project in Lae in Papua New Guinea, and then, for three months, with their other son, Ben, who lived in a small village in the Solomon Islands for a decade with his wife, Violyn, and their children. Helen worked with the women to produce paper earrings.

After returning from the Solomons, Helen stayed with her mother, Mavis, for some months while Don went to Kununurra and Halls Creek for relieving work.

They purchased 20 Turner Place in Kelmscott in March 2012. This was a four-bedroom house and two-bedroom granny flat, on 1¼ acres. This property had similar features to what they had enjoyed in Narrogin – a creek and paddock, in a rural setting.

A few months later, Mavis came to stay with Helen because of declining health. Helen nursed her until she died there, in the beginning of 2013.

In 2014, Ben and his family moved from the Solomons to Perth – for the education of their three children. They lived in the 'Rose Cottage' granny flat on the Turner Place property for three years. In 2018, they purchased their own property close by in Seville Grove.

Baha'i activities

This was Helen's first experience of living in an area where there was a strong Local Spiritual Assembly. She tutored several Ruhi study circles and conducted several public workshops (including *Noble Have I Created Thee*). Some Baha'i celebrations were held at Turner place – including pony rides in the paddock.

Arts & crafts

Helen was secretary of the Armadale Society of Artists (ASA) in a time when the organization was undergoing major transitions. She exhibited about four times a year with different exhibitions through the ASA, including a pop-up shop.

Helen participated in a plein air painting group and with another art group. This presented her with opportunities to experiment with other art styles. Don said she produced some of the best that she has done. In particular, she developed a method of watercolour painting on wood[21] – this enabled the colours to be more vivid and did not have to be framed behind glass.

She conducted several art and craft workshops for children and for adults.

Helen completed a course in Art Therapy – a subject that has always interested her.

She undertook some short-term community arts projects in the Pilbara and out on the Ngaanyatjarra Lands.

---

[21]   How to paint with watercolours on wood – Chapter 28

In April and May 2016, Helen was invited by Nintirri (a community organization in Tom Price) to work with indigenous people at Wakuthuni to produce crafts that could be sold at the Karijini Experience. This was a week of festivities of cultural

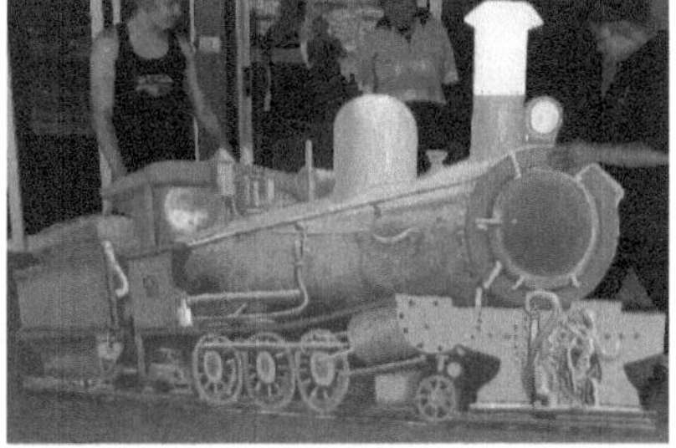

activities at the Karijini National Park. She also painted the stage sets for a play called *The Spinifex Train*, which was developed in Tom Price for the festival.

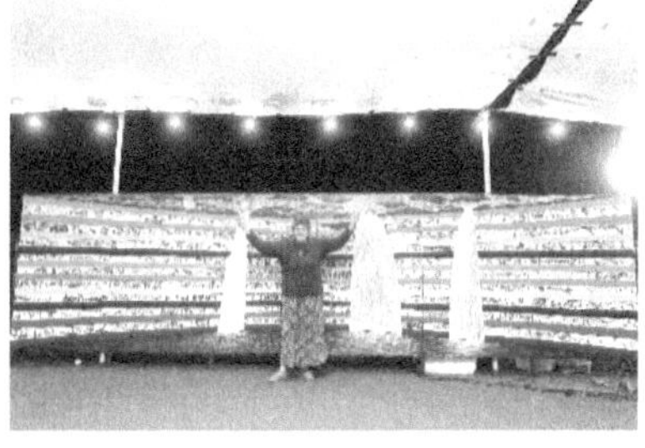

In May 2017, Helen was the community artist for the Karijini Festival Experience again. This time she produced a collective artwork some seven metres long and 3 metres high, involving about 150 people.

In mid-2017, Helen returned to the desert to arrange a community mural in the remote Indigenous community of Jameson while Don relieved staff at Jameson and Blackstone. The huge mural was 40-metres long by 3-metres high, on the side of the community store, with sixty aboriginal people working with Helen[22].

Helen and Maya-Rose Chauhan arranged for about twenty-five friends, musicians, singers and composers to share. 'an afternoon of music to cheer the heart and uplift the soul'. This was in her home in November 2017.

---

[22] Helen described how she conducted the Jameson community mural project – Chapter 32.

Histories

Helen always said that we all should live in the present – not the past or the future – and she did not share Don's enthusiasm for family history. However, in later years she took an interest in recording some aspects of the development of the Baha'i Faith in Western Australia. This started as she was gathering stories of the experiences of isolated believers throughout Australia when she was producing the *Bush Honey*. In 2015, she recorded her own experiences[23], and also arranged for her Narrogin diary[24] to be placed in the National Archives. She took this a step further when she compiled histories of the Pilbara, Kimberleys and the Southwest, as well as with indigenous people[25].

Around this time, four half-century reunions were arranged by friends from her school days, university, occupational therapy and St Andrews. This timing was wonderful because Helen's health would have prevented her participation if these reunions had been held a little later. It was a reminder of her deep friendships that had endured over all those years.

..ooOOoo..

---

[23] Transcript of Helen's recoding of her experiences as a Baha'i – Chapter 25.

[24] A diary of Baha'i activities in Narrogin has been lodged with the NSA Archives - and Don has a copy.

[25] Don has copies of Helen's notes on the development of the Faith in the Pilbara, Kimberleys, Southwest, and indigenous people.

14

Final years

Activities between intermittent illness

Three years prior to Helen's passing in July 2021

Written by Don

In 2017, for the reunion of Occupational Therapy students, Helen wrote: *At 72 and in good health, I am so grateful for a life so filled to the brim with so many opportunities … … and hopefully, God willing, my journey isn't over just yet.*

As things worked out, it was only five months later that the first indications of cancer were detected.

At the time it was detected, she had no symptoms of cancer, but Helen suffered severe side effects as soon as she started chemo-therapy. Her aversion was due to a rare condition.

She died three years later, but in between further unsuccessful treatments, she was able to do some of her best artwork and Baha'i activities. And she enjoyed special times with the family and many friends. Helen died without pain at home with her husband and three children holding her hands on 3rd July 2021.

Now, to look back over those three years to see how it all unfolded.[26]

---

[26] Don has a detailed record of her illness over the three years, and visits from friends in last six months.

The first indication that anything was wrong was in April 2018 when Helen felt some abdominal discomfort which she thought was food poisoning after a meal at a food-hall the night before. However, the GP suspected appendicitis which, after a test, proved to be the case. Appendicitis is most common in children but can also occur in adults. She went to the Armadale Hospital, and it was decided that she should have an appendectomy straight away. She was transferred to RPH and had a successful laparoscopic (keyhole) operation the next day.

This might have been the end of it, but a month later, Dr Rao asked her to come into RPH for an outpatient appointment. Helen thought this was just for a routine follow-up to confirm that the appendectomy was successful. However, Dr Rao explained that it was normal practice to check when doing the appendectomy, and this had indicated some cancer. Further tests revealed an adenocarcinoma on the ileocaecal valve and three small defined spots on the liver. Dr Rao recommended surgery.

The surgery, in July, was successful, however, chemotherapy was recommended as an 'insurance' – a precaution in case there were still some cancer cells that were too small to show up in the tests. This was arranged with Dr Kibaru at Fiona Stanley Hospital as an outpatient. It started in August 2018 and was intended to run for eight cycles.

After the very first treatment of chemo, Helen's body reacted so badly she was hospitalized for four months and could not eat. She became very weak and was close to death.

She was discharged by the end of 2018 but was still frail, and it took a few more months before she was strong enough to go for walks and eventually some swimming. She was beginning to be able to resume most of her normal activities.

She was well enough, in the middle of 2019, to spend two weeks in Darwin with Joe and his family.

A year after the initial treatment, she was able to face another series of cycles – this time at lower dosages. This started in August 2019. She ended up with eleven cycles over the next year or so – with further tests and stops and starts because of the side effects.

The second treatment was in October, and three more in the next two months.

Helen's treatments were interrupted in December when a cupboard fell on her leg. She had been in grand-daughter Jasmine's bedroom, where the little girl had stepped inside the drawer of the cupboard, and it toppled down and gouged a wound out of Helen's leg. She required hospitalization for two days, and she took a while to recover.

Treatment was resumed at the end of January 2020 and continued for four more cycles in February and March.

The side effects were still of concern, and there was a break of seven months. During this time, Helen felt well and very active, walking several kilometres every day, occasionally swimming, and undertaking many normal activities.

She was quite productive with some good painting being produced and was entering these for sale at the ASA pop-up shop at the Armadale shopping centre. She ran some workshops on watercolours on wood.

Helen had many phone conversations to support to James Gibson in Narrogin, and Gabielle McGuire in Balgo.

Although she was feeling better, the experience of such a serious illness prompted her to prepare for her passing. Around this time, Don and Helen went to the Pinaroo Cemetery to select a burial plot and to design a burial plaque.

In October and November, Helen had her tenth and eleventh cycles.

She continued to experience the persistent side effects, in varying intensities, of pain, diarrhea, nausea, hair loss, skin peeling, tiredness, poor appetite and loss of weight. It was decided to suspend treatment, and review this after the next test.

Despite these side effects, in December, Helen was still going for walks or the swimming pool most days. She was active with her art work. Remarkably, she was running four study circles and was a participant in a fifth. These naturally came to completion at the Christmas break, with the thought that others would start again in the new year. However, within weeks her condition deteriorated.

Periodic tests had been showing that the cancer had spread but not quickly. It seemed that the present treatment was retarding the cancer, but not stopping it. Alternative treatments were considered but rejected.

A marked change was evident in January when tests showed the cancer had grown considerably. Helen was experiencing more pain, was eating small meals, and had lost weight. The cancer, rather than the side effects of the chemo treatment, was taking its toll. Helen became noticeably weaker and only moved between her bed and the lounge room – and could not easily leave the home. Dr Kibaru arranged for Silver Chain palliative care to start. Initially, they visited every week or so.

Helen accepted that she was not going to get well again. She was not fearful. It would have been more difficult if there had been some 'unfinished business' such as great difficulties or uncertainties with any of the children or grandchildren. But Helen was confident that life was working out well for each of them. Probably her steadiness helped those around her to accept her inevitable death, even though this was not being spoken about directly.

Joe, Amica and their three boys came down from Darwin for three weeks in January, and the boys were able to spend time with their grandma while she was able to happily engage with them.

Helen arranged the details for her funeral service with Joe as the master of ceremonies, musical selections, and recorder performance.

She had written a final message, to be read after her death[27]: *Please make my funeral a joyful time with singing and music, laughter and happiness, and something beautiful.*

Helen did some study circle sessions (Book 8.3) with Ruth in January.

In February, at urging from Dr Manya Yazdani Zonozi, a friend, Helen decided to try chemotherapy yet another time – with another doctor, Dr Keeney at St John of God Hospital. In March and April, she had low doses for five cycles, but she was becoming weaker with the cancer.

At the end of April, Helen decided to stop all treatment– and to let nature take its course.

Joe and Amica stayed again (this time, without the boys) for the first two weeks of April.

During April, with Don's assistance, Helen arranged for the packaging of documents, photos and examples of art and crafts produced when Helen was at Blackstone. This 'Blackstone Collection' was sent to Thisbe Puric of NPY Women's Council in Darwin.

It was becoming clearer to everyone that Helen was getting weaker. Many friends made a point of visiting her, with the feeling that this might be their last opportunity to be with her. These visits were not somber – they were full of warmth and appreciation of all the good times that had been shared over the years. Elizabeth Hof, from school days, came on many occasions, and they

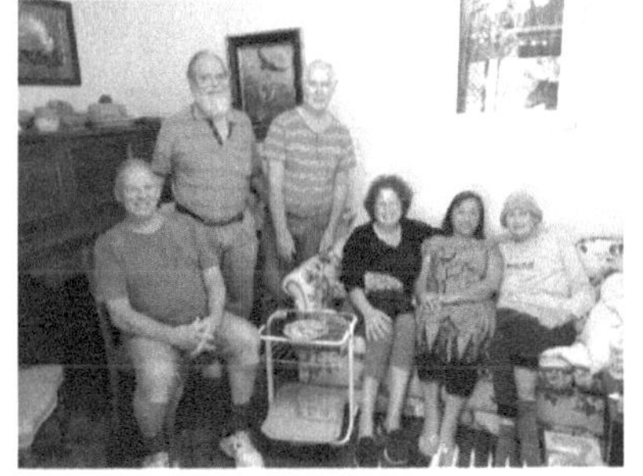

---

27 Final message held by Don.

watched movies together and chatted. There were visits by the occupational therapy students, notably Ronnie Naughton. And a friend from studying medicine, Annette Finn. Special friends travelled from afar and stayed with her a few weeks – Maxien Bradley from Queensland, and Mahshid Ferdowsian from Albany. Also, Verona Lucas from Fiji was in WA and visited her several times as well as having Zoom sessions. There were three visits by Glyn Marillier, who later played the recorder at the memorial celebration. Ruth's and Ben's families frequently visited. Helen's siblings Bev, Cyn, John and Russ gave a lot of support. And the nephews all visited. Many other friends visited in those last six months[28].

It was good that Helen was able to spend lovely times with family and friends, and she prepared herself and others around her for the inevitable.

One amusing occasion was on 1st May when Helen was invited to participate in a Zoom session for the 50th anniversary of the formation of the LSA of Dundee in Scotland in 1971. Dundee is next to St Andrews, where Helen was living and where she married Don in 1974. In thinking about the Zoom, because Helen was wearing a beanie when she was losing hair from the chemo treatment, she did not want to draw attention to the fact that she was ill. So she and Don decided to both wear beanies, and sit themselves up in bed for the Zoom – and explain that it was a cold night in Western Australia. They loved seeing and hearing friends from so long ago – especially Ronald Taherzadeh, who had officiated at their wedding.

Don and Helen updated their wills in the middle of May.

Mahshid stayed for the first two weeks of May, followed by Maxien for the last two weeks of May.

Joe came down from Darwin for a week at the end of May.

---

[28]   Friends who visited are listed on documents held by Don.

Silver Chain began coming more frequently. Their focus was on managing the pain. As Helen was becoming weaker, the nurses were coming more often. In May, they arranged for a hospital bed to be placed in the bedroom because she was getting very weak. Her GP, Dr Skellern, rang each week to check the pain medication was working okay.

On 1st June, Helen wrote a note: *My thinking is developing quite confidently with so much clarity … I am hoping to have sufficient mental energy to write down some of my thoughts. They are becoming crystal clear and every day endowed with more clarity and growing wisdom. My journey at the moment is very much defined by pain and energy levels.*

Up to June she managed to interact strongly with visitors, but she became markedly weaker in just her last three weeks. The Silver Chain nurse was coming about four times week to check on pain and give some bed baths. They would come again anytime if there were concerns.

It is significant that her last visitor was Joyce Drummond from Wakuthuni on 25th June. Her last phone conversation was with Maya Rose Chauhan on 28th June.

The family knew Helen did not have long, so Joe arranged to come. Because of the Covid restrictions, he had to obtain a special permit to travel from Darwin to Perth because Helen was in her last days.

On 3rd July, the nurse came in the morning. Helen was stable, but very weak. She could not talk much, but did not show any confusion.

Don wrote: *Joe caught his flight from Darwin about lunchtime, and I monitored the flight's progress and kept telling Helen: "He is leaving Darwin about now", and "Joe's flying over Kununurra now". "Half-way". "Joe has landed in Perth and will be here very soon". Helen could hear but couldn't fully respond. I think she might have been waiting for him. Ruth and Ben came and Joe arrived around tea-time. Helen had almost stopped her pain medication, and she showed some signs of a withdrawal reaction from the addictive morphine (she had such an episode a few months previously), and so I called the nurse back in the early evening to check. When the nurse arrived, she could see that Helen was very close to death. Without saying it, she gave me a look to indicate that it was time, and she said, "I will go into the other room and leave the family alone".*

All four of us held Helen's hands and quietly spoke to her. I said to Helen that it is so good that we are all together. I said to the children, "This is a special time. We will never forget this moment."

Helen died a quarter of an hour after the nurse had left the room. This was just two hours after Joe had got here.

Helen died in the evening of 3rd July 2021.

Her sisters and brothers came straight away.

On the death certificate, Dr Skellern recorded the cause of death as "Metastatic bowel cancer (months), Colon bowel cancer (years)."

Two days after Helen's passing, the Baha'is arranged a Zoom gathering[29] with 125 connections. Stories were shared by Mahshid Ferdowsian, Charmaine Burke, Violette Brentnall, Lorraine Inje and Lorraine Lobo and Shanks.

The funeral[30] was at Pinaroo on 14th July.

There were messages of condolence[31] from more than 100 individuals and families

A month later, a memorial-celebration[32] was held at the Armadale Town Hall. There with stories from Bev Thornton, Trish Halloran, Dianne Isgar, Lorraine and Andrew Shanks, Charlie Pierce and Mahshid Ferdowsian. And a poem by Ruth and a song by Ben.

---

[29] Bahai Zoom video and transcription – Chapter 18.

[30] Transcript of the funeral – Chapter 16.

[31] Condolences – these are held by Don.

[32] Memorial-celebration video and transcription – Chapter 17.

In the periods after her passing, several events were dedicated to her memory – a children's class in Armadale, an institute camp in Hedland, a meeting of the Armadale Society of Artists, and the Albany Summer camp. *The Helen Gordon Retrospective Exhibition* was held in Narrogin in August 2022.

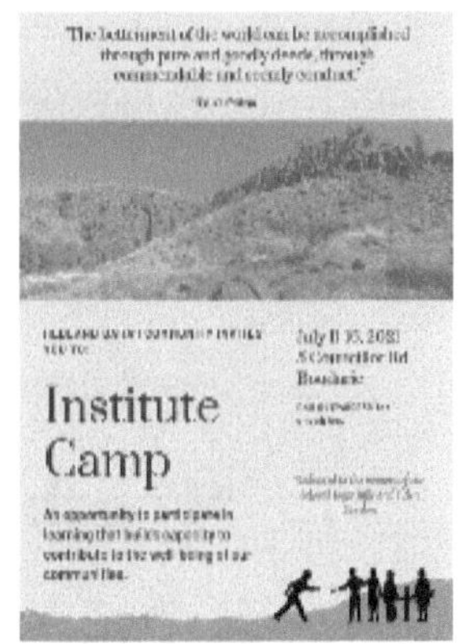

People were invited to send stories to Don, for inclusion in this book. These were sent by Maxien Bradley, Elizabeth Hof, Allison Stewart, Verona Lucas, Charmaine Burke, Ellie McLean, Maryam Bell, and Ronnie Naughton. Many others made contributions in so many ways.

..ooOOoo..

15

"For the love of Thy beauty"

Obituary in Feb 2022 edition of 'Australian Baha'i'

Written by Don

Helen Gordon, nee Mitchell, departed this world on 3 July 2021, after a vibrant life of 75 years.

Helen asked "For the love of Thy beauty" to be inscribed on her gravestone. This phrase was revealed by 'Addu'l-Baha in the context of those leaving their homelands to travel to teach the Faith. Helen pioneered to many parts of Western Australia – the Kimberleys, Pilbara, Great Southern and desert areas.

She was inspired by the beauty she saw all around her – in Baha'u'llah, the arts and in Aboriginal communities.

She brought these together in service with disadvantaged women and children through art and craft activities.

Helen wrote. "*I believe the artistic process is essential to the development of the human spirit. It can give birth to new thoughts and ideas, new ways of looking at the world, new perceptions; heal the wounded soul; be a channel for the creative mind; and, when directed towards a common purpose, become a strong force for the uniting of diverse peoples*". She equipped herself for this by undertaking training in occupational therapy and art therapy.

Her life was full of highlights. She grew up in Perth and embraced the Faith in 1970. This was in the early days of the Faith in WA and Helen served on the first Local Spiritual

Assembly in Perth.

She married Don Gordon when they were both on working holidays in Scotland. On returning to Western Australia. Helen was alongside her husband in his social work in Laverton, Derby and Kununurra. Helen also spent three months in Micronesia to assist in the election of the National Spiritual Assembly.

Then Helen and Don lived for two decades in Narrogin, where her three children grew up, followed by three years in the remote WA Aboriginal community of Blackstone and a decade in the mining town of Tom Price in the Pilbara. Her final decade has been in Kelmscott, Perth where, for the first time, she was part of a large Baha'i community rather than an isolated believer.

Helen promoted the Faith wherever she lived. She did this by tutoring Ruhi books and Baha'i activities, but mostly by the example of her life. She encouraged other isolated believers by visiting many in small country towns by telephone link-ups and newsletters – firstly "Bush Eagle" and then "Bush Honey" through the Outback Project.

She brought people together and enhanced personal growth by running activity groups, teaching in TAFE, setting up art centres and arranging community arts projects. This included murals and spinifex paper.

She also developed her own artwork. She explored ways of expressing complex concepts in a visual form, in how the arts can facilitate spiritual understanding and growth.

Her greatest joy was seeing beautiful development in the lives of her eight grandchildren and children Joseph, Ben and Ruth. All are active in the Faith.

An exhibition of Helen's arts and crafts will be held in Narrogin in July.

More information about Helen's life, service and Baha'i activities, may be found by writing to:

don.gordonl@hotmail.com.

Helen Gordon expressed her faith and shared it with others through her art, such as this piece she created a couple of years ago.

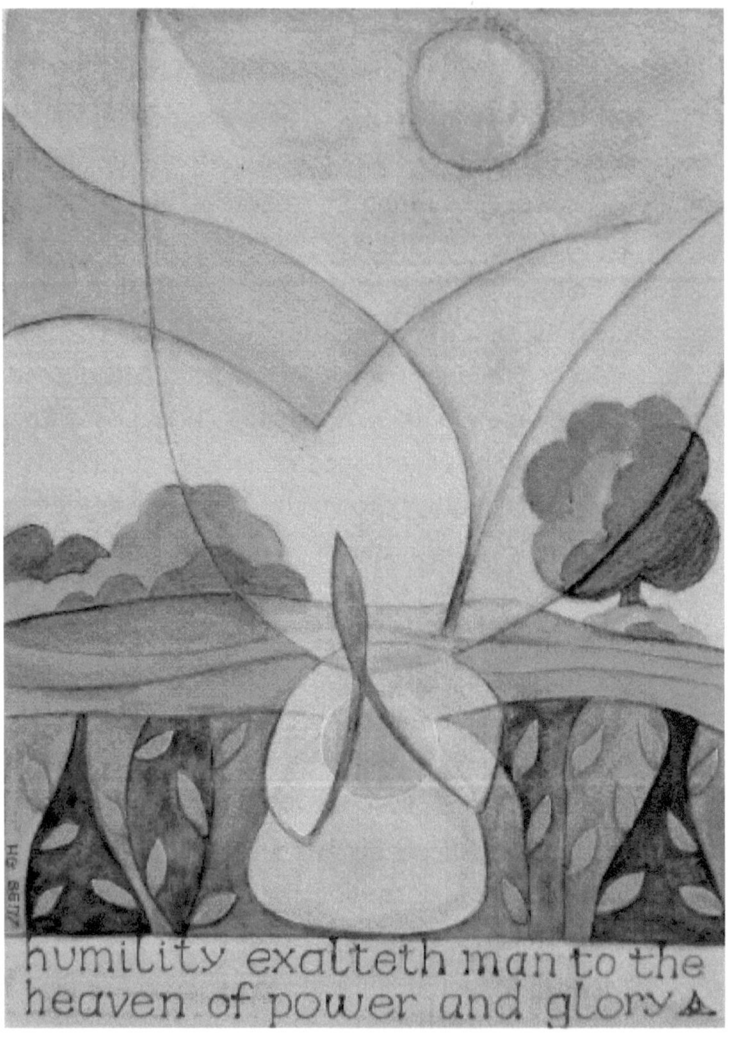

..ooOOoo..

Funeral of
Helen Gordon, nee Mitchell

Born 14th Aug 1945, died 3rd July 2021
Burial on 14th July 2021 at Pinnaroo Cemetery

View at https://etributes.seasons.com.au/etributes/helen-gordon

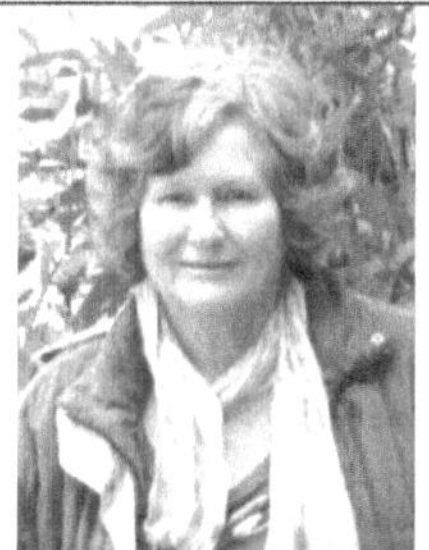

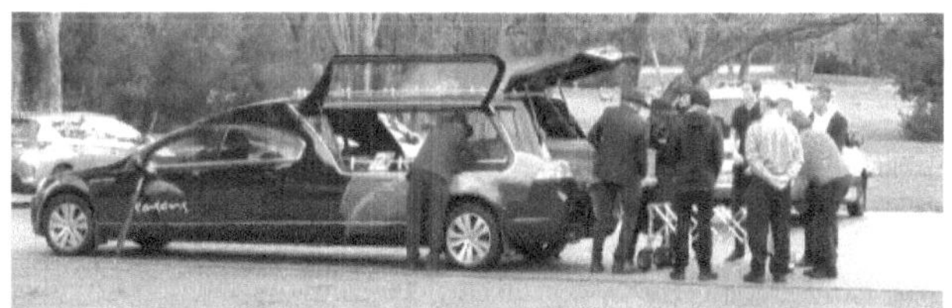

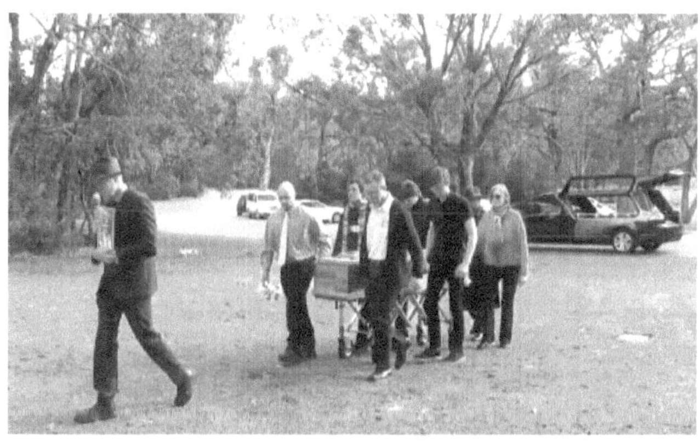

Introduction

MC: **Joseph Gordon** (son)

Dear Friends and Family, thank you for coming. Welcome, everyone.

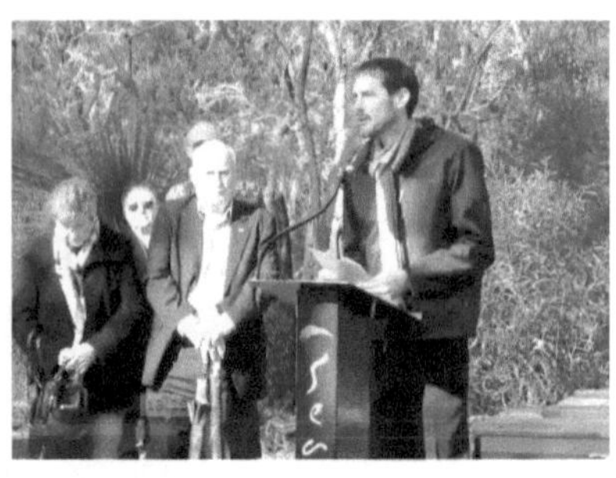

Today we gather to honour Helen; we will miss her dearly; she had so many beautiful qualities. I'm sure we have many stories we could share; she touched the hearts of many. Stories aside, we want this to be a time to reflect on our own memories of Helen, and the joy she brought us.

The ceremony will go for about an hour, if the weather gets bad, we'll need to shorten the program a bit, and if you need to run to your cars, by all means do so. There are extra umbrellas here if you need one, just remember to put them back when you're done.

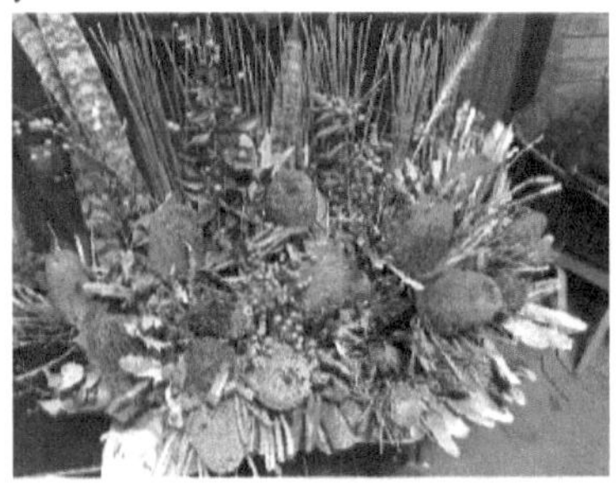

The ceremony will be very simple; there will be several songs and prayers played throughout, which Helen has chosen. And a few words from her husband Don and sister Cynthia.

At the end, a special prayer will be recited by Ben, which is one of the obligatory prayers to be recited during the Baha'i burial, and in which we will all need to stand for. The prayer will symbolise the end of the ceremony.

If weather permits, we plan to go the coffee shop here. You're, of course, all welcome to join us.

I'd would like to begin by acknowledging the Traditional Owners of the land on which we meet today and pay our respects to Elders past, present and emerging.

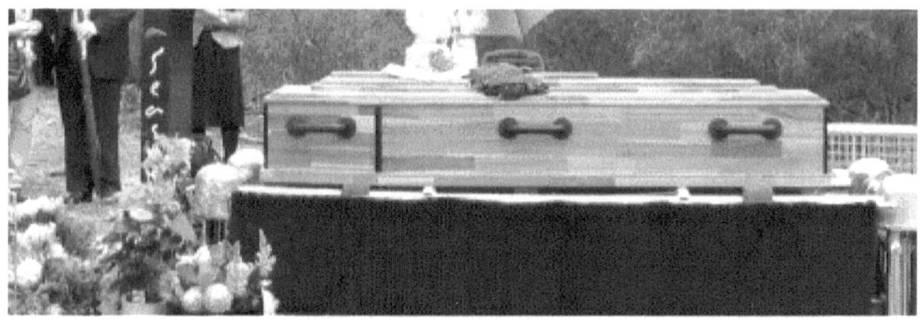

Message from Helen

Joe: Helen wrote this message for her funeral:

Helen's message: *I would like to thank you all for coming and hope this will be a time of happy memories. I have had a wonderful life, the most transformational moments being discovering the Baha'i Faith and marrying my husband, Don. We have three children, two strong boys, Joe and Ben and our daughter Ruth, who, to me, will*

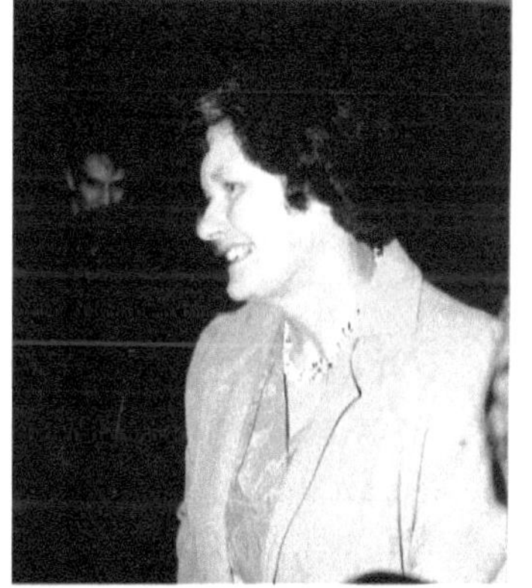

always be the most beautiful girl in all the world. They have all gone off the edge of my world and done incredible things with their lives, including bringing eight grandchildren into our lives. We have become a close extended family associating and assisting each other where we can.

I hope some of the music selected will bring joy to your heart, and maybe as you mingle together, you will find a new friend. I am sure we will meet again in the next world.

Much love to you all.

Joe: The piano piece you heard earlier is by Lisa Smith, a Baha'i friend, and it was one of Helen's favourite pieces of music to listen to in the evenings … just beautiful.

The next song which we would like to play is *Wind Beneath my Wings* by Bette Midler. Helen would like to dedicate this song to

Don, who has been such a hero in her life, and the wind beneath her wings.

After the song, Helen's sister Cynthia, will share some stories from their early childhood. This will be followed by Don, who will give a brief account of the years they shared.

Wind Beneath My Wings
Lyrics by Jeff Silbar and Larry Henley (Source: <u>LyricFind</u>),
Sung by Bette Midler

Oh, oh, oh, oh, oh.
It must have been cold there in my shadow,
To never have sunlight on your face.
You were content to let me shine, that's your way.
You always walked a step behind

So I was the one with all the glory,
While you were the one with all the strength
A beautiful face without a name for so long.
A beautiful smile to hide the pain

Did you ever know that you're my hero,
And everything I would like to be?
I can fly higher than an eagle,
For you are the wind beneath my wings.

It might have appeared to go unnoticed,
But I've got it all here in my heart.
I want you to know, I know the truth, of course I know it
I would be nothing without you.
Did you ever know that you're my hero?
You're everything I wish I could be.
I could fly higher than an eagle,
For you are the wind beneath my wings

Did I ever tell you you're my hero?
You're everything, everything I wish I could be.
Oh, and I, I could fly higher than an eagle,
For you are the wind beneath my wings

'Cause you are the wind beneath my wings,
Oh, the wind beneath my wings.
You, you, you, you are the wind beneath my wings.
Fly, fly, fly away, you let me fly so high.

Oh, you, you, you, the wind beneath my wings.
Oh, you, you, you, the wind beneath my wings.
Fly, fly, fly high against the sky
So high I almost touch the sky
Thank you, thank you.
Thank God for you,
The wind beneath my wings.

*****

Cynthia's speech – Cynthia Belonogoff is Helen's sister.
Joe: Cynthia is going to give an account of the early years of Helen's upbringing. Then dad will talk more about family life.

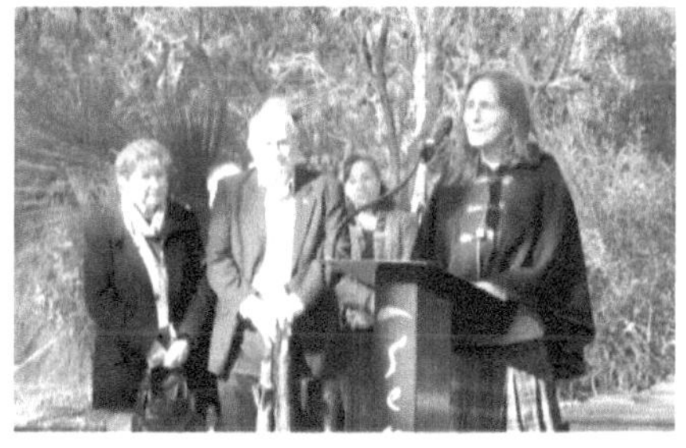

Cynthia: It's hard to encapsulate a person like Helen in a few minutes. My first memories of Helen were when I was a very small child. My older sister, Helen, had started school and she would come home, and she would teach me everything she'd learnt at school. She would have made a wonderful teacher, but Helen, from a very early age wanted to make people better, and she had wanted to be a doctor so she could make people better. She, in fact, started a medical degree but changed course part of the way through and became an Occupational Therapist but the aim was the same – to make people better.

If you believe in fate, then fate brought two Perth people together in, of all places, Scotland where Helen met her future husband Don, who was indeed the wind beneath her wings.

Helen was always a spiritual person, but struggled a little bit with conventional religion and was always looking to find her 'tribe' and she found this in the Baha'i community, a group of like-minded people, simple in their belief of God. Baha'u'llah believed that the whole earth was one country, and all the people were its citizens.

Helen, as the wife of a native welfare officer, I think it would be fair to say that she didn't just become part of that team but threw herself wholeheartedly into that, and there would be many people in the far-flung native communities who would remember her with great love, and she became life-long friends with many of them.

Helen was always meant to be a mother and became a mother to three gorgeous children who are a great credit to her.

I think it's also very true that she didn't just live her life through her children. She was a very talented artist, calligrapher and photographer and we are greatly blest to have reminders of her in all our homes.

We mourn greatly her passing, but we celebrate her life – a life well lived. A life of service to many people. She was just a beautiful, beautiful person.

I'll just finish with something the prophet Baha'u'llah said and that was – *"Do not be content with just showing friendship in words, embrace wholeheartedly all those you meet"*. That encapsulated Helen beautifully.

Goodbye, my dear sister. I will miss you terribly.

<u>Don</u>: Today is a time for reflection – not for a lot of words. Thank you, Cynthia for what you have said. It was lovely. I want to just add a few things.

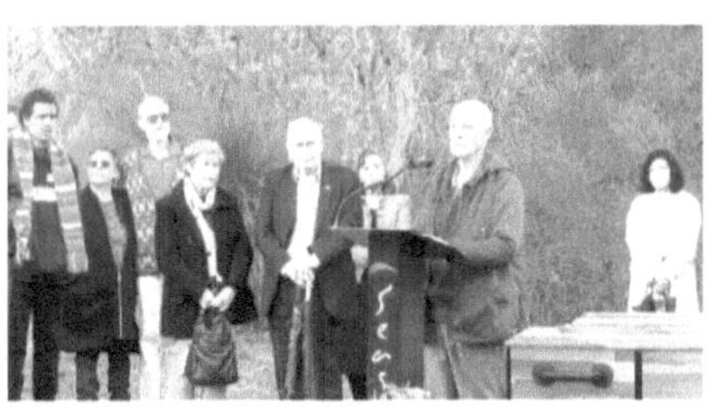

First of all, there will be an opportunity for more people to tell stories and to share experiences in a month's time when we have a memorial and celebration. That will be in the Armadale Hall, and it will be lovely then for people to have more time to freely express what they want to say in appreciation of Helen.

Helen had a wide range of deep friendships. She touched, and was touched by, the many ups and downs of people she became close contact with. These were enduring connections with friends from school days, from university and from occupational therapy. She has many friends among the Baha'is and artists. She was fortunate to engage with brave, resolute and noble aboriginal women in Blackstone, Tom Price, Hedland and Carnarvon. It is so good that many of you are here today and have made contact in recent days. One of Helen's many gifts to me has been in getting to know you all.

Helen's favourite animals are seals. Her favourite colour is mauve. Her favourite sport was ice skating (quite some time ago!). Her favourite flower is the desert rose. Her favourite places are Australian bushland and desert landscapes.

But there are four big things which energized Helen – her passions: our children, the Baha'i Faith, art and the community

First in her heart are our children. We are so happy for our three children, Ruth (with Colin), Ben (with Violyn), and Joe (with Amica). They have each found a place in life and are really contributing to the world around them. Nothing is ever easy, but they are successfully raising their children – our terrific eight grandchildren – Matthew, Hannah, Oirae, Weyburn, Jasmine, Luca, Dara and Kai.

The major force in her life is the Baha'i Faith. Helen expressed this in own words some years ago: *"After much painstaking investigation and reading and meeting with Baha'is from all over the world, I decided to become a Baha'i myself in 1970. I was immediately caught up in the only Local Spiritual Assembly in Western Australia at that time. There was a small but strong youth group – who would go singing Baha'i songs at various functions and were continually travel-teaching in country areas. I came to understand what the Baha'i Faith was, became deepened in my knowledge of the administration, and was nurtured and supported by the wonderful spirit of the Baha'is. It was sometimes difficult and painful, but mostly an exciting and rewarding journey into the world of the spirit and the processes of true human development. I have changed considerably and overcome many difficulties and set the course of my life in a totally different direction."*

(At this moment, in a back row, Weyburn fainted. He soon recovered.)

Thirdly, she was passionate for arts & crafts. Helen arranged for the words *"For the love of Thy beauty"* to be inscribed on her burial plaque which will be placed in the ground here. And Joe placed these wonderful words on her coffin that Ben made. Helen was skillful in a wide range of crafts, and she loved to distill complex projects into easy steps which others could learn and do things themselves – such as earrings, spinifex paper and jigsaws.

So, there we have it. So many things coming together. Helen was motivated towards the growth of our children, art, community and her Faith. These four passions were not separate. Each supported the other. Helen integrated them into the person she is – to create a great force – the wonderful person we admire, adore and honour today.

Dearest Helen.

<u>Joe</u>: Thank you, Dad and Cynthia, for those lovely memories. We now have a song and two Baha'i prayers selected by Helen.

The Holy City by Harry Secombe; this spoke true to Helen's belief in the Baha'i Faith.

Prayer for the Departed by 'Abdu'l-Bahá and sung by The Humming Birds choir. This starts with the words "O my God! O Thou forgiver of sins, bestowed of gifts, dispeller of afflictions!"

The final prayer is from *The Tablets of the Divine Plan*, written by 'Abdu'l-Baha to the Baha'is of Canada and Greenland. The prayer is titled to *The spreaders of the fragrances of God*.

The Holy City (The new earth)
Lyrics by Frederic E Weatherly, sung by Harry Secombe

Last night I lay asleeping,
There came a dream so fair,
I stood in old Jerusalem
Beside the temple there.
I heard the children singing,
And ever as they sang,
Methought the voice of Angels
From Heaven in answer rang:-
"Jerusalem! Jerusalem!
Lift up your gates and sing,
Hosanna in the highest
Hosanna to the King!"

And then methought my dream was chang'd,
The streets no longer rang,
Hush'd were the glad Hosannas
The little children sang;
The sun grew dark with mystery,

The morn was cold and chill,
As the shadow of a cross arose
Upon a lonely hill.
"Jerusalem! Jerusalem!
Hark! How the Angels sing,
Hosanna in the highest
Hosanna to the King!"

And once again the scene was chang'd,
New earth there seemed to be.
I saw the Holy City
Beside the tideless sea;
The light of God was on its streets,
The gates were open wide,
And all who would, might enter,
And no one was denied.
No need of moon or stars by night,
Or sun to shine by day,
It was the new Jerusalem!
That would not pass away.
"Jerusalem! Jerusalem!
Sing, for the night is o'er,
Hosanna in the highest
Hosanna evermore!"

O my God! O Thou forgiver of sins

O my God! O Thou forgiver of sins, bestower of gifts, dispeller of afflictions! Verily, I beseech Thee to forgive the sins of such as have abandoned the physical garment and have ascended to the spiritual world. O my Lord! Purify them from trespasses, dispel their sorrows, and change their darkness into light. Cause them to enter the garden of happiness, cleanse them with the most pure water, and grant them to behold Thy splendors on the loftiest mount.

By 'Abdu'l-Bahá, sung by The Humming Birds choir

O God, my God! Thou beholdest this weak one

O God, my God! Thou beholdest this weak one begging for celestial strength, this poor one craving Thy heavenly treasures, this thirsty one longing for the fountain of eternal life, this afflicted one yearning for Thy promised healing through Thy boundless mercy which Thou hast destined for Thy chosen servants in Thy kingdom on high. O Lord! I have no helper save Thee, no shelter besides Thee, and no sustainer except Thee. Assist me with Thine angels to diffuse Thy holy fragrances and to spread abroad Thy teachings amongst the choicest of Thy people. O my Lord! Suffer me to be detached from aught else save Thee, to hold fast to the hem of Thy bounty, to be wholly devoted to Thy Faith, to remain fast and firm in Thy love and to observe what Thou hast prescribed in Thy Book. Verily, Thou art the Powerful, the Mighty, the Omnipotent.

By 'Abdu'l-Bahá, revealed to the Bahá'ís of Canada.

Prayer

Joe: Could we all stand for a special 'Prayer for the Dead', which Ben will read. The prayer has two parts, the first part is said once and in the second part, each line is repeated nineteen times. After the prayer has finished, the coffin will be lowered and there will be two more songs by Nancy Ward to close the ceremony.

Thank you once again for coming. She has been surrounded by all the love that you have given her, and our family as well.

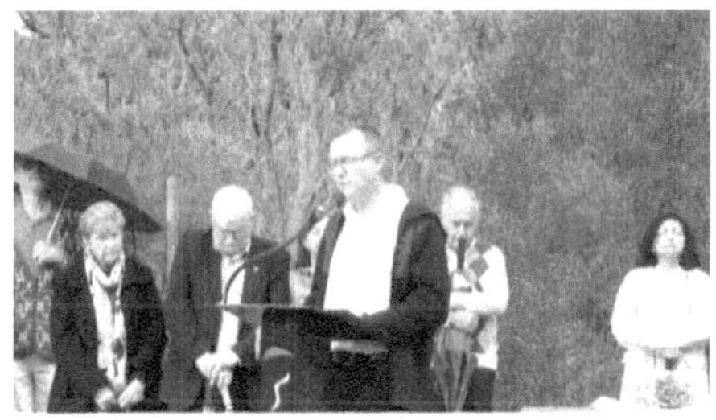

Ben: *O my God! This is Thy handmaiden and the daughter of Thy handmaiden who hath believed in Thee and in Thy signs, and set her face*

towards Thee, wholly detached from all except Thee. Thou art, verily, of those who show mercy the most merciful. Deal with her, O Thou Who forgivest the sins of mankind and concealest their faults, as beseemeth the heaven of Thy bounty and the ocean of Thy grace. Grant her admission within the precincts of Thy transcendent mercy that was before the foundation of earth and heaven. There is no God but Thee, the Ever-Forgiving, the Most Generous.

Alláh-u-Abhá (6 times),

We all, verily, worship God. (19 times)

We all, verily, bow down before God. (19 times)

We all, verily, are devoted unto God. (19 times)

We all, verily, give praise unto God. (19 times)

We all, verily, yield thanks unto God. (19 times)

We all, verily, are patient in God. (19 times)

By Bahá'u'lláh, read by Ben Gordon

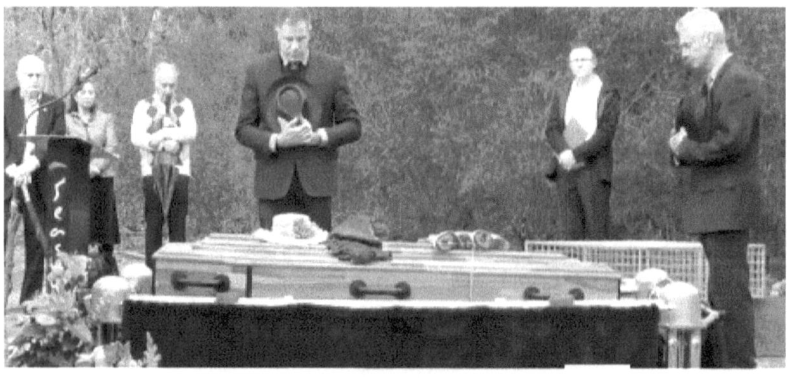

Planters of trees

Lyrics and sung Nancy Ward

In the last days, in the days of judgement, the Lord shall say to the planters of trees, "Come up, come up higher, your names shall be exalted. For while others were sleeping, you were labouring planting trees, and though the wine of the fruit is forbidden the faithful, the wine of the love of God shall flow for you"

Lyrics and sung Nancy Ward

Love revealeth, with unfailing limitless power the mysteries. Love revealeth the mysteries latent in the universe. Increase my astonishment.

..ooOOoo..

17

Memorial & Celebration

at the Armadale District Hall on 14th Aug **2021**

Helen Margaret Gordon, nee Mitchell
born 14th Aug 1945, died 3rd July 2021

View at https://1drv.ms/v/s!AkrT5JHAzTrTuUin6ulcTTb8MGN_?e=NA5QgI

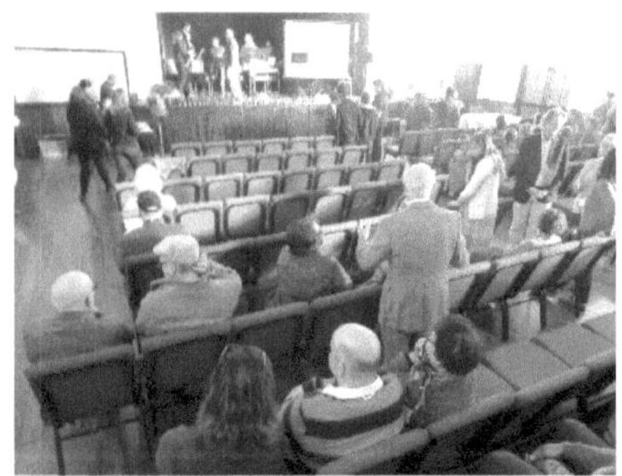

<u>Set-up</u>:

At one side of the stage, there was a screen for a slide show with photos to match some of the speeches, and it also showed many of Helen's paintings. Along the front of stage were about fifty seedling plants which people took home as mementos. There was a memorabilia table in an adjacent room. A feast of food which guests had brought was set out with a display of flowers. On the side walls were six large posters with photos of phases of Helen's life – early years, Scotland, family, outback, arts and Baha'i.

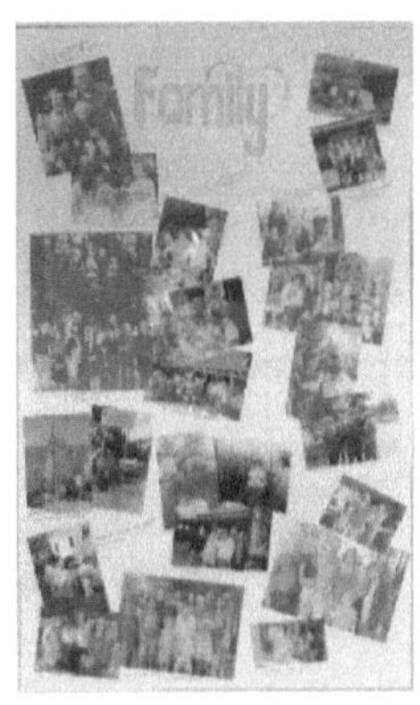
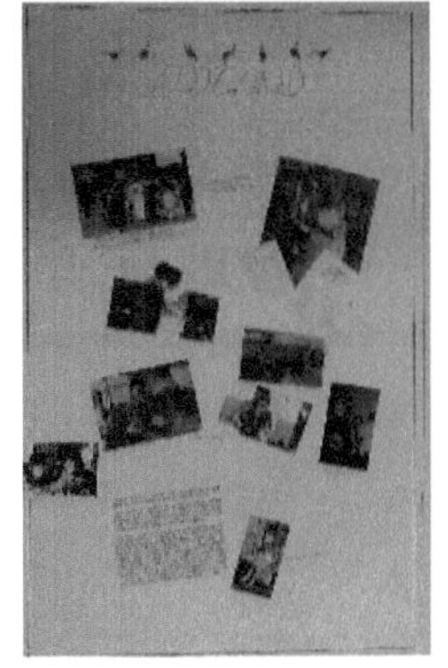
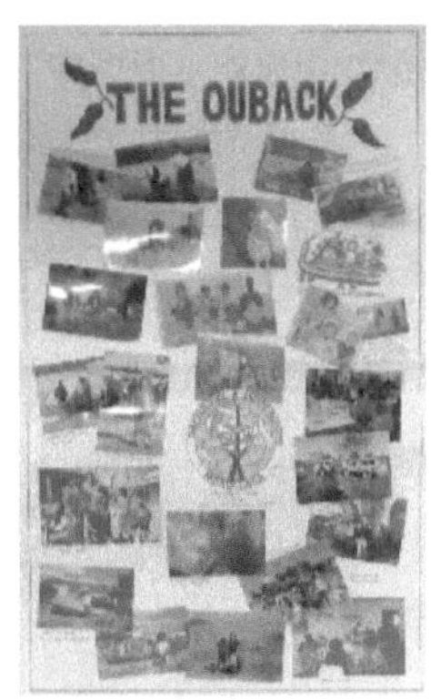

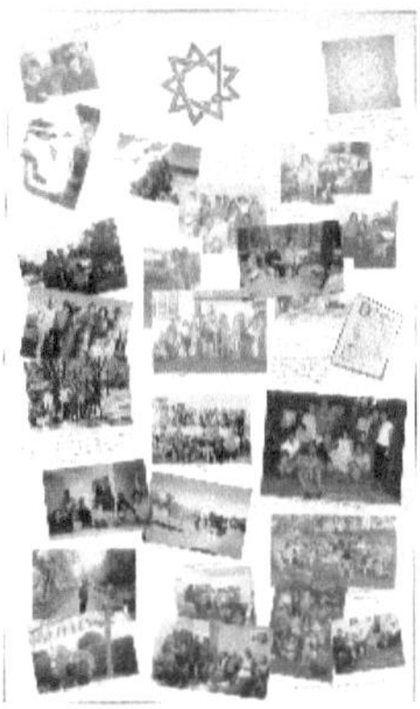
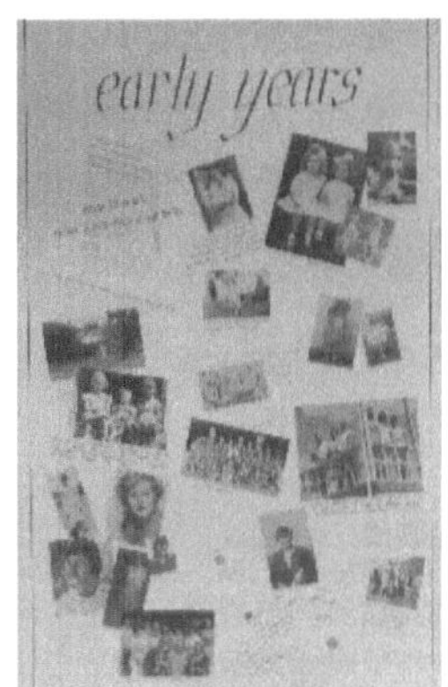
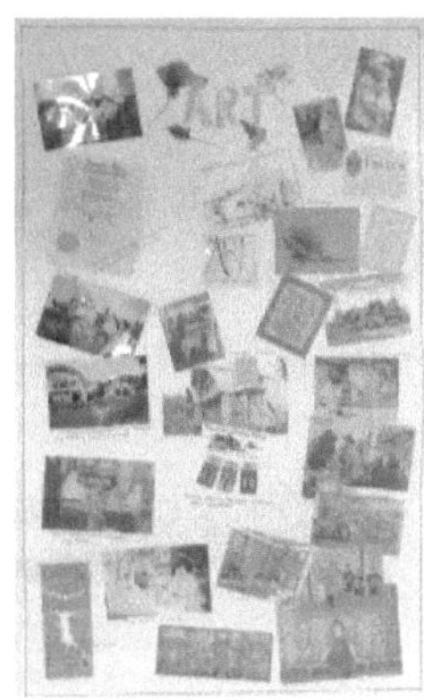

Welcome – by Joe (MC)

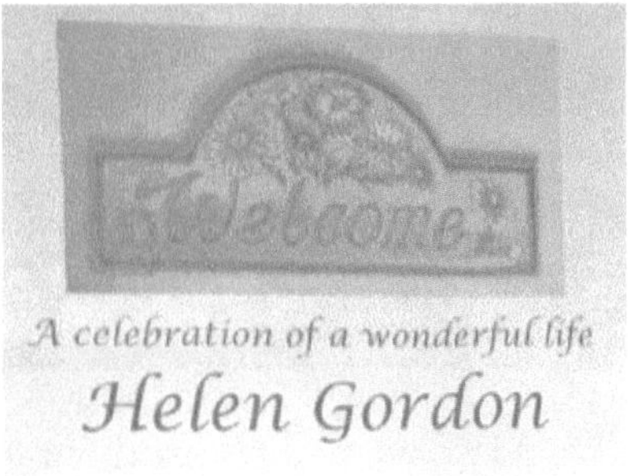

Joe: Welcome. It has been over a month now since Helen's passing. We all knew that that time would come but I certainly underestimated how much love surrounded her. And that has been expressed by the many kind words and continued support we've received. You might ask how much love is there for Helen, well it can fill the Armadale District Hall, but now we are joined by many more friends and family across Australia who have joined over Zoom. So welcome also to those who have managed to join with Zoom.

I believe joining us over Zoom are Don's sisters (Judy and Cindy) in Brisbane, my family in Darwin (who fell sick and couldn't make it), Verona in Fiji, Shona & John in Northam, Mahshid in Cairns, Ruhi in Albany, Jenny in Tom Price, Edna in Bridgetown, Narelle in Jameson, Maxien in Longreach and many in Hedland, Carnarvon and other places. I hope you have been able to connect OK. Just a note – we also plan to record the program.

This evening's will be a memorial but also a celebration. While we mourn the passing of dear Helen, mother of three, partner of Don for 47 years. We also have so much to be grateful for. As Helen said, she has had a *wonderful life*. So tonight, we thought we would share some stories and celebrate with some of the things she enjoyed and loved doing. She loved working with all forms of arts and craft, music, and connecting with family, friends, and community. She enjoyed making fresh bread, learning with others and uplifting the material and spiritual wellbeing of community groups.

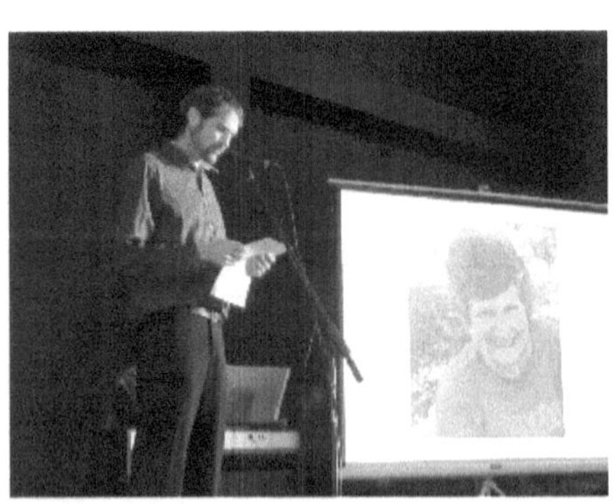

We have some of Helen's artwork and memorabilia which you can have a look at. And the memory boards where you can share your ideas and stories. You can write directly onto it or add a note or attach a story as you like. Also, we will be producing a memory booklet which will be a gathering of these stories about Helen's life. We will let you know when it is ready – probably in September. Please email Don if you would like to contribute anything.

The formal part of the program will consist of some short stories and poems interposed with musical items. After, we'll break for a light meal, followed by some good old Scottish Country Dancing. You will also find that some children's activities have been organised.

Peter Knol & Lisa Haese-Smith – 'The Holy City'
('The New Earth' – Lyrics by Frederic E Weatherly.

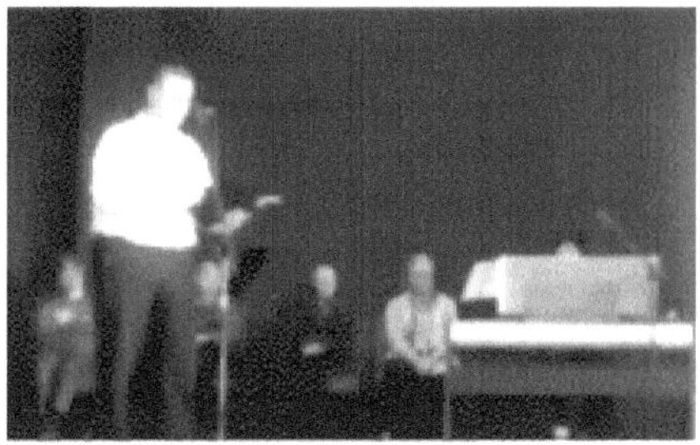

Joe: We now have the pleasure of hearing Peter Kohl sing the *The Holy City*. He is accompanied by Lisa Haese-Smith. This song had special significance to Helen because she saw the new Jerusalem as the symbol of the new earth transformed through the Baha'i Faith.

> Last night I lay asleeping,
> There came a dream so fair,
> I stood in old Jerusalem
> Beside the temple there.
> I heard the children singing,
> And ever as they sang,
> Methought the voice of Angels
> From Heaven in answer rang:-
> *'Jerusalem! Jerusalem!*
> *Lift up your gates and sing,*
> *Hosanna in the highest*
> *Hosanna to the King!'*
>
> And then methought my dream was chang'd,
> The streets no longer rang,
> Hush'd were the glad Hosannas
> The little children sang;

The sun grew dark with mystery,
The morn was cold and chill,
As the shadow of a cross arose
Upon a lonely hill.
"Jerusalem! Jerusalem!
Hark! How the Angels sing,
Hosanna in the highest
Hosanna to the King!"

And once again the scene was chang'd,
New earth there seemed to be.
I saw the Holy City
Beside the tideless sea;
The light of God was on its streets,
The gates were open wide,
And all who would, might enter,
And no one was denied.
No need of moon or stars by night,
Or sun to shine by day,
It was the new Jerusalem!
That would not pass away.
"Jerusalem! Jerusalem!
Sing, for the night is o'er,
Hosanna in the highest
Hosanna evermore!"

Bev Thornton – story of early years

Joe: Helen was the oldest in the family and has two sisters Cynthia and Beverly and two brothers John and Russell. Now there is a funny story where, Helen's mum, Mavis, was listening to the kids next door calling out over the fence to Helen and Cynthia – calling "Hel, Cyn!" Mavis was quite taken aback, and she made sure her third child's name could not be abbreviated to something so vial as 'hell' or 'sin', and so she named her third daughter Beverly. So Bev as we like to call her will be reflecting on a few stories of their times together.

<u>Bev</u>: I have been very lucky to have two older sisters, and Helen was the eldest. What a wonderful sister she was.

I have got many memories. Some of which I call second-hand memories – like what I was told by others in the family.

When I was about 18 months old, apparently I developed a taste for snails – fresh from the garden, of course – very French. Helen would be sent out to fetch them out of my mouth. So, she was looking after me from an early age.

Helen was always willing to share – probably not including her Royal Show lollies that I once "shared" with my mouth and stomach without consulting her.

Then there was the somewhat infamous story about the "dinner burning in the oven". The story was that we were away from home at the 'Block' where we were building our house over a number of years– that's what we did in those days. Helen was at home, sitting doing her homework less than a metre away from the stove on which something was cooking. She was a very focused person (unlike me) and she didn't smell something burning just that far apart. This became a family favourite story circulating within the family – for teasing Helen. I actually only remember it from the telling. But it can't have been too bad, because I am sure I would have remembered if I didn't have my dinner that night.

We shared a bedroom – Helen, Cynthia and myself. It was

just two beds long. There was Helen's bed under the window as you came into the room, then my bed here, they just fitted, and Cynthia's was over there. We were quite close, but we didn't think anything of it. We were very happy. There were not many disagreements but I remember waking up at 4 o'clock one night and the window was open and I was scared of the dark – afraid of what's out there. So, I closed it and then Helen opened it and I tried to undo it – and we fought about it. I think she won.

Later, when the house was built, we moved to the 'Block', and we each had our own bedroom – almost unheard of in those days. It was such luxury. But we didn't have any doors for a while. There was no back or front door.

In more recent times, I used to go up and visit with Helen and Don in Tom Price when the Nameless Festival was on and also when she ran a spinifex paper-making workshop. She loved to share her knowledge and passion with others.

Helen first came up with the idea of making paper out of spinifex grass when she and Don were living at Blackstone. Looking around at what resources were at hand – she could see lots of spinifex. She then developed a recipe that used very ordinary, safe ingredients and equipment that was easy to source – such as elbow grease, patience and a blender. So easy, it was a simple matter to soon be the proud producer of something beautiful.

Helen lived as she believed she should, and helping and nurturing others was always central to this. How lucky I am to have had her as my big sister.

So many memories – too many to share them all tonight. But she was a wonderful sister who will always be in my heart.

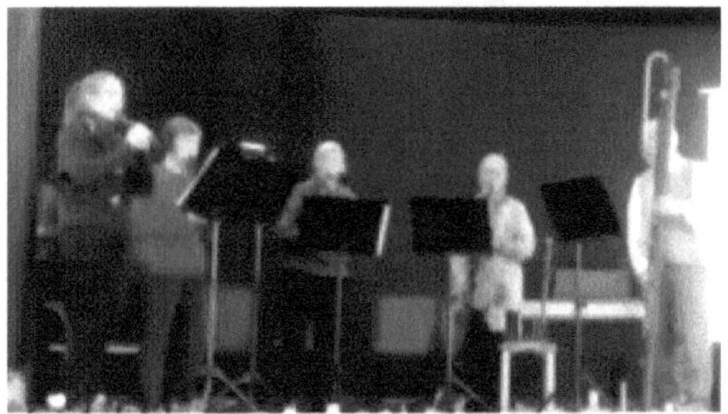

Joe: Helen was part of the recorder group in Narrogin which played in local events and annual weekend camps with the Western Australian Recorder Guild at the Agricultural College in Narrogin. Ruth was involved with this as well.

A central figure at those camps was Glyn Marillier who conducted the workshops. Glyn is a professional recorder player, pianist, composer and teacher.

Helen recently renewed her friendship with Glyn. She asked him whether he would play at her funeral and Glyn suggested a program which Helen agreed to.

We will now hear the first of six pieces from the REMSWA Players. I will introduce them more formally before their next item.

Their first piece is titled *Westron Wynde* which is a song of yearning by an unknown composer from the time of Henry the Eighth.

This will be followed by *Barcarolle* which is a gentle lullaby composed by Glyn Marillier. It is a soft farewell with Helen in mind.

Matthew and Don – Gypsy stories

Joe: Helen's eldest grandchild, Matthew, will read a story about Gypsies. This will be introduced by Don.

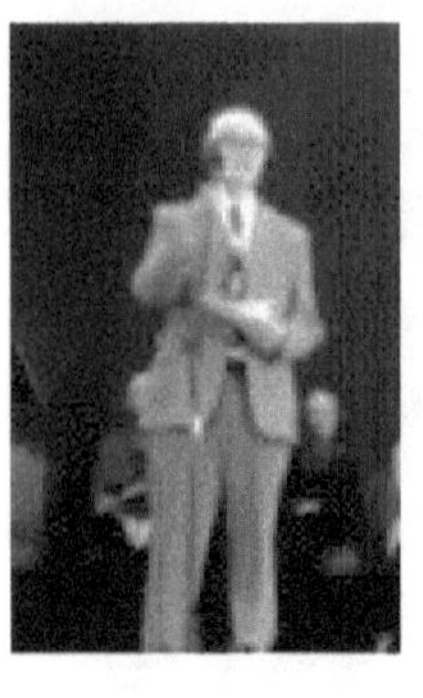

Don: I shocked my grand-kids when I came here today. They all said, "How come you are dressed so fancy. We have never seen you dressed so good." Well, I was dressed like this forty-seven years ago. This is what I wore at our wedding. Helen's dad took a video of the wedding. It is 47-year-old technology, so it is pretty rough. It is just brief with three phases. We were in St Andrews in Scotland, and we had a formal registration at the government office – you will see that. And then the Baha'i wedding at another place –at the Catholic Chaplaincy. And then we paraded through the streets of Scotland, St Andrews, with bagpipes in front. It was quite grand occasion. So you will see a little bit of that. Then there are shots of us after we were married, at a gypsy caravan site where I was working – Matthew will read that story after this video.

Comments while the video was playing: there is no sound. That's the registration office. We loved each other. That's my mum and dad, and Helen's dad and mum. That's the government registrar. And that's Annette Finn who Helen studied with at Uni and she happened to be over there at that time. Now we are walking out as a married couple. We are coming into the chaplaincy. Helen's cape was made by her mum, and we have got that on the memorabilia table out in the foyer. This was after the marriage ceremony. And bagpipes through the streets.

Our honeymoon was with Gypsies and we were there for several months. It was a brief time, forty-seven years ago, but it set a pattern in Helen's life which she developed in place after place. Wherever she went, time and time again, in different settings, she drew out the hidden capabilities of disadvantaged women and children through art, crafts and the Baha'i Faith. She supported their abilities, personal expression and growth – and thus community transformation.

I was working there with the Gypsies which were a subculture of families who kept on the move. They were not Romany Gypsies but were known as 'travellers' or 'tinkers' and they called themselves 'going about folk'. A few had a flashy caravan towed by a Range-Rover or Ford Transit, but most were very poor and some lived in tents or had a cart pulled by horses. They would camp in small groups wherever they could – on the verges of motorways or the bottom of a farmer's paddock – before they were forced to move on. Never welcome, always pushed on, always moving.

Scotland's first legitimate camping ground was being established in 1974 and was subject to criticism from townspeople so it was arranged that I would live there to help set it up, to avoid controversy.

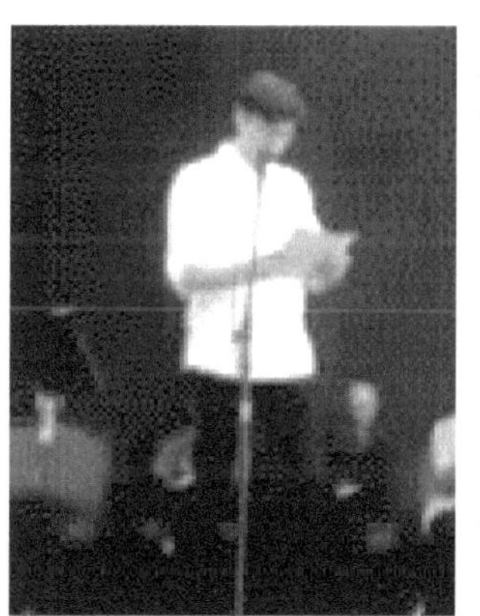

<u>Matthew</u> will now read what Helen wrote at the time.

"We were married in St Andrews but then moved to near Glasgow where Don was working as a warden on a gypsy caravan site.

"The gypsy site was a circle of twelve caravans with just a communal water tap, a small shed containing a primitive chemical toilet and no shower or bath. After a week or so the smell of the chemical toilet made me quite nauseous and I longed for a good wash. The caravan was so small we had no room to store anything. So we thought how could we solve these difficulties? We would take out the wood fireplace which took up a lot of space and replace it with a kero heater and a cupboard. And the very tiny room at the end we would make into a bathroom. We bought a gas ring and a large urn and then proceeded to make a bath, using a disused bath thrown on to the tip as a mold and buckets of fiberglass from a fiberglass factory only walking distance away.

We asked all the gypsies to decorate our bath with felt pens before putting on the final coat of fiberglass. They then all watched in amazement as we squeezed our flexible bath into the caravan. And I thought very soon they will learn from us and want us to help them make a bath and improve their living conditions. After a couple of weeks of enjoying our lovely hot baths, we began to realize why gypsies mostly have wood fires in their caravans and even in the best of caravans, never keep water inside. The sun doesn't shine much in Scotland and the steam from the urn seeped into the wood and it started to grow mould and smell damp all the time. The kero heater wasn't strong enough to dry it out.

"That was the beginning of a continual exchange in learning between ourselves and gypsies. The children couldn't read or write; they couldn't tell the time and didn't know the days of the week. So, starting in our little caravan, and then moving into a disused double-decker bus which one of the gypsies towed to the site, we started a school for the children. We taught them to read while they taught us how to use other people's rubbish. Our school desks and chairs came from the tip, still in good condition. The books, six huge bags full, were being thrown out by the library because they were finger-marked. With no help from the local school — they just weren't interested — and us stumbling on trying out different teaching methods, the children started to learn. They were quite undisciplined but bursting with enthusiasm and were very creative and imaginative.

"Life was based on relationships, not ideologies. When life is in the raw, words without actions are meaningless. One lady, Isa, had eleven children and her mother dying of cancer, all living together in one small caravan. She cooked and washed all day but even had time to bring me a bowl of soup when I was sick. Another family of six lived in a primitive tent made from an old tarpaulin wrapped around sticks. I felt I was just beginning to learn what life was all about, not passing exams, but sharing and helping each other. All the learning and knowledge you might gain is worthless without it.

"The campsite was now working fairly well. Don had established regular meeting procedures whereby they could consult and make decisions about how

they wished the campsite to be run. This was the first permanent site in Scotland where Gypsies could legally reside so a warden had been appointed to make sure everything went well at the beginning — to solve the initial difficulties as, while most gypsies wanted a place where they could stay, they were not accustomed to working together except in small tight-knit family groups. And so the time came when a full-time warden was no longer necessary. The social work department were close to getting a full-time teacher to continue the children's education.

"I was pregnant with our first child and suffered quite badly from morning sickness. So we decided to move back to Australia. It was hard to say goodbye. They insisted on us taking some of their treasured possessions with little crystal vases and ornaments and there were hugs and tears on both sides."

REMSWA Players

Joe: We are going to hear another recorder piece from the REMSWA Players. Let me introduce the members:

Glyn Marillier who plays the bass, great bass and contra bass recorders.

Irene Batini plays alto and tenor recorders.

Elizabeth Kelly plays the tenor recorder.

Irene, Elizabeth and Glyn were all foundation members of both the WA Recorder Guild and its successor, the Recorder and Early Music Society of WA (REMSWA). Each have taught both recorder and piano at various levels from primary to tertiary for many years.

Liz Whan plays tenor and great bass recorders. She has been an enthusiastic recorder player since starting to learn it as an adult since 1987 and is now the much-loved President of REMSWA.

Emily Taylor plays alto and soprano recorders. She recently came from South Australia with a double degree in music and engineering — a wonderful addition to the Recorder and Early Music scene.

This next recorder piece is *Bist du bei mir*. It is an aria from an opera by Stoelzel in which the leading lady requests that her beloved remain with her to the end.

Trish Halloran – Art stories

Joe: Helen, for many years, was secretary of the Armadale Society of Artists and worked closely with Trish Halloran who is the president of the society.

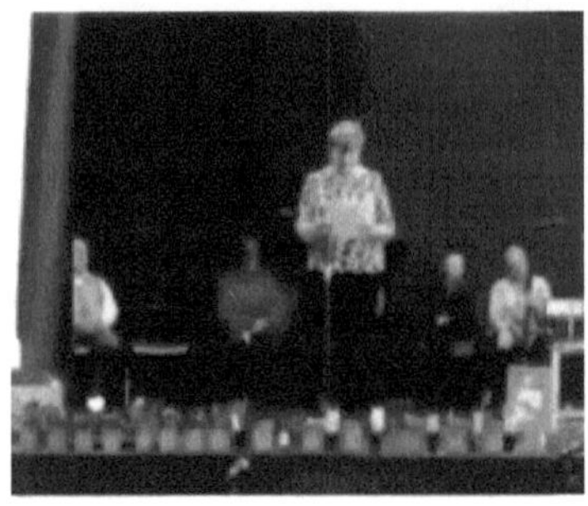

Trish: My name is Trish Halloran and I am here tonight as a friend of Helen and also as the president of the Armadale Society of Artists representing the Armadale Society of Artists family. I am honoured to be asked by Don and the family to speak at Helen's memorial-celebration. Don asked for stories. Well, I am not so good at stories, and I couldn't really think of a tale to tell. But I do have words and thoughts about Helen, and I would like to share them.

I am so glad that I got to say goodbye to Helen in person. We had a beautiful hour just talking together and reminiscing about her life and experiences over the years. Helen had clearly come to expect and was in a comfortable place and had no regrets as she bravely faced her fate. In fact, she felt blessed to have had such a great life. Helen put her family as priority and was a loyal friend to many people who are here today or those who can't be here – maybe looking on from Zoom. I left that room feeling sad and also so grateful for having known Helen. Helen had many friends in the Armadale Society of Artists (in short, ASA) and will be remembered by us all in a different way – as a teacher, painting companion, or as a dedicated committee member. Helen was our ASA secretary for more than six years – from

2014 to 2019 – and stepped down only due to her illness. Helen loved her time on the ASA committee and was always interested in hearing the news of what was our latest challenge that might be happening at the time. Helen was a dedicated ASA secretary who brought her intelligence and writing skills to us in dealing with the bureaucratic processes. Helen drew upon her extensive knowledge and wisdom from dealing with past art groups, especially her time with aboriginal communities, and in the Pilbara region. One of her favourite roles each year was, funny enough, standing right here on this stage, where Helen was doing her incredible work with the ASA. She looked after the sponsors for arts and organising the art awards and looking after our judges. Helen went beyond the normal role and was the sponsor of herself on one of the events.

Well, maybe I have a little story I will just add. The ASA has a pop-up shop in Armadale and Helen had a display of her artwork. I decided, as I did not have any of Helen's paintings, that I'd like to buy one. I decided on a small painting I was drawn to because I knew Helen loved the

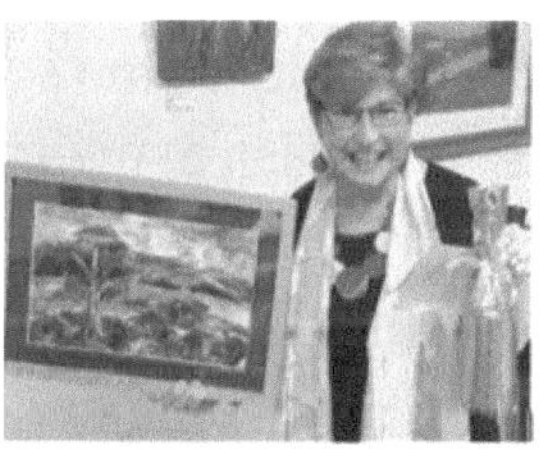

colours of the Pilbara. When I went to visit [in her final months], I let her know that I had bought the painting. I was really glad of that because she was thrilled/chuffed and it made her so happy. She said that she loved that little

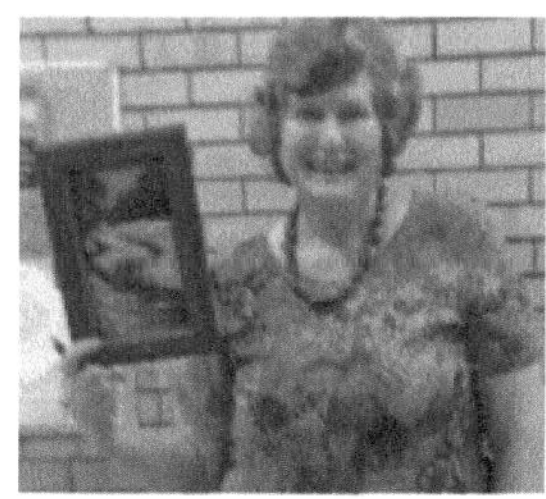

painting because it brought back special memories that she loved the scenery in the Pilbara region. Following along from that, some months later when we were doing a special feature in our newsletter about Helen, I was on the search for photos. I came across a photo of Helen at our monthly meeting at Creyk Park and she was holding up this Pilbara painting. She had in fact won the challenge with that painting. In dedication to Helen, the ASA had a painting challenge in July – a painting with vegemite – so I decided as a special tribute to Helen, to do a Pilbara scene. Well, Helen brought me good luck because I won the challenge and a bottle of red wine. So, to finish off, we will open that bottle of red wine sometime and we will be thinking about this little story – and here's cheers to a really beautiful person. Thank you.

REMSWA Players – 'Scherzo and Cantabile'

Joe: This recorder piece, *Scherzo and Cantabile* is another of Glyn's compositions. It is a joke and a song. Imagine little scurrying animals in the spinifex and the song of wind in the she-oaks.

Aboriginal communities – Dianne Isgar

Joe: For three years, Helen and Don were at the Blackstone Community in the semi-desert area near the corner of WA, SA, & NT. Helen managed the community office and women's centre – which included many arts & crafts.

After Helen left, Dianna Isgar took up the work in Blackstone.

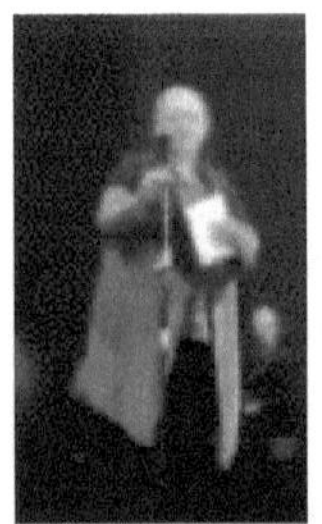

Dianna: I knew Helen most, and of course Don, and I want to share some of our experiences. I knew of Helen and Don before I even met them. I was brought out as a reliever to Blackstone in an administrative role and when I went into the office, I saw the wonderful work that Helen had done there. I couldn't believe how well Helen had structured the place to make good working conditions for the local community and I had staff with me who really ran and managed much of the community. And it was Helen's skill in setting up processes, in the way she pulled jobs together, the way she spent time and educated people. It was wonderful. It was sometime later that I actually met Helen in very sad circumstances of a funeral, but I got to meet her and formed a relationship – a friendship formed over her skills not mine, but Lord knows I used them as much as I could. I was the arts manager at the time and Helen helped us set up a paper-making program and that paper-making program got us the funding to build our Art Centre. Helen came many times back in very sad circumstances. She came to offer support and respect to the family after a terrible, terrible incident that blossomed into a great opportunity and shared experience. For that I shall never forget. I still work out of Blackstone and my job is now very different. I put enormous energy into developing programs for local workers. Coming down on the plane, I was thinking about this, and I realized that inspiration for the effort I have put into the indigenous employment program is from Helen. Just that time to go into the office and seeing how she had structured the place. There's not a lot I can say other than that she was valuable, inspirational, kind, and will be sorely missed.

Joe: There was a video of the spinifex paper making.

REMSWA Players – 'Hymn of Thanksgiving'
Joe: This recorder piece is a *Hymn of Thanksgiving* which is a serene thank you for a life well lived. It is a bit of a workout for the bass recorder, just to make it interesting.

'Pumpkin soup' – poem by Ruth
Joe: As well as a day of remembrance and celebration, today is also Helen's 76th birthday. Six years ago, Ruth wrote a poem for Mum's 70th Birthday which captures a regular day in Helen's life. Now, Mum, truth to be told, would often get fully absorbed with her projects, which meant she frequently forgot about the

pot on the stove or the dish in the oven. Other people find that alarms and timers useful to prompt them to check their cooking, although, for Mum, it was often the smoke alarm that prompted her.

<u>Ruth</u>:

> T'was Grandma from good old Perth
> That caught the cooking craze
> She boiled up some pumpkin soup
> to feed us for many days
>
> She turned away the trusty timer
> that had served us well before
> And put the pot a boiling
> Then left and shut the door.
>
> The pumpkin gently simmered
> and bubbled in its pot
> The steam gently rising
> as the vegies softened up
>
> But as we all well know,
> steam doesn't last
> for the vegies start to blacken
> when the moisture all has past
>
> Meanwhile somewhere close
> Grandma paints a scene
> Lost in her creation
> brush flicking specks of green.
>
> A smell wafts by unpleasant
> as Grandma paints a tree

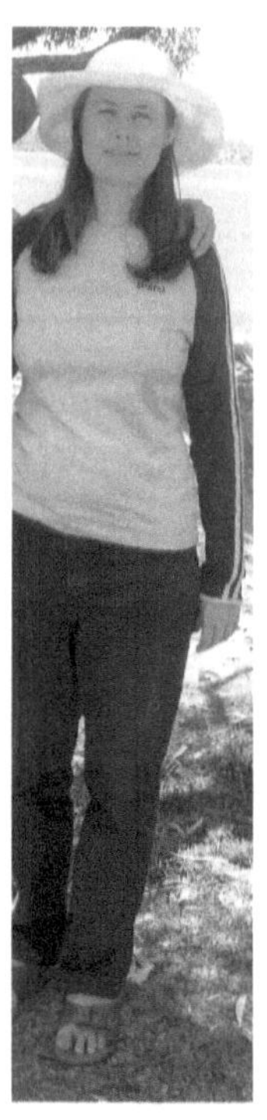

she thinks it might be coming from
her long forgotten tea.

Suddenly a sound shrieks out
the smoke alarm is beeping
'The Soup' she cries out loudly
suddenly realizing

She stares into the blackness
of the bottom of the pot
sadly reminiscing
of the soup that now is not.

Never mind says Grandma
with a swish of her hand
pulls out a bowl to announce
pancakes for lunch ié grand

And soon sitting around the table
the pumpkin quite forgot
focus now on pancakes
steaming, fresh and hot.

'Helen's soup' – a story by Lorraine Shanks

Joe: On the theme of soups, Lorraine will share a story titled 'Helen's Soup'

Lorraine and her husband Andrew Shanks, with their children Safira and Cailan, live in the mighty metropolis of Wongan Hills.

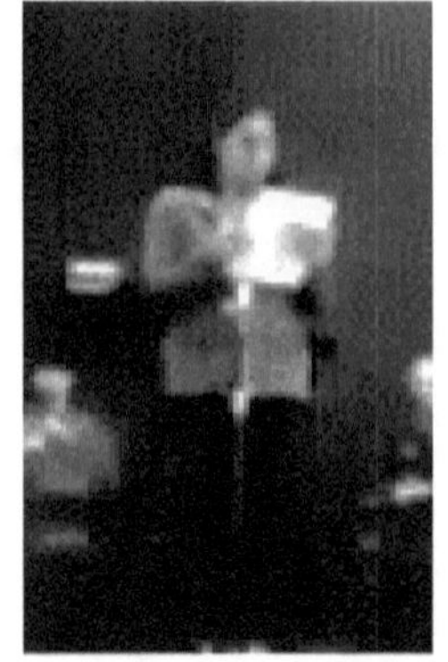

Lorraine: To give a little background. We were very fortunate for the time we lived in Wongan Hills, a little town in the regional areas two hours north-east of Perth. Helen would often visit our family. I remember one trip, when Safira was a baby, Helen with Joyce and Tadgee from Tom Price stopped with us on the way to the Summer School. We would have many wonderful visits of Helen and Don – one of the most eagerly awaited guests for our children. So here is a story about these times.

"I'm not eating it. I want Helen's soup!"

"This *IS* like Helen's soup" I protested.

"This is yucky. It's not like Helen's soup." Cailan was not giving up. (This is a true story.)

"Helen made a vegetable minestrone and Dad has made a vegetable minestrone," I patiently explained, not prepared to give up either.

"Dad's soup is disgusting!"

Now, for all of you who know 'Dad' – more affectionately known as 'Shanks' – you know that he CAN cook. He has a particular flair for cooking and even his soups are delicious. This soup had the lot – fresh herbs from the garden, a sprinkle of parmesan on top – it smelled divine and tasted even better.

Helen, on the other hand, would always describe herself as a simple person. "Nothing fancy," she said when she came to visit and brought with her a vegetable soup for lunch. And her soup was also delicious – but honestly, quite comparable to the one that Shanks had made for dinner a few weeks later, that our kids were now refusing to eat.

And it wasn't just the soup. It was Helen's bread too. "Why can't you get Helen's bread recipe?" It was Safira's turn to complain now.

"Because I already know how to make bread," I replied, somewhat sarcastically – patience having now given way to frustration.

"But Helen's bread was better," Safira continued.

"It was very similar to mine." I stopped. There really was no point continuing the argument.

Helen's bread. Helen's soup.

It wasn't what she put in them.

It was Helen.

My children weren't responding to the ingredients, the cooking time or the presentation. It was the COOK that they were responding to.

Helen.

Mother of regional WA. One of the longest-standing members of the WA Baha'i community. Someone who in all honesty, I have to say that I never felt would not be with us. Like her character – dependable, solid, hardworking, I expected that she would just keep on going.

We were blessed that Helen and Don made regular visits to see us in Wongan Hills, after we moved back out of Perth in 2008. When they came, it was clear that they weren't just visiting us – Lorraine and Shanks – but the entire family: our two children, Safira and Cailan too. We all felt the love pouring out from Helen and Don each time they visited. No other visitors, in fact, were received with greater anticipation and eagerness by my children (well, all of us really) than Helen and Don.

My children soon came to discover Helen's qualities for themselves……the qualities that she somehow sneaked into her soup and bread. She was creative. Patient. She listened. She paid attention. She was humble, simple, practical. She really had no trace of ego, although she was a brilliant artist and highly capable in whatever she turned her hand to – whether it was tutoring study circles or making deep and lasting connections with indigenous friends. She was dedicated, thoughtful and prepared. She rarely complained. She was faithful, steadfast, and independent. She was, in truth, one of the best people that I have ever known.

Shanks can't make 'Helen's soup' any more than I can make 'Helen's bread', because, at least in my case, most of the qualities of the cook are not evident in me. But maybe that is the challenge, and legacy, that Helen has left for us all. In a recent devotional, "a life well-lived" was a tribute that came from the lips of many. And poignant words from her son, Ben, reiterated the point: "We are not here because Helen died, we are here because she LIVED".

It really feels like we have lost someone irreplaceable, who had qualities far above the ordinary person, but I know that Helen would disagree with me absolutely. As with all those dedicated servants of Baha'u'llah who have ascended to the Abhá Kingdom, maybe the best tribute we can pay to Helen is with the example of our own life.

But I know that my children will always prefer Helen's soup.

REMSWA Players – 'Rejoicing Dance'
Joe: The final recorder piece was also composed by Glyn Marillier. It is *Rejoicing Dance* which is a jolly piece in which all the recorders get a chance to kick up their heels.

Charlie Pierce – Stories – Early Baha'i activities
Joe: Charlie Pierce has known Helen for more than fifty years. He going to talk about Helen's Baha'i early life.

Charlie: Like Don showed you his wedding clothes, I'm wearing trousers from the late 1960s and early 70s when, for a young person we wore flares. I first met Helen when she was Helen

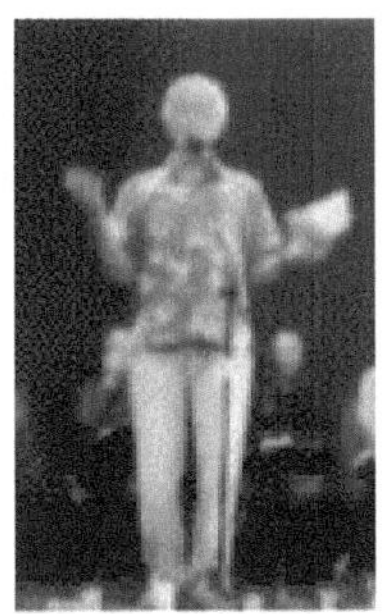
Mitchell in 1968 when I was a very new member of the Baha'i Faith, very enthusiastic. I went to a discussion evening which we called a 'Fireside', in the home of John Handley in Bentley. There was one of the young Baha'is called Verona, and she brought along her friend from university, Helen. I remember this meeting because Helen was so argumentative, she would not except any idea that Baha'u'llah, the founder of the Baha'i Faith, was a new messenger of God, and this was a new era. She would not have a bar of it. That's my first memory.

Now let's move on five years later to 1973. Helen had married Don. I had married Barbara, and we had gone to the New Hebrides in the middle of the Pacific, to help with the work of the Baha'i Faith. We had saved up, after a few years, a little bit of money which we wanted to invest, and we thought, "Well, let's get a block of land, if we can." We passed through Perth, and we met Helen and Don. Helen said to us, 'We've just come back from Albany and have actually bought a block of land in a wonderful place near a national park called Goode Beach. Lots of blocks going there." So, we said, "OK, we will get one too." So I ran out and we bought this piece of land for $3000. This was our entire life savings. That's where we are living now. We have this link with Helen and Don that we are now back in Australia and living in the one place that Helen recommended that we should go and live.

Memory number 3. Over the forty years of us being in the New Hebrides, now Vanuatu, every few years we managed to have a short break and visit my family in England and Barbara's family in Melbourne. But we would always pass through Western Australia, and we had a habit of linking with Helen and Don and their children who are the same age as our children. I remember on one occasion, they were now living in Narrogin, and Helen was so excited about her garden. She said, "Look what I have produced." And she showed us how she had spread newspaper all over the soil to suppress the weeds and had grown a wonderful crop of beans. I remember that because it was natural fertilizer. She was so excited about her method of gardening.

Memory number 4. Helen went to the Marshall Islands, and she came back through the Solomons, and she wanted to visit us in what was now Vanuatu. She had Ben with her, and he was very small. Helen wanted to help with the Baha'i community, and we visited one family who had a child who was handicapped. Helen went to the family and used her training as an occupational therapist and helped the family to devise activities to stimulate this little boy. That was a wonderful example of what Helen would do when she travelled – practical help for people. She came back. That evening Ben developed a fever and he began screaming in the middle of the night – he screamed and screamed and screamed. So Barbara said, "Take him to the hospital." We came down the stairs to take Helen and Ben in our little car. When I started the engine there was another huge scream because inside the radiator there was our cat and we had Ben screaming and the cat screaming – but the cat survived. By the time we got Ben to the hospital, he was better.

My last memory was much more recent. Since we came back from Vanuatu, in the last few years, we have been living in Albany and we have been involved in an annual summer camp. Some of you in this room have come to that camp. One of the regular people who came to the camp was Helen. She always had an art workshop, and I can remember on many occasions when she would just enthuse the adults, children and youth with this love of art. I remember once she had us all creating something from a leaf.

Can I summarize Helen? For me, she is the gardener, the

carer, the artist, the lover of humanity, the educator, a person of resolve and strength.

Joe: Thanks, Charlie. Lots of fond memories.

Joe: Isla McDonald is singing her song which she has composed in memory of Helen. Isla's song was based on a quote from

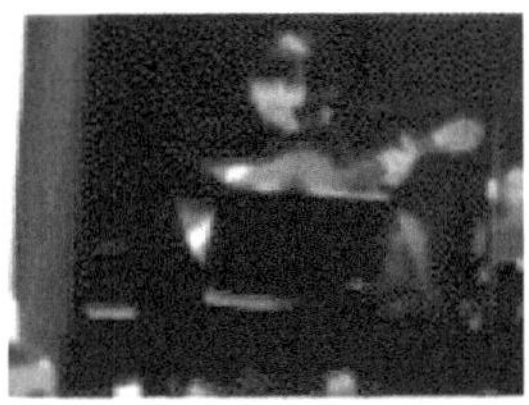

Abdu'l-Baha: *"Shine ye like unto the sun and roar and move like unto the sea; impart life to mountain and desert like unto clouds, and similar to the vernal breeze, bestow freshness, grace and elegance on the trees of human temples."*

Joe: Ben has created his own composition about Mum.

Ben: This is a small song that I have thought of while driving the truck one day. It not that good, but it's for Mum. Well, it's for all mothers in general. Because for me she was just Mum, before all the other things that she did, and she was really good at it – being a mother. So, this is for all the mothers who are here and all the mothers who not here.

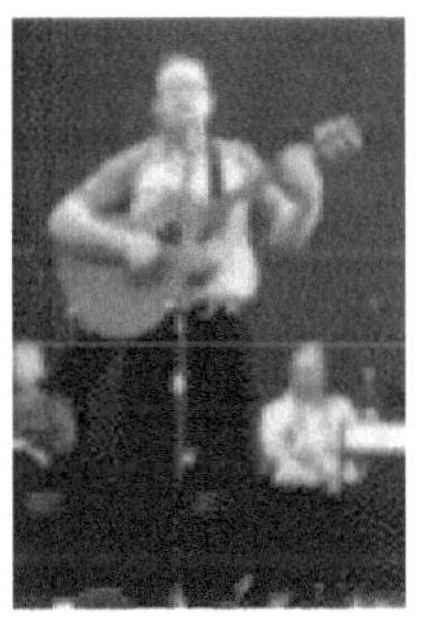

> Love is the only reason
> We have come this far.
> See the light that's shining
> From her sacred heart.
>
> When the sound for her forgiveness
> Is all that you can hear.

You know she's been beside you
For all of these long years.

When the colours of the world start to fade,
And you feel like you have gone and lost your way,
You close your eyes and you can see her face.
She will call your name.

When all that you have longed for,
And all you've left behind,
And all you've ever wanted,
But never seemed to find.

When all you hear is silence,
You begin to realise
You have seen it all
In your mother's eyes.

Chorus
She can light the darkness.
She can lead the way.
Love is her religion.
An angel in disguise.
A place you can go to,
Like when you were a child
You will always be reflected
In your mother's eyes.
You will always be reflected
In your mother's eyes
All she has, she can give you.
You can take all you need.
Love and light is shining.
She gives and gives for free.

So never take for granted,
The tears that you cry.
When memories have faded,
With the passing of time.
When all you hear is silence,
You begin to realise,
You have seen it all,
In your mother's eyes.

Chorus
She can light …..

Weyburn – piano

Joe: Weyburn is Helen's grandson. He will be playing Grieg's *Morning*.

Closing remarks by Joe

Joe: We will soon complete our formal program and break for a light meal and then some Scottish Country Dancing.

We would just like to say how much we appreciate the thoughtful support which we have received in the past months. It has been overwhelming.

We would like to thank the many people who have contributed in so many ways to this evening – those who have been on this stage and those who have helped with the setting up, flowers, sound system, projector and the food. It has come together so beautifully.

Thanks everyone for coming. Some of you have travelled from far away to come here. It is wonderful to have you here.

There are some seedlings here which you are welcome to take and plant as a memento.

We thought we would close with a few words brought together by Mashid Ferdowsian, who has been a long-standing Baha'i friend. Unfortunately, she cannot be here tonight because she is stranded in Cairns with the Covid lockdown. She sent through a message last night. It summarizes who Helen was. This is read by Padma Wong.

This will be followed by the last item of this program – children singing two songs which you can join in with the lyrics on your program.

Dear friends and family.

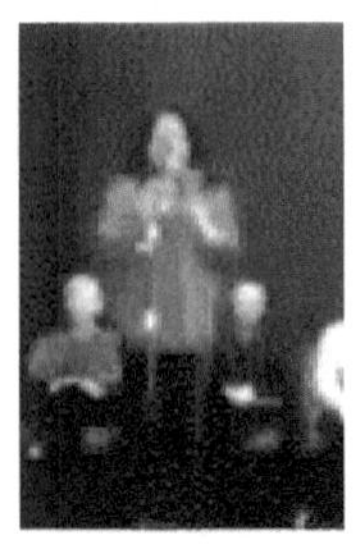

I wish I could be present on the Memorial of our dear Helen and share my feelings, but hope that these lines will convey my message.

These last weeks, since Helen's passing, I have been even more aware of her character and her love that has encompassed every one of us in so many different ways.

I also learnt a lot about Helen's many hidden talents, from her skating, dancing, singing, to her painting, creating and sharing her art.

Her industrious ability to make things so beautiful and precious out of cardboard, paper and grass is just unique and praiseworthy.

Helen's ability to mingle with everyone easily, and to befriend strangers without any hesitation is something we have all noticed.

The connections she kept with her childhood friends and school mates and university classmates was sign of genuine attraction and personality that comes from a deep understanding of Divine love.

Helen's services to connect isolated people with each other

through *Bush Honey Magazine*. Her study classes that continued till the last days of her physical life are also another connection with her spirituality.

We are so lucky to have Helen's memories and her friendship in our lives, and hope we could follow her lead in our lives.

My hope and prayers are that in our eternal journey, we will be able to recognise each other and be a creative source together.

My love and praise go to Don as an encouraging and supportive husband, and their children who are carrying the same capacity and love that their mum had.

I hope you enjoy the memorial and make Helen's spirit happy.

Loving greetings from Mahshid Ferdowsian

Children's Class & Junior Youth – two songs –
  'Happy by You' and 'Put a little love in your heart'
(The lyrics are on the program hand-out)

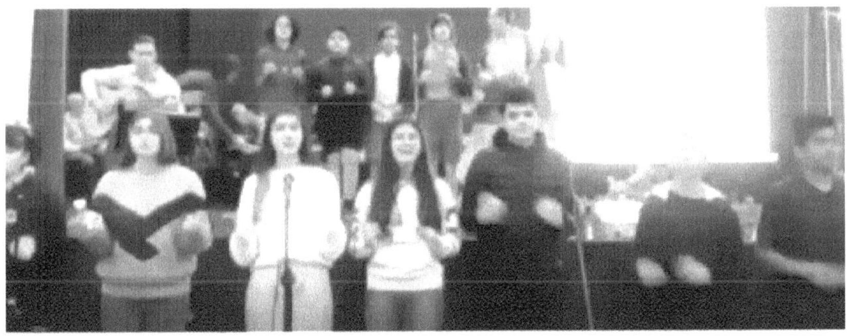

..ooOOoo..

18

Reflections about Helen

Gathering of Baha'i friends

6th July 2021 via Zoom with 125 connections

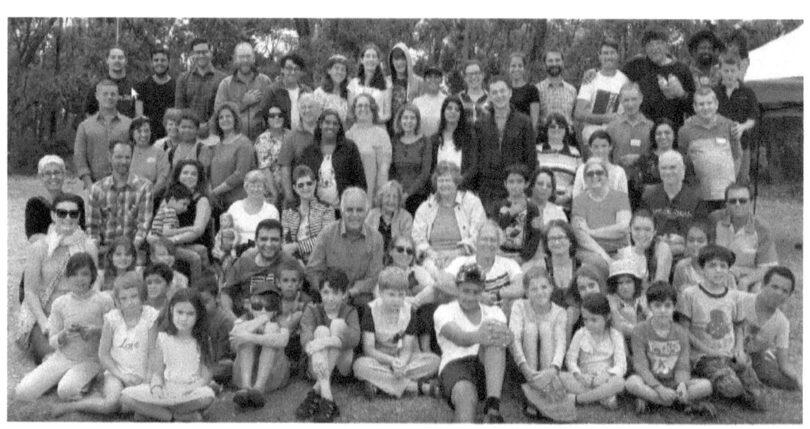

Albany Summary Camp about 2017

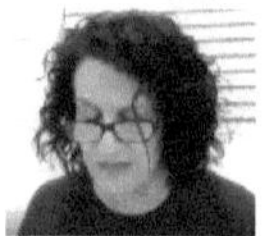

Farideh Mohebpour – **Prayer: in Farsi**

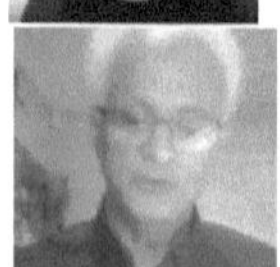

Dariush Farrokhi – **Prayer: "He is God. Exalted is He. The Lord of loving kindness and bounty. …."**

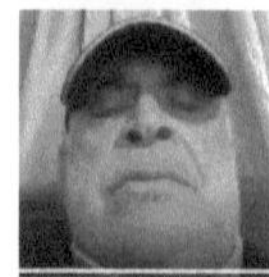

Benny Debestan – **Prayer: chant in Farsi**

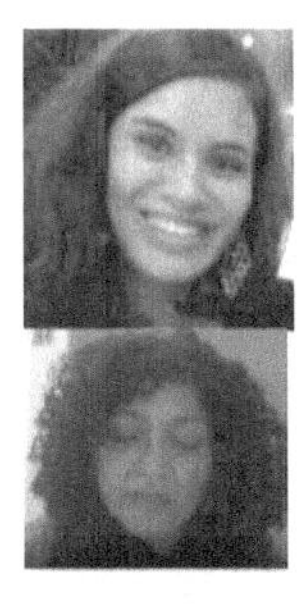 Shameem Taheri-Lee – Prayer/song: "Oh, Son of Man. Thou art My Dominion …."

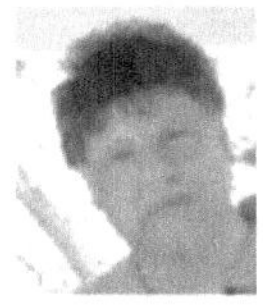 Manya Zanozi – For my dear friend Helen who, with her art, had so much beauty. Hidden Word: "From the sweetened streams of Thy eternity, let me drink, Oh my God …:"

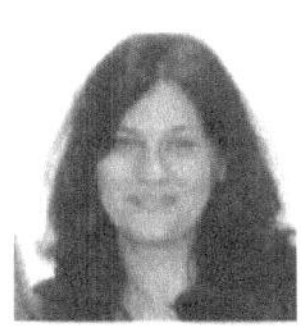 Peter Tidman – Song: "Until we meet again, may God hold you safe in the palm of His hand. …."

Forighieh Hajijafar: – Prayer: "Oh my God. Oh my God. Verily Thy servant is humbled before the majesty of Thy divine mercies …."

Debra Singh: – Thank you so much, friends. I am just wondering if we can now ask Don and the rest of Helen's beautiful family if they want to say a few words.

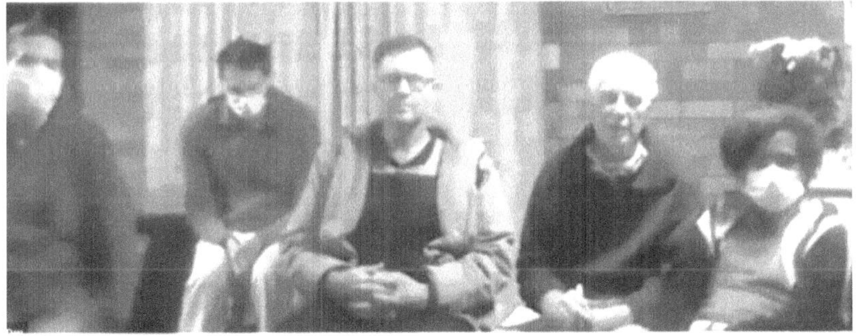

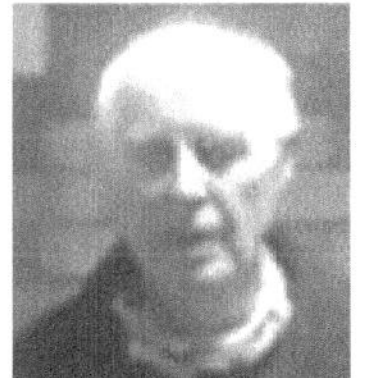 Don Gordon: First of all, thank you very much everyone for coming together like this. It is quite overwhelming to see so many wonderful friends going back so many years. It is Helen I must thank for leading me to connect with so many of you. I can see your faces and there are so many that we can't see on the screen.

I have got to know a little of your journeys and I am so impressed with the heroes and giants that Helen has enabled me to meet. I thank you all for the opportunity to meet with you and be part of your lives – mostly as a spectator of course, from my point of view. It has been quite, quite wonderful, so thank you so much for that.

Helen's journey with cancer started about three years ago and at times it has been very, very rough and then there has been some good times in between. She became weaker over recent months but it was just in the last week and a half that she became very, very weak. So strangely it has been a happy time for us – wonderful times together over recent months and also it has been an opportunity for friends to connect and re-connect and it has been quite a remarkable time. Helen was happy with the time she spent in these last few months. In the last week she was not able to talk and it was lovely to just spend time with her (without talking). Joe was in Darwin and fortunately he was able to get down to arrive in Perth just two hours before she passed. So it has been very good and we are so happy that our family is here. Violyn and Ben, Weyburn, Oirae and Jasmine. And Ruth and Colin and Hannah – Matthew unfortunately was having to work tonight so hopefully this is being recorded so Matthew can catch up with something of what was been happening here tonight. And Joe arriving just in time – It was great that Helen could hang on long enough to have time with him. And Amica and the boys, maybe you are connecting somewhere but we can't see you on screen. We can't quite see you. I guess, somehow Helen is linked into this conference too. I am sure someone told her which buttons to press. So she is here too. Thank you everyone. That's all from me, thank you.

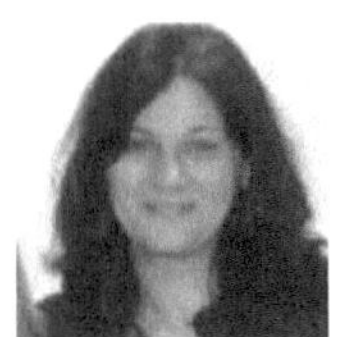

Debra Singh: Is there anyone else in the family who would like to share anything?

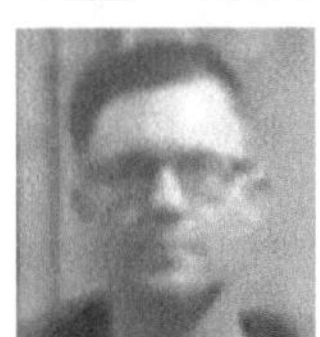

Ben Gordon: I just thank everyone for coming. I know we are not really here because Mum died. We are really here because she lived and the way she lived. She is here every second and it gives a chance to think how we could live that way. So that is what we can take away when we leave here tonight.

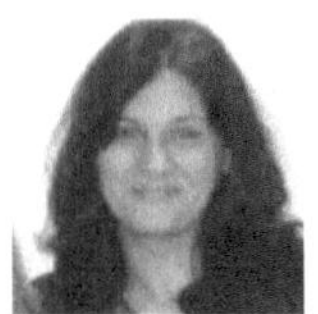

Debra Singh: Thank you so much Ben. I think it is so true. The words which come to mind are "A life well lived" when it comes to Helen's life. We might now move to Lorraine Injie. Lorraine was a dear, like a daughter I'd say, to Helen, and she is going to also share some of her memories.

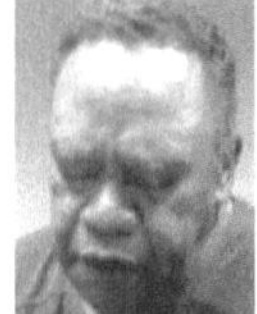

Warren Injie: If you can hear in the background, the Torres Strait Islanders are getting ready for their NADOC celebrations and so I'll open the door a little for background.

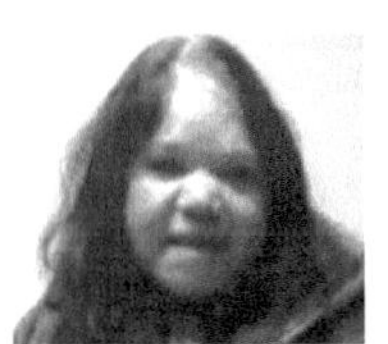

Lorraine Injie: Firstly, on behalf of all of us when we offer our sincere condolences to Don and the family and everyone else. I think I speak for all of us when I say that someone is in Geraldton right now. I would like to start by saying a prayer: "Oh Lord, Oh Thou who whose mercy has encompassed all …."

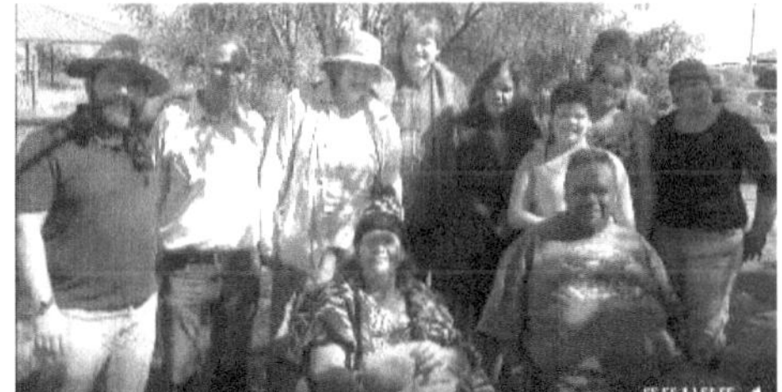

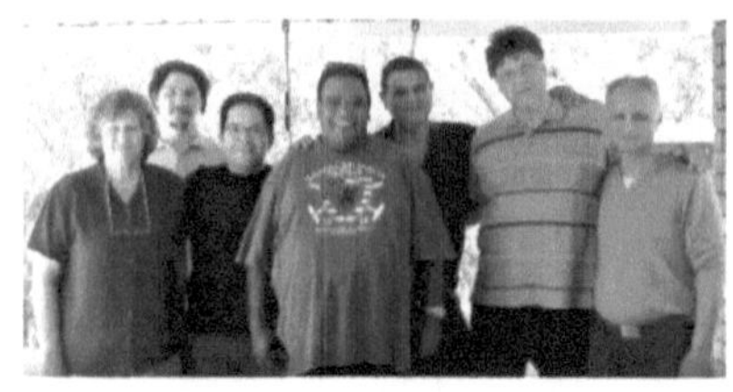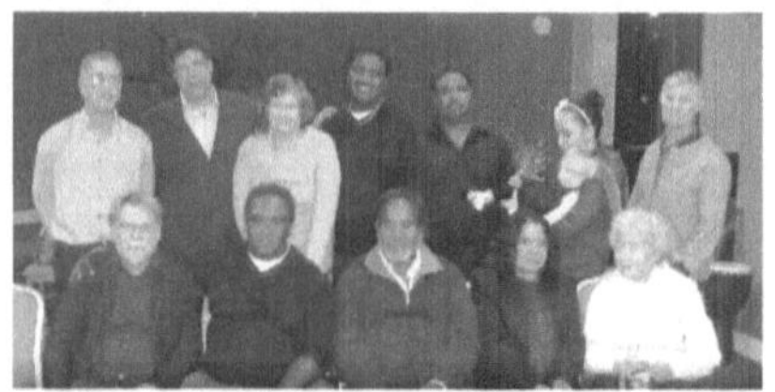

We were blessed when we were younger, sister came into our lives in 1990. She became close and was very acceptable of my mum (Joyce). They spent a lot of time talking and planning their trips to Perth. Sometimes I worried about them driving so far. I would hear the story sometimes I think I had the right to be worried because they seemed like they were hard trips. Often, they would travel at Xmas, to Summer School and sometimes they did it rough – camping on 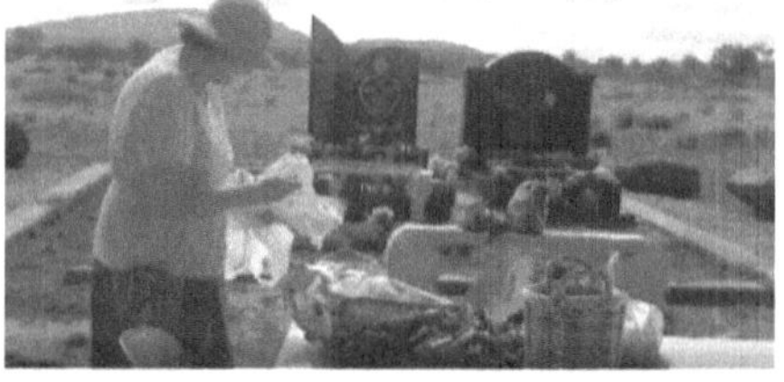 the side of the road or sharing a swag. Quite often I would go to Bellary and I would find them sitting on the verandah and yarning and talking about the plants. Talking about the things they had to do, but both of them living life to the full. Last May, we were planning our next Karijini Experience and she got sick. I had organized her accommodation, but when I got there, she hadn't come. I saw her a month or two later and I heard that she had the cancer. Later that year, I remember Samandar calling me and saying I think you should come and go to the hospital to see her. We got to the Armadale Hospital; she was almost ready to bounce out of bed and go home. After eight weeks, she had eaten her first meal after being on the drip for so long. But I was so shocked when I saw her that I did not think she would survive the next year, but she did and then next time I saw her, she was home. She was walking and gardening, and painting and organizing classes. We couldn't stop her. She kept going. I think the last year she packed as much as she could into the rest of her short life. She lived life to the full. I can see her talking to my mum. I'll always see her at that memorial. I can hear her laughing and I know she will always be with us. Perhaps, if she is with my mum I know they will be watching over all of us.

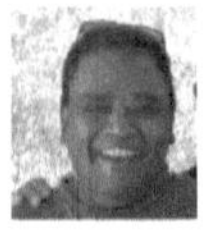 Warren Injee: **Yinhawangka language**

Slim Dusty (recording) – Song: "Until we meet again, may God hold you safe in the palm of His hand ….." ..

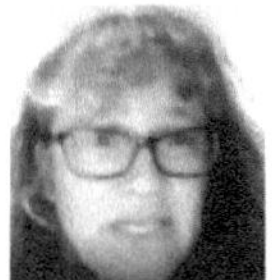 Dale Fuluna: **Shall we invite Charmaine to speak.**

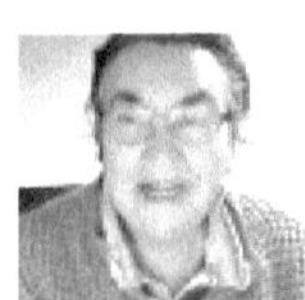 Charmaine Hale: I have too many memories to cover them all, so I am just going to talk about the early days. I became a Baha'i in July of 1969. It was at Heytesbury Road in Subiaco where Charlie Pierce was staying at the time. It was a long time ago, but in that same year, Helen had started to attend firesides and other Baha'i events. She didn't declare; she didn't become a Baha'i. She went over to Sydney to visit for some reason, I don't know why, and apparently while over there she just happened to go to

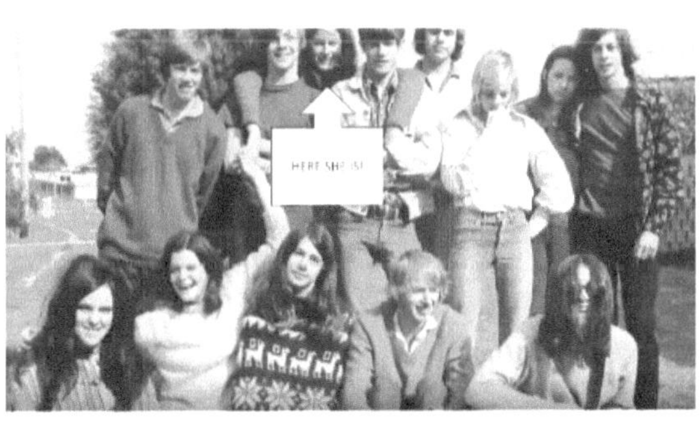

the Baha'i Temple and met up with Joy Stevenson – and declared! But she swore Joy to secrecy because she wanted to come back and surprise everyone. It was a failure. (That photo has Mike and Wendy Cater at the back, Rosemary and Jenny, Tony Deamer, Bryn Deamer. Helen there. Yes, lots of pictures. And oh dear that terrible picture of me at the front holding the guitar). Helen came back to a youth gathering that was being held and, as she walked through the door, all of us said, "Congratulations" because the Baha'i grapevine is much faster and much surer than anything in the world, absolutely. So she could not surprise us at all. Which was really funny.

As a Leo myself, Helen and Tony were all Leo's, so as a kind of celebration of our birthdays and her declaration, there was a party held at Helen's house and we all went along to that. That was very exciting. Helen and Maxien Bradley (Lethbridge) studied occupational therapy together (at WA Institute of Technology) and Pam Poulter was over here. Helen and Maxien shared an apartment in one of these old-fashioned, Victorian style multi-story buildings on the way up to Kings Park. I can remember going there quite a few times. They were very excited when they had finished their studies and had saved up like mad and all three of them took off to England [separately] which was kind of a standard ploy for young people in those days to get away from your roots I suppose. Maxien at that time was not a Baha'i when she left but she became a Baha'i at an Intercalary gathering in South London in 1972 and she went off pioneering to Ireland. Helen went up to Scotland where she connected with Don. Interestingly enough, they had known each other in Perth.

I didn't see Helen for a few years. When she came back, we reconnected and by that time I think she came back just before

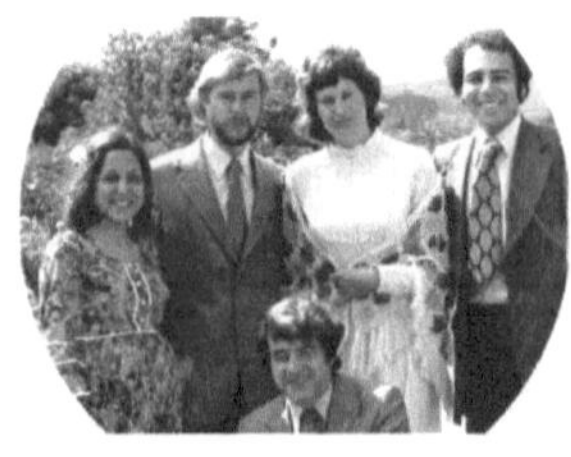

I went interstate so there was a gap there. Every time we met up it was as though there had been no gap at all. It was quite incredible.

When Brian and I went to Africa, to Malawi, we had some pioneers from Ireland (Mercede and Ronald Taherzadeh) come to stay with us. It was fascinating because they said "Oh, you're from Australia. Do you know Helen because we were witnesses at her wedding."

And of course I did. Small world being a Baha'i. It really is.

Anyway, after we came back from Africa, we moved to Collie and at that time, Helen and Don were in Narrogin with their three kids. On school holidays, because they were pretty isolated from other Baha'i children, as were we, either we would travel over to Narrogin and camp out at Helen and Don's place and the kids would get together and play, or else they would come over to Collie and camp out at our place. I always remember Ruth, when Rory was born, she used to hold Rory in her arms and call him Rory, baby Rory – absolutely adored him.

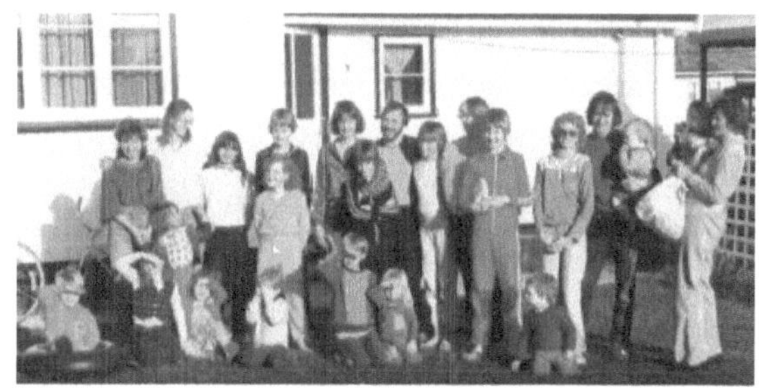

There we were – the mob in this photo. Lots of children there. You can tell there are heaps and heaps of red-heads from Rob McMahon and his wife, and myself and our kids. And Don Bruce and Marie. And Lisa and Helen. Too many memories.

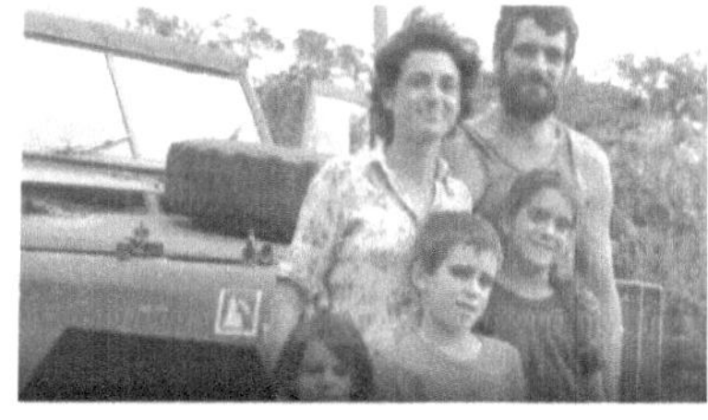

Maxien appeared on the scene. Maxine and Jim were foundation members, along with Pam Anderson, myself, Ali Thorne who is now Ali Hutchin, and Greg and Sandy formed the first Bunbury assembly.

I can remember Helen trying to teach herself the flute when she was in Narrogin.

Then we caught up again when I was at Mount Lawley campus. Helen had come down from Blackstone with a whole lot of women for an art exhibition that they held at Kings Park. Across the court yard of the art centre, we recognized each other. Shrieks, yells galore, catching up after all that time, talking art as we always did when we got together.

Chandra caught up with Helen when she did her youth year of service up in Tom Price and then came back to Perth for six months and went off to Sydney for a couple of years and worked in the National Office there.

2018, after Brian had died, I visited Helen, and that was when I discovered that she had cancer detected. I spent some time with her. My grandson dropped me off for the day. That was nice.

Just too many memories. But all good. All really good. We didn't always agree on things. I think we were very alike in nature. Sometimes caused pressures, but we always found a way to resolve things. I always learnt heaps from Helen.

That's enough from me.

Dale: Thanks Charmaine. Is Mahshid Ferdwosian here.

Mahshid Ferdowsian: Yes, I am here. Thank you for the opportunity from myself and Ruhi and the Albany community. I would like to give my love to Don and family.

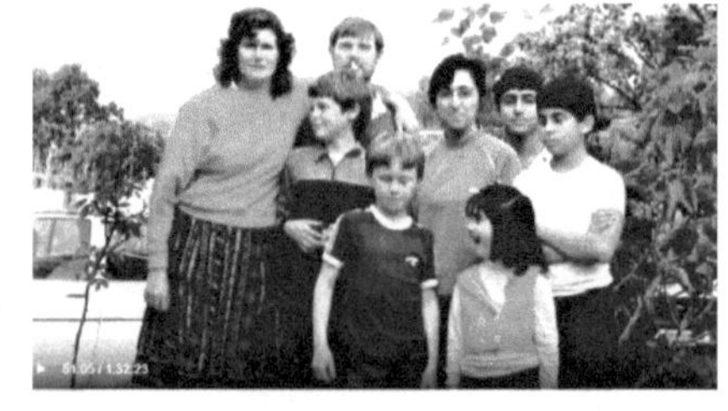

I would like to start with a small Hidden Word from Baha'u'llah which I have been reading since yesterday and it is so befitting. "Oh Son of Justice, Whither can a lover go but to the land of his beloved? and what seeker findeth rest away from his heart's desire? To the true lover reunion is life, and separation is death. His breast is void of patience and his heart hath no peace. A myriad of lives he would forsake to hasten to the abode of his beloved". I feel this is Helen. She was heavenly from the beginning. The love that is bringing us together tonight is the love she had for all of us. We all felt very special when she talked to us.

There are so many memories, very much alive in my mind. It started from the beginning when we came to Australia in 1985. The first place we visited after a month was Narrogin and met the family and fell in love with them. Our children are almost the same age, more or less, and that was a lovely connection. Shadi and Ruth were good friends and visiting each other during the school holidays. When they moved to Tom Price, we visited them there. My special time was when I visited Blackstone. I was invited there to help with the women and children. It always left wonderful, wonderful memories in my heart and my mind. So to me Helen is always alive and will be alive, and that is because of the character and love she had for everyone. We are all feeling very close to her. Thank you for the opportunity. Don and children, we love you very much and we will catch up very soon.

Dale: Violette Brentnal, would you be happy to share?

Violette & Trevor Brentnal: Alláh-u-Abhá friends. Alláh-u-Abhá to Don and all the family, Joseph, Ben, and all of you.

I had heard about Helen but did not come to know her until we moved to Alice. Actually, the first member of the family we came to know was Joseph. He came for one year of service to Alice, and then Helen and Don used to visit from Blackstone. We had the bounty to get to know them and love them.

We got to visit them in 2001 in Blackstone and we learnt that Helen had a very good idea to make paper out of spinifex. All the women in the women's centre were making paper out of spinifex which was very successful for the arts. Then Helen organized marketing it and started a sort of income for the women there.

I remember in 2002, when the convention was on. Helen came a few days before, and I think Don was there too. They were staying with us. My children were going to a Catholic school where they had to go to religious studies which was about Catholic studies. They used to ask too many questions with the teacher. One day the teacher invited my youngest son to come and present the Baha'i Faith to a 45-minute class, this very close to the convention and Helen and happened to be staying with us. I asked Helen if she would do that as it would be nice if someone who was born in Australia, to present that. Very quickly she organized it with my youngest son and another family were visiting for the convention had a daughter. She organized the three of them with songs and material for the presentation. It was a big success at the school and apparently the children were talking about it for many weeks.

That photo was what we had for the 2002 convention, those boxes from Hidden Valley camp that is the entrance for the convention and that was 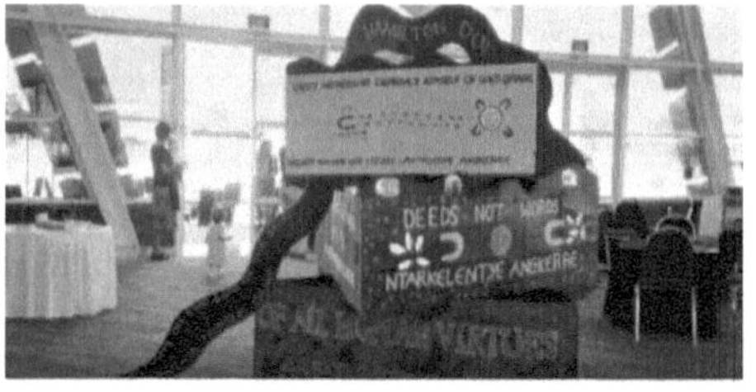 all Helen's work with all our indigenous friends from Hidden Valley, Alice Springs and Santa Teresa.

They used to visit us every so often from Blackstone. One of the times that they were visiting us in 2003, we had bought a place which had a big shed which we wanted to make it into a hall, so we had a place for meetings and all that. It came to the point that we didn't know what we wanted to do with the floor. We couldn't tile it because it was a bit out of our budget. We were talking to Helen, "What can we do?" She said, "You have a paint shop next to you. Let's go to the paint shop and pick up some paints." I said, "OK." We walked to the shop because the place we had bought was in the industrial area. She picked out a few colors and then told us to move all the cars out of the large garage. She started to make seven or eight different patterns on our shed floor. She said "Which one of these patterns do you like?" We started choosing and then there was a meeting and the Baha'is came and looked to see which ones we like. Anyway, the biggest one she had done was a dot painting which she had done very quickly with a sponge. That became the design for the floor of the hall and Helen showed Trevor how to do it. Before we could paint it, we had to do an acid wash because it was a garage floor and was full of grease and oil and things. We did an acid wash with five Baha'i youth on a year of service, one afternoon and it dried overnight. The next morning Trevor and one of the Baha'is did an underlay painting and then made the pattern which Helen had shown us what to do. It was just concrete, but beautiful. It only cost us $500 – the whole floor. Everyone could not work out what it was. Whoever would come, they would take their shoes off and try to feel the floor. They would say, "What is this? It is so beautiful. It is not a tile. It is not lino." It was absolutely stunning, and it was all Helen's idea. You wouldn't believe it – it was so beautiful. It was wearing off after some years but in the beginning, it was so beautiful.

We had a few camps with our indigenous friends. We were trying to do Ruhi book one. Helen came – we had two camps with Helen and one of them was in the middle of nowhere in Anne-Marie's motherland and we had only a few trees there, but it was not hot weather. It was in May. One of our Baha'i friends, Shane Foster, got a generator and a fridge. It was in the

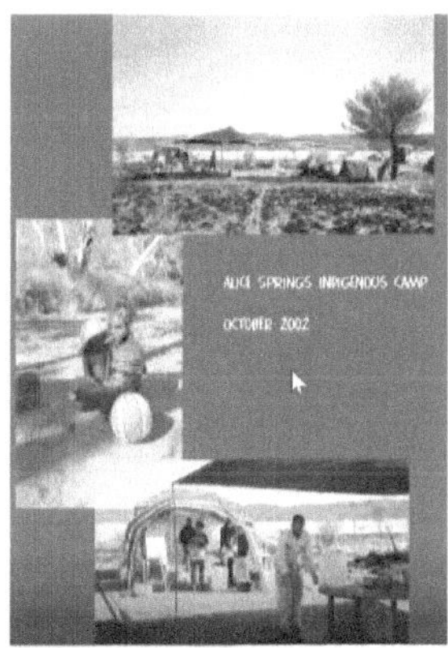

middle of nowhere and we held the camp. Helen had brought all her art materials. And big canvases which she just rolled on the ground. All the sessions Helen ran were the most attended. It was all so exciting for everybody getting involved. Then there was another camp a few months later and Helen came again, and again she held all these art 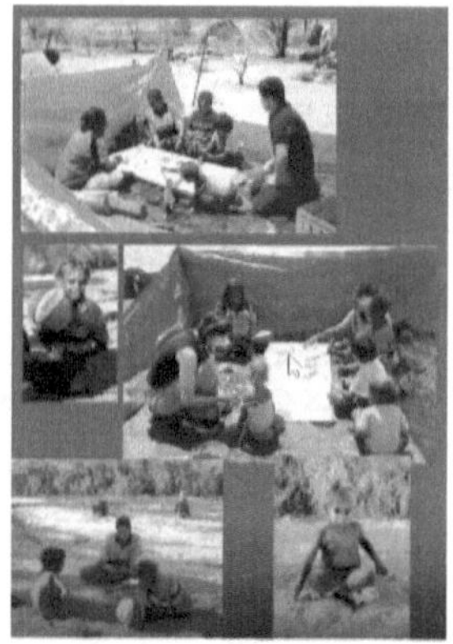 sessions, and it really made a such a big difference. We would read quotes and we would say "Okay, now let's paint this quote. Now what does this mean to you?" And we would do a painting. It was beautiful.

We had lots of help from Helen in Alice Springs and Don was always in the background supporting Helen.

Then Ben came to Alice for service. He declared in Alice and 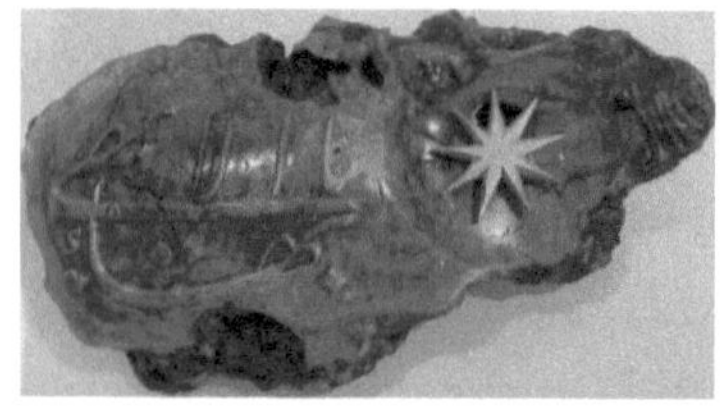 after that he went to Haifa. On one of Helen's trips, she said that Ben had made this beautiful artwork of Ya Baha'u'l-Abha out of roots of olive trees there. Helen said, "I am going to Haifa and I could bring this carving back. Would you buy it and put it in this hall because it is so fitting?" We said, "Sure". So, she brought the beautiful piece of work of Ben which was hanging in the hall until we sold that place and it is now hanging in our room when we moved here. We have lots of gifts of Gordon's in our house. And memories.

Helen had so much to do with Alice and the spirit of the Faith and whatever made it nice and beautiful.

When we last visited Helen which was seven weeks ago, she asked us to choose one of her paintings because I love her paintings. We chose one that is so real – it reminded us of our time in Africa. It was a store on the island

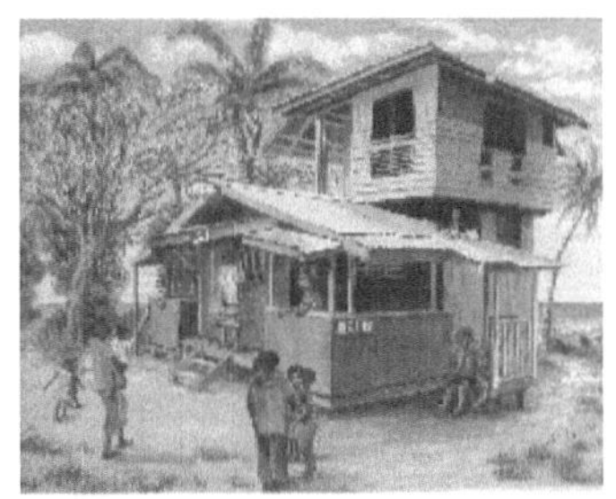

of Malaita where Ben was pioneering. We really treasured it and that is the one she wanted us to have.

Trevor has brought another painting. We bought that from the women's centre in Blackstone. It is at top of our bed and we see it every day.

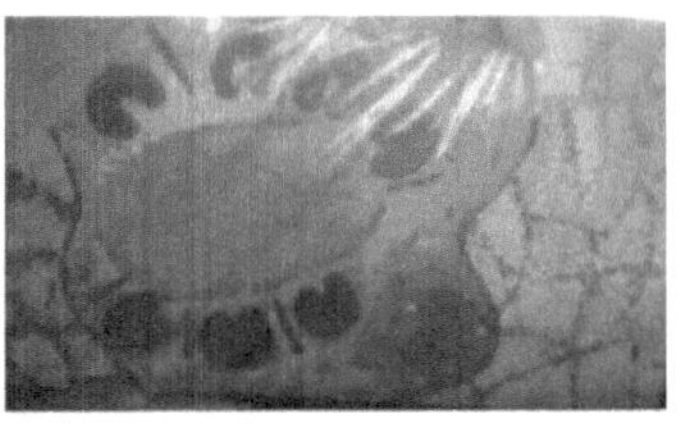

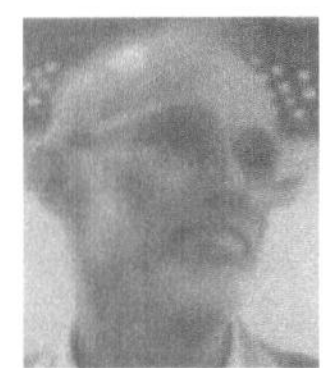

We love Don, Joe, Amica, Ben, and Violyn. Violyn, Ben's wife, saved my life in Samoa. We went visiting in 2000 to Samoa. I jumped into a natural water hole and another guy jumped and caused me to fall over a cliff. It was maybe four metres down and Violyn grabbed me. If she hadn't grabbed me I would have broken many bones and I might have died. She grabbed me and she was nearly falling in too, but then a Samoan guy held onto a tree and pulled me to the other side. Then later, Violyn married Ben. In the Baha'i world, it is so small.

So there are a lot of memories of the Gordon family. They are really part of our family. We love them so much.

I love Helen so much and I know that she is with us and she will help us with the teaching and getting the work going.

That's it. I talk too much, sorry.

Dale: That's fine. Thank you, Violette. Next, I would like to invite Lorraine to say a few words.

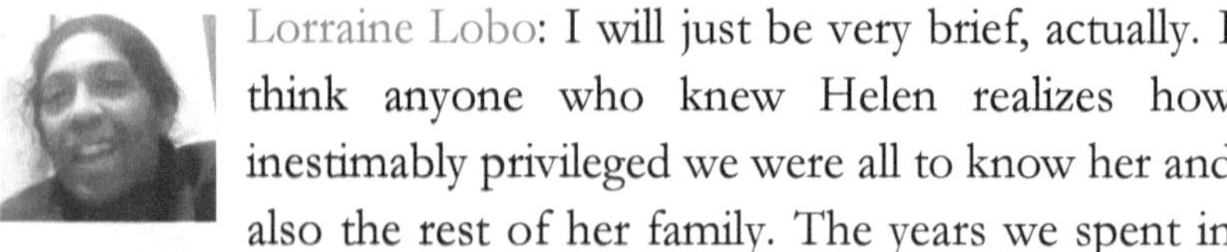

Lorraine Lobo: I will just be very brief, actually. I think anyone who knew Helen realizes how inestimably privileged we were all to know her and also the rest of her family. The years we spent in Tom Price were brief but were very formative. It is interesting that today, our family have been helping Shona and John Earnest move house (in Northam) and they were pioneers in Tom price at that time.

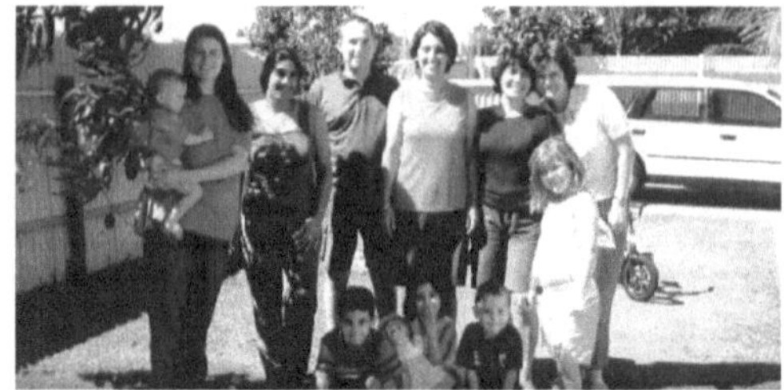

All these were connections forged so long ago – twenty years ago – are still so deep and strong now.

The memories I want to talk about tonight are the recent memories of Helen and Don and the family. Since we moved to Wongan Hills they always made a point of visiting us. The love they have for all the regional believers is so powerful. It is strong.

That picture there is something that I want to talk about. Helen visited here in Wongan Hills so many times. My kids have grown up all their lives here, and to have Baha'i

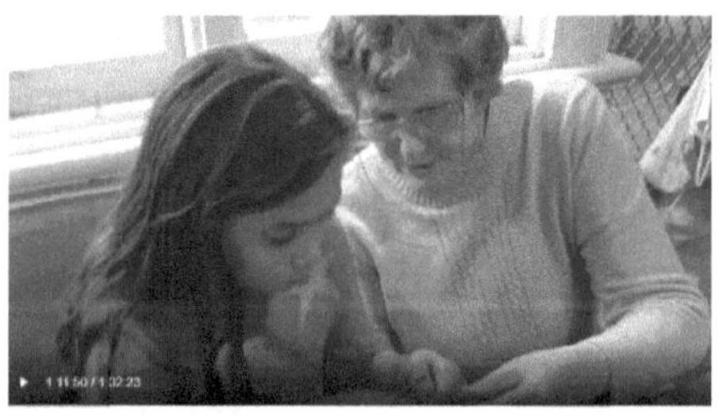

visitors was always special. But, particularly with Don and Helen, they didn't come just to visit Shanks and myself, but they made a point of spending time with our children. I remember Helen came once. She always be used to bring clay, and she wouldn't just give them the clay and say go off and play with it – she would spend time with them, showing them what to do. Teaching them. The picture is teaching Safira how to knit.

I remember a previous time when Safira was very little, maybe three or four years old, when we got out the plasticine to entertain the children while we were quietly talk to Helen and Don. But no, Helen got involved in the plasticine herself and she made this spectacular bilby out of the plasticine. I never wanted to squash it up after that and return it to the plasticine box. It was all that love and care, not only for us, but for our kids. I think they might be as heartbroken as we are that they won't have Helen in their lives anymore.

But we have her memory and her passion for being in the outback. She was a simple person, a creative person, a practical, humble person. I can't say enough about her.

I might ask whether the rest of my family have something to say – they're all still a bit emotional, I think.

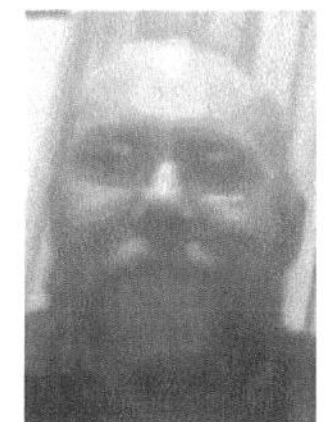

Andrew Shanks: I think as somebody mentioned before – the unconditional love she had for all of us.

In the photo there, I was the scruffy bearded fellow who turned up at her door after meeting some Baha'is in Tom Price – and she was welcomed with open arms. I ended up doing Book 1 there. When others would come there to the house, they take their shoes off – but I didn't wear shoes, so I would just wear some special socks

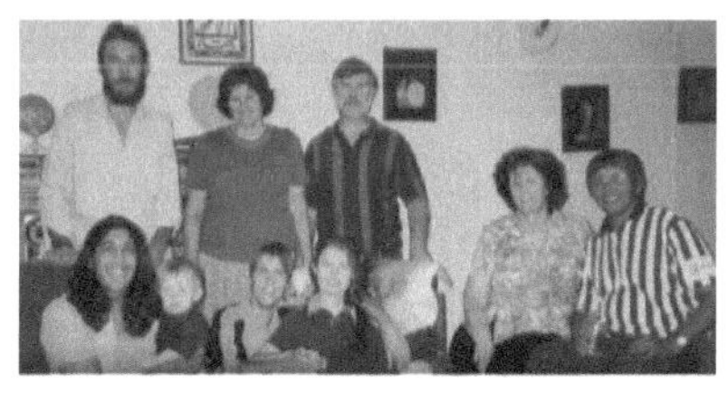

which I'll have to keep the floors clean.

There is so much love the family has given us over these years. Others have mentioned spinifex paper and for our wedding Helen sent down some spinifex paper and some red dirt and desert flowers from the Pilbara. It was never a simple thing – she always went out of her way to make it even more special. Lorraine has mentioned about with our kids. Memory, many wonderful memories.

Dale: Thank you, the Lobo/Shanks family. I will invite Debra for some final words.

Debra Singh: Friends. I just want to thank everyone for attending this gathering and celebrating this beautiful life of Helen. I think we all feel very assured that she is with us. She had this mighty soul, and she will be releasing so much energy that we can all draw on in this coming year – and what is ahead for all of us.

Thank you, Dale, for all the effort you have put into this evening. I know that she has been working at this all day. It had a rocky start, but it was all beautiful.

Thank you, Helen's family, for joining us. It has been very special.

Kate mentioned today that Mr Hall has asked the Universal House of Justice to pray for Helen.

Thank you so much everyone. I will say good night.

Dale: Could I have one person volunteer to say or sing a prayer – one last one for this evening – and then we will go our separate ways.

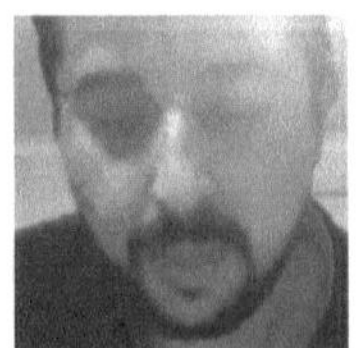

James Gibson: For Helen and her safe progress in the next world. Prayer: *"He is King, the All-Knowing, the Wise! Lo, the Nightingale of Paradise singeth upon the twigs of the Tree of Eternity …."*

..ooOOoo..

19

What was driving Helen?

Written by Don

"for the love of Thy beauty.": Helen arranged for this phrase to be inscribed on her burial plaque, and the words were placed on her coffin. This has special Baha'i meaning[33] and the phrase also had other meanings for Helen – the beauty of her family, beauty she saw in other people, beauty in nature, and the beauty in the range of arts and crafts which she created and which she encouraged others to produce. And, it can be said, in the beauty others saw in Helen.

Helen's favourite animals were seals. Her favourite colour was mauve. Favourite sport was ice skating. Favourite flower was the desert rose. Favourite places were Australian bushland and desert landscapes. Favourite singers were John Denver and Nancy Ward. The favourite pieces she played on the piano were Galway Bay and Danny Boy. And her favourite cooking was making bread.

Her frequent saying is: *Few of my plans have come about – but all of my dreams have come true.* Helen often joked about *taking a road less travelled.* She wrote: *If I had lived a hundred or more years ago, I think I would be an explorer, sailing on a ship to unknown lands, or riding across the desert to find the next waterhole.*

Less typically, and in a different tone, as part of an art therapy

---

[33] "For the love of Thy beauty" – this phrase appears in many Baha'i writings. They are listed at the end of Chapter 23.

course in 2016, she wrote the following.

A fairy tale about me: Once there was a little girl who fell into a sea of turbulent water. She was still floating but didn't know where she was. There were many creatures in the water. Some were friendly, others tried to harm her. But always, the waves enveloped her and carried her on. At times she nearly drowned. She longed to put her foot on dry land, to feel the earth beneath her feet. Occasionally, she would come to a small island but just as she was feeling safe and happy, another wave would come and take her away.

This tale was prompted by a terrifying incident when she was swimming off one of the Perth's beaches in her youth. She felt she was being caught in an undertow and was afraid she might be dragged further out. In her desperation, she just managed to hook a toe on to a rock which held her long enough to then catch the movement of a wave as it began to come back towards the shore. This had such an impact on her that she spoke about this experience on several occasions, many years later. Helen's comment about her fairy tale was: *This is my journey through life – a journey sustained by faith, to provide me with wisdom, understanding, compassion – a security that is beyond this material world, a heart that reaches out to all people and the ability to perceive beauty in almost anything. So now my feet are on the ground. I am not moving anymore. And that which has grown inside me through all these trials and difficulties, will hopefully at last bear fruit.*

At another time, Helen described herself in this way: *I find myself to be: Composed yet searching. Calm, but ready to act. Organized, but not rigid. Controlled, yet feeling. Complex, but of one mind. Empty, yet overflowing. Shaped and molded by the storms of life, this creative soul is gathering, understanding, strength, and wisdom - moving ever closer to some invisible destiny.*

And further *I have realized there is a place of peace and light in my soul which can illuminate and guide the ideas that I have in my head. These are really just thoughts that rationally sound good, but they may not be right for me now. Or they may not be right at all, even though outwardly they may*

So this is what inspired, motivated and impassioned Helen. She was not 'driven' in the sense of anxious energy – but rather in the sense of having a clear focus and sustained determination to do what she thought was right.

In day-to-day practice, for Helen, she was driven by four forces: her family and friends, her faith, her creativity, and community service.

She did not see these as separate – none of them can be seen outside the context of all the others. Each added strength and purpose to each of the others. Her final message was about her husband and children, about the Baha'i Cause progress, and about wider community service and the world of humanity. This book has drawn all these together, but, for a general overview, they are considered one by one, in the following chapters:

- Family and friends – chapter 20
- Baha'i activities – chapter 23.
- Creativity – chapter 21
- Community service – chapter 22

..ooOOoo..

20

Family & friends

Written by Don

Throughout this book, there are many specific stories of Helen's family activities and connections with friends. Now, in this section, there is a general overview.

Family

Quite some years ago, when Helen and Don were preparing their wills, while she was in normal good health, without an inkling that her days were numbered, they each wrote their own 'final message' for the family – to be read after their deaths: Helen wrote:

> *I would wish you all to know that at every moment of my life I have lived it to the best of my ability to be the very best wife to my husband and mother to my children, … and my deepest wish has been that you would all be animated by the love of God, and connected with each other … and I pray that you will all carry on the same between each other and with your own families. My love will always be with you. Remember that every test and challenge is a part of our growth preparing us for this next realm of existence, just as a baby grows within the womb of its mother preparing itself for this world. Keep growing, overcome all concern for self, that some measure of God's eternal spirit may be reflected in you.*

Although it is not remarkable to say that a mother's family is central to her life, it cannot be taken for granted, and with Helen this was particularly strong. Don commented at her funeral that: *The children are first in her heart. Helen was so happy that her three children have each found a place in life and are really contributing to the world around them. Nothing is ever easy, but they are successfully raising their children – her terrific eight grandchildren.*

Helen always made a point of encouraging Joe, Ben and Ruth in their hobbies as they were growing up, and these became significant in their working careers. All are strong the Baha'i Faith.

She took delight in how the grandchildren were developing – Ruth and Colin's (Matthew and Hannah), Ben and Violyn's (Oirae, Weyburn and Jasmine) and Joe and Amica's (Luka, Dara, and Kai). She encouraged the grandchildren by spending time with them in arts and crafts.

As she was preparing for her funeral, Helen wrote this speech for Joe, as MC to read out:

> *I have had a wonderful life, the most transformational moments being discovering the Baha'i Faith and marrying my husband, Don. We have three children, two strong boys, Joe and Ben and our daughter Ruth, who, to me, will always be the most beautiful girl in all the world. They have all gone off the edge of my world and done incredible things with their lives, including bringing eight grandchildren into our lives. We have become a close extended family associating and assisting each other where we can.*

She did not let Don know beforehand but, for the funeral, she dedicated to him Bette Midler's song: *Did you ever know that you're my hero, and everything I would like to be? I can fly higher than an eagle, for you are the wind beneath my wings.*

Helen's siblings, Cynthia, Beverly, John and Russell have

remained close to each other. This has been extended to their spouses. They can count on each other for support – this was in evidence when Helen was so ill in her final years. They have always enjoyed each other's company and met for various reasons quite often – for a book club, games nights, and special occasions. They always gather for a luxurious breakfast on the Saturday before Christmas. This closeness was fostered by their mother, Mavis, who always made a point of encouraging the connections between the families.

The linkages with the next generation have also been maintained: Beverly and John 'JT' Thornton's children (John, George, Chris and Tim), John and Maria's (Adam, Luke and Blake), George and Cynthia's (Natasha), and Russell and Sharon's (Miles and Sarah).

Friends

Helen's friendships began though shared interests in the arts, the Faith, or with communities, and these grew to be rich bonds.

When Helen was becoming quite ill, she thought she should let some of her friends know what was happening. She asked Don to make a list and he started writing down some names and Helen suggested a few more as Don continued to list them. He got to the bottom of the page, and still more on the next, as the pages filled with more and more names. Don joked that his own list would be small. Maybe it's a 'man thing' – it seems that women build friendships in ways that men do not maintain to the same extent.

It is not appropriate to include this list in this book. Many friends have been named in the course of the various stories told here, but it had not been possible to give due recognition to the many people who became such significant parts of Helen's life.

It was fortunate that, in her final years, she was able to

reconnect friendships from school, OT, university and Scotland.

She didn't stop valuing the connections between people. Remarkably , even in the message she arranged to be read at her funeral, she acknowledged the potential for relationships to be sparked between people from different networks attending her funeral: *Maybe as you mingle together you will find a new friend.* And indeed, this did happen.

At the reflections gathering on zoom two days after Helen's passing Don said: *It is quite overwhelming to see so many wonderful friends going back so many years. It is Helen I must thank for leading me to connect with so many of you. … I have got to know a little of your journeys and I am so impressed with the heroes and giants that Helen has enabled me to meet. I thank you all for the opportunity to meet with you and be part of your lives – mostly as a spectator of course, from my point of view. It has been quite, quite wonderful, so thank you so much for that.*

Don expanded on this at the funeral: *Helen had a wide range of deep friendships. She touched, and was touched by, the many ups and downs of people she came in close contact with. These were enduring connections with friends from school days, from university and from occupational therapy. She has many friends among the Baha'is and artists. She was fortunate to engage with brave, resolute and noble aboriginal women in Blackstone, Tom Price, Hedland and Carnarvon. One of Helen's many gifts to me has been in getting to know you all.*

..ooOOoo..

21

Creativity

Written by Don

Throughout this book, there are many specific examples of Helen's own work and the community arts that she facilitated at in various places. Now, in this section, there is a general overview.

Helen wrote: *I believe in the artistic process as essential to the development of the human spirit. It can give birth to new thoughts and ideas, new ways of looking at the world, new perceptions; heal the wounded soul; and be a channel for the creative mind. When directed towards a common purpose, it becomes a strong force for the uniting of diverse peoples.*

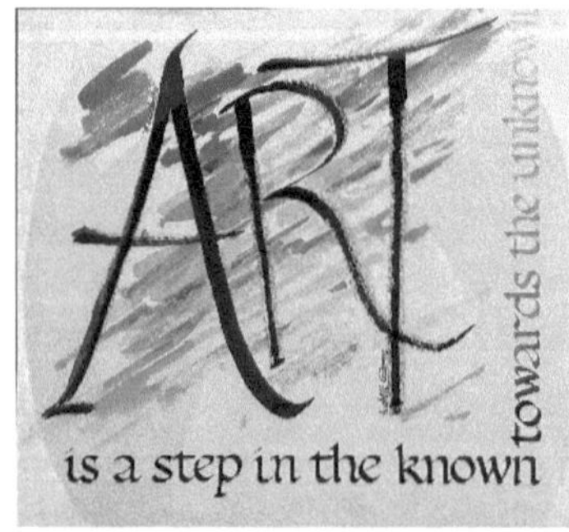

Helen often referred to two quotes which inspired her work – *"Art is a step from the known to the unknown"* by Kahlil Gibran and *"for the love of Thy beauty"* from the Baha'i writings[34]. She also quoted *"All art is a gift of the Holy Spirit. When this light shines through the mind of a musician, it manifests itself in beautiful harmonies. Again, shining through*

---

[34] "For the love of Thy beauty" – this phrase appears in many Baha'i writings. They are listed at the end of chapter 23.

 – by Abdu'l-Baha in *The Chosen Highway*, p. 167.

Helen's own arts and crafts

Helen endeavored to express spiritual concepts through the visual arts. Her skills and versatility in a range of creative forms can be seen in her picture book[35].

Painting & drawing:

She used many mediums – acrylic, pastel, watercolour, charcoal, and inks, in various combinations. This was on canvas, spinifex paper and wood. Her styles included landscapes, sketches and abstracts.

In Tom Price, she exhibited and sold through Pebble Mouse Studio Art Gallery, her own gallery in the old Masonic Hall, PACT exhibitions and the People Exhibit at the Nameless Festival. There were regional exhibitions in Port Hedland and Cossack. She did not win many prizes, but at the Cossack Art Exhibition she was highly commended for *Roots in the Pilbara* in 2006, and for a work for *Beauty is in the Eye of the Beholder* in 2008. She exhibited many times with the Armadale Society of Artists.

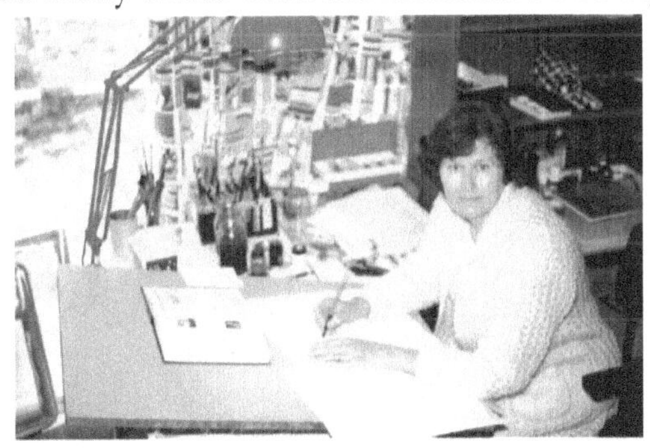

---

35 "Let your spirit fly" picture book – available from on-line bookstores.

Calligraphy:

Helen was a member of the WA Calligrapher's Guild for fifteen years. Her work was printed in the annual Calligrapher's Diary for about ten years and a selection of her work has been on display at the WA Art Gallery with other work by WA Calligraphers. She taught calligraphy at TAFE and conducted workshops privately.

Photography:

Helen's photos were mainly scenery as well as abstracts[36]. Following her father's example, she did her own developing in the black-and-white days of the 1970s.

Crafts:

Her crafts included bush baskets, pyrography, mosaics, collage, bookmaking, clay, and painting on ceramics. Papier mache included bowls, decorated frames for pictures and mirrors, and making small 3D objects. She was also skilled in dressmaking and knitting. She worked with raffia, wood and fibreglass.

Printing:

Helen had her own screen-printing business for fifteen years in Narrogin – doing the designs, screen cut-outs, photo-stenciling, and making the screens. She also did linocuts, woodcuts and monoprints. She produced T-shirts, posters and cards.

Graphic design:

She designed numerous labels for products, logos, pamphlets, newsletters, posters, and banners.

---

[36] Examples of her abstract photographs are in "Let your spirit fly".

Other creativity

Helen's ingenuity was not confined to physical arts and crafts.

Music:
She played the piano, recorder and flute.

Writing:
She wrote some poetry – a few of these were the basis for calligraphy. Helen wrote simple story books for her grandchildren. She produced newsletters for isolated Baha'is – *The Bush Eagle* and *The Bush Honey*. She wrote diaries and other accounts of her experiences – some of these are included in this book. Late in her life, Helen compiled histories[37] of developments in the Baha'is Faith that she had been part of.

Building layouts:
She recognised the practical importance of spaces for activities she was involved in. Her designs included the Kununurra women & children's centre, Narrogin solar house, Blackstone women's centre, Tom Price Cultural Centre, Alice Springs investment residence, Streich Avenue granny flat. And student accommodation at Mummowee farm in Hunter Valley. Maybe, in another life, she would have been an architect.

Inventiveness:
Helen created a weaving loom for people with one arm, papier mache leg splints, and sandals out of car tyres (for people with leprosy). Also, she devised techniques associated with large wooden jigsaws, earrings, spinifex paper, and watercolour on wood.

---

[37] Don holds copies of Helen's histories.

Organisational:

She used her vision and imagination in the numerous organisations and projects she developed. In Blackstone, this included Papulankutja Artists and the Women's Centre. In Tom Price, it was PACT, the Cultural Centre and Nameless Festival. In Kelmscott, it was the Armadale Society of Arts and arranging Baha'i celebration events.

Own training

To equip herself for her own creativity Helen undertook formal training in the piano grade 6, and Cert IV in Visual Arts and Contemporary Craft, as well as many short courses and workshops to broaden her skills.

To equip herself for assisting others, she completed an Associate Diploma Occupational Therapy, Diploma in Art therapy, Cert IV in Workplace training, and the Associate Diploma in Art Teaching.

Community Arts Projects

Beyond her own art work, Helen encouraged others in their arts and crafts. This was partly for people to learn new skills, but mainly as a means of their growing in confidence – to realize something which they already had within themselves. This was transformation. She helped people with little experience to learn how to produce saleable products that they were proud of. She saw this as a channel for personal growth, people working together to strengthening their communities, and potential financial independence of individuals and small communities.

With her imagination and practicality, Helen was skilled in re-envisioning the production of craft items – to work out appropriate technologies and processes – and then distilling complex projects into easy steps that others could learn.

Helen worked with people through her employment with TAFE and other organizations and also voluntarily running workshops and community projects. This was mainly with women and children, particularly in aboriginal communities.

She conducted projects in many of the forms of arts and crafts which she had pursued in her own work (as above). Some of her ideas are described in her suggestions for activities in the study circles[38]. In this book, some particular crafts are singled out:-

- **Earrings**: This was a small craft industry making earrings out of paper that Helen encouraged in the Solomon Islands, Papua New Guinea, and Port Hedland. The method is detailed in Chapter 31.

- **Spinifex paper**: This was made from grasses in desert areas. The paper could be enhanced with pressed flowers. It was used for painting with red sand as well as acrylics – also cards and decorative note paper. Helen set this up in Blackstone and Jameson, and also held workshops in Tom Price. The background to this is described in Chapter 10 and the process is in Chapter 30.

- **Large wooden jigsaws:** See Chapter 10

- **Murals**: Helen was involved in many community murals – mostly at her initiative, and also with her daughter Ruth. These included many in Tom Price – at the schools, bus shelters, drive-in theatre, sports pavilion,

---

[38] How to use creative arts in Ruhi study circles – Chapter 26.

and hotel – and later at the Karijini Experience. Also in Palmerston, Bridgetown, and Jameson[39]. She decorated the floors the old Masonic Hall and Cultural Centre in Tom Price, and the Alice Springs Baha'i Centre. The methodology is detailed in Chapter 32.

- **Organisational**: Another kind of creativity, using her vision and ability to break down tasks in do-able steps was in evidence at the Blackstone office and Women's Centre. Helen described her methods in Chapter 9.

..ooOOoo..

---

[39] Jameson Mural – Chapter 32

22

Community Service

Written by Don

Throughout this book, there are many specific examples of Helen's community service. Now, in this section, there is a general overview.

In her final message,[40] Helen stated that she had done her best for the progress of the wider community, and she urged her family to continue: *to be servants to the world of humanity according to their calling.*

In a talk at a reunion of Occupational Therapists in 2017, Helen concluded: *I have worked all my life with people on the edge of mainstream society and developed a set of skills for enabling them to feel worthwhile, encouraged and keen to develop their potential. … My whole life has been oriented around the use of activities for healing, self-development and community engagement. … I am so grateful for a life so filled to the brim with so many opportunities to explore my talents, develop my potential and hopefully put in a little to make this world a better place, particularly the gift of working with the Indigenous people.*

Most of her work has been with disadvantaged people, particularly aboriginal women and children, through arts and crafts. This has been voluntary and through various organisations.

Her experiences in Blackstone have been detailed in this

---

[40]   Helen left a final message, to be read after her death – Don holds this.

book, and she was also engaged with the communities of Jameson, Mulan, Billiluna, Balgo, Wakuthuni, and Bellary.

In addition to the work specifically with indigenous people, Helen was enthusiastically engaged with the Nameless Festival and Cultural Centre in Tom Price and art societies in Tom Price and Armadale. Also, she was involved in a wide range of organisations in Narrogin as the children were growing up.

..ooOOoo..

23

Baha'i Activities

Written by Don

There are many specific examples of Helen's Baha'i activities[41] throughout this book. Now, in this section, there is a general overview.

Her faith was the major force in her life. In her final message[42] she stated that, at every moment of her life, she had lived to the best of her ability to contribute, in whatever way she could, to the development of the Baha'i Cause. Helen expressed this some years ago: *After much painstaking investigation and reading and meeting with Baha'is from all over the world, I decided to become a Baha'i myself in 1970. I was immediately caught up in the only Local Spiritual Assembly in Western Australia at that time. There was a small but strong youth group – who would go singing Baha'i songs at various functions and were continually travel-teaching in country areas. I came to understand what the Baha'i Faith was, became deepened in my knowledge of the administration and was nurtured and supported by the wonderful spirit of the Baha'is. It was sometimes difficult and painful, but mostly an exciting and rewarding journey into the world of the spirit and the processes of true human development."*

---

[41]   Helen's Baha'i activities are described in the chapters on all the stages of her life and, in particular chapters about the Marshalls (Ch 6), Israel (Ch12), Stories (Ch 24 & 25) and study circles (Ch 26).

[42]   Helen's final message is held by Don.

In an interview,[43] Helen spelled out the two essentials as she saw them: "The journey of a Baha'i is always away from self to God" and "Finding your part in the plan of God".

The phrase "for the love of Thy Beauty' was special to Helen. The various quotes are at the end of this chapter.

Helen promoted the Faith wherever she lived. She did this by Baha'i activities, children's classes and Ruhi books, but mostly by the example of her life. Some highlights were as follows:

- She was brought up, with her family, within the Methodist church.

- She had an early interest in religion and had a dream about the New Jerusalem.

- Her first contact with the Faith was in 1968, through her university friend Verona Mauger (now Lucas). This was at a time when there were very few Baha'is in Perth. Helen attended many activities but did not decide to become a Baha'i until the end of 1970.

- She was among a small, but energetic group of Baha'i youth. This was a significant time[44] because many of these young people went to live in the Pacific to promote the Faith.

- Helen helped form the LSA in Perth.

- She went on pilgrimage to the World Centre in Haifa in 1974 and also spent a month there in 2004[45].

- Over the years, she formed many, enduring friendships with other Baha'is.

---

[43] In 2015, Helen was interviewed about her experiences as a Baha'i – Ch 25.
[44] Don has a history of the Baha'i youth in Perth in the late 1960s & early 70s.
[45] Haifa – Chapter 12

- Helen's activities in Narrogin[46], Tom Price[47] and Kelmscott[48] are described in the various chapters. Also, the Marshall Islands[49]. Helen described[50] her experiences with indigenous communities, particularly in Blacktone, Billiluna, and Balgo.

- Helen completed Ruhi books 1 to 13 herself and tutored in these.

- She made records of the history of the Faith in areas she was involved in.

- Helen was an isolated believer in the bush but she supported others who were isolated by producing the *Bush Eagle*, and the *Bush Honey* through the Outback Project. She also connected with others by visits to other country towns, and by phone link-ups for study circles.

- When she settled in Perth in 2012, this was the first time she was part of a strong Baha'i community – after four decades in isolated areas.

..ooOOoo..

---

[46] Narrogin – Chapter 7

[47] Tom Price – Chapter 11

[48] Kelmscott – Chapter 13

[49] Marshall Islands – Chapter 6

[50] In 2015, Helen was interviewed about her experiences as a Baha'i – Ch 25.

"... for the love of Thy Beauty"

The phrase *"for the love of Thy Beauty"* is in several Baha'i Writings, which are urging *"Forsaking their homes"*, *"leaving homelands, families and children, to travel to foreign countries to diffuse Thy fragrances and promulgate Thy Teachings"*, *"being afflicted by trials in longing to meet Me"*, *"curbing of the desires of a corrupt inclination and observing the precepts laid down by Thy most exalted Pen"*, and *"observing My commandments"*.

The context of these quotes are:

"O Divine Providence! Awaken me and make me conscious. Cause me to be detached from all else save Thee, and captivate me by the love of Thy beauty. Waft upon me the breath of the Holy Spirit, and suffer me to hearken to the call of the Abhá Kingdom. Bestow upon me heavenly power, and kindle the lamp of the spirit within the innermost chamber of my heart. Release me from every bond, and deliver me from every attachment, that I may cherish no desire except Thy good-pleasure, seek naught besides Thy Countenance, and tread no path other than Thy path. Grant that I may enable the heedless to become mindful and the slumberers to awaken, that I may proffer the water of life to those who are sore athirst and bring divine healing to those who are sick and ailing. Though I am lowly, abased, and poor, yet Thou art my haven and my refuge, my supporter and my helper. Send down Thine aid in such wise that all may be astounded. O God! Thou art, verily, the Almighty, the Most Powerful, the Giver, the Bestower, and the All-Seeing." ('Prayers of Abdu'l-Baha', 8)

*These, O my God, are Thy servants who, **for love of Thy beauty**, have forsaken their homes, and been so stirred up by the gentle winds of their desire for Thee that they have sundered every tie in Thy path.* (Baha'u'llah, 'Prayers & Meditations', CI)

*Lord! Dispel the darkness of these corrupt desires, and illumine the hearts with the lamp of Thy love through which all countries will erelong be enlightened. Confirm, moreover, Thy loved ones, those who, leaving their homelands, their families and their children, have, **for the love of Thy Beauty**, traveled to foreign countries to diffuse Thy fragrances and promulgate Thy Teachings. Be Thou their companion in their loneliness, their helper in a strange land, the remover of their sorrows, their comforter in calamity. Be Thou a refreshing draught for their thirst, a healing medicine for their ills and a balm for the burning ardor of their hearts.* (Abdu'l-Bahá 'Revealed to the Baha'is of the United States & Canada')

*Awaken me and make me conscious. Cause me to be detached from all else save Thee, and captivate me by **the love of Thy beauty**. Waft upon me the breath of the Holy Spirit, and suffer me to hearken to the call of the Abhá Kingdom.* (Prayers of Abdu'l-Baha)

*How great is the blessedness of him who, **for love of Thy beauty** and for the sake of Thy pleasure, hath curbed the desires of a corrupt inclination and observed the precepts laid down by Thy most exalted Pen!* (Bahá'u'lláh, 'Prayers & Meditations', CLXXVIII)

*From My laws the sweet-smelling savor of My garment can be smelled, and by their aid the standards of Victory will be planted upon the highest peaks. The Tongue of My power hath, from the heaven of My omnipotent glory, addressed to My creation these words: 'Observe My commandments, **for the love of My beauty**.' Happy is the lover that hath inhaled the divine fragrance of his Best-Beloved from these words, laden with the perfume of a grace which no tongue can describe.* (Bahá'u'lláh,' The Kitáb-i-Aqdas'

If adversity befall thee not in My path, how canst thou walk in the ways of them that are content with My pleasure? If trials afflict thee not in thy longing to meet Me, how wilt thou attain the light in **thy love for My beauty**? (Bahá'u'lláh, 'The Arabic Hidden Words 50')

The Pharisees did rise up against the Messiah ... and they cried out that He was not Messiah. ... ... He told them, "I am God's Son ...." Therefore, they passed the sentence upon Him ... and they hanged Him on the cross, where He cried out, "... I love this cross, out of **love for Thy beauty** *..."* ('Selections from the Writings of Abdu'l-Baha: 19)

..ooOOoo..

24

A horse from Baha'u'llah

Written by Lorraine Lobo

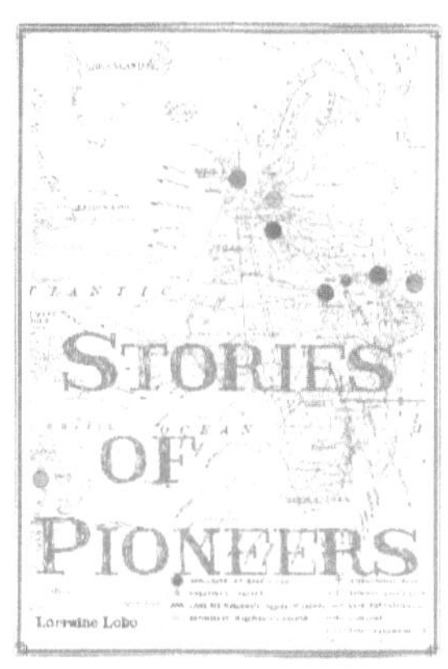

This story is from a booklet of nine stories written by Lorraine Lobo in 2018. Helen first met Lorraine in Tom Price where she was the schools Guidance Officer.

The boy's crestfallen face tore her heart. What on earth had she been thinking? Why hadn't she thought to ask her other children whether they would like her daughter's horse instead of just selling it without a second thought? But now it was too late. The horse was gone, together with any dreams that her son had entertained about playing at being a cowboy. Perhaps it was for the best the expense involved in keeping a horse was one that the family could ill-afford anyway. Oh well, it would all be forgotten by tomorrow.

But it wasn't. The very next day, a horse appeared in their paddock. From where it came, nobody knew. Enquiries were made, questions were asked, until a neighbour arrived to say that her horse kept straying out of its paddock and that she just didn't know what to do about it anymore. She didn't have the time or money to fix her fences, so – she apologized – it would very likely happen again. If only she could find someone to look after the horse for her ….

Helen could not believe her ears, but then again, why not? Baha'u'llah had always looked after her and her family, sometimes in the most mysterious of ways. Was this not just another example of the bounties and blessings that He showered upon those who arose to pioneer and serve Him? The neighbour quickly struck up a deal with the ecstatic boy – she would provide the feed and saddle if he would look after her horse. And, yes, of course, he could ride the horse. In fact, why didn't he ride to their farm and help to round up the sheep – he could play at being a cowboy!

It wasn't the first time that Helen Gordon had experienced such blessings. They had been happening ever since her first foray into regional towns in Western Australia, with her husband Don and their three children. From the Trappist monk in Derby who instantly fell in love with Baha'u'llah's Writings, giving her the courage to keep on going with organizing public meetings. And to the retired shearer who adored her son so much that he had taken him under his wing and taught him how to use his hands – something that his white-collar father would never have been able to do. Blessings indeed.

The list went on. While others in her town often relocated to the city for their children's high school education, or sent them to outlandishly expensive boarding schools, it seemed to Helen that everything she had ever dreamed of for her children's education would rain down from heaven! An aeronautics course for her engineering-minded son. The cheapest pony club and ballet lessons imaginable for her daughter. And what about the retired electronic engineer and his workshop full of equipment that her other son, electronics-crazy son, was given the run of? Really, the list was endless. It was almost embarrassing. No private school in Perth could compete with what Baha'u'llah had arranged for her children's education!

But, it was also hard won. When Helen and Don moved to Narrogin for Don's work in 1980, they were the only Baha'is there. They had another choice – Bunbury, which had an established LSA and a lovely Baha'i community. But Helen chose Narrogin, precisely so that she would be able to open another town to the Faith, although she would be on her own in doing so – even her husband, though supportive, was not a Baha'i.

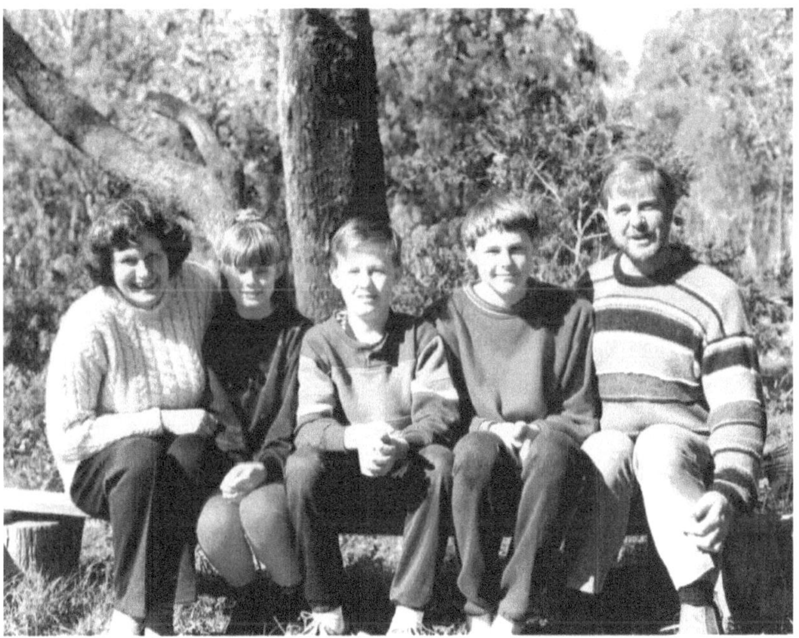

But despite all the bounties and minor miracles, there was still a fear that gnawed at her heart … how on earth would her three children grow up to become strong, steadfast Baha'is with no Baha'i community surrounding them? … with no other Baha'i children, or youth, as they grew older? They didn't always celebrate Feasts. The local school would only allow her to teach her *own* kids during religious education time – and in a tiny closet at that! The kids attempted to do Baha'i children's classes via correspondence but that also had its difficulties.

Many, many times Helen felt that she had sacrificed too much – but her concern was only for her children, not herself. On the other hand, her faith had only deepened, as she realized the true empowerment that came with standing on her own two feet – having stalls with Baha'i pamphlets, holding public meetings, entering street parades – all to proclaim the message of Baha'u'llah. Her capacity had only seemed to increase by being the sole Baha'i in her town and she started to feel sorry for the Baha'is whom she felt were being paralysed into inaction in the midst of large Baha'i communities in the city.

But again, her concerns for her children proved to be wholly unfounded. Baha'u'llah had protected their spiritual development too. At one point, her daughter was the only youth in the whole of Western Australia who accepted to attend the very first Collis Featherstone Teaching Project, being held in Wollongong, New South Wales.

In later years, as she and Don moved to various other regional areas, she watched with great joy as all three of her children embraced the Faith and became devoted, capable Baha'is in their own right. At every step of the way, through crisis and victory, Baha'u'llah had been there with her and confirmation upon confirmation had strengthened her courage and resolve. In the end, Helen realized that her nineteen years of service in Narrogin – the whole time spent as the lone Baha'i family there – had been the catalyst for spiritual development and capacity-building that would have been impossible to achieve anywhere else.

..ooOOoo..

25

My experiences as a Baha'i

45 years – 1970 to 2021

Transcription of a recording by Helen Gordon

This is a transcription of a 107-minute audio recording of an interview conducted by Parisa Mohebi of the Mundaring Local Spiritual Assembly. The interview was in Kelmscott on 21st December 2015. Helen died five years later, at the aged of 75 years. There is an endnote about the transcribing process.

Early years

I was born in Geelong in Victoria in 1945. When I was two, my father (Bill Mitchell) moved to Perth to work as a reporter for the Australian Broadcasting Commission. My mother (Mavis) brought myself and baby sister over here soon after my father had started, but he got tuberculosis straight away and he was in hospital for two years before recovering.

So that was our beginning here in Western Australia. I remember we had a house in Kensington and my mother had six children altogether. We lived in a tiny two-bedroomed house, but I don't remember feeling deprived in any way. It was quite a lively sort of neighborhood, full of very interesting people. So that was my growing up.

I studied medicine for three years, then Occupational Therapy and a Bachelor of Science.

When I was 25 years old, I became a Baha'i and was on the first Local Spiritual Assembly in WA.

I went to Scotland for a year or so and was married there, to Don Gordon. My husband is not a Baha'i but is very supportive of me as a Baha'i. Our children are Joe, Ben and Ruth. And we have eight grandchildren.

Don and I returned to WA in 1974 and we lived in Laverton, Derby, Kununurra, Narrogin, Blackstone, Mulan and Tom Price. We also spent short periods in many other aboriginal communities and in non-western communities in three other countries for short periods. We retired to Kelmscott in 2011.

New Jerusalem[51]

My parents were Methodist. I used to play the organ as a teenager and I taught in Sunday School. I became very interested in religion. I was always asking the ministers of the church, "What does this mean? What does that mean?" They were not very interested. There was "Oh Helen, don't worry about those things." I was particularly interested in prophecies and I used to read the Book of Revelations in the Bible. I loved that particular passage in the Book of Revelations, "I, John saw the Holy City, New Jerusalem, coming down from God out of heaven". I was so fascinated by this idea of this New Jerusalem. One day I had a dream that I would see it. This is while I was quite young – I was about 12 or 13 when I had that dream. Then I forgot all about it and my life continued on. I was still in the church.

I started my university studies. I got a scholarship to study

---

[51]   Helen asked for the song, 'Jerusalem', to be played at her funeral and it was also sung at her memorial-celebration – see Chapters 16 and 17.

medicine at WA Uni.

While I was studying, I met a friend, Verona. She's now Verona Lucas but she had the surname of Mauger then. We used to share a lot of stuff – we both loved in the guitar, singing, art, ice skating, meals at the refectory, and going on little holidays together. Lots of conversations about life and people. She was not interested in religion at all. I shared with her my dream – that I dreamed I would see this New Jerusalem, but I said, it's just a dream. I think, we were just talking about it. It wasn't like something that I was hanging my life on or anything like that. We would share our thoughts and she said "I'm not interested in religion at all."

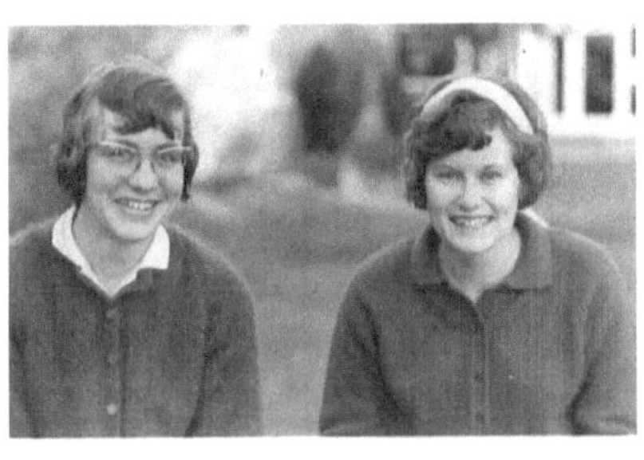

We had been close friends for four years and one day, she came to me and she said, "I found the New Jerusalem."

I said, "What do you mean? That's ridiculous. Don't be stupid."

She said "It is here."

I said, "What do you mean?" My whole body – I was all quite goosebumps all over me. It was sort of like, "No way, this couldn't be!"

She said, "Yes, it's the Baha'is."

There was just Margaret and John Handley, the first pioneers in Western Australia. There were no local assemblies or any administrative bodies at all. This would have been in the late 60s.

Verona and the Handleys had decided to hold youth meetings each fortnight in their home in Bentley. Verona asked me to the first one. This would have been in June or July in 1968.

I was compelled to go and find out about it, so I went to the fireside. I didn't immediately say, "This is it" or anything. I just kept going. But Verona was absolutely on fire with it. She really thought it was amazing. And I was so amazed at her – the difference in her. She was just alive, she just lit up with this whole thing of the Baha'i Faith. I thought, "Well, what is it?" I just kept thinking about it and then I read some books that they gave me. Sometimes I thought, "I'm not gonna go to this meeting any more. It's not really right." There were only less than six Baha'is in Western Australia at that time. It was very sort of on the edge. Then I would think on Friday night, "No, I've got to go, I've gotta go". So I would go.

At one of these meetings, I had a big argument with Charlie Pierce about the appearance of the new Manifestation of God.

Gradually, gradually it took me, from the time I first heard about it, two or three years to think about it. I was a member of Christian organization called the Evangelical Union at the WA Uni. There were a lot of ties. My parents were Methodists. There was a lot of things I had to think through before I could commit myself to being a Baha'i. Then, actually to try it out, the minister of our church would always be saying, "We need a new spirit in the church. We need a new spirit in the church". He was always trying to get everyone to commit themselves to Christ – all this sort of thing.

So one day I very bravely went up to him and said, "Look, I found a new spirit but it's not here. It's with this other group." He just laughed at me. Like I'm asking, "Why don't you just come along and meet them." And he did, which I have to give him full credit for because he didn't have to.

So he did come, and it's actually that what decided for me that the Baha'is were right. He kept putting John Handley down. He was talking to him, and he was telling me that claim was ridiculous: "If Christ had come again, I would have seen him. He would have appeared before me."

I started thinking, "He is not right. His thinking is not right.

How could that be that Christ would just appear before him?" In a little weak voice, I said, "But maybe this is just how God spreads his message – through people." And I said, "Maybe He's telling you now. Maybe He is giving you that message through John, you know, like". But he totally rejected that. And then that really pushed me, that this must be right. John just answered his questions very well. I could see that there was not much logic to the way my minister was talking. And there was a lot of logic and truth in what John Handley, the Baha'i, was saying.

That minister? Unfortunately, he had a nervous breakdown six months later and he left the church. I don't know what happened to him, but he was no longer the minister of our church and I don't know what happened to him because I was only young. It wasn't like I was an adult and following up what happened to him. I didn't know.

Declaring in Mudgee

I had changed from studying medicine and did two years study of Occupational Therapy and was working as an OT at the Claremont Mental Hospital. At the end of 1969, I went on holidays to NSW to visit Verona, who by then was doing her Masters in bio-chemistry in Sydney.

I attended the Baha'i Summer School in Yeerinbool. I went to a meeting with Verona where Jim Heggie, the first Baha'i youth in Australia, gave a talk on Noah's Ark. He explained the meaning of Noah's Ark, how the Ark was the covenant that God makes with man. Then this whole thing of the parables, everything, I just suddenly saw that they had a spiritual meaning. It was not just a story. It wasn't just a story about a physical happening. Whether it happened physically or not is irrelevant – it was the spiritual content of the story that was the real meaning. That was really like drawing back the blind. Ah, it was just like, so true. This is true.

I travelled around with Verona and her two brothers, Alan and Geoff. We went on a trip around the eastern states. Firstly, to Yerrinbool, where we met the Handleys, then to Sydney to meet Elaine Pearman and visit the temple. We visited Kosciusko and then northward up the eastern seaboard to Rockhampton. Verona talked about the Faith all the time. We came back the inland way via Mudgee where we visited Joy and John 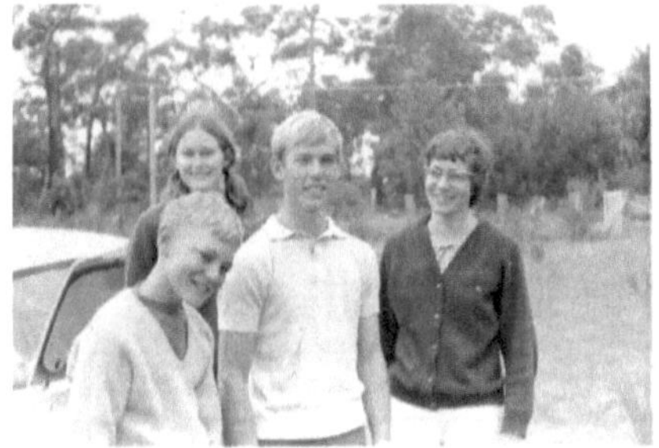 Stevenson. I remained with the Stevenson's while Verona and her brothers returned to Sydney to send Alan back to Perth after his holiday. Joy was quite a remarkable Baha'i. She was a member of the National Assembly of the Baha'is of Australia, and a counsellor. I think she eventually was at the International Teaching Centre in the World Centre. It was there, at Mudgee, that I said that I wanted to be a Baha'i. This was in January 1970.

From Sydney, I took back some Baha'i books for my family, so I could give each of them a Baha'i book.

I had asked Joy to keep my declaration a secret because I wanted to surprise everyone. However, when I got back to WA, I attended a youth gathering and as walked through the door, they all called out "Congratulations".

So that's my journey, how I become a Baha'i. It took a bit, but I just felt right about it. I wouldn't say it was courageous or anything to do it. I felt quite right about it.

Reactions

Was there any opposition from the people in my church? They said that I was on the wrong track, this is ridiculous. It wasn't the right thing. They couldn't see. Our church used to teach that you had to be saved. You had to come to Christ. You had to go through Christ – that He was the Way, the Truth and the Life – as it says in the Bible. But I'd already worked out that if my parents had been Buddhist, I would have been born into a Buddhist family. Would God just have no interest in me? No way. I'd already sorted that out. So, I already had this concept and had studied Buddhism and few other religions, and I could see that there was truth in those religions. I couldn't see how God could abandon most of the world and would just be looking after the Christians. So, I mean, I only saw it in those very broad terms. I didn't have any problem with the fact that, somehow, I wasn't going to be saved. It becomes a fear thing – "Oh, I've been staying the church because otherwise I might not be saved." I don't like those fear-based things.

My parents were okay. My father got to a stage where, though he was still sort of socially connected with the church, but he didn't really believe by then. He'd gone right away from religion, for all sorts of reasons. My mum still had a strong faith, but she wasn't really concerned about my beliefs. When Dr Muhajir came here in those days, I invited him to give a talk in our house and I thought, "Ah, my parents." But at the last minute they decided they were gonna go out for dinner so I could have the house to myself. I thought, "Oh no, this is why I got this guy." That didn't really work. But yeah, they didn't really show much interest, but they didn't cause me any problem. They were quite happy for all of us. All of my sisters and brothers all went different ways. I've got a sister who is interested in Buddhism. I've got a brother who's a Deacon in the Anglican church. They followed their own path, but none of them have gone the same way as my parents. My father really encouraged us all to be independent in our thinking and he was a great thinker himself. He was a very well-known and used to be a public speaker, an orator. He was a journalist and then later he was the first public relations officer for the WA government. He was a very outspoken thinker. We were lucky in that he encouraged us to think for ourselves and follow our own path. So I was fortunate there. But I don't want to talk too much about myself.

As soon as I got back, after Sydney, an NSA member asked me to move into the Perth city area. I had no idea what a Local Spiritual Area was, but this is what I was supposed to do – I was to move into the LSA area. By then there were enough people, nine, to form an LSA[52]. And it happened that a friend of mine said to me, "I've got a flat. Would you like to share with me?"

It was her mother's flat in the middle of Perth – an old-fashioned, Victorian style, multi-story buildings in Mount Street. This friend, Maxien Bradley (nee Lethbridge), had studied Occupational Therapy with me. She eventually become a Baha'i as well.

During that time, I came to understand what the Baha'i Faith was, became deepened in my knowledge of the administration and was nurtured and supported by the wonderful spirit of the Baha'is.

The first book we studied was *God Passes By* with Soheil Taheri as our facilitator.

There was a small but strong youth group – who would go singing Baha'i songs at various functions and were continually travel-teaching in country areas. We had a singing team that would entertain anywhere – mainly held together by Charlie Pierce with his very profound musical skills and Fiona McDonald also had a superb voice. We also had a community car painted bright yellow with BAHAI UNITES MANKIND on the side. Everyone took turns in driving it to their work so that mostly it was thought we had a fleet of these cars[53].

---

[52]   There was already one LSA in WA – in the South Perth area, but Helen helped form the second LSA - in the city of Perth.

[53]   This was a remarkable time with young Baha'is in WA. Many soon left to

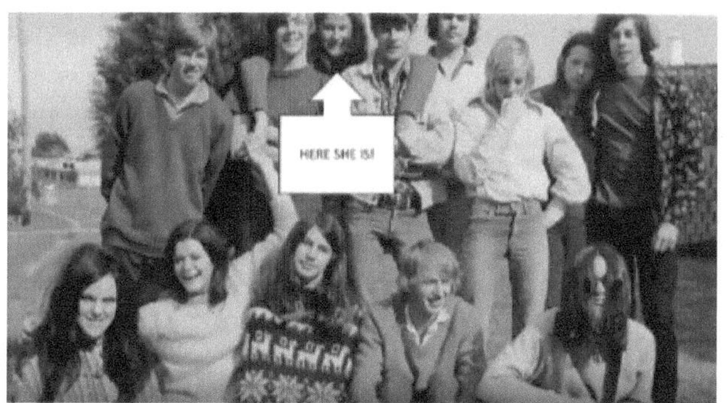

Mike & Wendy Cater at the back, Rosemary, Jenny, Barbara, Tony
Deamer, Bryn Deamer, and Charmaine in the front right with the hair

I remember Dr Muhajir coming to Perth and talking about
the need to move out of the city and for Bahais to start moving
to country towns. He had a map of WA and pointed to various
towns all over WA. Why doesn't someone go here and then here.
I think he had no idea of how incredibly small some of these
towns were. Even though we were such a small group there was
a lot of talk of moving away from Perth and starting Baha'i
groups in country areas. Also, the call came for pioneers to the
Pacific and five members of our small community went to
Vanuatu and Fiji at different times.

Baha'i Society at UWA – 1971

I went back to do a Bachelor of Science at the University of
WA, full-time. Another Baha'i had enrolled full-time
(Charmaine Burke), and one part-time (Minoo Fozdar). With
three Baha'is at the university, we decided to form a Baha'i
Society. It was a bit hard because the other two left soon after
we started it, so I was left as the only one with the Baha'i Society!
I began to feel very insignificant and powerless, and wondered

---

become long-term pioneers in Pacific Islands. Don has a history of this time.

how I could keep this going. This was my first taste of being just on my own as a Baha'i.

I decided to do beautiful silkscreen posters so that they looked like we were a very professional organization. I left space on the posters to write in different topics – every week I just changed the subject to advertise. The posters had a great effect. Even some people stopped to write comments on them – sometimes blasphemous comments were written across them like "This isn't true."

I had booked a room to have meetings but mostly no one came. Even when we had all three of us, only one or two people were enquiring so I wasn't expecting many people to come. But the small group of people with whom I was studying – there was only six of us doing third year human anatomy – would ask me during the afternoon's practical work, how the meeting went. There was a Jewish fellow – we'd have to dissect a body, and he was opposite me. He was always saying to me:

"What did you talk about in the meeting?"

I said, "Oh yes, we talked about this, and this, and this." So I would give my talk to him over dissected bodies and bottles of formalin. My prayer was always, "Please don't let him come to the meeting and see no one there." It was just me sitting alone in the room eating my lunch. It wasn't so bad because you could meet up with the other Baha'is afterwards and have a bit of a laugh about it.

So that is how it was. But it did keep going, then more people came in. I was only there for a year to complete my Bachelor of Science.

I had a job as the first Occupational Therapist in the maximum-security ward at Claremont Mental Hospital and this opened up many opportunities to teach the Faith there, particularly with the doctors.

Travels – 1972 to 1974

I went on a working holiday to New Zealand[54] and then
Ireland where I attended Maxien's wedding. Then St Andrews
in Scotland where they were trying to establish an LSA. Don and
I were married there. I have known him a little through mutual
friends in Perth, and he was also on a working holiday. He got
some work with gypsies near Glasgow and we had our first few
months of married life living with them on their caravan site[55].
And then we came back to Western Australia.

Laverton & the Kimberleys – 1974 to 1979

I have been in lots of different places around WA. My
husband got a job with the Community Welfare Department in
Laverton. It is 350 kilometres northeast of Kalgoorlie. A very
small town, right out in the desert. Don was working with
aboriginal communities there. Then from there we went up to
Derby, which is right up in the Kimberley region. Then we went
to Kununurra after that. So we stayed in the Kimberleys for
about five years, and all our three children were born there. In
those places I used to always have my little Baha'i stall at the
markets.

One time I organized a public meeting in Derby. It was very
interesting because there was another Baha'i who was working
at a cattle station as a teacher. She was Jackie Appierspach who
had become a Baha'i in Perth then took this station job. (She
eventually went back to America or Canada and I've lost contact
with her now.). She was teaching just a few children at the cattle
station away from Derby because often station people used to
have School-of-the-Air for their children, who needed a teacher

---

54   Helen wrote about her adventure on the Routeburn Track – Chapter2.
55   Helen wrote about her time with the gypsies – see Chapter 4.

to help guide them. So she was working there and we both got together. We decided to have this public meeting in Derby. So we advertised the meeting and we got it all ready. We had a little projector, with slides of the Holy Land. We planned our talk and really prepared it well. We had some Baha'i books there. No one came and then half an hour after the starting time, suddenly this fellow came walking in with a beaming face. He was Brother Dan, a Trappist monk, which means they mostly live in silent meditation. Anyway, he had seen our poster about the twelve principles. He very quickly said that he believes that there has to be a new prophet come to bring all the religions together – and that it won't come from Christianity itself. It was just amazing. Then we showed him the Baha'i books. Straight away, he wanted to look at the Baha'i writings and other books. So we showed him *Gleanings*, and as he read it, he said, "This is true." He was just immediately, completely, right there with the Faith. So we gave him a copy of the book. He did not live in Derby. He went back to his place where he lived – One Arm Point – quite a remote location, several hundred kilometres away. I corresponded with him for about three years, but he never became a Baha'I, that I know of.

Probably there were little sparks of things like that happening when we had meetings or occasionally people would really show a lot of interest, but not always become a Baha'i. I always taught the Faith wherever I was, but it didn't always result in me creating a Baha'i community where I was. But there a lot of people who heard about the Faith from me just being in that place. The fruits of that effort might come up somewhere else – who knows.

While we were in Kununurra, Don had three months holidays and we went to the Marshall Islands in the Pacific Ocean. Jackie Appierspach had been there and she suggested this to us. I lived on this tiny island and taught the Faith there in the villages[56].

One of the highlights of teaching in remote areas was when I was out of Blackstone – but that was after Narrogin.

Narrogin[57] – 19 years from 1980 to 1998

After had been in the Kimberleys, and we decided we wanted to be closer to Perth, for our three little children growing up. But we didn't want to live right in Perth. We moved to Narrogin, 200 kilometres south of Perth. We lived there for nineteen years.

Our children grew up there and I would teach them Baha'i classes at their school. At that time, although I was allowed to have my own children in the class, I wasn't allowed to have other children. The structure for other children with other non-Christian religions was not set up yet. That was my way of teaching my children because it was very hard to do it at home as they didn't see why they should do it. There's no other Baha'i children and all that sort of thing. From time to time there was some other Baha'is who moved to Narrogin for short periods, but no children. Then they moved away. There weren't any other Baha'i children, so our children grew up quite removed from much contact with other Baha'is. They were attracted to the Faith but it was really hard because the boys particularly, started seeing that their dad was not a Baha'i. Why didn't he believe in God? Why didn't he, and all this stuff. So they moved away from it a little bit. Then a few years down the track, all of them became Baha'is – very committed[58].

I put the 'Baha'i Thoughts' in the local paper, *The Narrogin Observer*, every week for sixteen years. I got it in for $3 a time,

---

56   Helen wrote about her time in the Marshall Islands – see Chapter 6.
57   Helen kept a diary of Baha'i activities in Narrogin – in the NSA Archives.
58   Lorraine Lobo wrote about Helen's experiences as an isolated pioneer in Narrogin – see Chapter 24.

and they kept it at that cost for the whole sixteen years, which is amazing. For the price, I wasn't allowed to put my name or anything on it, so they just put it anywhere. It might be on the front page or third page or the last page – wherever they had a little space, they would pop it in.

After about eight years a lady, called Elizabeth Eaton, had been reading them, and she contacted the paper to find out who was putting in these 'Baha'i Thoughts'. She came to me and she said, "This is what I believe. I want to know more about this religion." She was a Mormon. I said, "That's fine", and she said, "Well, I'll organize a meeting and I'll invite my friends and you come and talk to us". So that's what I did. She did everything. She wanted to start with the Baha'i prayer so I gave her a Baha'i prayer book. Then she would ask for a topic and I would talk on it. So she opened up these meetings. I didn't feel all that prepared for them. I had been living in Narrogin for so long and not having talked about it much with anybody, it was quite a big learning curve. Then they decided that the great interest was in the return of Christ. We decided that we would study the Book of Revelations in the Bible (which included the New Jerusalem). I very quickly got a whole heap of Baha'i books on this subject, and then I actually made my own notes, and really honed up on it. I had as much information as I could and compiled it into a little book.

I said that I only want to study those passages that 'Abdul-Baha has given a meaning for those passages. So that is what we did. We would all read these passages. We went through them. We were meeting every week. It went on for six or eight months.

We got a whole group of people joining, so there were Christians and Mormons. It was probably about six of us altogether. In that group there was one single mother who had two children, one of whom was a friend of my daughter's. There was another who was a Mormon lady who was dying of cancer, she was in the group. Another lady was a Christian but not really strongly connected with any particular church. And then there was this Elizabeth Eaton, a Mormon.

The Mormon church got extremely worried because they could see that there was a couple of members of the Mormon church coming. They were worried that I was taking away parishioners. I was quite friendly with some people from the Mormon Church, so that was quite difficult.

A lot of things happened in that time. People connect with each other about various things. We were helping this lady who was dying. There was a lot going on. It was more than just the meetings; it was all the connecting up with everyone. We kept taking food around to this lady dying of cancer and it just went on and on. Then suddenly my own son, Joe, became very ill, and he was in hospital. So I said, "Look, my son is seriously ill and I really can't do these meetings anymore." Anyway, Lyn, one of the other ladies in the group said, "Well, I'm gonna keep it going. This meeting has been started by God, and it is not going to stop". So she kept it going for a while. For me, I felt we had gone through all these things, a lot of it, we'd been through my little book, and it was almost coming to an end, and something had to happen. I wanted people to either study more, or other things. Anyway, it went on for about another month or more — it kept going but finally stopped. It was quite an event.

Then finally Elizabeth left Narrogin and I heard that she contacted the Baha'is up in Perth but I don't know that she actually became a Baha'i. I lost contact with her.

Every year we put on a big Baha'i display at the agricultural show. We made this great big thing out of three-ply — a globe map of the world. We put all the counties on it then we had 'Baha'i Unites Mankind' across it. We had a model of the Baha'i temple in Sydney. It had been made Pieter De Vogel, who at that time was the secretary of the NSA, and he had made one for each state. We put this model of the temple there and then we had our great big world. We would really go to town. Sometimes we had pony rides for children (our daughter had a pony) and other activities for children. I had pamphlets and big display boards with information about the Faith. One time, we won first prize for our display at the show.

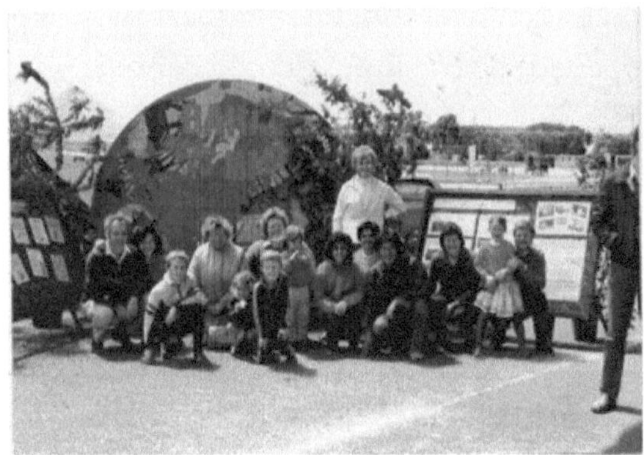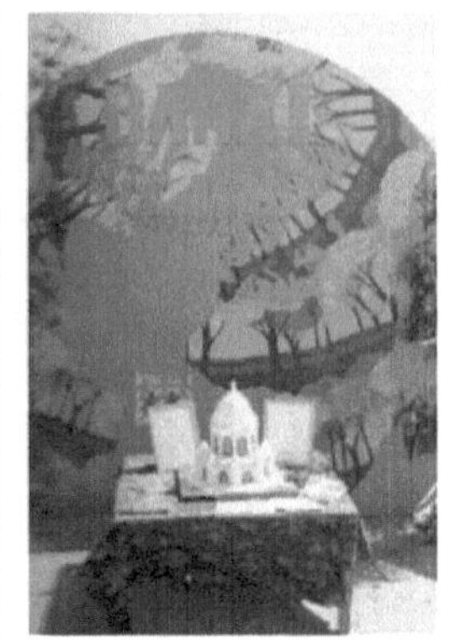

It invited a lot of discussion. People would come. Christians would come and talk to us about "This isn't right" and "Christ is the only one." We would have discussions, "Do you believe in the resurrection?" It was time of intense discussion with a lot of people. A few Baha'is from Perth would help. So that happened every year at the agriculture show.

We used to have weekend deepenings, maybe once a year. Baha'is would come from Perth. One time it was quite a big event with about fifty people. A friend, who was a Christian, used to help me prepare it all. She would help me with the children's activities. She never became a Baha'i.

I was the only Baha'i in Narrogin for most of the time. A few times we had some Baha'is living there for short periods, then they left. At various times were Marie and Phyllis Coles, John and Susan Koshkusan. There is no one there now. There is a lady who has been inactive from a long time ago. She doesn't want contact with Baha'is now. There was another lady, Colleen, but she has moved to Mount Barker quite recently.

Over the years, I kept contact with the other Baha'is in the south-west – in Collie, Bunbury, Harvey and Albany. They would visit us for the day or stayed for a night or so. And similarly, we visited many others. There were real connections between our families.

Also, I linked with other isolated pioneers by writing a newsletter – *Bush Eagle*[59].

We left Narrogin at the end of 1998.

Blackstone[60] – 1999 to 2001

After Narrogin, our children went up to university and whatever. We decided that we would do either Australian Volunteers Abroad or something like that – just for a couple of years. But we realized that it was a bit silly. We got concerned about going to another country as we had previously been travel-teaching in the Marshall Islands with very young children. We saw some groups, like AVA, that were really not very effective. In the three months we were there travel-teaching, we realized that we were limited in what we could do because, even though it was claimed that English was the second language, it really wasn't. It was just that some people could understand a bit of English. They talked in Marshallese. You really need to be fluent in the language of the people. So we started going away from that idea and Don saw some jobs for remote places in WA. We felt, in that way if something came up with our children, I'm not depending on my mum and dad to sort it out – we can just go back because we're not too far away.

---

59   Copies of the Bush Eagle are in Don's possession.
60   Helen wrote about her time in Blackstone – see Chapter 9.

So we took this job out of Blackstone. It is where the three states meet (WA, NT & SA), but just inside the border of Western Australia. It is 2000 kilometres east, half of it on gravel – it takes a few days to get there. We were both employed – Don was the CEO, and I was managing the office and doing all work with the women, and other things. It was a tiny community of 200 aboriginal people. We absolutely loved it there. I love the people, really.

I have never taught the Faith so much as when I was out there. I just found so many opportunities. Many people would ask me about the Faith. The Aboriginal people knew I was a Baha'i but I never tried to sign people up to the Faith or anything, because it wasn't appropriate.

We had an astounding number of professional workers coming in and out of this community, and because we were managing it, we often had people staying with us. There was some accommodation for visiting staff which was close to our house, so people would come and meet us. A lot of scientists, such as botanists, would come there to explore the pristine desert environment. And anthropologists. We had the Minister of Education fly in because he wanted to see this aboriginal community at first hand. Then there was the head of Mental Health and a few of his entourage, because there was some mental health issues and he wanted to see how it worked in this community. So all these people came in and out. We ran the community quite differently to staff from most other communities so a lot of people would ask:

"Why are you doing it this way?

"What's your philosophy?"

I said, "Well, I'm a Baha'i. I don't see myself as being above the people here."

We were not controlling their lives or anything like that, but we'd laid down rules that we think are fair, and all this sort of thing.

I had a diverse role. Originally, I was paid as an office manager, just to manage the community office. I trained a lot of people to actually run the office. White staff from other communities didn't believe that I had taught these 'bushy aboriginals' how to use computers. But they're actually exceptionally good. Much better than me. They were very good at just inputting information and that's what you have to do. Like with payrolls and things like that. I had a wonderful girl who just had memorized this whole payroll system. I still hadn't memorized it because it's not my natural thing, managing an office. She was just off with it.

Very quickly I saw that there was no one coordinating the women's center and so I used to leave the staff I had trained in the office, and I was over with the women. This was my passion.

I set up activities in the women's centre. We ran a play group. Meals for the old people. Secondhand clothing. Sewing our own clothes. We had a lot of industrial type activities, like making giant jigsaws that we used to sell and send all over to schools. And then they used to do a lot of dot paintings. I started Papulankutja Artists as an outlet for all their creative activities. Towards the end, I started a spinifex paper making industry. So there was a lot of things.

I had quite a few Baha'is come to stay for short periods. Mahshid Ferdowsian came out and worked for a month teaching sewing and hairdressing, and things like that. Then I had some youth come out and helped the people write their own books – that was Maryam Bell. All of our children actually came out and worked there as well. All of them for different times, for different purposes. At different times, Joe and then our son-in-law, Colin ran the swimming pool there – a big indoor swimming pool. Our other son, Ben, was motorbiking around Australia and he ended up there, as a project supervisor running the CDEP employment program. He looked after all the buildings and the infrastructure. He worked with some of the local people and he would manage all that. Our daughter, Ruth, came out and helped the play group. So there was just a lot. We had our whole family actually because it was a wonderful experience for them too. Sorry I'm getting a bit off track from Baha'i teaching.

I could tell you a really interesting teaching story. We were away. We used to have to take some time out every now and again, and we had someone looking after the place for us. There was a guy from health – the health department had a nursing post there – and he stayed in our house. I said that I was happy with anyone staying in our house because there's a shortage of accommodation for visiting people.

I said, "Yeah, just let them stay here, that's fine".

Anyway, he was staying there. Later on, when we came back, even though you have people looking after things while you are away, usually they don't do a lot of things that have to be done – so I had a lot of work to catch up on and we were up till midnight trying to get everything up to date. Then this same guy came over.

I whispered to Don, "Oh no, I am exhausted. He just can't stay here."

So he said that there was no problem – he slept on the sick bed in the nursing post. So that was alright, he had found somewhere to sleep. Then, about 5 o'clock, about tea time, at 4:30, I had just come home to have something to eat and I saw this guy coming over towards our house. "Let's tell him, he just has to go."

I had to open the door and I said, "Hi there," trying not to sound too rude.

He said, "I was coming to say that, while I had been staying at your house when you were away, I had read some of the books. There was one book in particular that fascinated me". It was *Baha'u'allah and the New Era*. I said, "Oh, really."

Suddenly energy flooded through me. "Come in for some tea." So he stayed for tea and I gave him the book.

That type of thing happened. Some other beautiful things happened with the Aboriginal people. There wasn't a church building in Blackstone – it wasn't a strong Christian community but there were a few Christians there. One local lady ran the play group, and she was really concerned about the young children and she wanted to help them to have some spiritual teachings. She was trying to run a little Sunday School. She would come and ask my help.

I'd say "Why don't you teach about the oneness of God? Or why don't you teach them about …."

I gave her my virtues book. She would come and ask me about a lot of things. We had really in-depth discussions. It was really wonderful. In the end, she was running Baha'i classes, in effect. It wasn't called a Baha'i class, but there are a lot of Baha'i concepts that she would actually teach because she loved them. She really connected with them.

Some people criticize me that I never asked some of these people to be Baha'is, but if they had asked me, "I want to be the same religion as you," I would never have said "No." But, in my position, I could not be seen to be proselytizing. You're actually in a very sensitive environment. I saw one CDEP supervisor, who is a Christian, try to convert people. He used his position to influence people – it was not right. I never set out to influence them. I really just answered their questions. I would say what I believed. I didn't say, "This is what you should believe." So that's how I approached it.

There were some wonderful events that happened. Sometimes I would go out bush with the women and I would boil the billy and sit there and just chill out for a bit in the bush. That was my way of getting a bit of peace and quiet. They used to run around everywhere getting goanna's and wichity grubs – collecting bushtucker which they love to do. So they would do that, and I'd do this. Usually, I'd take a little container of flour to cook a bit of damper in the end. Anyway, it was the Baha'i Fast this time, and so I didn't eat or drink during the day and it was quite a hot day. We were out, and then on the way home the sun set, and we hadn't got back. So, I'd taken in preparation, some watermelon and some water with me. I had it in an esky.

I said, "The sun has just gone down and I have to stop, if you don't mind." I said, "You could come and join me. In my religion, we have a Fast this time of the year and we don't eat and drink. So I need to sit down and just have something, and I can share with you."

So we sat down and we were all sitting in the red sand. We gathered around. I handed them each a piece of watermelon and we ate this. Honestly, if you could describe what reverence is. I could never ever, I mean, this was just total reverence – for me – for what I believed – and for what I was doing. Yeah, like it's something you can't actually talk about reverence. You can, read reverence is da da da. But, actually, reverence is something that is beyond words. All the virtues are beyond words. We use words to describe them, but the actual nature of it, the entity of it, is something that is beyond words. They showed such reverence and respect for me. I will never forget it. They just asked me … they said, "Wingula (that was my Aboriginal name), do you believe in the same God as us?"

I said, "There is only one God. The God of all of us. We're all one. It doesn't matter, your skin is black, and mine is white. It doesn't make much difference, does it?"

I got on very well with them. They looked at me and they said, "Is your religion the same as ours?"

I said, "Well, we all have a different way of approaching our belief in God. There are many different prophets. I believe in

Baha'u'llah who is the latest of the prophets". I talked just very simple, and they just listened quietly. It was just that – a beautiful exchange of conversation. It was done in that whole atmosphere of reverence, and to this day, I've carried that in my heart. I just know what it is. They gave it to me. I didn't give it to them.

There was a couple of youths in our community who were actually unusual, to be mixed blood. Mostly they are full blood aboriginals there. They were girlfriend and boyfriend. They were quite keen. One was trying to study to be a nurse and other wanted to be a mechanic. They left the community – they would be there sometimes and then they would leave. They went to Alice Springs. There was a lovely young Baha'i called Kurt Branso from Alice Springs. He had come and worked at Blackstone for a while. I'd got a few Baha'is just visiting but he came and actually worked in the store with us. He was part islander background – from Samoa, I think. He had quite a strong affinity with all the young people there. And so they came, these two young people actually visited him in Alice Springs, and they used to come to all his firesides and everything. They were quite keen but I don't think they became Baha'is in the end. So that was another thing that happened so far as teaching the Faith goes.

There was a lot of amazing moments like that. But I've been unhappy about just acquiring numbers into the Faith. I think it's very important that people understand, particularly with indigenous people. I've seen a lot of quite meaningless, even destructive, gathering of cards in Aboriginal communities. I've seen the consequences from that later. But it's not so many times.

There was a Local Spiritual Assembly in Alice Springs but we didn't form one in Blackstone because I didn't try to get people to sign up to become Baha'is. I just couldn't do it. If someone had said, "I really want to be a Baha'i" and were really determined, I would not have stopped them, but it didn't get to that point. I thought it was important that they understand the concepts.

Relationships are quite difficult with indigenous people. I always kept away from any reciprocity, so I never tried to give them things. I never entered into any arrangement whereby I was giving them something. Occasionally, if I had this watermelon, I would share it around, but it wasn't like I would give something to someone as a way of forming a relationship because sometimes misunderstandings come from it. Nomadic people, their philosophy of life is to take what they can from the environment and then to move on. If you become a resource, then the relationship is almost broken. So I didn't go into that. I didn't allow that to happen.

Joe lived in Alice Springs for a while. And Ben went to stay in Alice Springs after he had been in Blackstone and was very involved with the Baha'i youth there. He was not a Baha'i at that time, but then he went to a tiny, remote community – Patja – and decided to become a Baha'i out there – with no other Bahai's around. He was soon off to Haifa.

I have so many stories. I could talk for years, but these are just a couple of examples. It was quite a unique time.

Billiluna – 2001

After we left Blackstone, we went to Alice Springs. I said to Don that I would really have loved to have gone to Billiluna in the Kimberleys because there was an LSA in that little community. Philip Obah[61] lived 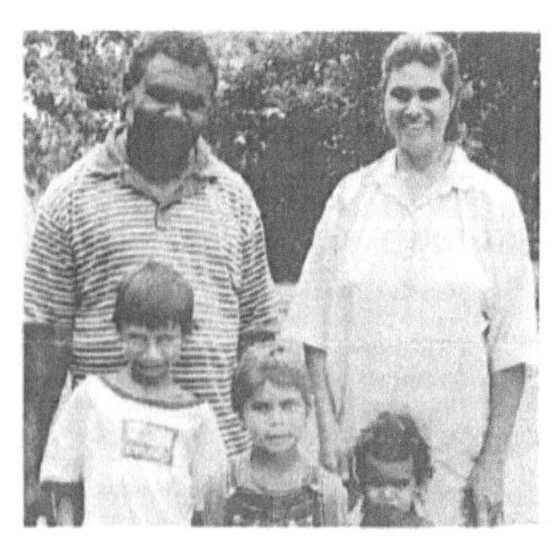

---

[61]   Philip Obah died in 2021 and his obituary is in the February 2022 edition of the Australian Baha'i – the same edition that carried Helen's obituary.

there, and he was on the National Assembly at that time. They wanted to go back because his wife, Sue, had left that community when she was four years old. Her father was a white man and so she wanted to go back and find her roots again.

They were driven back to Billiluna from Alice Springs by my son, Joe, so I had that connection there. I said I'd like to see how an LSA works in a similar sized aboriginal community to what Blackstone was. I was thinking, "How could this be?".

When we got to Alice Springs from Blackstone, Don got rung up and was asked, would he do a relieving job right up in Mulan, just for six months. Mulan happens to be the community right next to Billiluna. I said, "Oh my God, this is amazing." Those things don't happen easily. So we took it, and we went up to Mulan. Actually, it's better that Don wasn't the CEO of Billiluna because it meant I could just drive around there. I drove to Billiluna and visited them like I was just a friend. So I stayed in their house. I was able to just be a visitor, you see what I mean, whereas if I'd been working in the community, I would have been not able to have quite as close a relationship with them. So that was a really amazing time.

I was there when Philip was writing his book. It was about the similarities between the way Aboriginal culture is set up and how the Baha'i Faith is set up. They have elders, which are comparable with our counsellors. There are a lot of things. Just the way they have meetings and things like that. They were actually doing paintings to illustrate this. It was an interesting time to be there. Really, really interesting.

When I arrived, Philip wasn't that keen for western people to come in there. But when he saw the yellow ute (Joe had given us his Toyota), he recognized it, so he thought, "Oh it's Joe coming back," and he was really pleased. But it was me who had arrived. I said that I was Joe's mum. So he welcomed me and it was really good what he said, "I don't like some of the western people who come here because they teach from the outside-in. But we have to do things from the inside-out. Some of the Baha'is here, they drink, they smoke, they gamble (cards) – all these things. We have got to work from the inside. We have to make them strong on the inside and then they will forget about these things. Rather than just from the outside, you stop doing these things but the inside is still not resolved." He taught me quite a lot, actually.

It was interesting when Philip was there because he would go off to the National Spiritual Assembly meetings from Billiluna. It took him a week to get to Sydney. A tiny plane would take him up to Halls Creek, then Kununurra, then across to Darwin, and then Sydney. It would require a long journey and so he'd be away from the community. While he was away, everything sort of quietened down. Nothing much happened. Then as soon as he came back, there was this great spiritual awakening. He used to show pictures of where he had been and what he had been doing, discussing or whatever. He would show it on the little viewer onto the corrugated wall of the shed of the house they were in. There's this corrugated picture. It didn't seem to make any difference; they weren't worried about that.

This was before the Ruhi process, not long before. I didn't go around teaching the Faith, in that sense. I just sat down with them, and I showed the women how to make bush baskets. Making baskets out of grasses and creepers and things like that. They were interested in that. I said that they can sell these because they had a store there where tourists used to call in. They could make other crafts and things. We got a sewing machine and made clothes. It was just doing productive things. I could be here for another day telling you about the experiences I had there.

While we were at Mulan, I assisted setting up small craft industries, sewing, silk screen printing and basket-making.

I witnessed the Walmajarri people of the three communities

of Mulan, Billiluna and Balgo being awarded Native Title to the land surrounding Lake Gregory. And also Lake Gregory being designated as the Paraku Indigenous Protected Area. Both these events had government ministers, lawyers and other personnel all flying in to camp on the edge of the lake. It was my job to organise the food – under very basic conditions!!

I visited Billiluna about three years later (when Don was working at Balgo for a few weeks). Philip and Sue had left and their families left. It was just Rachel there and she had the Baha'i library and the sewing machine and all that. It was still going, sort of. But I believe now, she has left, so I don't know what's happened to everything that was there – all the books and some Baha'i books and things. I don't think there are any active Baha'is there now, as far as I know. But I haven't been back since that time, to Billiluna itself.

Tom Price – 2001 to 2011

After we'd been up there in Mulan, we moved to Tom Price, because our first grandchild was born there. We decided to be there with our daughter and son-in-law.

We lived in this mining town for eleven years – from 2001 to 2011. In that time Don worked for several aboriginal organizations.

There was a LSA there and I had many wonderful experiences, including connecting with other Baha'is through the Pilbara cluster. And a lot of involvement with the nearby indigenous communities of Wakuthuni and Bellary. But for now, instead of focusing on Tom Price[62], I will talk about Balgo.

---

[62] In this interview, Helen did not describe her experiences in Tom Price but these are in Chapter 11.

Balgo – 2004

There was a time in Tom Price when Don was taking just whatever jobs he could get, and there was a little bit of a space when he had no work. So I said, "Well, I'd really like to go back up to Billiluna to see what's happening now." So he just rang up a few other communities and found that Balgo, which was another neighboring community, had a job going for a few weeks for someone to work in the office there. He took that, and we went up there.

I had the most amazing experience. At that time Patsy Mugadell had been the delegate for the Kimberley Region at the National Convention that was held in Alice Springs. She had been down to that. The convention was in 2003, and our visit was in 2004. I caught up with Patsy. That was the most amazing experience. That was probably even more so than visiting Billiluna.

While I was at Balgo, it felt I was on a roller coaster with Patsy. First of all, when I met up with her, I quickly summed up her life. She was the radio announcer there. They have a local radio system whereby they have music and a way of communicating ideas, and things that are happening, and all that sort of thing. Well, she was a very astute person, a very capable person. But she drinks, smokes, and gambles. When I went into her house, I could barely have even sat on a chair that was there. It was so filthy that I couldn't almost bear to even be there.

She said, "Oh, come over and we have tea together one night." Cockroaches running around everywhere. Mice.

I thought, *My God, this is incredible.* I had heard all sorts of stories about Patsy, so I swallowed hard and said, "Okay, alright." I said that I would cook up something. I went along with my billy of stew and was determined not to eat anything else at all. Anyway, we sat outside fortunately.

She told me, something that happened. There had been some Baha'is calling in there, 'Art Works'. Apparently, they had been quite effusive, teaching and all that. She said, "How could I do that? Don't they realise how I'm the one who has to live here, and they're doing all this stuff? I don't want to be associated with this."

I said, "Look, Patsy, if you don't want to be associated with it, if you're not wanting to be a Baha'i anymore, you don't have to be." I was quite strong with her. I said "I'm here, I just come to see you as a Baha'i friend. If you don't want to have anything to do with me, you don't have to." She quickly snapped out of it and she said, "Oh yeah, I do. I do want to."

Finally, she said, "I'd like you to come and meet some of my friends."

I thought, *What's going to happen now?* She took me to the back-blocks of Balgo. It is a very terrible community. It's been a Catholic stronghold. The Catholics went in there at the beginning of the century, like 1900 or something. They have this great big Catholic church there. The priest almost runs the thinking of the community. There is a lot of destructive behavior going on there.

At the time we were there, they had just built a new office and it had bars on all the windows. Nobody could go in and out of the doors. It was so different to Blackstone where we had people coming in and out easily, and no problem. But this was just like a prison. Some guys had flown in just at the time we were there – had flown in to bring new computers for the office, and people had stoned the plane so it couldn't take off again. There had been an assault on a nurse at Billiluna, and so the health service had removed all the nurses from Mulan, Balgo and Billiluna – they were connected with each other. Removed everything, so all that had gone. So there was no nurse in the community. This had happened. The new storekeeper – they regularly had new storekeepers – the new storekeeper had his windscreen smashed. There was very strong racist type of feelings going on.

So anyway, Patsy took me to the back-blocks of Balgo, where they were having a barbecue. Barbecuing a kangaroo. We were just sitting around all together there. I was the only white person. They were just chatting. It was like a depression there – it was so strong. What they were talking about was that the old people were not passing on the Lore because the young people don't respect them. Not respecting what they're teaching them, so they are not passing on that Lore anymore. Some people decided they had to sleep beside the plane to stop people vandalizing it again.

There was a couple of people who had done a bit of training with the nurse, so trying to help keep their health clinic going.

There was all this discussion going on. I didn't say anything. I just sat there. Just listened, listened, listened. Then I said – it just came out of me – "Don't think that you're the only ones who are looking for the right way.

I can't remember what was the particular word I used. "You are not the only ones searching. It's not just in this community that things are not working out – that people are searching – trying to find a possible right path in life. It's not just here." I said, "In a way, if you worked with, and thought about the white staff who came into this community, they're such a few. They haven't got their families. They haven't got any connections with them. They haven't got their support. They're just so few people and they've come here to help … if you work with them. You can all help each other. Don't get into a state where you think this is the only place where people are struggling and searching. This is going on all over the world. Even in the middle of big cities. I think people are wandering lost, and not sure where to go. So hold hands with the white people in this community. You have to somehow resolve this, so that you can work together to make this place a beautiful place to live."

That's all I said, it just came out of my heart, and I just left it. I wasn't expecting replies or people to have a conversation.

After that, we got on really well then, Patsy and I. She took me to a church service that was being held as a funeral. I went to that. She was sitting there saying, "Isn't this disgusting." The whole thing was led by the priest with the whole Catholic regalia, rituals and stuff that goes on. She said, "How can they stand it. How can they put up with this?" She was really quite angry about how everyone just followed on and did what the priest said.

Then Patsy said, "Why don't we go out bush and say some prayers?" This was a turn up. So, we went out to this beautiful ridge that looked right out over the valley. It was just the most spectacular scenery. We sat there amidst the spinifex while her young son, who had come with us, he went around lighting fires everywhere to catch goannas. These spinifex bushes were on fire. I don't know how you could let someone going about lighting fires like that. We sat there.

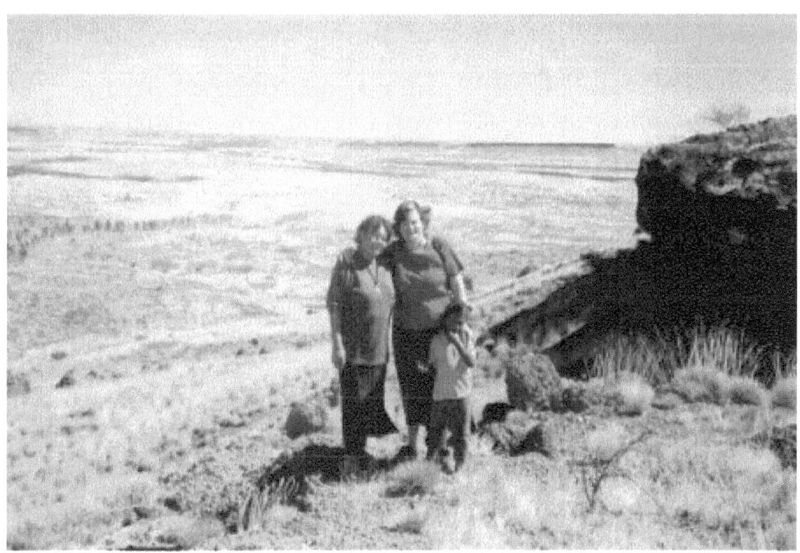

I travelled with a few books: *Seven Valleys* and *Hidden Words* and a few prayer books. I didn't have much with me. We just got there and said some prayers. Then this little boy – he was a really wild little boy – he couldn't read, and hardly went to school – he came around and sat next to us. He just sat there and I said, "Would you like me to sing you a prayer?"

So I sang, *Oh God, educate these children*. I was just saying this simple prayer, and he calmed right down. He just sat there. I said, "Would you like me to sing it again?"

And then Patsy was absolutely amazed and said, "I've never seen him listen to anybody like that. This little boy … I felt a really strong connection with him. It was very strong and he just sat beside me and just quietened down. He wasn't running around doing stupid things.

There are a few other things. An amazing thing happened. Patsy took me down and showed me all the women's dreaming sites. We spent a whole day driving through the valley, seeing all these dreaming sites which no western people are ever meant to see. She explained, "These stones are very special. This means this … and that is …." We went through the whole valley.

After that, we all eventually went back and then I said, "Patsy it's almost time for me to leave. I've only been here for three weeks and tomorrow I'm leaving. We have to say goodbye to each other. I'll come up and just say farewell."

When I went up there, I could hardly believe what I saw. She had completely cleaned the house. It was spotless – scrubbed the walls, everything was absolutely stunning. She had cleaned up outside. The yard was all rubbish collected. The whole place was just immaculate. She had had a picture of 'Abdul-Baha and she put his picture on the wall. What books I had, I had left with her, and she said, "I have been reading that book, *The Seven Valleys*. Ah, that is the most amazing book." It just did something to her.

Unfortunately, this was when I had to leave, so I left, and that was it. I thought that's it, I'll probably not see Patsy ever again. But we bumped into each other soon after – it was so funny.

After we left, we went up through Halls Creek. Patsy, she gambles (cards), and she had obviously bet on some money and had told me that she wanted to get enough money to buy a vehicle. I didn't think much about it at the time. When we went to Halls Creek, we camped just in our tent. We were driving out to go to Fitzroy Crossing and to go back home to Tom Price. As we were driving along, suddenly this four-wheel drive came haring along the road from behind, much faster than should have been, driven by Patsy's older son, who hasn't got a license. She went right past us and then she suddenly saw us. *Beep. Beep. Stop. Screech. Stop.* She jumped out of the car and she just came out and she hugged me. This is only about three days since we left Balgo, and she gave me a big hug. She said to Don, my husband, "Did Helen tell you about our magic day?"

I've actually caught up with Patsy again, in quite an amazing way. After we had left Tom Price to come here to Kelmscott five years ago, my husband got a short-term job to go up and do some work in Halls Creek. So we're up there. Patsy now lives at Halls Creek and I wondered if Patsy was there. I thought, *I'll ask around.*

They said, "Yeah, she's in the community.

So we went down there. We met up at the pub (she still drinks). She got some other friends, and we had a devotional meeting together. I was talking about 'Book One'. She said, "Why can't we start it here?"

I said, "Well we could, but maybe it's better that you come down, and you're away from your environment. You could stay with me in Kelmscott and we could do it in Perth."

I had in mind an intensive workshop. Patsy was quite eager. She was keen to learn more about the Faith and I spent evenings and days reading from the writings and saying prayers.

Then she organized this amazing trip. We went out collecting all the bushtuckers – bush potatoes, bush tomatoes. We went for many kilometres. A whole group of us.

That was Patsy. I assisted her with a resume in 2011 but I don't know what's happened to her now. I tried to write to her, but never got a reply.

I had almost forgotten all these things. There's all these little scenarios, and I forget the details now. I still don't know what it actually all meant.

Kelmscott – 2012 to 2021

After Tom Price, we retired to Kelmscott. There are so many activities in the Armadale community. I am on the LSA. This is my first experience of living in a large, strong Baha'i community after being an isolated believer for many decades

Ben was in Bahai' World Centre in Haifa working in building maintenance. He was wanting to marry Violyn Hoahania from the Solomon Islands – she was working in the gardens. We were keen to meet her and, as Ben's parents, we were allowed to visit there for four weeks. This was in 2004 and it happened that America was about to invade Iraq and so pilgrimage had been suspended and we, Don and I, were almost the only visitors at the centre. We had the special opportunity to meet with several members of the House of Justice and other key figures[63].

In 2011, we spent a month in Lae, where Joe and his wife, Amica, were supporting the Rays of Light schooling program – Preparation for Social Action. Then three months with Ben and Violyn in the Solomon Islands. Altogether, I had four visits to the Solomons.

---

[63]   Helen described her time at Haifa in Chapter 12.

There are so other many things. Last year I conducted a workshop on the Seven Valleys in Annemieka Braud's Mummowee Farm in the Hindmarsh Valley in South Australia.

Isolated Baha'is

I've been an isolated believer for forty years of my life because we have lived in rural and remote areas for most of my married life. Occasionally, I've been in a Baha'i community, but we've lived out in the desert. My husband worked with Aboriginal people – managing communities, remote communities, developing aboriginal groups. Trying to get them together to form an organized body that's incorporated and has a voice, and so they can speak for themselves and have their own path of development. Whereas most of the aboriginal people tend to be sort of lost in the western environment – the way the western world is.

So mostly I've been quite isolated, and at first I felt, "Why did I do this?" Remote places. I used to feel sorry for myself, that I was so separated from the rest of the Baha'i community. Then after a while, I started to feel quite blessed because I really had to develop my own thinking, and my own path, and I had to be very strong in what I thought. Well, there were many times I'd be quite tested because, if you're the only Baha'i, I see all my friends go to church and have a lovely social group around them. Even though often my friends were religious people, I was a little bit cutoff from that spiritual sharing with others. Sometimes I would even go to church if they had a meeting or something and I thought it was okay for me to be at – I would go along just to be with people who believed in God. But it didn't always work out for me to stay in that group or keep going because when they found out what I believed, they used to feel uncomfortable. I didn't want to make them feel uncomfortable – that was not my purpose. Sometimes it was interesting, often my Faith would wane a bit. How do I keep going with this?

There was very little support for isolated believers. I received the Australian Baha'i Bulletin magazine. Sometimes I would actually make a big effort to go to a meeting in Perth and to the Summer Schools. Occasionally I would get a letter or people would ring up to say they would come down and visit, mainly when I was living closer to Perth, in Narrogin. Sometimes that was difficult because people didn't understand what it was to be in a remote place – sometimes they did things that were not appropriate for a country town. I don't want to criticize anyone, but an example was when I was living in Narrogin, I was rung up from someone who had a teaching committee in Perth. They asked would I ask some of the organizations in town if they would like a speaker to speak on child education or something like that. So I wrote to several groups in town because they're always looking for speakers. Several responded and said, "Yes, they would like someone to come and talk". So I let Perth know. Then they wrote back and said, "Tell them that we will be in Narrogin on a particular day". And I said, "Well, you can't really do it like that. They have their meeting times, and you have to come at the time of their meeting". It all fell apart and I felt it had a really very bad effect. It was not good. They just didn't understand.

Or sometimes they would say that we have a public meeting in Narrogin. Often in the early days, that's how we did things – with public meetings. So I'd advertise the meeting, everything, speakers can talk on this, and then the last minute I'd get, "We can't come". So I'd have to do it on my own. I'd have to quickly get myself together to give a talk, which I wasn't that good at, at that time.

My message to people visiting to support pioneers is that they should listen to what the pioneer says and answer their needs –

not just do what you feel comfortable doing. Don't ever go to their place and just sit around – teaching is by actions, not words. Ask if you can help out in some way – weed the garden, sweep the floor, pick up rubbish in the town – anything except just sit around. Make yourselves useful.

[Note by Don: Helen did not have an opportunity to review this transcript. However, I am certain that, although she has mentioned a couple of examples of things going wrong with people visiting, she really appreciated the tremendous support on the many occasions when things went well.]

I remember that, when this Faith started, people weren't in perfect comfort and that they sacrificed a lot to travel to take their Faith to outlying areas and even give up jobs and houses – the comfortable house or wherever they were living to go move somewhere else. I would hope one day that the same spirit would come back. But I don't see it yet, at the moment – that spirit of sacrifice, where people really move for the sake of their Faith and go to another place. It's really hard. We've got youth going out to these places, and I appreciate what they're doing with this focused effort, but they are only there for a limited time – they know they are there, and then they leave. I still think that there has to be a level of sacrifice for things to work. If people go to places, sometimes if people want to really pioneer, they leave where they are at, and go – their life is now in this other place. That's hard. It's not easy. Particularly if you live in a city, then you move to country town, it takes a while to get used to a different way of life and a way of thinking. But I think in the end the people are much, much richer for it.

Now, looking back I think I lost nothing from leaving the city. Nothing at all. I only gained. Even my children becoming Baha'is. They became very strong Baha'is.

I served on the Outback Project for seven and half years; I've just resigned because I am now living in Kelmscott and have a

lot of commitments in a very active, busy Baha'i community –
so I just can't do everything. The Outback Project is under the
National Assembly. It was trying to reach out to all the outback
people, right cross Australia. To support them, make them feel
connected. It's very important to keep that connection with
people who are out in remote areas – so they feel connected, and
they feel they still part of everything. Otherwise, how do you do
a study circle if you're one person out there, a long way from the
city. The Outback Project arranged study circles by Skype and
phone link-up, so they don't feel left out from part of the whole
development of the Faith. So that's something that I really, really
enjoyed doing. I used to do the newsletter *Bush Honey*[64], and all
the statistics and we had 917 people on our list. So it's a lot of
people to keep track of.

The Outback Project was very successful at that time, but I
think now it's probably moving over to doing it within each
region because the numbers were getting so big. It's now
probably time for a bit of a change – to have it more regional. I
think eventually the Regional Councils will have their own
outback support – the councils are starting to do that anyway.

Baha'i spirit

I remember many of the beginnings of the Faith in WA. I
suppose all of us were so imperfect in our understanding. I
didn't even know what an LSA was when I became a Baha'i. I
have seen so much change in this time since I became a Baha'i
in 1970. It's really only forty-five years, but just how much
change in growth has taken place is really, I suppose, a testimony
to the Faith itself.

What is it that attracts people to the Faith? I just recognized

---

[64]   Editions of Bush Honey are available through Don.

the spiritual. There was some spirit there that I must have been searching for, and felt connected with. But it was beyond just an intellectual understanding of the Teachings, if you see the difference. Gradually, over time that intellectual understanding has been added to it. I'm very conscious, when I'm teaching, or when I'm telling people about the Faith, to be sharing that spirit along with the actual intellectual content of the message. We can talk about equality of men and women, and all these things, but there's a spirit in the Faith, so if you don't connect that with a person's heart, it doesn't matter how much you might tell them, you're not going to influence them. That's something that I've learned. I think the Faith generally is going that way anyway – that we don't engage in Ruhi Study circles simply to convert people, or don't engage in social economic development to convert people. In fact, it's very much disapproved, now. I think that's really good. Even though we now have these Ruhi study circles developed, it's just raising our consciousness and our understanding. But it's not the essence. I think that the essence is something like you smell the fragrance of the rose and how beautiful it is, and then eventually you look at the rose and you see all the petals and how it's made. But that in itself doesn't give you the fragrance of the rose, if you know what that means. That's something that I would like to share.

The other thing is that a lot of the original development of the Faith has been with a great deal of sacrifice and also an acceptance of things being less than perfect. I remember the very first summer school that we had here in Western Australia. It was in Dwellingup. It was just friends of the Faith who actually left their house and went to live in the bush, and allowed us to use their house. It was a very simple little wooden house and we all slept on the floor together. Putting down sleeping bags on the floor. It was so simple. We cooked outside – barbeque or whatever. We just walked 500 metres down the road to the little scout hall. We had our meetings there. It was all very simple. We were so excited about being together and the spirit was so strong that we just didn't think about discomfort or probably the flies and mosquitoes and I don't know what else. We weren't really conscious of those things. I see now, often people expect such perfect comfort when we all get together. That's something that still comes from within the Baha'i community, particularly from people in the cities.

My message to the Baha'is in the future is: **The journey of a Baha'i is always away from self to God.** We keep that in mind. The battle is always with our own selves, and I think it's not an outside battle. It's not with the institutions of the Faith or the external environment that we're in. So if we get that out of our mind – that we can't teach the Faith because of the people around us. Or we can't because of this, and this, and this. Forget about all those external things. The battle is always within, so if you overcome that internal battle of fear of maybe people not thinking the same way as you, or not appreciating the message that you have. Also getting rid of those things that might distract you or move you away from your true self. Because that's what it's all about in the end – to bring us closer to that part of us that is being created by God, that spiritual self.

This is our journey. This is the main journey that we have. If we focus on it and if we take responsibility for our own spiritual development, we actually attract people to us and we bring people along with us. In a way, this is what teaching is to me. It's not just self-development in terms of what psychologists would view. Also, there's a lot of new age talk about this, and a lot of people are into meditation and all these sort of things. But I think that sometimes these are very self-orientated things too. To get rid of this self-orientation – to be God centered and to rely on God. The total independence is really total dependence on God. A lot of people think, and a lot of discussion now, is about developing self-confidence.

Actually, self-confidence comes from total trust in God. A lot of people are very confused about this, with the way it's talked about in the modern world. It's, "Well, you can do it. You know you're this … You're that … You want to do it, then go for it." All that sort of thing. Whereas real happiness and real satisfaction in life comes from **finding your part in the plan of God**. That's my only prayer now for my life – that I'm part of this plan of God. Whatever, and if I can be.

My prayer is always, "Find me my place in this plan of God". What is it that I can give that would be most relevant? Everyone has capacities. Everyone has talents. Lay those there for God to use – "Please use me. Please find me my part in this plan." This is the source of happiness – of real joy – of real self-confidence in a way. There's a lot of talk with psychology and all those in the modern western world that takes us away from this and makes us focus on ourselves all the time. The secret is to be not so focused, but reliant on God – trust in God. Ask for help. Ask for Him to guide you; ask that you find your pathway in this world. It doesn't mean that you're running around doing every Baha'i activity that's available because you could fill up your life with Baha'i activities.

But there's a pathway for you before God. It may just be a quiet thing. Like, at the moment, I am very concerned with my grandchildren. I need to be here with these children just for this time. That's not something that you would write up in a Baha'i journal – 'She looked after her grandchildren.' That is a very personal thing between you and God. You know yourself whether you're doing it for God.

I'll finish with a beautiful *Hidden Word*:
If thou lovest Me, turn away from thyself,
If thou seeketh My pleasure, regard not thine own,

That thou mayest die in Me,
And I may eternally live in thee.

I think that is the main message. The other message is an affirmation. There is a lot of talk now about affirmations, but I think this is the greatest that anyone could have:

With the hands of power I made thee,
And with the fingers of strength I created thee,
And within thee have I placed the essence of My light.
Be thou content with it, and seek naught else,
For My work is perfect, and My command is binding.
Question it not, nor have a doubt thereof.

There are many others. The secret is to always be nurturing that inner itself, and the self that brings us close to God.

..ooOOoo..

The story of the interview in 2015

Notes by Don Gordon

Soon after Helen died in July 2021, I was reflecting on her life and noticed that, in a subdirectory on her computer, there was a file just labelled 'Helen Gordon'. There was no indication of what it was about, so I opened it up and found that it was an audio recording of Helen talking about the Faith. Helen had never mentioned the recording to me, and I did not know it had existed (I think I was working away up north at that time).

I wanted to contact the interviewer to find out how the recording had come about, who it was intended for, and whether there was a transcription. The only clues I had was that the document was saved on 25th Dec 2015 and the audio had some brief interjections by a female interviewer, but no name.

At first, I thought that it might have been arranged by Graham Hassall who is the go-to-person for Baha'i History in Australia, and I knew that Helen had some contact with him. However, when I rang him, he said that he was not aware of this interview, but would like a copy.

Then I thought there might have been an interchange of emails to set up the recording. Unfortunately, when I looked at Helen's old emails, there were none before 2017 because this is when she changed from Yahoo to Gmail. I was surprised that I was able to find the right password for Helen's old Yahoo, so I quickly discovered that <u>Parisa Mohebi</u> from Mundaring was the one who had organized the interview.

In Parisa's email to Helen on 15th Dec 2015, she stated:

> *We met at the unit convention the other week. I've been doing several voice-recordings of people in the community (Mundaring) on my humble tablet. These are informal recordings where people can share memories and the story of their life as Baha'is as well as before they were Baha'is. I have done four already. I think these stories will be very interesting for people now and the future to listen to and will be a useful addition to records of local history. The duration can be as long or short as you would like to make it. At this stage, I am keeping the recordings on a computer file and I may possibly forward them to the NSA for their archives some time in the future. Of course, I will email you a copy. You are under no pressure to respond in the affirmative. I am just putting the idea out there.*

Helen emailed back:

I did not know Parisa, but I rang her straight away because
her phone number was in the bottom of her email. She told me
that, six years ago, she had undertaken five interviews of people
involved in the early days of the Faith in Western Australia. She
said that there wasn't a transcription, but she thought the audio
recordings could be placed in the archives of the relevant Local
Spiritual Assemblies.

I thought that audio is wonderful for getting a sense of how
Helen was expressing herself, but many people find it difficult
to sit down to listen right through such a long recording. A
transcription is easier for people to find the sections which are
of greatest interest to themselves.

Transcription

I did this transcription in September 2021. There is some
minor editing such as removing 'um' and 'you know'. Headings
and photos have been added. There are some extra details from
Verona, Maxien and Charmaine. Also, I have fill in a few gaps
with what Helen had told me from time to time, and some details
from what she had written in 1992, 1997 and 2020 – these
original documents are on my computer, as well as the unedited
2015 interview.

..ooOOoo..

26

How to use creative arts
in Ruhi study circles

"All Art is a gift of the Holy Spirit. When this light shines through the mind of a musician, it manifests itself in beautiful harmonies. Again, shining through the mind of a poet, it is seen in fine poetry and poetic prose. When the Light of the Sun of Truth inspires the mind of a painter, he produces marvelous pictures. These gifts are fulfilling their highest purpose, when showing forth the praise of God." Abdu'l-Bahá

Introductory Thoughts

- Art activities in Ruhi Study Circles should be used to enhance meaning, uplift the spirit and facilitate learning. They should not take a lot of time but play a supportive role. If you all want to have a creative day or time specifically for more extensive creative activities that is good but the participants should know that is what they are coming to.
- Creativity is a virtue that is the property of every human soul. As we create, we connect directly with our soul. We can be creative through visual arts, drama, music, poetry, dance, arranging flowers etc.
- We don't have to be professional artists to use this virtue.
- We can be creative in simple ways.
- We need to be a little patient with each other and allow us all to make a start with this process.

- It is important that our creativity uplifts our spirits, supports the spirit of the Faith and enhances our understanding of what we are studying.
- It must not be careless, aimless or frivolous as is often found with the arts in the world today.
- Be flexible in how you use the arts – Who are the people in your group? What are their interests? They may have skills they can bring to the group – music, dance, drama etc. As a tutor you don't have to only draw on your own expertise. Utilise the talents of those participating.

Method

- Write down all the constraining requirements – length of time, cost of materials, number of people to be involved, and access to resources. Various talents of your study circle participants – it may take a little time to discover these.
- Meditate, brainstorm, write down or take note of every idea that comes along even if it might seem a bit silly at first. You may need to do some research as ideas come up.
- Decide on the best ideas, gather your materials and equipment, and DO IT.
- The following are simple ideas that take minimal resources and almost no preparation.

Making connections

- Jigsaw picture – cut a piece of card (A3 is a good size but can be bigger or smaller) into as many pieces as there are people in the group. The pieces should be in a jigsaw shape. Choose a quote or a theme and everyone draws their interpretation of this on their piece. Coloured pencils or felt pens work well. You then stick the pieces together on another piece of card the same size. This really brings out the individuality of people and their different ways of looking at the same thing. This is unity in diversity. A good starting activity as it really brings home the whole principle of the Ruhi Study Circles that everyone's contribution is important and everyone's interpretation is valid and everyone can make a contribution to the whole.

- Introduction games – there are many books with these in them.

- Washing hands with perfumed water – don't do every time – not a ritual

- Secret friend – You are given one person you have to think about, care for and make sure they are happy in the group and maybe at the end you can make or bring a very small gift for that person.

Learning Quotes

- Write out quote in large print. Cut out each word or short phrase. Ask them to put it together – verbally or sticking on.

- Write the quote on a blackboard or white board and rub out one piece at a time.

- Visualisation of the quote – drama or drawing – act this out (can be done in pairs like charades) or illustrate this with the quote written in somewhere.

- Sing the quote, clap in time to a beat maybe with a drum.

- Make your own fridge magnet. Cut a round or square piece of card and stick a fridge magnet to the back (these can be bought in sheets from craft shops)

- Make a folding book with decorated cover pieces. Write quotes to memorize on the pages and decorate.

- Make a decorated bookmark with a quote on it.

- Decorate a frame to put around a quote
- Each person in the group is given one part of the quote to read – not in order but at random – then the group has to say the quote as if they are one person. People have to concentrate to work out when their turn is coming.

Meditation

- Working with clay, plasticine or play-dough while listening to music.
- Tissue paper pictures: Using coloured tissue paper and a glue stick, shape the tissue paper to make a pattern.
- Finger painting – this can be messy – mix paint with cooked cornflour to make a thick paint.
- Drawing with wax crayons – this is very easy and effective.
- Music with quote slowly and repetitively read – also good for memorizing.
- Deep breathing with simple arm movements while saying the quote.
- Repetitive Quotations – as in the Mana songs

Illustrating principles

- City of the human heart: Make a heart attached at the top so it folds with 2 halves. On one half write on the outside how you present yourself to the outside world and, on the inside, how you feel yourself to be. On the other half write how you would like to be on the outside and the inside. If possible, the song from Manna "O man of two visions" could be a good meditation for this activity. This can be very personal and does not have to be shared.
- Make a spiritual fruit that would attract someone – out of modelling clay, paper – you could have a choice of

simple materials to draw from.

- Spiritual Pathway – each person writes on a cobblestone then you make a pathway. The cobble stones can be glued to a long roll of brown paper to make a path.
- Write a poem – senses. Haiku. Each letter of a virtue expanded out.
- Role play attitudes and principles.
- Use Puppets – even simple finger puppets are lots of fun

Creating Beauty

- Imagine you have in your hand something precious – describe it and people have to guess what it is.
- Meditation piece in the middle of the group – a collection of shells or flowers or stones.
- Each person brings along a flower or leaves and put them all together in a vase.
- Seeing the beauty in each other – "See me beautiful" – say what you see in each other. This is a very powerful thing and needs to be handled well.

..ooOOoo..

27

How to make various craft items

Some ideas for community groups

There are endless ideas for art and craft activities, many of which can be found on the internet, providing such a wealth of information. Interest here is in developing simple but attractive crafts that can be made at a community centre, or in the home. Materials should be easily acquired and inexpensive. This activity can pass on to their friends and children to provide a meaningful activity in the home. If done well, the crafts can be sold for additional source of income for the individuals or for the group.

Papier mache bowls

These are made from strong cardboard (obtained from used packaging boxes) and are cut using simple patterns. They are then folded to the shape required and covered with paper (the cheapest paper towels from Coles – single ply) and glue (flour and water or starch). You can then make them very smooth by sanding them when they are dry and rubbing them with a multipurpose pre-mixed filler (from the hardware store) although this is optional. They are then painted first with a white or black undercoat and then a design is painted on with acrylic paint. The surface is then coated with a water-based varnish to make it waterproof. These almost pass as ceramic bowls.

Pyrography

This is burning designs on to wood with a hot wire. It requires a burner but can also be done with a piece of fencing wire heated in the fire (this is how they do it in the desert).

Painting flowerpots

This is an easy activity. You can use old flowerpots cleaned up or buy new ones – the plastic ones are quite cheap. I would suggest using house paint which can be bought in sampler jars of different colours as acrylic paints are more expensive and not so durable for outdoor use. You could even put plants in them and sell them that way. Cuttings don't cost anything.

Bush Baskets

These can be made from grasses, leaves, vines – as long as they are strong and flexible – often best when green. They can be woven with string, twine, cotton, wool, strips of material or raffia and have beads, gum nuts, feathers and other objects woven into them.

Sewing

With a simple basic sewing machine, you can make simple items. Curtains – very simple that slide on a rod can be easily made. It is hard to get short colourful curtains and I have always found this to be very popular. You can buy bolts of coloured curtain material from Spotlight. The other item I have found to be popular is sewing basic skirts out of good quality stretch knit fabric with an elastic waist. We used to make them to measure and they took about half an hour to make. We sold them for about $10 but it would depend on the cost of the fabric.

Origami Earrings

Earrings can be made for almost nothing from old magazine

pictures or any decorated paper or even plain coloured paper. I have the instructions sheets for these and also a lot of earring findings and rings.

..ooOOoo..

28

Watercolour Painting on Wood

Prepared for a workshop by Helen Gordon 10 Dec 2019

Introduction

Recently there have been several explorations into using watercolour on other backgrounds that are not the conventional papers. You can now buy watercolour canvases, Ampersand clay board, Rowney watercolour board, and may be others. Those that I know are fairly expensive. You might use them for a really well finished artwork but you couldn't afford to play around on them.

I love painting with watercolour but don't like the method of framing with glass so that when you look at the picture you see a reflection of the window opposite. Also you don't see it with the same immediacy that you view an oil of acrylic artwork.
Also it is expensive to frame a watercolour in the traditional way. This set me on a journey to find a way to do watercolour without a matt or glass and find a cheaper way to produce a finished piece of artwork. Most of us are not going to be top artists and don't have unlimited resources to spend on our art.

This is a process that I am still developing but these are the instructions for how I go about doing this at this moment in time. I am pretty happy with what I am doing now and mostly prefer to use this than paper—even for Calligraphy which I pursued for many years in the past. It requires some simple preparation but the materials are very cheap, even cheaper than paper and all you need to finish it off is a simple frame. If you pursue this method I am sure you will develop your own variations and methods. You are welcome to contact me if you have any queries or problems.

Phone: 0439679000 Email: helen.m.gordon19@gmail.com

Instructions

Preparing the Painting Surface

I use 2 different methods—one requires no paper and you paint directly on to the painted wood. The other, which I prefer, you stick a sheet of wet art paper on to the wood and then coat the wet paper with a gesso:

- The wood base can be any type of wood that has a smooth surface. I use 3mm mdf board because it is smooth, easy to cut, a thickness that is both strong enough and thin enough to easily put into a simple frame. A 90cm x 1.20cm sheet of 3mm mdf board from Bunnings costs $8.00. it can also be bought wth a simple shiny white backing. Many bought frames already have a mdf backing board. You can just remove the matt and glass and prepare the mdf board for painting on. If you do this I tend to put a card or foam backing board or even another piece of wood behind it but not absolutely necessary.

- Sand down the edges so they are smooth and with some moderately fine sand paper lightly sand the flat surfaces. Thoroughly clean off the dust with a damp cloth so they are completely clean.

- Place the board on some blocks so the board is raised a little off the painting table. This prevents the edges from sticking to the under surface.

- The paint is a 50/50mixture of Dulux Ceiling White and Art Spectrum smooth white Clourfix Gesso

- I mix about 500mls at a time and keep in an airtight jar.

Surface A—

Using just painted wood

- Using a cheap foam brush about 2-3 cms wide. dip in water and dry so the brush is damp but not dripping wet. Put your brush into the paint and paint the surface of the wood. Keep the brush strokes going in the same direction - I prefer the length rather than the width. Allow to dry, coat 2 more times then sand down with a non-clogging fine sand paper. I then do the same again so there is a total of 6 coats.

- The board is now ready to paint on. I mostly do several boards at one time.

Painting on the Prepared Wood

- Depending on the size of the board I first draw lightly with a pastel pencil or H pencil a frame between 4 and 6cm. This defines the area to be painted and is effectively the matt. I quite like leaving a slightly rough edge for the frame—this seems to suit this method but you can make it very defined if you wish. You can also put borders around it.

- You then paint your picture similar to how you do normal watercolour painting but with less water as it doesn't soak into the surface in the same way as it does on paper. There are some other differences which you learn as you go along. You can play around with it much easier than you can with paper. You can also correct mistakes too by just painting the gesso over the area you are not happy with however I try not to do this. You need less paint than on paper and the colours really reach their full brilliance with the pure white background (watercolour paper is mostly cream not white and contains a lot of size)

Instructions

Preparing the Painting Surface

I use 2 different methods—one requires no paper and you paint directly on to the painted wood. The other, which I prefer, you stick a sheet of wet art paper on to the wood and then coat the wet paper with a gesso:

- The wood base can be any type of wood that has a smooth surface. I use 3mm mdf board because it is smooth, easy to cut, a thickness that is both strong enough and thin enough to easily put into a simple frame. A 90cm x 1.20cm sheet of 3mm mdf board from Bunnings costs $8.00. it can also be bought wth a simple shiny white backing. Many bought frames already have a mdf backing board. You can just remove the matt and glass and prepare the mdf board for painting on. If you do this I tend to put a card or foam backing board or even another piece of wood behind it but not absolutely necessary.

- Sand down the edges so they are smooth and with some moderately fine sand paper lightly sand the flat surfaces. Thoroughly clean off the dust with a damp cloth so they are completely clean.

- Place the board on some blocks so the board is raised a little off the painting table. This prevents the edges from sticking to the under surface.

- The paint is a 50/50mixture of Dulux Ceiling White and Art Spectrum smooth white Clourfix Gesso

- I mix about 500mls at a time and keep in an airtight jar.

Surface A—

Using just painted wood

- Using a cheap foam brush about 2-3 cms wide. dip in water and dry so the brush is damp but not dripping wet. Put your brush into the paint and paint the surface of the wood. Keep the brush strokes going in the same direction - I prefer the length rather than the width. Allow to dry, coat 2 more times then sand down with a non-clogging fine sand paper. I then do the same again so there is a total of 6 coats.

- The board is now ready to paint on. I mostly do several boards at one time.

Painting on the Prepared Wood

- Depending on the size of the board I first draw lightly with a pastel pencil or H pencil a frame between 4 and 6cm. This defines the area to be painted and is effectively the matt. I quite like leaving a slightly rough edge for the frame—this seems to suit this method but you can make it very defined if you wish. You can also put borders around it.

- You then paint your picture similar to how you do normal watercolour painting but with less water as it doesn't soak into the surface in the same way as it does on paper. There are some other differences which you learn as you go along. You can play around with it much easier than you can with paper. You can also correct mistakes too by just painting the gesso over the area you are not happy with however I try not to do this. You need less paint than on paper and the colours really reach their full brilliance with the pure white background (watercolour paper is mostly cream not white and contains a lot of size)

29

Working with Paper Mache

All types of structures can be made from paper mache, from very small, delicate constructions, like flowers, jewellery, mobiles to very large figures like animals. It also lends itself to decorating all manner of objects like frames, boxes etc. Once dried and sealed the structures are strong and durable

Materials

White tissue paper
Paper towel
Plain flour
Wallpaper paste
Old cardboard
Masking tape
Aluminium foil
String – varying thicknesses
Light chicken wire and cane
supports for large structures
Acrylic Paints
Brushes
Protective Sealer

The Process

Step 1

Construct the base structure with wire, cane, cardboard, foil etc. depending on what you are making. This could be very simple or quite complex

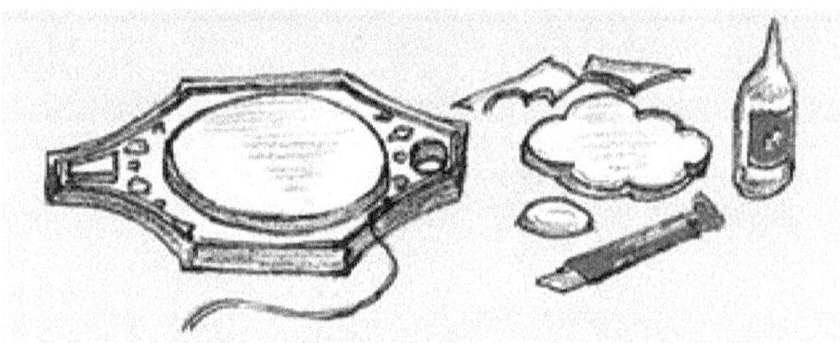

Step2

Cover the structure with many layers of paper towel and/or tissue paper. This process is time consuming and must be done well for the structure to be strong and durable. This is done by pasting glue on individual sheets of paper and smoothing them on.

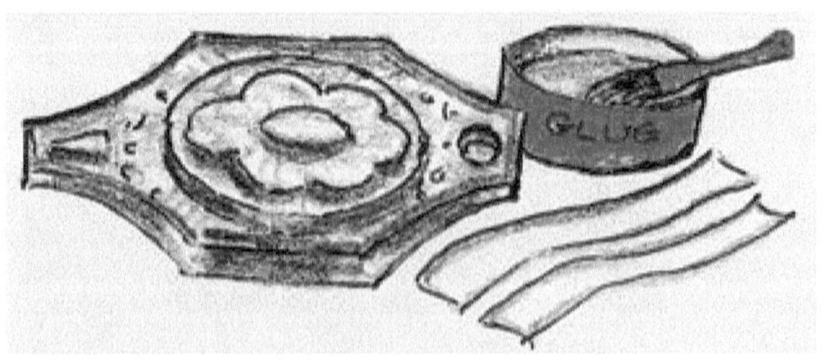

Step 3

The completed structure needs to dry
thoroughly - for small objects this
can be speeded up , if necessary,
using a hair dryer, fan, oven or
microwave, but be careful not to
overheat them.

Step 4

The structure is painted with acrylic
paints. Once the paints are dry it is
coated with several coats of a
colourless sealer, to provide a
waterproof, and durable finish

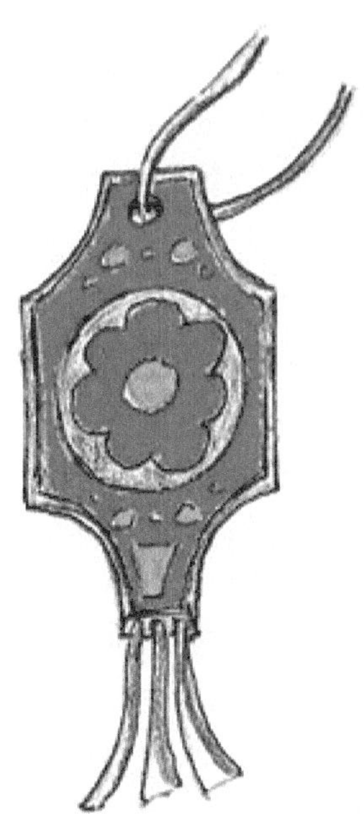

30

How to make spinifex paper

In 2004, Ngaanyatjarra Media produced 'Tjanpi Paper Palyara' - an 11-minute video of Helen demonstrating how to make spinifex paper[65].

Unique product

Spinifex paper is a unique product that has a multitude of uses and applications and is distinctly Australian, aboriginal, and from the desert, and is not being produced in this way anywhere else. It is light weight to send away. There are ready markets.

Practical and cost effective

Apart from minimal cost for some initial equipment the running costs are almost zero. Most of this initial equipment has already been acquired.

The raw materials (apart from the soda ash – easily obtained by truck from Perth) can be obtained locally.

The advantage of the spinifex paper-making is once set up, it requires no costly materials, so if a product isn't successful nothing is lost – there is an infinite supply of the raw material. You don't need highly paid technicians to operate expensive equipment. Anybody who is interested can acquire the skills.

The most expensive piece of equipment is the commercial blender (approx. $1400). However, in total the equipment cost

---

[65] Don has a copy of 'Tjanpi Paper Palyara' by Ngaanyatjarra Media

less than $3000. There is little maintenance or risk of danger.

Suited: with people and the environment in which they live.

A very safe and simple process has been developed to make this fibre paper using soda ash, and most of the processing is done in a sheltered outdoor environment.

This is feasible in a remote community, with limited resources, and people with limited experience and skills.,

Strong support base to ensure continuity

The process can involve the whole community. It has a wide back-up for continuity in training, artistic development and marketing being a partnership with the school and the Papulankutja Artists.

Potential for employment & training

In remote communities, employment and training opportunities are limited, particularly for young people. Most children who attend the local school remain in the community or marry into neighboring communities.

The monetary reward will come through Ab-Study and traineeship funding once the children reach fourteen years and nine months of age. The school will direct the formal level of literacy; numeracy and work experience or training that is appropriate for each student, linking this with the skills and learning processes of this enterprise. After they reach sixteen, they can be employed on CDEP.

The basic skills are all easy to learn but are able to be developed to a fine art as expertise improves. There are also some highly skilled areas in developing the finished product.

Mostly, it will be the older high school age children who will be involved in conjunction with adults from the community. Being set up as a small industry it will provide training in a number of skills, development of work ethic, and a purpose for furthering their academic studies. The children will also have an academic program that runs parallel to this. At the moment, there are very few opportunities within the community for the children to apply any of the skills they are being taught at school.

The skills they acquire can be applied to other areas of work.

Skills that can be acquired

- Working co-operatively to produce a finished product that belongs to the group rather than to an individual.
- Paper-making is both a series of tasks and an art in that care and thought is required to complete a successful product. There is always room for improvement and variation in how the product is completed. Thus, while some tasks are simple and repetitive, you are always working towards a product that is exciting and has an infinite variety of possibilities.
- Carpentry skills in making frames
- Watermarking skills – some of this requires soldering.
- Artistic skills such as various forms of printing (block printing seems to be the most popular) painting in many different media.
- Designing products
- Framing skills when work is finished off in frames.
- Packaging and posting finished work
- Marketing the products to various outlets – this requires computer skills and the use of the internet
- Bookkeeping skills – it would be hoped that the grassroots financial management could be done by the participants in the project.
- Organisational skills in keeping a flow of work between all the different aspects of making and completing the paper.

- Work ethics – getting to work on time, being paid for the time worked. Taking responsibility for a finished product and its delivery to an outlet.

1. The process of making paper from spinifex

Collecting the spinifex

Spinifex grass is collected by hand – some care is taken to get the right variety.

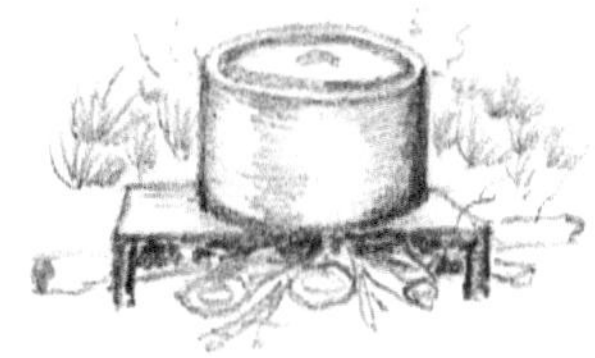

Softening the spinifex

The spinifex is then cut into small lengths and heated in a pot with some soda ash until soft.

Breaking the spinifex down into a pulp

This can be done by pounding and by using a vitamiser. A commercial vitamiser is used for the process

Making paper from pulp

The paper is pulled on prepared frames, couched on to cloths and then pressed. Paper can be made very small or quite large – the largest that has been made so far is 70cm x 50cm.

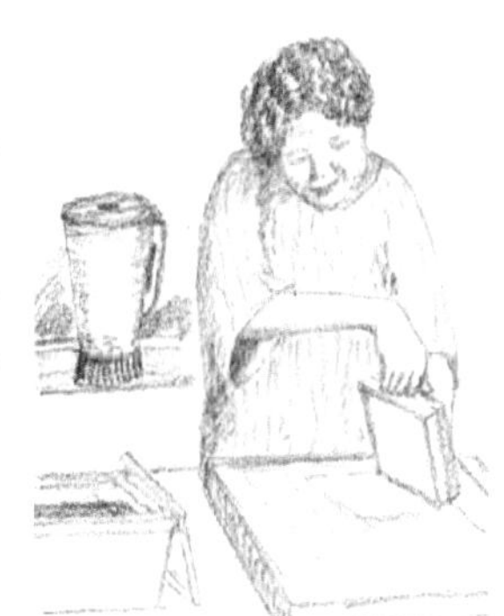

Drying the Paper

Ideally, the paper is allowed to dry slowly overnight but the process can be sped up.

2.Materials for making spinifex paper

Collecting the spinifex

- Transport to areas of suitable spinifex – some varieties are more suitable than others
- Gloves to protect your hands – soft leather gloves are best
- Bags to put the spinifex in
- Scissors – The grass mostly breaks very easily in your hands, as it is fairly brittle. However, it can be cut with grass cutters or scissors.

Softening the spinifex

- This can be done slowly in black pots or more quickly by heating.

Equipment and materials required are –

- Black Plastic buckets
- Scissors or grass cutters to chop the spinifex
- Large stainless steel or enamel cooking pot
- Portable heating element
- Soda Ash

Breaking the spinifex down into a pulp

- Rubber Mallet
- Vitamiser (4 litre commercial)
- Large Fine Sieve for washing
- Buckets to put the pulp in

Making paper from pulp

- Troughs for putting the paper pulp in – size depends on the size of the paper you are making
- Cotton cloths a little larger than the paper required – from secondhand sheets

- Couching Pad (made from foam and towels)
- Mould & Deckle (frames – one of which is covered with a mesh) for "pulling" the paper
- Pressing boards – at least ½ inch thick and waterproof – melamine board or clear-lacquered particle board or ply.
- Press – this can be made from a metal frame and a car jack.

Drying the paper

- Whitecoat masonite
- Blankets or towels

Watermarking

- Solder Iron
- Fuse Wire or copper wire (about .5mm -1mm thick)
- Wire Cutters
- Needle and Cotton

Making Moulds and Deckles

- Lengths of wood 1.8cms squ
- Screen Mesh – coarse – about 8T or fibreglass flywire
- Mitre Saw
- Drill with a fine bit and 3cm nails to suit
- Wood Glue
- Thin nylon cord
- Set Square
- Sandpaper
- Filler
- Johnson's waterproofing compound &/or clear finish
- Staple gun & staples – 8 mm or $5/16^{th}$ inch

3. Creating products out of the paper

Tourist Products
- Greeting Cards
- Notepaper
- Small books
- Stories about the area printed on it
- Decorated with native flowers, leaves and grasses

Fine art products
- Speciality Papers
- Paintings – Chinese style, leaving the paper as a background
- Limited Edition Prints of lino, wood cuts and silk-screening
- Charcoal sketching

..ooOOoo..

31

How to make paper earrings

Tawaimare Earring Project

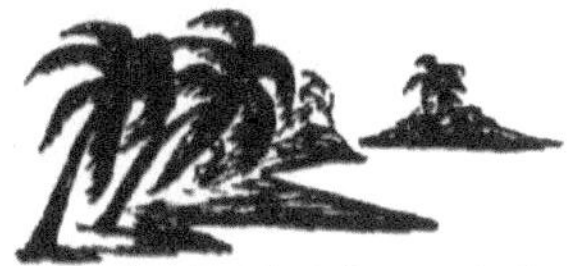

A small industry making earrings from paper and grasses and bark has started in the SW villages of Malaita in the Solomon Islands. In this place where there is almost no cash economy, life is labour intensive with subsistence farming and no electricity, water, sewerage or transport systems so water, food from the gardens in the hills, have to be carted, and everything is done by hand. The industry empowers the women by giving them a means of earning some money without leaving their homes. It requires minimal equipment and no special area to be set up permanently. It develops creative skills without being physically tiring.

At the moment, it is mainly the villages of Tawaimare, Heo and Puna'nu'u that are involved. The earrings are bought through the Taiwaimare secondhand shop which is run by a local woman. They also sell the raw materials and tools required to make them.

They are then freighted to Australia, packaged and marketed. The freight costs for materials and sending the finished product back to Australia is relatively little compared to the value of the product.

Even though they attended workshops to learn how to create the earrings, they are now coming up with their own ideas.

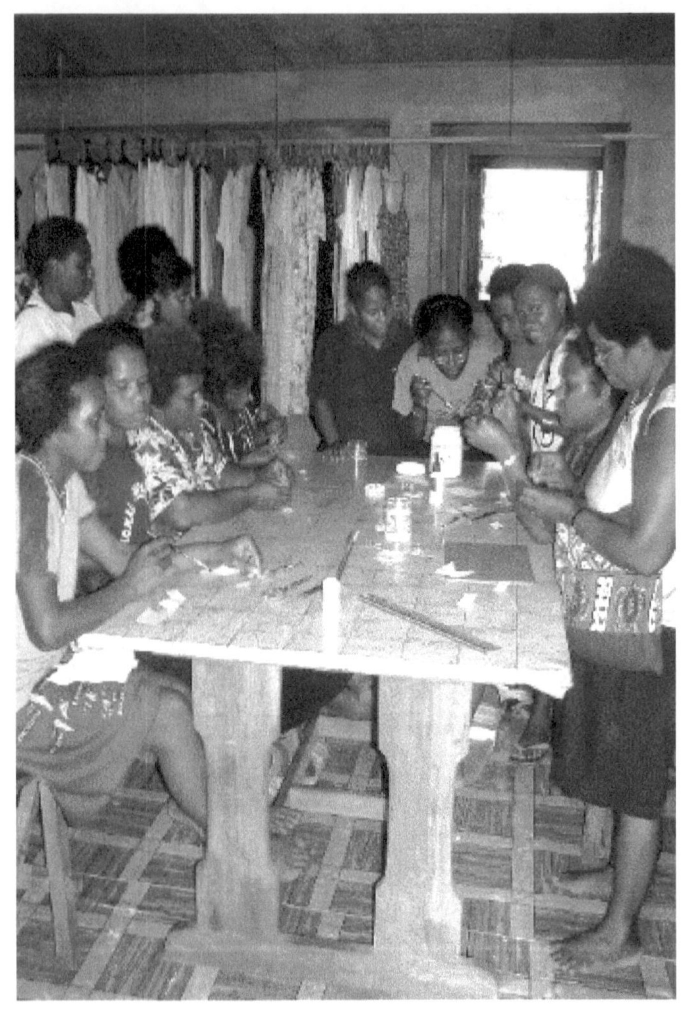

Tawaimare Earring Project

Instruction Sheet for Earrings– Cone Shape

Materials needed: Pack of paper & Earrings (6 pairs per pack), craft glue, earring varnish, brush, cotton string, scissors. pointed stick, cardboard template, cup of water to wash brush & small cloth.

NOTE: Brush must be placed in water immediately after use and washed thoroughly. Dry brush before reusing again. **The detail is important. Keep fingers and working surfaces clean. Wipe off excess glue with a soft damp cloth.**

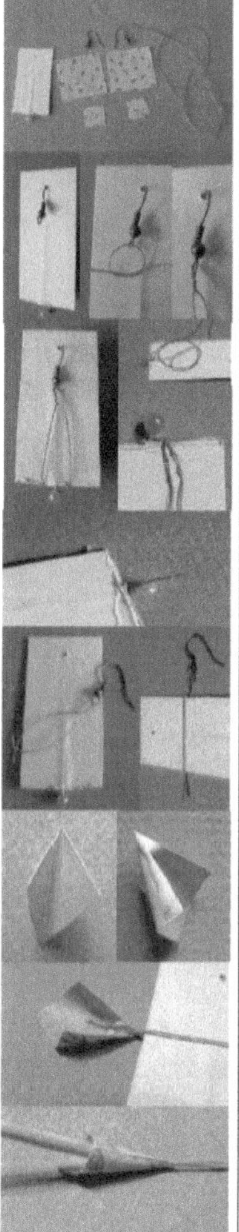

- For each pair you need 2 large pieces of paper and 2 small pieces of paper, 2 earrings and 2 strings and a template card plus glue and varnish.
- Hook the earring into the hole in the template as shown.
- Thread the string through the ring at the base of the earring and tie a knot in the middle of the string.
- Tie another 5 knots alternating left over right then right over left to make the knots strong.
- Loop the ends of the string around the pin head at the bottom of the template.
- Tie 6 knots the same as before pulling the strings tight. Then tie another knot with both strings together as shown. Pull tight close to the other knots.
- Cut the string off about 1 cm.
- You now have a strong knot at the top and a strong knot at the bottom with a loop in between. It is important to use the template because this makes sure that both earrings are exactly the same.
- Put the template through the loop sideways as shown.
- Take a small square and lightly fold it diagonally pinching on end firmly at the top.
- Glue the top and one side of the paper as shown.

- Place the paper under the bottom knotted string as shown.
- Carefully wrap the paper around into a cone so it covers the knot. It is helpful to use a pointed stick inside to press against as you hold the join until it sticks. This is the most difficult part and can take a bit of practise. Allow to dry.

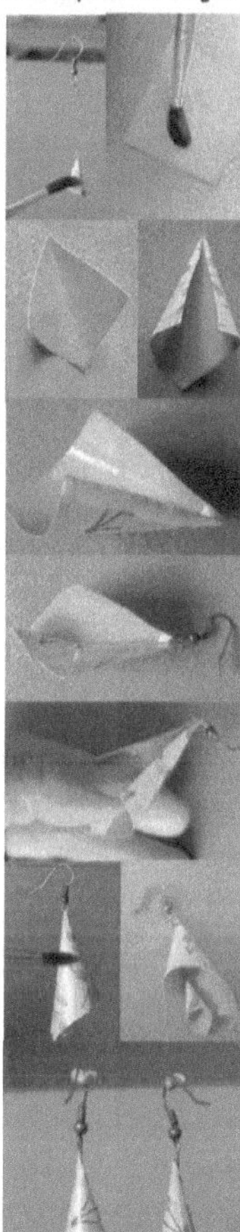

- Coat the small cone and the inside of the large square with varnish. Give them 2 coats allowing time to dry between coats. You can start the next earring while you are waiting.

- When the varnish is dry fold the large sheet of paper diagonally pinching it firmly at the top. Wrap the paper around into a cone moulding the shape to make it even.

- Glue top and one side of the paper as shown.

- Place the string holding the small cone to the earring in the middle of the large cone as shown.

- Put your thumb gently on the small cone then wrap the sides together shaping them until they are joined neatly. Take care to keep the top part neat and shaped nicely. Use the pointed stick inside as before to push against and make the pieces join properly

- When the glue is properly dry give the earrings 2 coats of varnish on the outside only

- When the varnish is dry carefully release the ring at the base of the earring so the string can slide a little and the earring can swing a bit from the top. The small cone should hang just below the tip of the large cone and both earrings should look the same. The glued joins should barely be noticeable.

Tawaimare Earring Project
Review Sheet for Cone-shaped Earrings

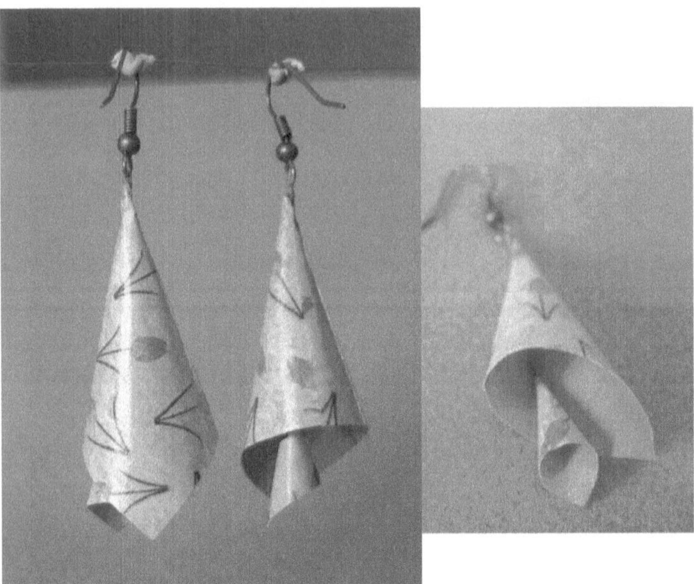

When making the earrings it is important that you pay attention to detail.

Points to look for are –

1. Joins are glued well and evenly. They should be barely noticeable and the top part of the joins on each cone must wrap around the knot leaving just the string coming out.
2. The cone must be evenly shaped.
3. The small cone should hang just below the larger one and the same for both earrings.
4. The large cone needs to be gently released from the varnish so it moves freely on the ring.
5. Varnish needs to be even and smooth.

Tawaimare Earring Project
Instruction Sheet for Earrings – Diamond Shape

Materials needed – Pack of paper & earrings (6 pairs per pack), Craft Glue (same as wood glue), Earring Varnish, brush, pin or sharp point, scissors, tweezers (not essential), container of water.
NOTE: Brush must be placed in water immediately after use and washed thoroughly. Dry brush before reusing again.
The detail is important. Keep fingers and working surface clean. Wipe off excess glue with a soft damp cloth.

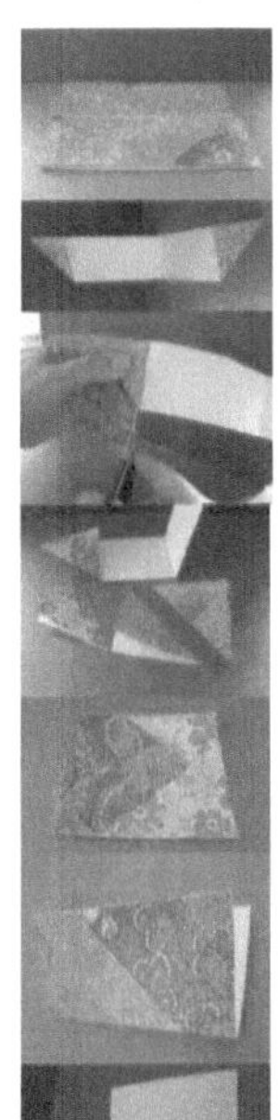

- There are 2 lots of 2 folded sheets of the same paper. Each pair of folded sheets makes 3 pairs of earrings. You need 2 squares for each earring.
- Fold the paper diagonally from each end working in towards the middle.
- Cut as shown and fold another diagonal.

- You will end up with 12 squares from the 2 sheets of paper.

- You will need 2 small squares of paper for each earring

- Flatten out the sheets of paper.

- Fold paper in half patterned side out and press firmly

- Open up and fold in half the other way and press firmly

- Open out

- Fold paper diagonally with the plain side out. Press firmly.

- Open up and fold diagonally the other way. Press firmly.

- Holding the paper on the patterned side bring the four corner points together allowing the paper to fold in as shown.

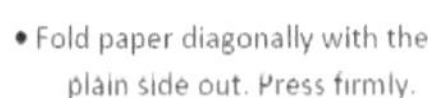

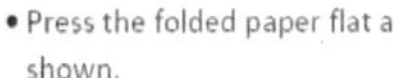

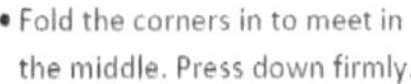

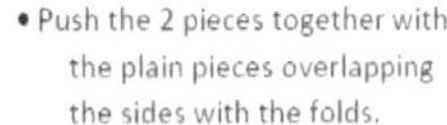

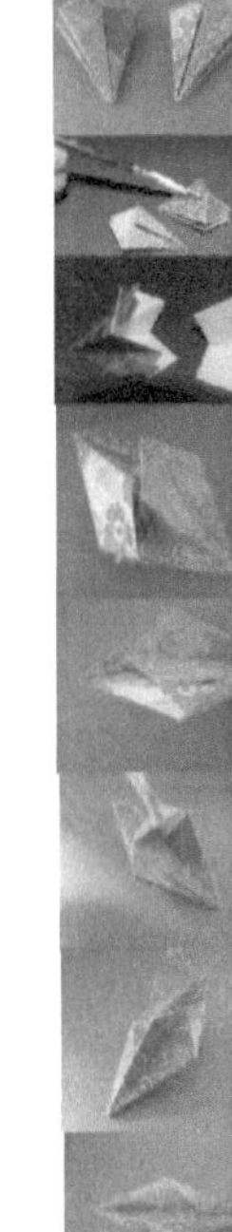

- Press the folded paper flat as shown.

- Fold the corners in to meet in the middle. Press down firmly.

- Turn over and do the same on the other side.

- You will need 2 squares folded like this to complete the earring.
- Glue the small flaps down. Allow to dry thoroughly.

- Open up the folded papers as shown.

- Push the 2 pieces together with the plain pieces overlapping the sides with the folds.

- Push together firmly so the 2 pieces are interlocked together.

- Glue the flaps down and press together firmly. Let glue dry.

- Push a pin through about 3mm from the top to put the ring through.

- Attach earring wire and paper construction on the same ring.

- Finish off with 2 coats of varnish. Allow about 30 mins between coats.

Tawaimare Earring Project

Review Sheet for Diamond-shaped Earring

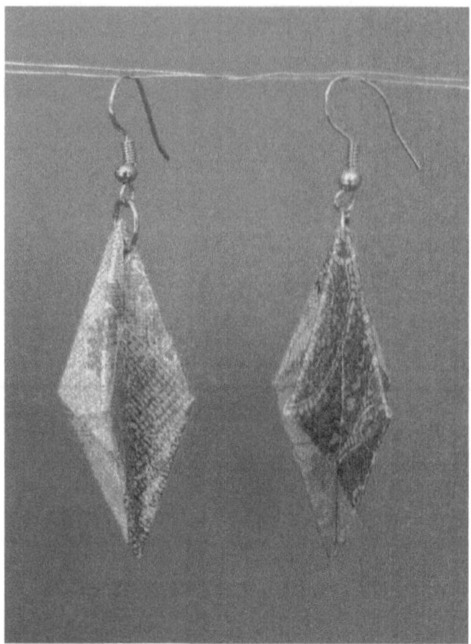

When making the earrings it is important that you pay attention to detail.

Points to look for are –

1. There is a neat point top and bottom
2. The points around the middle are joined closely – no gaps and are evenly spaced.
3. The unfolded flaps overlap the folded flaps. A flap from the bottom going up should alternate with a flap from the top going down.
4. This should look like one piece of paper and it should be hard to see the joins.
5. Varnish twice to give a hard waterproof surface.
6. The ring should be placed about 2-3mm below the top and closed neatly.

Tawaimare Earring Project
Instruction Sheet for Earrings - Fan-shaped

Materials needed: Earring pack (6 pairs of earrings in a pack), scissors, Craft Glue (same as wood glue), Earring Varnish, brush, pin or sharp point. Tweezers and ruler are helpful but not essential.

NOTE: Brush must be put in water immediately after use and washed thoroughly. Dry brush before reusing again.
The detail is important. Keep fingers and working surface clean. Wipe off excess glue with a soft damp cloth.

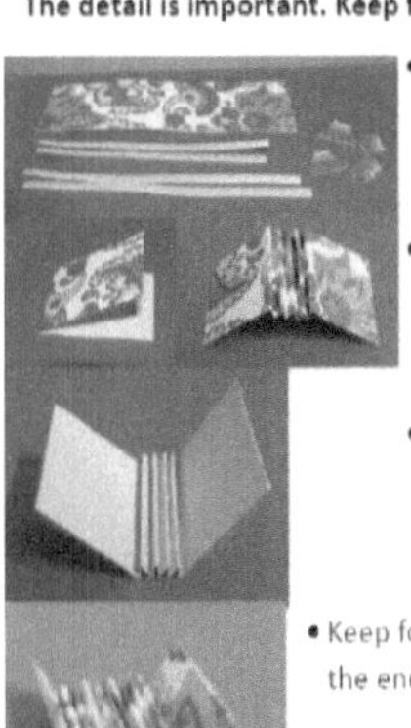

- For each pair of earrings there are 2 sheets of paper, 2 small & 2 large strips of card, 4 decorative pieces
- Fold the paper in half, then concertina fold from the middle out (3mm folds)

- Make sure folds are even and firmly folded

- Keep folding until there are 9 folds and the ends are facing up as shown

- Trim the ends so they are level with the top of the folds.

- Press the folds together firmly making strong creases.

- Glue one side of the short strip

- Glue the strip on to the outside fold of the paper

- Glue the tops of the folds as shown – use glue sparingly – don't allow it to dribble down the paper.

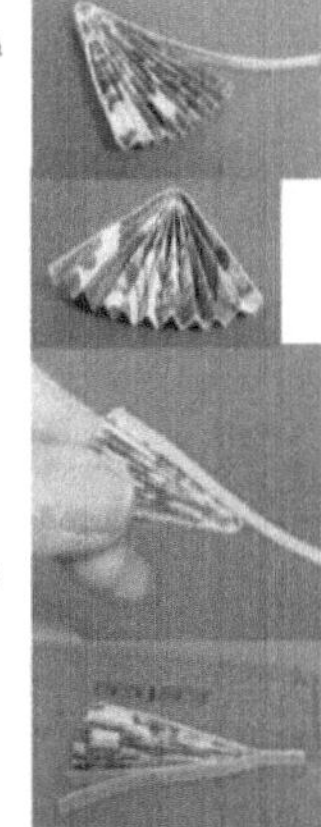

- Squeeze the top of the folds together wiping off any excess glue then paste the rest of the strip down the side of the other outer fold.
- Allow to dry thoroughly then spread out folds.

- Glue one side of the longer strip of card and paste on to the previous card strip.

- Allow a 1cm extension above the top of the folded paper then glue back down the other side.

- Stick decorative piece on front

- Stick decorative piece on back
- Allow to dry thoroughly

- Poke a pin through the centre of the strip about 2-3mm down from the top. Wriggle it around a bit to make sure the hole is big enough for the ring.

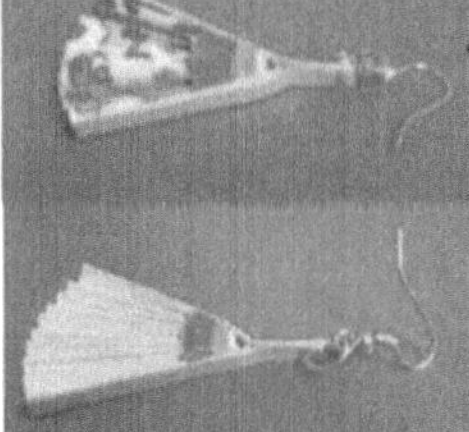

- Put the ring through the hole and add the earring wire, making sure it faces the right way.

Tawaimare Earring Project

Review Sheet for Fan-shaped Earring

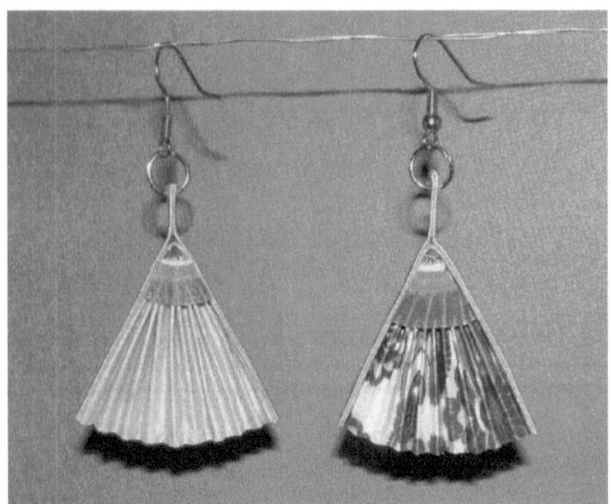

When making the earrings it is important to pay attention to detail

Points to look for are –

1. Folds are even and both fans are opened to the same size.
2. Strips of card are put on evenly coming exactly to the bottom of the folded paper and the same size extension at the top.
3. Decorative pieces are carefully glued and placed properly
4. Ring is through the centre of the card about 2-3mm from the top and joined neatlly.
5. Earring wire is facing the correct way.

Tawaimare Earring project

Instruction Sheet for Earrings – Leaf Shape

Materials Required: Pack of paper and earrings (enough for 6 pairs), Craft Glue (same as wood glue), Earring Varnish, brush, pin or sharp point, scissors, tweezers (not essential), ruler (not essential), container of water.
NOTE: Brush must be placed in water immediately after use and washed thoroughly. Dry brush before reusing again
The detail is important. Keep fingers and working surface clean. Wipe off excess glue with a soft damp cloth.

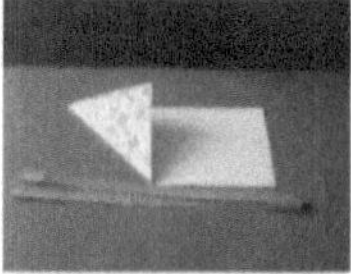

- Fold patterned paper diagonally making sure edges line up.
- Fold and cut strip in half Cut paper exactly along the edge as shown.

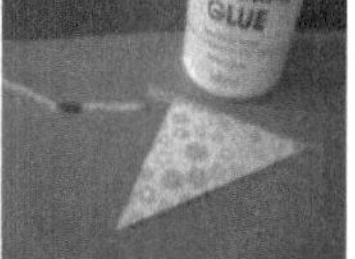

- Fold paper diagonally again and cut the same as before. You now have 2 diagonally folded papers and 2 edge strips to make 2 pairs of earrings.

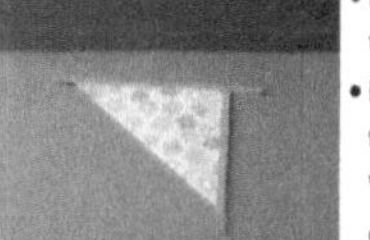

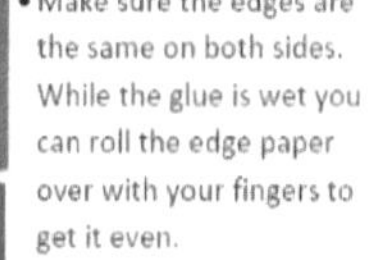

- Cut each edge strip in half again. Glue along one side with a brush – make sure edges are glued.

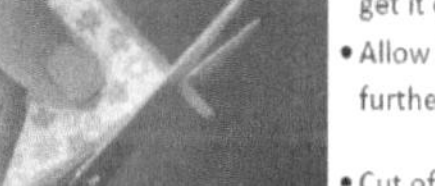

- Fold edge strips evenly over the cut edges
- Make sure the edges are the same on both sides. While the glue is wet you can roll the edge paper over with your fingers to get it even.
- Allow to dry before going further.

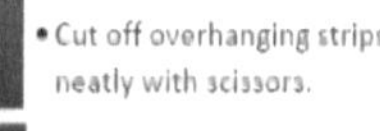

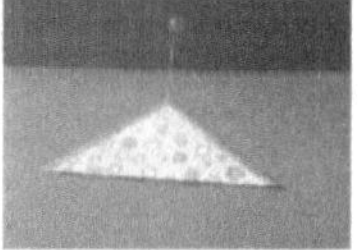

- Cut off overhanging strips neatly with scissors.

- Place a pin in the top of the triangle and make a hole for the ring.

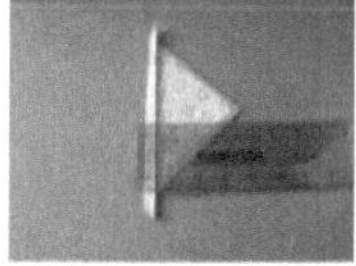

- Fold the long edge of the triangle over, about 4mm and press down firmly.

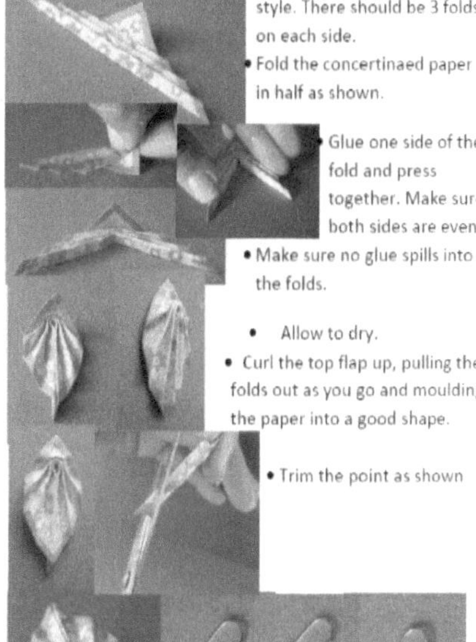

- Fold 5 more times concertina style. There should be 3 folds on each side.
- Fold the concertinaed paper in half as shown.

- Glue one side of the fold and press together. Make sure both sides are even.
- Make sure no glue spills into the folds.

- Allow to dry.
- Curl the top flap up, pulling the folds out as you go and moulding the paper into a good shape.

- Trim the point as shown

- Open larger ring by twisting the ring sideways (don't pull the ends outwards). Tweezers can be helpful with this. Place ring in the hole made by the pin. Join the small ring to the earring wire in the same way. Join the small ring to the bigger one.

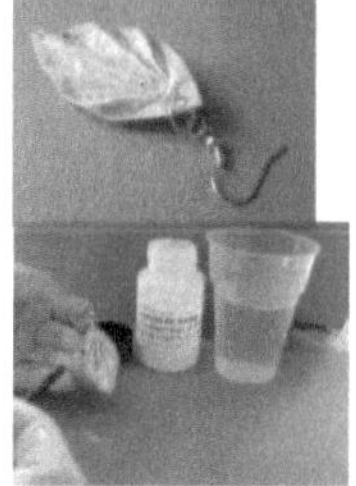

- The earring is completely constructed. Make sure it is joined correctly and they hang the right way. The cut point should be to the back.
- Varnish the earrings as shown.
- They need 2 coats (30 mins between coats) to make them hard and waterproof.

357

Tawaimare Earring Project

Review Sheet for Leaf-shaped Earring

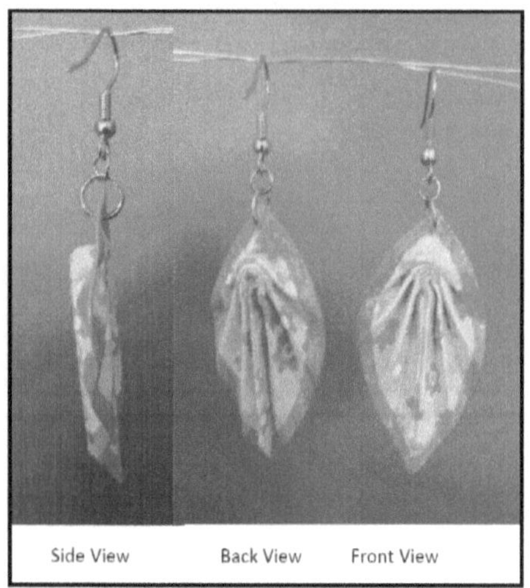

When making the earrings it is important that you pay attention to detail

Points to look for are –

1. Edge strip is the same width both sides and is glued on properly. Make sure the edge strip has dried well before folding otherwise it can slip off.
2. There is a neat point top and bottom
3. The folds are nicely arranged particularly on the front. Don't allow them to be glued together when you are gluing the middle section.
4. When you look from the side the earring should hang straight.
5. The rings are closed neatly.
6. Make sure you put on 2 coats of varnish – the earrings should be quite hard and waterproof.
7. Make sure they hang the correct way – with the join in the middle facing the back.

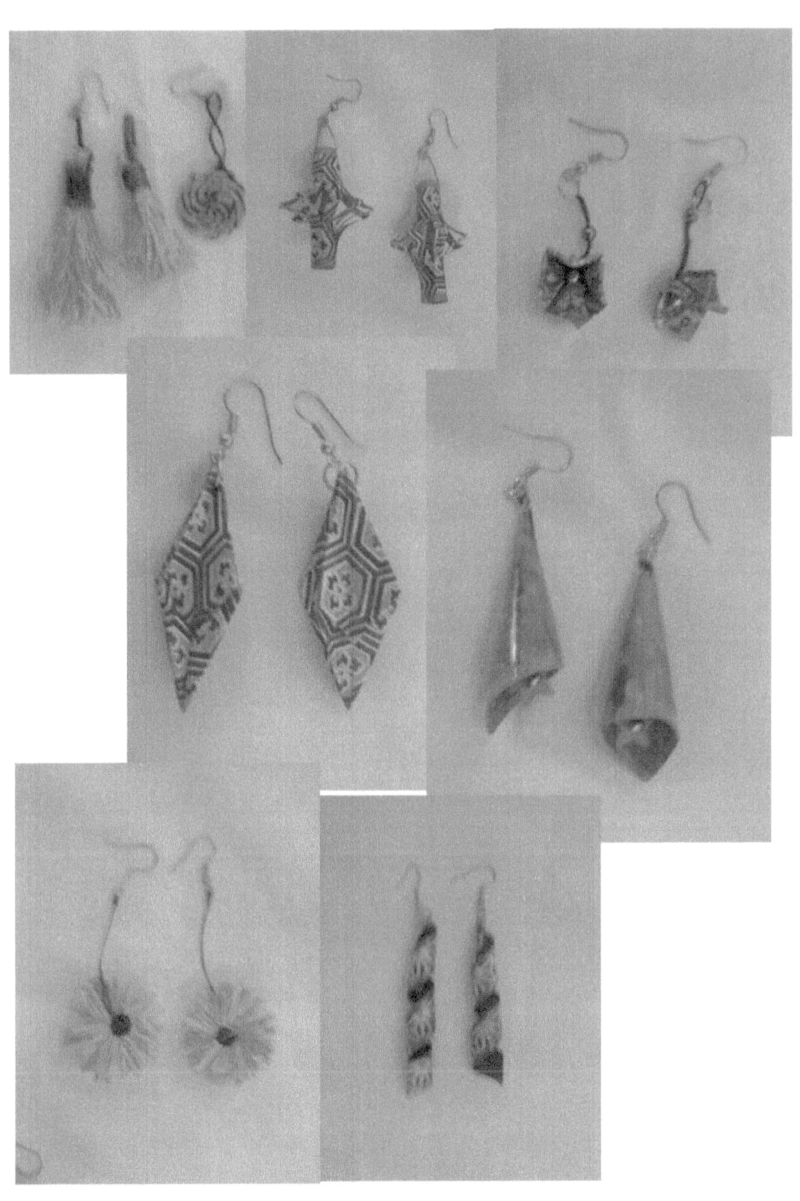

Tawaimare Earring Project

Instruction Sheet for Packaging

Make sure the area set aside for packaging is clean and free from dust.

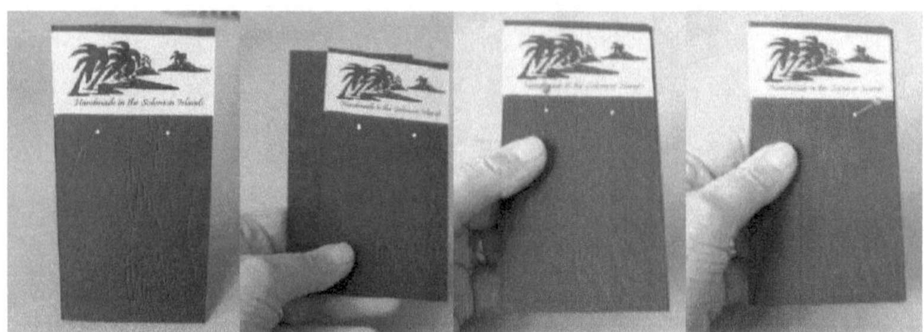

- Take the template which has 2 holes already in it and the label on.
- Place it over a blank card (rough side of the card up-this is the front)
- Poke a pin through the template where the holes are and into the card underneath
- You now have a blank card with holes in the right place.

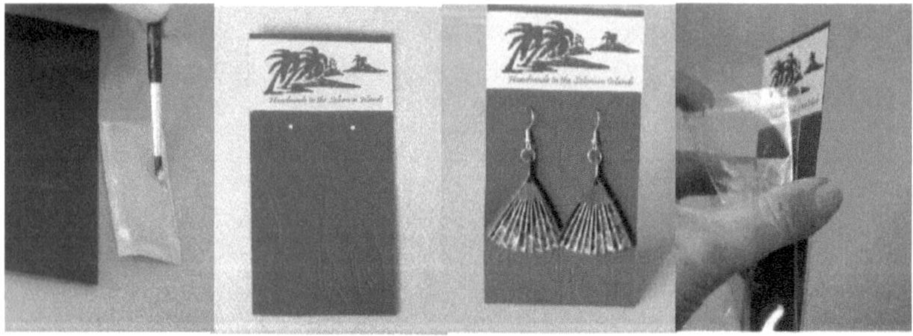

- Take the gold label and lightly glue the edges on the back.
- Stick the label on top of the card allowing a small black strip at the top
- Attach the earrings through the holes
- Slip the card with the earrings on into the bag. Make sure the bag seals at the back.

32

How to make a community mural

Jameson in 2017

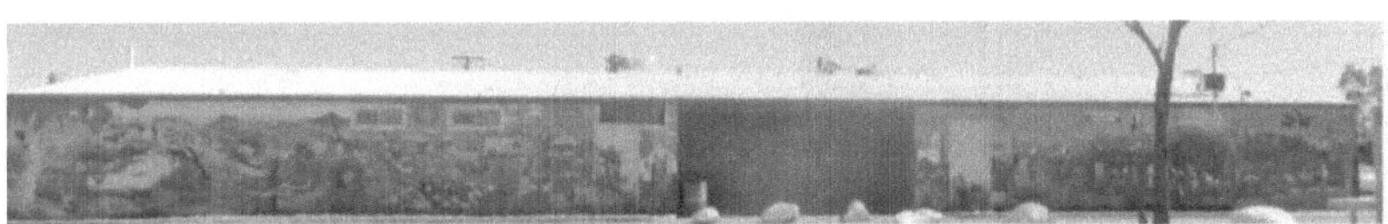

The Community Development Advisor, Ellie McLean, invited me to paint a mural on the side of the Mantamaru Community Store in the remote indigenous community of Jameson.

As the entrance to the store is in the middle of the wall, the mural had to be in two halves which collectively measured 40 metres in length and nearly 3 metres high. The wall had already had a coating of white undercoat on it so we could go straight into drawing up a design.

Preparation

I spent about three weeks doing workshops at the school and asking for ideas from the community members. Unfortunately, many of the adults in the community were sick or away or otherwise occupied so I leant heavily on the input and enthusiasm I received from the children at the school, particularly some very good drawings done by the high school children. A design was drawn up in the form of an outline drawing and then circulated around the community for approval, extra ideas, changes etc. Once the drawing was done there was a lot more interest from the adults and they liked the basic concept, and then came forward with a few more ideas.

We finally sourced a data projector that was working and one cold night in the middle of June we projected the drawings (after they had been photographed and put on to a computer) on to the store wall.

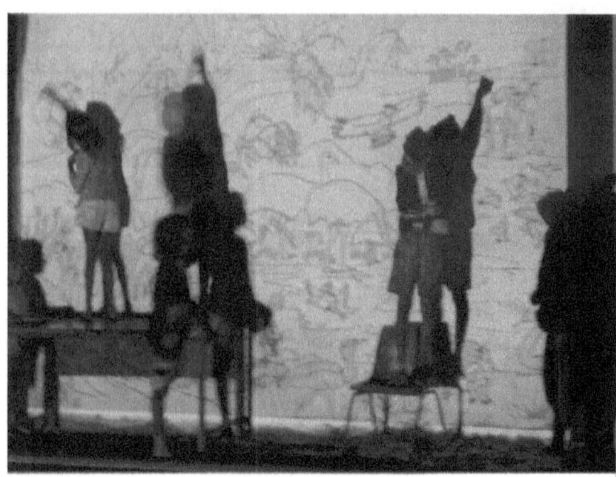

A few adults, but mostly children, traced the outline design on to the wall with marker pens. This was done in two stages – the left half first which took two nights to draw up and, after that was painted, we drew up the second half, which was all done in one night.

The mural was a collection of scenarios depicting a day in the life of people at Mantamaru, with the Tjitji Kutara story woven in as well.

Left Half

The first scene was about the animals around the waterhole in the early morning. This was painted by the primary school children. They were given at least one animal each and they could paint it as they wished. Some did them very realistically and others painted abstract designs inside the outline. They also painted some of the background particularly leaves and flowers and grasses. Adults painted the large trees.

The second scene is the Tjitji Kutara Story. This was mainly painted by Narelle Holland, an artist in the community.

The third scene is about the life of the community in the town and its surrounds. Many of the drawings for cars, houses etc. were done by high school children. Community members saw themselves in it and it attracted a lot of interest and participation.

The long dusty road joined these 3 scenes together.

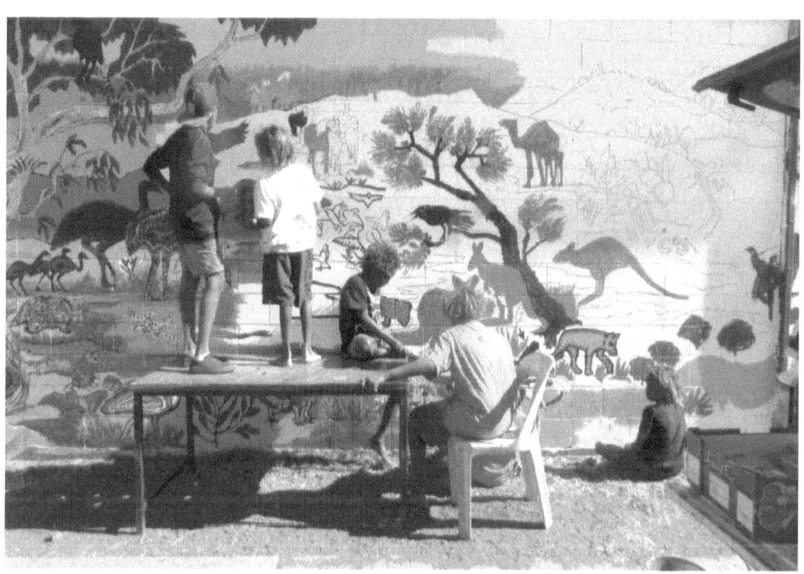

Right Half

The fourth scene is around the store which is a popular meeting place.

The fifth scene is about the sports, mainly softball and football, which occupy the weekends and are very popular.

The sixth scene is about hunting mostly done in the evening or early morning.

Engagement

The mural was a moment in time with a few people identifiable and the activities are about **now**. Bikes Palya were there for the school holidays so they painted themselves in helping children to make bikes from old parts and also fix them. As the mural went along people began to identify themselves with the figures and paint themselves in. For example, Bruce and Nicki, two footballers, painted themselves playing football. The children came over regularly from the school to paint and often collected there after school. Many adults joined in once the whole mural started taking shape, and a few made significant contributions – painting quite large sections.

Painting was a little dependent on the weather which at times was quite windy and cold. For about one week it rained so we couldn't paint at all.

Overall, twenty-four adults, nineteen primary school children, twelve high school children and five pre-primary school children were involved. So that is sixty people involved, some more than others. I think the highlight for me was the preschool children coming over to paint the flowers and grasses at the bottom. They did it with such care and attention and were so involved. I did the final touching up where needed.

The painting seemed to develop a life of its own with changes emerging as it went along. However, it certainly attracted interest and comment and input from a wide section of the community, black and white.

I would like to thank Ellie and Zarrin McLean who came many times after finishing their own work and both gave encouragement and contributed to the painting of the mural, and also thanks to Carol, the headmistress, and the teachers at the school for facilitating the children's involvement.

This was a moment in time for me as well as I am getting

older and this may be the last large mural I do, but have greatly enjoyed doing this. I love the combination of art and people bringing everyone together with a common vision.

..ooOOoo..

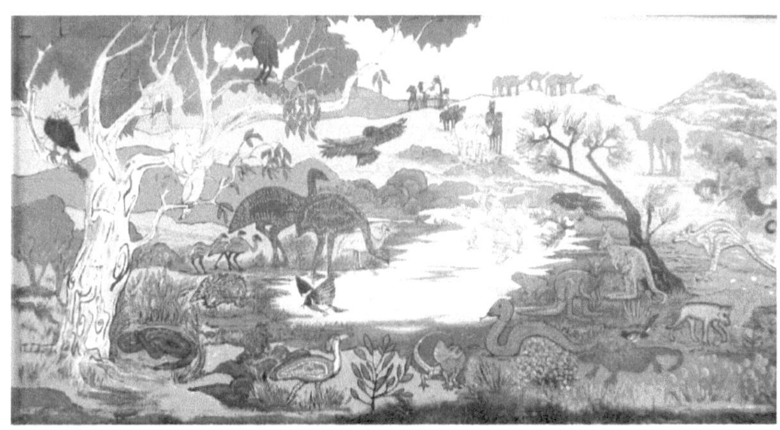

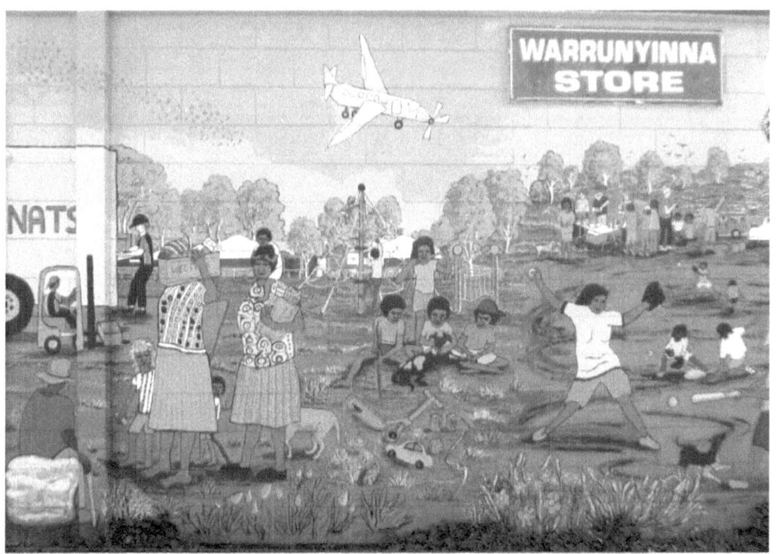

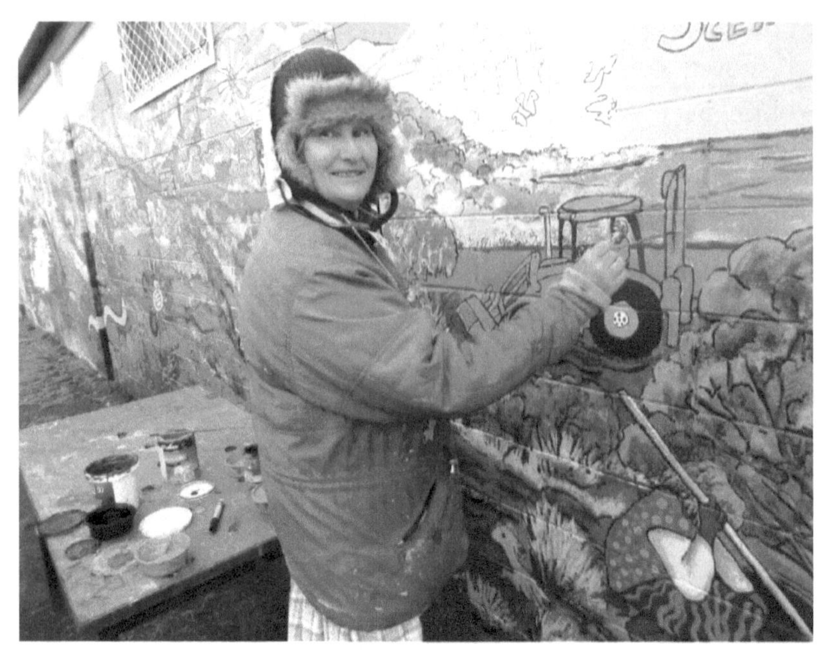

33

My life story, in brief

Helen's talk
at the Occupational Therapy reunion in Nov 2017

Getting started in life

I was born in Geelong, Victoria on the 14th August 1945 – at the exact moment all the bells were ringing for the end of the second World War. My parents began to settle in Ballarat, but moved to Perth when I was two years old.

I was the first born of six children. We lived in a small rental house in Kensington until I was fifteen and then moved to Riverton where my dad, over ten years, had built a house on five acres of land. It was quite a trek to Kent Street High School where I completed my schooling.

I was fortunate to win a scholarship to study medicine and went on to study for three years at UWA. Near the end of my third year, our house burnt down, and I lost everything I owned including all my notes and books for my studies. I still managed to pass but it was a time of crises and I started thinking deeply about why I was studying medicine. I then heard about an Occupational Therapy school starting up in Perth and the more I found out about this, the more I felt this was closer to my calling, as I was also very interested in, and good at, arts and crafts. So, I investigated transferring my scholarship, but they said this couldn't happen as it would be going backwards from Uni to TAFE. So, I firstly worked at Claremont Hospital as an OT assistant for a year and then applied for a Mental Health Scholarship which bonded me to work with Mental Health for two years after completing the course. I accepted. I was given the first year because of my previous studies, so I entered the second year of the OT course in 1968, and completed it the following year. Then I was back working off my bond at Claremont Mental Hospital. I then went back to Uni and completed a BSC with a major in Human Anatomy, my favourite subject at Uni. During this time, I also heard about the Baha'i Faith and became a follower of this religion. I would have to say this had a major influence on the direction of my life and my thinking in the years to come.

Scotland.

I then travelled on working holidays to New Zealand and then Ireland and Scotland until marrying in 1974. My husband, Don, had already got a job as the warden on the first legalised gypsy caravan site in Scotland – a place on the edge of Glasgow called Heatheryknowe. We lived in a caravan and worked with gypsy families and together we started a school for the children which was eventually continued with a special class at the local government school. At this time, late in 1974, pregnant with my first child, we returned to Australia

Early years of marriage

For 12 years my time was given to caring for our three children. Don was working for the Department for Community Development. First, we were at Laverton for about five months and then to Derby where Joe was born for about eighteen months and then Kununurra where Ben and Ruth were born. Overall, we were in the Kimbrleys for five years. During this time, we spent a short time in the Marshall Islands in the Pacific. Then Narrogin.

Narrogin

We established our home in Narrogin where we settled for 19 years. The children did all their schooling there. I took on a lot of voluntary positions, with the school P&Cs, the Brownies and Cubs, Pony Club etc. and involved myself in numerous local organizations particularly in art and craft, drama, and music groups. I also ran a silk-screen business from home and taught it at the Indigenous TAFE and practiced and taught calligraphy as a profession. I even learnt to play the flute – joining an orchestra that played for a performance of The Sorcerer. As the children grew older and were at school, I did many part-time jobs – managing a little art and craft shop, working as an activities organiser at the Narrogin Cottage Homes and then for several years as a Laboratory Technician at the Narrogin SHS Science Dept.

Blackstone

By 1998 our youngest child, Ruth, had flown the nest and was now in Perth, with her two older brothers, Joe and Ben, studying. My husband, Don had always worked with Indigenous people as a social worker, community development and other roles and now he was very keen to go to the outback again. We both applied for jobs in a remote indigenous community called Blackstone (Papulankutja) and were accepted.

I don't think anything could have prepared us for this experience – living with 200 very nomadic full blood aborigines who had only been twenty years living in a community and were still very tribal. We had to rethink almost everything we had learnt. Fortunately, it was a dry community – a crime to bring alcohol in – as, if there was any strife, the police were 1000 kilometres away in Laverton. The people were very wild and their culture so different to our own.

I don't want to embark on any details about this chapter in my life otherwise I would be writing a book, but it was a major life-changing experience. Just in brief my role as office manager and women's centre coordinator started with training some of the few literate women there to run the office and then I coordinated the setting up of the women's centre with a playgoup, HACC meals and arts and crafts including painting, basket-making, wood carving, jewellery-making, silk-screening, tie-dying, sewing etc. We had our own art and crafts shop and they had to buy their own materials. The output of these people was enormous and their creativity unlimited. I sold about 600 paintings with five exhibitions in Perth apart from all the crafts. Perhaps the highlight was the setting up of two small industries, something they were not familiar with – making jigsaws (large with Indigenous paintings on them) and making paper out of spinifex grass. For these activities they were paid on the CDEP work-for-the-dole employment program and the money from sales kept the women's centre going.

I became very close to many of the women and would have to say, when we left some three years later, it was like the end of a love affair. The connections we made over that time have dragged us back many times since then. I returned to Blackstone five times. Sometimes for short visits and a few times for several months. At the request of the community, I returned to re-establish the spinifex paper-making industry which I had started while working there earlier. This grew into a proper industry with a purpose-built centre and a full-time coordinator. At

Jameson, which is next to Blackstone, I organised for members of the community to paint a large mural on the side of the store.

Mulan

After working at Blackstone, Don accepted temporary work at Mulan, a remote indigenous community in the Kimberley. In that time, I spent some time at Billiluna and Balgo and witnessed the Walmajarri people of these three communities being awarded Native Title to the land surrounding Lake Gregory, and also Lake Gregory being designated as the Paraku Indigenous Protected Area. Both these events had government ministers, lawyers and other personnel all flying into camp on the edge of the lake. It was my job to organise the food!! I also assisted setting up small craft industries, sewing, silk screen printing and basket-making.

Tom Price

We then moved to Tom Price where our daughter Ruth and her husband Colin had their son, our first grandchild. During our 10 years in Tom Price Don had several jobs all related to Indigenous welfare, the last being setting up the Commonwealth Indigenous Employment Scheme all over the Pilbara. I travelled with him sometimes right out to the border of WA visiting all these small communities. I also worked in Wakuthuni community about thirty kilometres from Tom Price – setting up small craft industries. In the town, for four years, I ran a craft group for Indigenous primary school children after school. Don and I were also involved with the Nameless Festival and I helped get the Peoples Exhibit established where adults and children could exhibit their arts and crafts. I was an inaugural member of a local artists group called PACT (Pilbara Artists Coming

Together) and each year we held a pretty awesome exhibition. We were also very involved for many years in the establishment of the Tom Price Cultural Centre (for black and white). I tutored Indigenous children after school at the Enrichment Centre. I was involved with a lot of community arts projects there, painting murals, and banners mainly with the schools.

We left Tom Price after Don retired in 2011. We spent a month with our son Joe and his wife, Amica, who were coordinating an educational project in New Guinea, and we visited our other son Ben who had been living in a small village in the Solomon Islands for about ten years with his wife, Violyn, and three children.

Kelmscott

We retired to Perth, bought a house and settled down to suburban life after four decades out bush. I was able to nurse my mother until she passed away in 2013. I also did some studies in Art Therapy – a subject that has always been of interest to me. In 2014, Ben and his family decided to come back to Perth for the education of their children, so we live in close proximity and we have a lot to do with the children.

I was secretary of the Armadale Society of Artists and participate in their activities. Also, I undertook some short-term exciting community arts projects in the Pilbara and out on the Ngaanyatjarra Lands.

Finally

At 72 and in good health, I am so grateful for a life so filled to the brim with so many opportunities to explore my talents, develop my potential and hopefully put in a little to make this world a better place, particularly the gift of working with the

Indigenous people. Even though I was only employed officially for a couple of years as an Occupational Therapist, in the broader sense, my whole life has been oriented around the use of activities for healing, self-development and community engagement and hopefully, God willing, my journey isn't over just yet.

..ooOOoo..

www.ingramcontent.com/pod-product-compliance
Lightning Source LLC
Chambersburg PA
CBHW032143050726
47591CB00001B/60